Downsizing Democracy

Downsizing Democracy

How America Sidelined Its Citizens and Privatized Its Public

Matthew A. Crenson
Benjamin Ginsberg

The Johns Hopkins University Press

Baltimore and London

© 2002, 2004 The Johns Hopkins University Press

Printed in the United States of America on acid-free paper

9 8 7 6 5 4 3 2 1

The Johns Hopkins University Press
2715 North Charles Street
Baltimore, Maryland 21218-4363
www.press.jhu.edu

The Library of Congress has cataloged the hardcover edition of this book as follows:

Crenson, Matthew A., 1943–
  Downsizing democracy : how America sidelined its citizens and privatized its public /
Matthew A. Crenson and Benjamin Ginsberg.
    p.   cm.
  Includes bibliograhical references and index.
  ISBN 0-8018-7150-6 (hardcover : alk. paper)
  1. Political participation—United States. 2. Democracy—United States—Citizen
participation. 3. United States—Politics and government. I. Ginsberg, Benjamin. II. Title.
  JK1764.C74   2002
  323′.042′0973—dc21   2002005601

ISBN 0-8018-7886-1 (pbk)

A catalog record for this book is available from the British Library.

To Alene and Sandy

Contents

Contents

Preface

FOR MORE THAN two centuries, ordinary citizens were important actors on the Western political stage. Their vanguard entered political life with a bang in the eighteenth century, firing the shot heard round the world and responding with alacrity to the *levee en masse.* Over the ensuing decades, tens of millions more served loyally as voters, citizen soldiers, taxpayers, jurors, and the citizen administrators now disparaged as patronage employees. In these and other ways, citizens were the backbone of the Western state, providing it with the administrative, coercive, and extractive capabilities that allowed the West to conquer much of the world.

In return for their service, citizens received a variety of benefits including legal rights, pensions, and, perhaps most notably, the right to vote. The history of suffrage is often written so as to suggest that the opportunity to participate in national politics was wrung from unwilling rulers after bitter popular struggles. This tacit exchange of service for benefits, though, drew citizens further and more fully into political life. Citizen administrators became the mainstays of vigorous political party organizations. Expansion of the government's revenue base to include tens of millions of ordinary citizens also expanded the power of the representative and political institutions that encouraged popular compliance and negotiated conflicts of interest. Reliance upon citizen soldiers continually expanded the boundaries of participation as those asked to fight demanded the right to vote. In time, the government's reliance upon the support and cooperation of ordinary citizens had the critically important effect of expanding the universe of popular political involvement.

The era of the citizen is now coming to an end. Today, Western governments have found ways of raising armies, collecting taxes, and administering programs that do not require much involvement on the part of ordinary citizens. This underlying development has, in turn, opened the way for political elites to reduce their dependence upon popular political participation and to avail themselves instead of methods for securing and exercising power that do not rest on mass politics. In some respects, the symptoms of this change are most marked in America, where voter turnout has been declining for more than six decades as ordinary citizens have been banished to the political sidelines. Despite the nation's initial democratic exceptionalism, contemporary political elites have substantially marginalized the American mass electorate and have come to rely more and more on the courts and the bureaucracy to get what they want. We call this pattern "personal democracy" to distinguish it from popular democracy, a way of doing business that required elites to mobilize non-elites in order to prevail in the political arena. It is personal because the new techniques of governing disaggregate the public into a collection of private citizens. Their experience of democracy is increasingly personal rather than collective.

Ordinary Americans, in recent decades, have been reduced from citizens to what are in Washington frequently called "customers"— individual recipients of governmental services who are not encouraged to involve themselves as a group in the political or governmental process. Take, for example, the report of former vice president Al Gore's National Performance Review (NPR). The NPR, one of the few Clinton-era institutions endorsed by most Republicans because of its "businesslike" approach to government, generally fails to use the term "citizen" in its references to the people of the United States. Instead, Americans are deemed "customers" for government services. In its preamble to Chapter 2, "Putting Customers First," the report quotes Gore as saying, "A lot of people don't realize that the federal government has customers. We have customers. The American people." The transformation of citizens into customers is significant. Citizens were thought to own the government. Customers, by contrast, are merely expected to receive pleasant service from it. Citizens, moreover, are members of a political community with a collective existence created for public purposes. Customers are individual purchasers seeking to meet their private needs in a market. What is missing from the experience of customers is collective mobilization to achieve collective interests, and the omission is not just a matter of changing semantic fashions along the Potomac. In keeping with a customer-friendly orientation, government employees are advised to be courteous and more "user friendly" at all times. Agencies are admonished to provide friendly surroundings for customers and are advised to conduct frequent customer-satisfaction surveys. The NPR report, however, has little or nothing to say about how customers might actually influence the substance of federal programs and their administration.

The declining role of the American citizen became even more evident during the aftermath of the 2000 presidential election. The national news media claimed that the so-called battle for public opinion was every bit as important as the legal and institutional struggle for Florida's twenty-five electoral votes. This claim, however, was patently false. Although public opinion was not totally irrelevant—each candidate employed dozens of surrogates to trumpet his claims to the press—neither candidate made much effort to elicit popular support. Certainly, neither candidate heeded the calls of political activists like Reverend Jesse Jackson for mass demonstrations and protests. The two candidates' occasional public appearances were not really designed to bolster popular enthusiasm. They were intended more to strengthen the resolve of important political allies and to induce contributors to keep their wallets open to finance the battle, which was costing tens of millions of dollars. While their public appearances were rare, both Al Gore and Joe Lieberman spent hours on the telephone each day contacting contributors. GOP fund-raisers were active throughout the nation as well. Al Gore, for one, fully understood the minimal role of the mass public in the battle. In response to a television reporter's question on November 28 about the role of public opinion in the presidential struggle, Gore said, "I'm quite sure that [public opinion doesn't] matter in this, because it's a legal question." This was a rather significant observation from a candidate for elective political office.

During the course of the Florida struggle, the media also pointed with pride to the fact that an all-out battle between the nation's two major political parties was being resolved peacefully. There were no tanks or troops in the streets, as there might have been in other nations. On a typical day, fewer than a score of protesters stood outside the vice president's residence. The absence of political ferment was said by the national media to indicate the maturity of American democracy and Americans' profound respect for the rule of law. Yet the absence of expressions of popular political emotion, the paucity of demonstrators, and the near absence of any kind of popular political action or protest during the course of the battle for the presidency should not be seen as a symptom of America's political well-being. Quite the contrary. The struggle over the presidency involved a few hundred—at most a few thousand—political leaders and activists. Perhaps a few hundred thousand others watched the battle on the television networks or regularly followed newspaper accounts. Most Americans, however, paid only mild attention to the Florida struggle. They assumed it would eventually end and were, as the polls suggested, prepared to accept either outcome. Little popular feeling was expressed and few demonstrators were in evidence, but not because Americans are so mature. Perhaps, instead, Americans failed to become agitated because most knew the political struggle they were witnessing did not involve them.

If further confirmation was needed, the declining importance of the citizen in the American political process was underlined again in the aftermath of the 9-11 terrorist attacks on New York and Washington. President George W. Bush addressed the nation to calm fears, to inform Americans of his plans, and to call upon the citizenry to do its part in the face of the crisis. What exactly was the part the president assigned to ordinary Americans? We were advised to sing patriotic songs, think patriotic thoughts, and, above all, to go shopping. In other words, the government had little need for citizens and could think of little for them to do besides buoy up the economy and stay out of the way. More than two centuries ago, Americans entered the political arena with the shot heard around the world. Today, perhaps, they can be seen exiting that same arena holding the credit card accepted around the world.

We have written a new introduction for this first paperback edition of *Downsizing Democracy*. In it we set the subject of citizenship and personal democracy into a broader political science context. This allows us to show how our analysis relates to ongoing questions that political scientists raise about politics and citizenship in America.

Introduction to the Paperback Edition

THE DISCIPLINE of political science itself bears witness to the emergence of personal democracy. The evolution of its disparate schools of thought reflects the growing privatization and political incoherence of the American public, the political disengagement of ordinary citizens, and the development of access and influence in policy-making that does not depend upon popular support.

Political science, as Theodore Lowi has pointed out, is not just a detached academic pursuit devoted to the study of political activity. The discipline is a political phenomenon itself, and its dominant intellectual currents follow the prevailing tendencies in American politics.[1] Political science, in fact, seems a distinctive expression of the country's exceptionalist claims. A nation brought into being to serve a conscious purpose, defined by shared political belief, and explicitly designed in a written constitution seemed to call up a science of politics. The emergence of political science as an academic discipline only formalized the kind of intellectual enterprise that was already at work in the *Federalist Papers,* and though it would not come to be known as "political science" for almost a century after the ratification of the Constitution, it was present at the creation nevertheless. To Bernard Crick, and to many other political thinkers abroad, the discipline was not just the science of politics, but the *American* science of politics.[2]

Political Science Looks at Citizens

Because its practitioners have been concerned with civic education as well as political scholarship, political science has had an enduring interest in American citizenship, yet it has often been harshly critical of the vehicles through which citizens achieved collective mobilization. As a product of the Progressive Era, the academic discipline of political science shared many of the Progressives' apprehensions about the unwashed, uninformed, and unreasoning rank and file mobilized by the country's unprincipled political party organizations. The parties, in fact, seemed entirely foreign to the spirit of American exceptionalism. They were coalitions united, not by high political purpose, but by competition for office and profit. Perhaps Americans were so unified in their political principles that they had nothing to fight about but boodle.

Though the discipline remained critical of parties, its position shifted slightly after World War II, when the American Political Science Association formed a Committee on Political Parties. Its final report, "Toward a More Responsible Two-Party System," would appear in 1950.[3] Written largely by E. E. Schattschneider, it advanced the argument that programmatic, disciplined, and "responsible" parties could overcome "the depressed state of their reputation," which reflected "their past indifference to broadly conceived public policy." The parties' operating practices, said the report, had "fixed in the public mind the idea of spoils, patronage, and plunder." By presenting clear policy choices to the citizens, however, responsible parties might not only restore their public reputations but also reverse the decline in electoral mobilization that reflected their organizational decay.[4]

The Committee noted in particular that strengthened political parties might develop "greater resistance against the inroads of pressure groups." While not entirely hostile to the interest groups they saw proliferating in national politics, the Committee members were concerned that such groups threatened to increase the incoherence of public affairs. They needed to be integrated into responsible parties, each of which articulated a "working formula of the public interest in its *general* character."[5] The responsible party, in other words, was a framework for engineering compromises among special interests that added up to a larger public interest.

The Pluralist Paradigm

Responsible parties were a work of political imagination reacting, in part, to the political reality of pressure groups, but it was political reality that most political scientists sought to describe and explain, and parties were a diminishing part of it. Instead of becoming more disciplined and "responsible," they continued to decay. Voters' party identifications continued to grow weaker. Political candidates ran their own campaigns for office and increasingly went their own ways after winning it. Interest groups, on the other hand, proliferated, and political scientists' accounts of group politics emerged "as perhaps the most imperial of literatures, not only in American politics but in political science generally."[6]

Groups had the apparent advantage of being more spontaneous and ubiquitous than parties. They were, as David B. Truman pointed out, a fundamental fact of human existence. They structured human experience, feeling, and thought. Political parties uplifted by reform might channel the hopes of citizens into an expression of the public interest "in its *general* character." But groups were vehicles for the actual and immediate preferences of those citizens, and therefore served as practical, not prospective, engines of democracy.

The public interest? That was a ghost. In his 1951 classic, *The Governmental Process,* Truman asserted that the group theory of politics did not have to "account for a totally inclusive interest, because one does not exist." In this, Truman acknowledged the influence of Arthur F. Bentley, who forty years earlier had been almost alone in his insistence that the interest of the social whole could not be actual and observed, because the whole itself had no behavioral existence. Only the groups that made it up were real.[7]

By exorcizing the public interest from American politics, Truman and other group theorists legitimated the "special" interests that found expression through pressure groups. There was no longer any higher interest from which to look down on them. At the same time, lobbying overcame its disreputable status as a desecration of democracy because it was simply the activity through which the citizens worked their will on government. Group politics was a process of democratic competition and maneuvering among an array of citizen interests. Public policy reflected the equilibrium reached by this process, and government was the institution that registered, legitimated, and enforced the result. Group politics, in other words, was an alternative to party democracy—another mechanism of popular sovereignty. According to Elisabeth Clemens, citizen participation in interest groups began to expand just as Progressive reformers were attacking the political parties' monopoly on grassroots mobilization.[8] But in several respects, the interest group was less closely identified with the doctrine of popular sovereignty than political parties had been. Parties lived and died by the politics of numbers; majority-formation was their stock in trade. Interest groups, on the other hand, could achieve their ends outside the orbit of electoral democracy by employing a command of expertise and information, or by exploiting the resources of wealth and political access. Like the political party, moreover, the interest group was a deeply flawed institution even when it came to mobilizing citizens. Truman and most other advocates of "group theory" accepted as unavoidable the fact that interest groups were actually controlled by just a small minority of their most active members or full-time staff employees. They usually resolved themselves into "a leadership and a led."[9] The leadership, of course, might be responsive to the led. But even if interest groups failed to achieve internal democracy, they might contribute to the preservation of the larger democracy in which they operated.

Political sociologist William Kornhauser regarded groups as a layer of insulation that protected social and political elites from the erratic, extreme, and precariously rational movements of mass sentiment. Citizens themselves could become a threat to democracy, and groups were needed to ground them, to contain them, and to counter the alienation that might send them careening off into extremist mass movements.[10] In a later formulation that echoed Kornhauser's theory of mass society, Robert Putnam argued that groups became vital assets in the accumulation of generalized "social capital"—surety for the good conduct of democratic citizens.[11]

Just as groups helped to maintain moderation in the political behavior of citizens, so citizens moderated the group's pursuit of its animating interest. David Truman pointed out that the constituency of one interest group was likely to overlap with the membership base of other groups. The implication, Truman argued, was that group leaders had to take account of interests other than the ones to which their own group was devoted. A single-minded campaign to advance the group's agenda at all costs was likely to alienate members who also belonged to other groups with other concerns.[12]

Overlapping memberships also moderated the political conduct of group members themselves. Early voting research showed that citizens who belonged to multiple groups with conflicting political inclinations tended to respond to their conflicted status by becoming less attentive to politics and less likely to participate in elections. Political scientists did not always regard this tendency toward political apathy as a diminution of democracy. In fact, it might create just the frame of mind that helped to assure citizen rationality. "Cross-pressured" voters were more open-minded than the committed partisans whose group affiliations were all politically aligned with one another. A "sizable group of less interested citizens" might be "desirable as a 'cushion' to absorb the intense action of highly motivated partisans." According to Bernard Berelson, politically passive and indifferent citizens could contribute to the survival of democracy: "If everyone in the community were highly and continuously interested, the possibilities of compromise and of gradual solution of political problems might well be lessened to the point of danger."[13]

By the 1960s, political scientists engaged in the study of both group and electoral politics had converged on a "low-citizenship" model of democracy, a kind of democracy that could be sustained, and even enhanced, by only modest levels of popular interest and participation.[14] The subsequent critiques of this position, instead of unifying the discipline around a new democratic consensus, sent political scientists along two sharply diverging lines of argument, neither of which succeeded in returning citizens to the center of American politics.

Two Roads to Personal Democracy: The New Institutionalism and Rational Choice Theory

Both critiques began by questioning the assumption that citizens with shared interests could be expected to form organizations devoted to the advancement of those interests. But they differed fundamentally in their approaches to this question. One congregation of political scientists—the rational choice theorists—emphasized the obstacles to group formation and collective expression inherent in the logic of individual action, while the other turned toward the structure of state institutions as a constraint on the influence of organized interest groups and a source of protection for the unorganized.

Exponents of group theory had not ignored the problem posed by unorganized interests. David Truman called them "potential interest groups," and among them he included the bearers of such basic political values as "constitutionalism, civil liberties, representative responsibility, and the like." While denying the existence of a public interest, therefore, Truman seems to have rediscovered something like it in the broadly shared concerns of his potential interest groups. And he proceeded to argue that when unorganized interests were challenged by organized ones, they might be galvanized into action. Once under threat, potential interest groups could become actual interest groups.[15]

But, according to E. E. Schattschneider, unorganized groups were still at a disadvantage in the "pressure system." It was dominated, after all, by organized groups that reflected the privileged, upper-class interests of those with the resources needed to organize. This built-in bias not only called into question the democratic claims of group politics but also demonstrated the importance and validity of the distinction between special interests and public interests. Because pressure politics involved only a limited segment of the nation's citizens, it could hardly speak for the broader "potential" groups that stood silently outside the system.[16]

Schattschneider's remedy was to enlarge the arena of political decision-making by means of the responsible party system that he had outlined ten years earlier in the report of the APSA's Committee on Political Parties—"a competitive political system in which competing leaders and organizations define the alternatives in public policy in such a way that the public can participate in the decision-making process." But he also perceived a more spontaneous equilibrating mechanism in American democracy that checked the power of the private interests emerging from the country's capitalist economy. Government and business were "power systems" in competition with one another. Big business was checked by big government.[17]

Schattschneider did not seem much concerned that the democratic state itself might be penetrated by private interest groups. The involvement of political institutions, he thought, had a democratizing effect on group conflict. Moving the clash of private interests into the larger public sphere brought the will of the majority into play, and it also tended to empower weaker interests because groups that monopolized private power were not likely to seek redress from public authorities.[18]

Grant McConnell and Theodore Lowi were more apprehensive than Schattschneider that private interests might undermine the autonomy of public institutions. Like Schattschneider, McConnell argued that the democracy of decision-making depended on the size of the political arena. The smaller the sphere of conflict and deliberation, the more likely it was that democracy would succumb to elite private interests. According to McConnell, however, the mere fact that an issue became the concern of government did not always succeed in enlarging the scope of conflict or achieving democracy. Cozy coalitions of interest groups, bureaucratic officials, and congressional subcommittees could define public policy outside the view of the public and beyond the reach of majority rule. Public decision-making did not necessarily mean open decision-making. Public agencies and programs could be colonized by interest groups that turned public authority to their own uses.[19] Theodore Lowi was also critical of the extension of "interest group liberalism" into the administration of public policy. It made "conflict of interest a principle of government rather than a criminal act," and it shut out all of the mass public "not specifically organized around values salient to the goals of the program."[20]

Both Lowi and McConnell complained that the conquest of government by private interests undermined the authority of the state to act on behalf of public interests, but in describing the problem they also identified potential solutions. The remedies were inherent in the centralizing tendencies of national institutions that might counter the centrifugal forces of group politics. Interests marginalized by pressure politics, McConnell suggested, could seek protection from "the centralized features of the political order—parties, the national government, the presidency." Lowi argued that a strictly law-governed bureaucracy might be able to resist the demands of special interests for special treatment, and McConnell shared Lowi's view that the formal impersonality of bureaucratic government had its virtues because it served as an antidote for the informal bargaining by which private interests sought to unravel the will of the majority as expressed in legislative statute.[21]

The current of thought evident in the work of McConnell and Lowi reflected a new appreciation of formal political institutions. Once a principal concern of political scientists, the study of formal government institutions had been largely abandoned for the more "realistic" study of group politics or individual political behavior. Formal institutions, even the Constitution itself, were mere epiphenomena with no independent being apart from the interests of the groups that supported them. Now the critics of group politics looked to public institutions—president, party, bureaucracy—as independent forces capable of resisting interest group pressures in order to protect unorganized interests and the public interest itself.

The so-called New Institutionalism may not have been born in these responses to group politics, but the kinds of arguments advanced by McConnell and Lowi certainly count among the antecedents that made political science receptive to the idea that political institutions were not simply the artifacts of social forces or individual interests, and one essential component of the New Institutionalism drew directly on the work of McConnell and Lowi. It rescued the state from its dependent status as an attentive bystander in interest group struggles and brought it back to the center of political scholarship, where it became an autonomous political actor.[22]

If political institutions were to provide protection to unorganized interests, they had to be able to resist the demands of organized interests. "The bureaucratic agency, the legislative committee, and the appellate court" had to be something more than mere "arenas for contending social forces." As James D. March and Johan P. Olsen pointed out, they were "also collections of standard operating procedures and structures that define and defend interests. They [were] political actors in their own right."[23]

By themselves, the claims of the New Institutionalism are relatively noncontroversial, but they have significant implications for democratic decision-making. An autonomous state that need not give ground to interest groups provides the matrix for a "new politics of public policy." It is a kind of politics that proceeds rather independently of the society that surrounds it. As a result, its deliberations become more deliberative. They are driven more by ideas and values than by mere group interests or individual preferences external to government. Policy does not simply register the balance of electoral or interest group pressures. "Ideas, and those who have mastered them," writes Martin Shapiro, "come to play a larger role than they would in pure preference politics."[24] Public officials, as Steven Kelman points out, are animated by more than a self-interested concern to accommodate the self-interested groups and voters who can advance their careers or get them reelected. They are guided, at least in part, by a public-spirited determination to make good policies—effective policies that succeed in achieving worthy ends.[25] Their political behavior may be colored by interest but cannot be reduced to interest alone, not their own interests nor those of the groups and voters who pass judgement on their actions.

The "power of public ideas" has taken its place alongside the power of money and the power of the people. "Evidence has steadily accumulated," writes Gary Orren, "that ideas and values are autonomous and do not merely rationalize action in accordance with self-interest."[26] Political institutions supply a framework that supports the ideas and values "that dwell in individual political actors, persist over time, and play a major role in shaping policy outcomes."[27]

Public officials guided by autonomous ideas, of course, may be that much less susceptible to the guidance of citizens and their opinions. Among the guiding ideas, however, is the conviction that policy-making should be open to all interests, even the unorganized ones. Some regulatory agencies have gone so far as to provide financial support so that disadvantaged groups could participate as "stakeholders" in the deliberations that shape policy.[28] But the new power of public ideas is not just a force that reserves a place in the political process for the interests of the weak and unorganized. It may also represent the response of public officials to a public that has become incomprehensible.

Government decision-makers take their cues from autonomous ideas and values, perhaps because they feel that they can no longer take their bearings from public opinion. The public is disorganized. Its opinions are incoherent. Today, it routinely elects a president from one party and a Congress dominated by the other. It is conservative in ideology but liberal on public programs.[29] Its diffuse and disjointed temperament can be accommodated, it seems, only by diffuse policies or those that allow the widest latitude to personal discretion. That might explain the recent emphasis on such public ideas as maximum feasible participation, devolution, privatization, and market-based policies of personal choice. All of them operate to suspend or obscure the public ends that policies are supposed to serve. All of them reflect the incoherent public opinion characteristic of a disorganized public. Revenue sharing was a prime example of an autonomously conceived, "ideational" policy that articulated, at best, a diffuse conception of the public interest. Its principal constituency was composed of government officials. Its early advocates were professional economists. Its ostensible goal "was to combine the advantages of raising revenues at the national level with the advantages of local discretion over spending."[30] Its practical effect was to expend $6 billion of federal revenue each year for nothing in particular. It was a policy tailored loosely to fit the disparate opinions of disorganized citizens in a personal democracy where citizen interests are rarely aggregated into collective interests through collective mobilization. Citizens become articulate through collective action. The voices of unmobilized citizens remain muffled, disaggregated, and obscure.

Schattschneider, McConnell, and Lowi recognized that citizens with shared interests might not be able to take collective action because of economic or political disadvantage. Economist Mancur Olson argued that it was logically impossible to do so, even for the advantaged. Interest groups presumably formed in order to advance group interests. Public policy satisfied those group interests by conferring a collective good on the membership at large. By definition, this collective good became available to all the members of the group, including those who contributed nothing to the collective effort necessary to achieve this good. Olson argued that rational, self-interested people would maximize personal advantage by placing themselves among the fortunate free-riders who consumed the group's collective good without paying any of the associated costs. Since economists assume that people are rational and self-interested, it follows that no one will voluntarily contribute to a group's campaign for a public policy favorable to its members, even if all members would be better off as a result.[31]

Olson's now familiar argument holds that members can be induced to join and contribute to the collective efforts of interest groups only if coerced to do so, or if their activism is rewarded with some private, individual compensation not available to free-riders—in other words, the sort of personal benefit that has become the currency of personal democracy. The same view of citizens is shared more generally by adherents of rational choice theory, an economic perspective on politics that self-consciously views citizens as customers pursuing their private interests.

Political scholarship has yet to advance a convincing program for reconstructing and reinvigorating the American public. For proponents of rational choice theory, in fact, the privatization of citizenship may seem a positive good. It releases us from the complications and contradictions of collective choice. But for most of us, the decline of public citizenship represents a serious lapse in democratic vitality. We cannot claim to know what will restore American citizenship, or even be certain that restoration is what we want. Simple nostalgia for the era of strong parties and high voter turnout tends to overlook its late-nineteenth-century accompaniments—sweatshops, lynchings, and labor violence. Citizenship encumbered by such miseries hardly seems worth restoring. Perhaps we need to envision something entirely new in the relationships between people and their governments. But before that alternative comes into view, we must first understand more fully where citizenship and democracy stand today. That is the aim of this book.

Notes

1. Theodore Lowi, "The State of Political Science: How We Became What We Study," *American Political Science Review* 86 (March 1992): 1, 4.
2. Bernard Crick, *The American Science of Politics: Its Origins and Conditions* (Berkeley: University of California Press, 1959).
3. Committee on Political Parties of the American Political Science Association, "Toward a More Responsible Two-Party System," *American Political Science Review,* 44 (September 1950): Suppl.
4. Ibid., 16.
5. Ibid., 19.
6. Frank R. Baumgartner and Beth L. Leech, *Basic Interests: The Importance of Groups in Politics and Political Science* (Princeton, N.J.: Princeton University Press, 1998), 44.
7. David B. Truman, *The Governmental Process: Political Interests and Public Opinion* (New York: Alfred A. Knopf, 1951), 21, 50–51; Arthur F. Bentley, *The Process of Government: A Study of Social Pressures* (Chicago: University of Chicago Press, 1908), 220–21.
8. Elisabeth S. Clemens, *The People's Lobby: Organizational Innovation and the Rise of Interest Group Politics in the United States, 1890–1925* (Chicago: University of Chicago Press, 1997), 35–37.
9. Earl Latham, *The Group Basis of Politics: A Study of Basing-Point Pricing Legislation* (Ithaca, N.Y.: Cornell University Press, 1952), 3; Truman, *The Governmental Process,* 139.

10. William Kornhauser, *The Politics of Mass Society* (New York: The Free Press, 1959).
11. Robert D. Putnam, *Making Democracy Work: Civic Traditions in Modern Italy* (Princeton, N.J.: Princeton University Press, 1993), 169, 183–85.
12. Truman, *The Governmental Process,* 159.
13. Paul Lazarsfeld, Bernard Berelson, and Hazel Gaudet, *The People's Choice: How the Voter Makes Up His Mind in a Presidential Campaign,* 2d ed. (New York: Columbia University Press, 1948), 60–64; Bernard Berelson, "Democratic Theory and Public Opinion," *Public Opinion Quarterly* 16 (Autumn 1952): 317, 327.
14. For an early and concise critique of the "low citizenship" theory, see Jack L. Walker, "A Critique of the Elitist Theory of Democracy," *American Political Science Review* 60 (June 1966): 285–95.
15. Truman, *The Governmental Process,* 51, 114–15.
16. E. E. Schattschneider, *The Semisovereign People: A Realist's View of Democracy* (New York: Holt, Rinehard and Winston, 1960), 29–36; see also Peter Bachrach, *The Theory of Democratic Elitism* (Boston: Little, Brown, 1967).
17. Schattschneider, *The Semisovereign People,* 120–21, 141.
18. Ibid., 38–41.
19. Grant McConnell, *Private Power and American Democracy* (New York: Alfred A. Knopf, 1966), 6–7, 162.
20. Theodore Lowi, *The End of Liberalism: Ideology, Policy, and the Crisis of Public Authority* (New York: W. W. Norton, 1969), 86.
21. Lowi, *The End of Liberalism,* 291, 298–99; McConnell, *Private Power and American Democracy,* 8, 107, 349.
22. The work of McConnell and Lowi is directly implicated in recent writing on the autonomy of the state. See, for example, Eric A. Nordlinger, *On the Autonomy of the Democratic State* (Cambridge, Mass.: Harvard University Press, 1981), 44–45.
23. James G. March and Johan P. Olsen, "The New Institutionalism: Organizational Factors in Political Life," *American Political Science Review,* 78 (September 1984), 738.
24. Martin Shapiro, "Of Interests and Values: The New Politics and the New Political Science," in Marc K. Landy and Martin A. Levin, eds., *The New Politics of Public Policy* (Baltimore: The Johns Hopkins University Press, 1995), 7.
25. Steven Kelman, *Making Public Policy: A Hopeful View of American Government* (New York: Basic Books, 1987), 261.
26. Gary R. Orren, "Beyond Self-Interest," in Robert B. Reich, ed., *The Power of Public Ideas* (Cambridge, Mass.: Ballinger, 1988), 24.
27. Shapiro, "Of Interests and Values," 5.
28. Ibid., 6.
29. Albert H. Cantril and Susan Davis Cantril, *Reading Mixed Signals: Ambivalence*

in *American Public Opinion about Government* (Washington, D.C.: Woodrow Wilson Center Press, 1999), 10–11.

30. Timothy Conlan, *From New Federalism to Devolution: Twenty-Five Years of Intergovernmental Reform* (Washington, D.C.: Brookings Institution Press, 1998), 65.

31. Mancur Olson, *The Logic of Collective Action: Public Goods and the Theory of Groups* (Cambridge, Mass.: Harvard University Press, 1965).

Downsizing Democracy

Chapter 1

From Popular to Personal Democracy

IN THE NINETEENTH CENTURY, America was exceptional for the vitality of its democratic institutions—especially its political parties. The country may have been slow to abolish slavery, but it was first to achieve universal white manhood suffrage; and by midcentury, when European states were taking their first hesitant steps toward mass democracy, America's dynamic party organizations were routinely mobilizing 70 to 80 percent of the electorate in presidential campaigns. Outside the South, even midterm congressional contests typically pushed turnout past 60 percent.[1]

Today, American politics is no longer exceptional for its feats of grassroots mobilization. In the midterm elections of 1998, for example, merely a third of the registered voters went to the polls. In the 2000 national election, barely half of all voters—but all nine Supreme Court justices—cast presidential ballots. Candidates are spending more than ever to turn out their supporters. They are employing the tools of mass communications to project their voices and images across a vast electronic electorate. But the citizen response has grown progressively weaker. Behind the receding waves of electoral mobilization, a new kind of American exceptionalism is emerging, one marked by rates of voter participation significantly lower than those that prevail today in the same European nations that once stood by and watched while the United States built the world's premier popular democracy.

Voting is the most common means of citizen participation, and the contraction of the electorate is the most obvious sign of the diminished role that citizens play in American politics. But the decline of citizen activism extends beyond the empty voting booth. Though the absence of nineteenth-century opinion polling makes it difficult to trace forms of popular participation other than voting, there are strong indications of a general decline in popular politics since the end of the nineteenth century.[2] The evidence of the last thirty or forty years suggests, at best, a stagnation in political activism. Contributing money to political organizations is the only activity to register an unambiguous gain since the 1950s, but it is unclear whether we should regard such financial donations as a sign of active involvement in politics or as a substitute for it.[3] Even the venerable institution of the citizen jury is increasingly giving way to a criminal justice system in which judges, lawyers, and private arbitrators are the only participants.[4]

Just how truncated the role of the ordinary citizen has become in America was made patently clear when President George W. Bush called Americans to action in the wake of the 9-11 terrorist attacks on New York and Washington, D.C. Did Bush ask Americans to sacrifice, to buy bonds, to volunteer for military service, or to donate blood? Not exactly. In point of fact, the president told Americans the best thing they could do for their country would be to shop more while the government went about the business of fighting terrorism. In other words, the nation's defense was best left to professional administrators and soldiers, and ordinary folks should avoid getting in the way.[5] Tens of millions of Americans displayed flags and clearly wanted to do something for their country, but their country seemed to have nothing for them to do. A few months later, during his 2002 State of the Union address, President Bush issued a call to Americans to commit themselves to community service. Precisely how they were to serve and to what end were left vague.

American democracy is not dead. It has, however, undergone a transfiguration, and so has American citizenship. These changes do not come from some vast conspiracy to deprive the general public of its place in politics. In fact, twentieth-century political reforms have given citizens unprecedented access to the political process. The introduction of primary elections, the use of referendum and recall, sunshine laws, legislative mandates requiring agencies to give public notice and hold public hearings before making policy changes—all would seem to have made the government more responsive to citizens than ever before. Through ACTION, VISTA (Volunteers in Service to America), Americorps, and the Peace Corps, the government has sponsored the activism of citizens committed to a vision of the public good, and it has extended the idea of citizenship itself to cover many circumstances of life once regarded as purely private. Gender, race, age, sexual preference, and physical disability now figure in the claims that we make upon the public. According to sociologist Michael Schudson, "a dimension of citizenship has come to cover everything," and he adds that the new political dimensions of life in the United States may compensate for the "slackening of voter turnout."[6]

But the new opportunities for citizen involvement have changed the nature of citizenship itself. The proliferation of opportunities for individual access to government has substantially reduced the incentives for collective mobilization. For ordinary Americans, this means that it has become standard practice to deal with government as individuals rather than as members of a mobilized public. At the same time, Americans of more-than-ordinary political status find that they can use the market, courts, administrative procedures, and other political channels to achieve their ends without organizing the support of a political constituency. In short, elites now have fewer incentives to mobilize non-elites, and non-elites have little incentive to join with one another. The two circumstances have operated in combination with one another to produce a new politics of individualized access to government and a new era of "personal democracy" for those in a position to take advantage of its possibilities.

Recent trends in popular participation are all the more striking because they seem to run counter to expectations. For example, the most powerful predictor of political activism used to be education, and although levels of education have been rising in the United States, political participation has not.[7] Personal democracy may help to explain why. Increased education, together with the increased accessibility of government, may have equipped Americans to get what they want on their own, without hitching their interests to coalitions of like-minded fellow citizens.

Just as curious as the combination of rising education and declining participation is the conjunction of the "advocacy explosion" in Washington with quiescence beyond the Beltway. Estimates of the explosion's magnitude vary, but everyone agrees that there has been a dramatic increase in the number of organizations represented in Washington, perhaps as much as a fourfold increase since the late 1960s. Yet the population explosion in organized interest groups has not been accompanied by any comparable increase in organizational activism among the public at large—except for the increase in financial contributions, which may actually represent a retreat from direct involvement.[8] Perhaps the most puzzling anomaly in contemporary democratic politics is the disparity between mass immobility and elite agitation.[9] The coupling of elite conflict with popular quiescence is inconsistent with expectations based on what might be called the neoclassical theory of political democracy. As developed by Robert Dahl, Maurice Duverger, V. O. Key, and E. E. Schattschneider, this theory asserts that high levels of competition or conflict among political elites will increase rates of mass participation as contending leaders and parties engage in rival efforts to mobilize political support.

V. O. Key credited the Jeffersonians with setting the stage for mass mobilization when they built local party organizations to "line up the unwashed in their support." The practice was distasteful to the opposing Federalists, but they were soon forced to do the same or risk exclusion from office and power.[10] Throughout the nineteenth century and well into the twentieth, party leaders and candidates waged political warfare like generals, recruiting and mobilizing regiments of voters whose numbers tended to grow whenever party conflict intensified. But some time in the twentieth century, the link between leadership competition and citizen mobilization weakened and then disappeared. Though partisan conflict in Washington has rarely been more rancorous than during the past several years, this rancor does not seem to have been translated into popular mobilization. Voter turnout, for example, once rose and receded with the intensity of partisan division in Congress; but by the late 1960s, surges of congressional conflict and tides of electoral activism no longer ebbed and flowed in concert, and voting itself was riding a downward wave that has not yet broken.[11]

Down to the end of the nineteenth century, American elites encouraged popular participation because they needed the active support of non-elites. In its infancy, of course, the United States had to win the allegiance of citizens already attached to states and regions. It was largely for this reason that the framers of the Constitution extended basic rights of participation and representation to common folk in exchange for their consent and support for a new government. Constitutional Convention delegate James Wilson explained that to "raise the federal pyramid to a considerable altitude," it would be necessary to give it "as broad a base as possible."[12] For at least a century after ratification, the federal government remained a small state in a big country. It depended on the support of citizen soldiers, citizen taxpayers, and citizen administrators in order to survive and govern.

The government's need for its people set the terms of political competition. Groups and parties contending for office and influence were virtually compelled to organize and mobilize citizens. Popular support was the currency of power, and in the struggle to acquire power, political leaders produced the high rates of participation that persisted until the start of the twentieth century. Left to themselves, many citizens—especially those with lower levels of income and education—would never have taken to politics. Limited political information, limited interest in public affairs, and primitive communications technology would have left many of them on the sidelines of the nation's public life. They became active because vigorously competitive leaders marched them into the public forum.[13]

As they sought popular support, politicians striving for power were compelled to offer concessions and inducements in exchange for the people's allegiance. At first, elites offered representation and participation. Later, they pledged more concrete benefits. Even today, contending politicians offer voters health benefits, social services, old-age pensions, and job security in return for their votes. Yet today, the promises seem more ritualistic than ever—designed less to mobilize new support than to retain the old and to placate important interest groups. There are fewer promises of new benefits and more pledges to continue existing programs while controlling their costs, fewer efforts to galvanize new constituencies and more fence-tending to retain a political base.

This is what happens when elites discover that they can do without the support and service of common folks. Rather than expand the range of public benefits to broaden their support base, elites promote the private market as a better source than government for education, health, welfare, and old-age benefits. Rather than expand the base of the federal pyramid through voter mobilization, elites disparage representative institutions as gridlocked and ineffectual. Term limits are proposed as a remedy for the ossification of these institutions; privatization, deregulation, and expansion in the role of the judiciary offer paths around the democratic deadlock.

The upper classes never relied exclusively upon mass politics to advance their political and economic goals. Facing the rise of popular democracy in the nineteenth century, they tried to ride the majoritarian tide by astutely deploying campaign contributions and lobbyists.[14] Reformers, who readily spied the hand of privilege that manipulated these political innovations, railed against the influence of "big money" in elections and interest-group lobbying in Congress.[15] But there was no reactionary conspiracy here to reverse the progress of democracy. The money and the lobbyists represented the elites' capitulation to democracy's electoral and representative institutions, and an acknowledgment that they would have to play the democratic game. By contrast, contemporary reforms that are supposed to democratize government—enhanced access to the courts and to the process of administrative rule making—may actually enable political elites to circumvent the arena of popular politics and exercise power without mobilizing democratic support.

The Making of Modern Citizens

The manifestations of the new era in American politics are subtle and wide-ranging. Consider, for example, the recent transformation of civic education in American public schools. Civic education's purpose is to teach young people a common set of political ideals and beliefs and to habituate them to the rules of conduct that govern public life in a democracy. Promoting good citizenship was one of the purposes for which public schools were originally created in this country.[16] The not-so-hidden curriculum used to concentrate on preparing students for collective political action, especially the electoral process.[17] Students held elections to choose team captains, class officers, and student government representatives. They even held mock elections that paralleled real elections.

Schools have not abandoned all of these rituals. But there is a pronounced shift from these electoral exercises to "student service learning." Maryland was the first state to make it a requirement for high school graduation, but other states are quickly following suit. Elementary and secondary school students are expected to "volunteer" for public service jobs with charitable, civic, and public interest groups. Student service learning is also a growing presence on college campuses, and there have been calls to make it a graduation requirement in the state colleges and universities of California.[18]

Traditional civic education tried to teach students that they could help to govern the country along with their fellow citizens just as they governed their classrooms, teams, and schools with their fellow students. Service learning imparts a fundamentally different set of lessons about citizenship. Citizenship is no longer about the collective activity of governing. Students are urged to produce the public services that a voting public once demanded from its government, frequently services that government has abandoned or is not prepared to pay for. Lessons in service have supplanted training for sovereignty.

One study finds that more than half of all service-learning students report that they have worked in environmental or beautification projects, which may not even provide direct assistance to other human beings. But the principal and intended beneficiaries of these programs may be the students themselves, rather than the service recipients. The service-learning experience is supposed to be personally rewarding and to bolster "self-esteem."[19]

The civic activities of young adults (ages eighteen to twenty-four) reflect a similar shift toward service activities. During the past twenty-five years, voter participation among young people has declined by more than twelve percentage points while their participation in quasi-public and private volunteer organizations like Americorps or the Jesuit Volunteer Corps has grown substantially.[20] In a recent study of local activists, sociologist Nina Eliasoph found parallel tendencies among adults in general. Activists tend to avoid "politics" in favor of community service projects. Talking about political issues, they believe, is wasteful because such talk seldom arrives at consensus or clearly defined conclusions. Perhaps more important, they are convinced that political issues are unlikely to yield to the efforts of community volunteers like themselves. They tend to concentrate instead on community service projects that they know will enable them to "make a difference"—especially projects aimed at the welfare of children. Not only were such efforts likely to be noncontroversial, says Eliasoph, but the volunteers "took a 'focus on children' to mean 'a focus on private life.' That meant that the only real changes regular citizens could make were changes in feelings."[21] Not least important were the feelings of the activists themselves, whose personal satisfaction depended on the conviction that they were "making a difference."

What passes for citizenship today often inverts the feminist dictum that the personal is political. It has transformed the political into the personal. Political activity should feel "empowering." It should enhance self-esteem. It should not engender confusion, ambiguity, or frustration.

An all-too-easy diagnosis of the new, service-oriented citizenship would locate its origins in a more comprehensive feel-good culture of self-gratification and self-esteem. But such a diagnosis would overlook the authentic sacrifices made by volunteers who actually perform tasks that are useful to their communities. And it would ignore the more authoritative efforts of political elites to recast the meaning of American citizenship: "Ask not what your country can do for you; ask what you can do for your country." President Kennedy's inaugural exhortation bore fruit in the Peace Corps and, later, in VISTA. The National Community Service Act of 1990 would embrace an even wider population of volunteers, and it supplied more than $200 million to fuel President Bush's "thousand points of light." President Clinton followed this initiative in 1993 with his half-billion-dollar Americorps program. For his part, President George W. Bush called upon the nation's schools to help bring about a "renewed spirit of patriotism" in the wake of the 9-11 terrorist attacks. Concretely, however, the president seemed to translate patriotism into something like service learning when he suggested that students could demonstrate patriotism by raising money to help Afghan children.[22] Bush's subsequent call for a renewed spirit of voluntarism has a similar ring.

These programs unquestionably inspire worthy people to worthy deeds, but they also represent a government-sponsored shift in our conception of citizenship. Rather than make demands of government, we now fulfill them ourselves, and in doing so we gain the personal satisfaction and certainty that we have actually performed a service and made a difference.

The New Science of Public Administration

While citizens have been encouraged to think of themselves as public servants, the more conventional public servants employed by the federal government have also been encouraged to adopt a new perspective on the citizens whom they serve. This new perspective emerged in the 1993 Report of the National Performance Review, the manifesto of the Clinton administration's campaign to "reinvent" government. The review is one in a long succession of studies designed to improve the functioning of the federal bureaucracy. Its predecessors emphasized the democratic accountability of public bureaucracy, which was one of the first points made by the first Hoover Commission in 1949: "The President, and under him his chief lieutenants, the department heads, must be held responsible and accountable to the people and the Congress for the conduct of the executive branch." The statement has all the banality of a self-evident truth. But, as political scientist James Q. Wilson observes, nothing like it appears in the Report of the National Performance Review overseen by Vice President Gore. The subject of democratic accountability is hardly ever mentioned. Nor do citizens figure in the report. They have been transformed into "customers," and the review's explicit objective, declared by the vice president, is "to make the federal government customer friendly."[23]

There is nothing necessarily undemocratic about this aim. The vice president's point is that federal employees should strive to meet the needs of their clients and treat them with respect—in other words, the government should be more responsive to its people. But there are crucial differences between citizens and customers. As noted above, citizens were thought to own the government, while customers merely receive services from it. Citizens belong to a political community with a collective existence and public purposes. Customers, however, are individual purchasers seeking to meet their private needs in a market. Customers are not involved in collective mobilization to achieve collective interests.

Customer service has also become the focus of training for public administrators in general, in a departure from an earlier emphasis on public responsibility. In the 1950s, political scientist Fritz Morstein Marx summarized the bureaucratic orthodoxy of the time: "Public responsibility . . . asserts the necessity of providing demonstrable public benefits and of meeting public expectations. . . . Public responsibility under popular government further demands the willing subjection of the bureaucracy to the laws as the general instruction of the representatives of the people."[24] But the authors of a more recent text regard the public as a collection of customers to be "managed" rather than a public to be served:

> You should work hard to cultivate outside group support for your mission. . . . When you deal with the general public you should expect its members to have a limited understanding of the complexity of most issues. . . . While it is to your advantage to have the public on your side, this may not always be possible. Your organization may have a mission that is in conflict with . . . community groups. . . . Your job is to uphold your organization's mission. . . . Be prepared to suffer through public outcries, insults and demonstrations while supporting your program goals.

But suffering can be minimized by effective management of the media, representative institutions, community groups, and the public at large.[25] Citizens have been demoted to customers; public administration, to customer relations.

The Politics of Social Capital

The narrowing political role of American citizens has done nothing to diminish the ethical elevation of citizenship itself. Citizenship, in fact, seems to have become an embodiment of the virtues and values in which American society is alleged to be deficient—civic consciousness, the sense of community, responsibility to others. Among academics, a recent "explosion of interest in the concept of citizenship" is partly a response to a perceived deterioration in the practice of citizenship.[26] The new requirements for community service in public school systems are introduced to reinvigorate a sense of public-mindedness weakened by a market-driven society that inspires the avarice of its consumers rather than the public spirit of its citizens. One of the more recent eulogies for the lost virtues of citizenship comes from a representative of the television industry, an institution often blamed for the erosion of America's civic community. Anchorman Tom Brokaw's best-selling book, *The Greatest Generation,* honors an entire generation of citizens who endured the hardships of the Depression and the hazards of World War II.[27] They are the measure of what we have lost and the model of what we should have become. In a sense, they are modern America's counterparts to the fallen soldiers glorified in Pericles' famous funeral oration, the citizen heroes who sacrificed themselves for the sake of Athens.

We are witnessing a radical divergence between the moral conception of citizenship and the political conduct of citizens. The mismatch is widely acknowledged and is conventionally attributed to deficiencies in the moral, cultural, or social resources of today's citizens, deficiencies that prevent them from acting on behalf of interests larger than their own.[28] The general diagnosis is that America has amassed money and power at the expense of its "social capital"—the interpersonal connections and mutual trust that used to sustain collective enterprises. In a book and a series of articles, Robert D. Putnam documents a general decline in civic engagement since the 1960s, a decline that has transformed us into a nation of increasingly solitary and mutually mistrustful citizens.[29] Even in our services to others, we have become more likely to act alone. Putnam finds an increase in "volunteering" since the mid-1970s, but it is accompanied by a decline of participation in community service projects.[30] Altruism itself has been privatized.

Though Putnam attributes an array of social and cultural ills to the erosion of social capital, the political consequences of that erosion must weigh most heavily in any assessment of American democracy and citizenship. Those consequences strike at the sources of political engagement. Formal associations and informal socializing once instilled habits of cooperation and elevated private interest into public spirit, but the social ties that sustained the practice of democratic citizenship have weakened or dissolved. This depletion of social capital has impoverished grassroots democracy, depopulated the public forum, and undermined the effectiveness of popular government, which the people have come to regard with growing mistrust.

By Putnam's account, three-quarters of the decline in civic engagement can be attributed to just two factors—television and generational change. Television made entertainment a private matter to be enjoyed in one's home. The diversions of an older America—visiting with neighbors, lodge meetings, church socials—now compete with a calculated campaign of amusement designed to capture an audience for commercials. Americans, long known as a rootless and mobile people, seem to have become a nation of stay-at-homes.[31]

They have also abandoned the public commitments of the self-sacrificing "civic generation" that pulled through the Depression, then fought World War II. Having missed the collective experience of the war and its unifying force, Americans born during the second half of the twentieth century turned inward. According to Putnam, the satisfactions of personal fulfillment and material comfort displaced an older attunement to patriotism and community. Though the new generation was hardly homogeneous, its ambitious Yuppies, New Age seekers, and channel-surfing couch potatoes had in common a detachment from the public concerns of their predecessors. But Putnam's picture of civil society in decay and citizenship in decline is curiously incomplete. It suggests that the patriotic generation of World War II rose to meet its public responsibilities because it was called upon to do so, and because the call seemed compellingly urgent and just. Putnam's picture neglects the possibility that that generation's successors remain politically inert because no one has issued a convincing summons for their support. What appears to be a failure of citizenship may in fact be a failure of political leadership.

Several of Putnam's critics seem to converge on precisely this oversight in the "civil society" argument, though they reach it from different directions. The late C. Everett Ladd, for example, challenged Putnam's central contention that we have experienced a decline in civic engagement. Though established group ties may have disappeared, Ladd argued, new connections emerged in their place. The new attachments, however, differ systematically from the ones that they succeeded. According to Ladd, "the trend is away from centralized, national organizations to those decentralized and local."[32] In other words, networks of civic involvement are increasingly detached from national institutions and elites. Social and civic interactions continue, but no national leadership stratum uses these connections to mobilize participants around larger national purposes.

Sociologist Theda Skocpol traces the fraying of civil society to an "unraveling from above." More privileged Americans have pulled out of cross-class membership federations that once linked local chapters to national organizations. They have thrown their support instead to staff-led advocacy groups with headquarters in Washington but little or no presence at the grassroots. Skocpol points out that some of the organizational keystones of civil society—like the PTA—were elite-generated federations created from the top down.[33] "Classic American association-builders," she observes, "took it for granted that the best way to gain national influence, moral or political, was to knit together national, state, and local organizations that met regularly and engaged in a degree of representative governance."[34] Such associations depended not only on the power of numbers but also on the dues of members. Today they can be sustained by foundation grants, wealthy patrons, direct-mail fund-raising, or the fruits of litigation.

Changes in government institutions, not the ebbing of civil society, have been responsible for opening up these new political niches for interest groups that get what they want without mobilizing a mass membership. To some extent, in fact, civil society is as much a product of political institutions as vice versa. Skocpol's cross-class federations were modeled on the federal structure of the government they were trying to influence. Civic traditions do not spring up spontaneously to undergird a passive state. The exercise of public authority often shapes civic culture and determines whether or not civic institutions take root in the society that surrounds government.

One of the first outings for Robert Putnam's argument about the citizen-forming role of civil society was a study of the effectiveness of regional governments in Italy that attributed their general success in the north and their disappointing performance in the south to a thousand-year-old difference in "civic traditions" between the two regions. Political scientist Sidney Tarrow responded that the difference in civic traditions might be a product of government itself. In the south, a succession of foreign occupiers found it advantageous to discourage the formation of associations or coalitions among the subject population. In the north, competing parties in the nineteenth century mobilized supporters by creating sports clubs, mutual aid societies, and recreational associations. Civil society was a product of politics, and so was its absence.[35]

Recent lamentations on both left and right mourn the loss of political consciousness among citizens, the waning of collective feeling, the disappearance of public spirit. We are lectured about our abandonment of old-fashioned communal virtues, our culture of self-involvement, our expectations of entitlement. As citizens, it seems, we are no longer good enough for our country. Above all, we have lost the discipline of self-sacrifice and given ourselves too completely to self-interest.

But self-interestedness, as historian Peter Riesenberg points out, has been the constant companion of citizenship.[36] Even Pericles recognized the intimate connection between the public sacrifices of citizens and their private interests. Political communities had to offer inducements to inspire good citizenship: "For where the prize is highest, there, too, are the best citizens to contend for it."[37]

Who Needs Citizens?

States offer "prizes" for citizenship because they have need of citizens. In classical antiquity, the extension of citizenship rights often followed from an escalation in the need for military manpower—especially foot soldiers. At the beginning of this century, historian Otto Hintze noted that in modern states there had been a similar connection between dependence on citizen soldiers and the extension of suffrage. The existence of militia forces was associated with the early onset of democracy, and even in more centralized and authoritarian systems, Hintze argued, universal military service eventually led to universal suffrage, if only after several generations.[38]

Armies, of course, had to be equipped, provisioned, paid, and pensioned—all of which enlarged the state's need for taxpayers—and the need for taxpayers gave states another incentive to extend the rights of citizenship. Long before American colonists demanded that representation accompany taxation, England had begun to recognize taxpayers as citizens. The step was taken not just to part taxpayers more peacefully from their money but to increase the wealth available to be taxed. Property rights, the right to practice a trade or engage in commerce, and the right to secure those rights through the courts all helped to enhance the prosperity of taxpayers and expand the state's revenue base.[39] In absolutist France, the transformation of taxpayers into citizens occurred later, but more suddenly, when a revenue crisis forced Louis XVI to summon the Estates-General for the first time in centuries.[40] Within a few years, almost everybody in Paris was addressing everybody else as "citizen."

The modern states of Europe invented modern citizenship not just because they needed standing armies and the money to pay for them but because the very existence of the state defined the conditions for citizenship. The modern state was a membership organization to which people belonged directly as individuals, not indirectly through their membership in families, clans, tribes, guilds, or status orders; and the state itself replaced this jumble of premodern political jurisdictions as the single, paramount object of political allegiance.[41]

Understood in this way, the connection between the modern state and modern citizenship is tautological. The definition of citizenship is implicit in our definition of state. But citizenship was more than a vertical relationship between subject and state; it also implied a relationship among fellow citizens, a common tie of blood, belief, or culture that united them into a political community. Beyond that, citizenship also has behavioral implications—a role in governing the state and the support of state authority. These involvements in governance were the activities denoted by Aristotle's definition of the citizen as one who rules and is ruled. The benefits of rulership were the prizes that citizens won for being of service to the state, and as Pericles observed, the more valuable the prizes, the higher the standards of citizenship were likely to be. His ancient observation, as well as the modern state's cultivation of citizen soldiers and taxpayers, suggests an alternative to the view that the recent decline in the role of American citizenship is a product of the citizens' personal characteristics, their cultural values, or their access to "social capital."

Citizens become politically engaged because states and political elites need them and mobilize them. If citizens remain passive, politically indifferent, or preoccupied with private concerns, the reason may be that our political order no longer provides incentives for collective participation in politics. The state may no longer need citizens as much as it once did, or perhaps citizens have become a nuisance to political elites, or it may be that citizen "prizes" have gotten too expensive for the state to afford.

Citizens, of course, do not disappear simply because they have become institutionally inconvenient. A political system engaged in the collective demobilization of citizens fashions other arrangements for the political management of its population. In general, American institutions operate increasingly to disaggregate and depoliticize the demands of citizens. The "reinvention" of American government has reinvented citizens as "customers." It has offered "stakeholders" easy access to the decision-making process as a low-energy alternative to collective mobilization. It emphasizes private rights at the expense of collective action. It is promoting arrangements for policy implementation that encourage individual choice rather than the articulation of public interests. It has reduced the occasions for citizens to congregate around "opinion leaders," and it has weakened the incentives for political entrepreneurs to organize public constituencies. It has begun to privatize not only many of its own functions but the public itself. American politics has entered the era of personal democracy.

A Short History of Personal Democracy

The routine operations of American government once relied on the large-scale mobilization of the public to a far greater extent than they do today. Conceptions of political democracy that focus on parties, elections, and pressure groups tend to overlook this fading dimension of popular sovereignty. But the complete citizen, as Aristotle observed, plays two roles—ruling and being ruled—and these roles have been bound to each other. The more government rule depended upon citizen cooperation, the more government submitted to the rule of citizens. As government has learned to manage the public business without the public, it has also diminished the occasions for the kind of popular mobilization that demands reshaping public policy or changing political institutions.

Some of the first steps toward the demobilization of American citizens date to the Progressive Era, when reformers sought to eliminate waste and incompetence from government by abolishing patronage and by crippling the political party organizations that mobilized working-class, immigrant voters who offended the Progressives' "public-regarding" conception of citizenship.[42] The Progressives' conception of an autonomous citizen independently evaluating candidates and policies was an early anticipation of personal democracy. But some of the most significant discouragements to the collective mobilization of citizens followed the end of World War II, perhaps the last and greatest summons to citizen duty in the nation's history.

These discouragements were expressions of the postwar conservative reaction against the New Deal. Both the Administrative Procedure Act of 1946 and the Taft-Hartley Act of 1947 were intended to curb the authority of New Deal regulatory agencies by holding them to formal standards of rule making and adjudication. The ostensible purpose of these enactments was to prevent the interest groups under regulation from "capturing" the agencies that were supposed to regulate them. The chief concern of congressional conservatives at the time was the privileged status of labor unions with respect to the National Labor Relations Board. To counter such interest-group influence in the regulatory process, Congress tried to open administrative rule making to the public at large by means of requirements for public notice and comment. To avoid bias in particular cases, the Administrative Procedure Act attempted to construct a firewall between the agency's rule makers and its administrative law judges. And finally, Congress decreed that an agency's decisions could be appealed to the courts.[43]

In the effort to eliminate factional bias from the regulatory process, Congress also reduced the incentives for citizens to mobilize and form interest groups. After the passage of the Administrative Procedure Act, pressure successfully exerted on an agency's rule makers did not necessarily extend to its adjudicators, and because the rule-making process was now open to the public at large, there was not so much need to organize groups and mobilize constituencies in order to gain access to rule making, especially since unfavorable decisions could be appealed from regulatory agencies to the courts. The postwar regulatory reforms were eminently democratic, at least in a formal sense.[44] It could be argued, in fact, that they opened government more fully to the participation of its citizens because of their notice-and-comment provisions and the opportunity to appeal agency decisions to the courts. The Taft-Hartley Act was explicitly justified as a measure that would protect individual workers from undemocratic labor unions as well as from the unfair labor practices of their employers. But since the new regulatory regime facilitated individual access to policymaking, it reduced the value of collective mobilization.

The legalistic mode of administration imposed by the postwar conservative reaction was extended, in the 1960s and 1970s, to types of policies that the conservatives could hardly have anticipated—civil rights, occupational health and safety, environmental protection, and consumer protection.[45] A further step in the progress of legalistic policymaking was the use of public interest lawsuits as instruments of regulation. The civil rights movement had used litigation to advance its aims since the 1940s—but it did so, in part, because the denial of voting rights to African Americans and their minority status meant that they were seriously handicapped in the usual arenas of democratic decision-making. Litigation, like the resort to civil disobedience, was a way to overcome their electoral disabilities. In the 1970s, however, public interest groups emerged whose chief democratic disability was not minority status but the very breadth and diffuseness of the disorganized constituencies that they claimed to represent. These groups devoted less energy to mobilizing their potential supporters than to litigation. Aided by responsive federal judges, these new public interest groups employed lawsuits against federal agencies—like the Environmental Protection Agency—to establish regulatory standards that the agencies were then required to enforce.[46]

What ensued was an "advocacy explosion." Organizations claiming to represent diffuse population groups such as consumers, children, the disabled, the elderly, or the public in general opened Washington offices not just to conduct traditional lobbying activities aimed at Congress or the federal bureaucracy but to litigate on behalf of their constituents. The relationship between the constituencies and the organizations claiming to speak for them, however, was often quite tenuous. Litigation required money, research, and expertise, but not the political mobilization of a popular following. The "membership" of these groups sometimes amounted to nothing more than a mailing list of faceless contributors who had never met with one another to discuss the group's political objectives or strategies. A few highly influential groups, in fact, were actually supported by foundation grants and legal fees won in court cases, and some received funding from the federal government itself.[47]

The legalization of national policymaking accentuated an emphasis on individual rights that has always been inherent in American ideas about citizenship. Public interest lawsuits aimed not only to assert those rights but to invent new ones, and in the process they changed the character of national political discourse. Legal scholar Mary Ann Glendon argues that the language of rights is a conversation stopper. It "puts a damper on the processes of public justification, communication, and deliberation upon which the continuing vitality of a democratic regime depends."[48] The successful assertion of a right trumps all other arguments. In some instances, of course, political argument can actually be stimulated by the contest between competing rights, or by the attempt to extend a recognized right to a new situation. Once established, however, a right can be invoked without engaging in the collective action that awakens and renews the common ties of citizenship.

The vast increase in interest-group litigation and the rights-based politics that followed from it may help to explain one of the previously noted anomalies of American politics.[49] By all accounts, the population of Washington lobbyists and interest groups has grown rapidly since 1970, to unprecedented levels, but there has been no corresponding increase in group membership among Americans at large. One possible reason for this disparity may be that some of the newest interest groups have begun to target ever narrower interests.[50] But an explanation with an even longer reach is that contemporary interest groups tend to concentrate more on litigation, research, polling, fund-raising, and media relations and less on mobilizing popular support. The handful of Washington-based interest groups that actually have extensive grassroots memberships, like the National Rifle Association and AARP, are connected with the vast majority of their constituents only by mail.[51] The interest-group struggle in Washington, like the clash of party elites in Congress, becomes increasingly disconnected from the mobilization of citizens, and the scope of citizenship itself narrows.

While Washington interest groups floated free from the constituencies that they claimed to represent, the federal government seemed to fasten itself more firmly to the grassroots. "Maximum feasible participation," was the controversial watchword of federal policy.[52] Requirements for citizen participation spread from one national program to another. Public bureaucracies and private interest groups seemed to be moving in opposite directions, but they were both dancing to the same music. Both public and private organizations sought to open the administrative processes of regulation and policy implementation to outside forces, but they accomplished almost exactly the opposite. "Maximum feasible participation" usually achieved only minimal mobilization of the public. In the Community Action Program, the Model Cities Program, and other antipoverty ventures of the federal government, the chief effect of participatory administration was to absorb and dissipate the political pressures generated by urban protest movements, often by co-opting the actual or incipient leaders of those movements.[53] The participatory programs also lacked substance. To allow for policymaking by the people, official policymakers had, after all, to refrain from issuing precisely designed programs with clearly articulated objectives. The immediate result, as political scientist Theodore Lowi pointed out, was that "the absence of central direction and guidance simply deprives the disappointed of something to shoot against. This is a paternalism that demoralizes."[54]

The absence of clearly formulated rules and objectives was also a formula for policies that would be difficult to justify and defend from attack, precisely because the policies and their purposes were not clearly or compellingly defined. When the Reagan tax cuts made deficit reduction the organizing purpose of federal politics in the 1980s, the last vestiges of community action were swept away, along with the revenue-sharing and block grant programs of the 1970s.[55] They suffered from the same political disabilities as their participatory predecessors—vaguely defined objectives and weak or politically diffuse clienteles.

What replaced community action was a new conservative policy regime that preached the virtues of the market not just as a substitute for big government but as an instrument of big government. Privatization and vouchers were supposed to free the public sector of bureaucratic inefficiency and unresponsiveness. But they also represented a new stage in the erosion of citizenship. Vouchers and programs of "choice" were designed so that public policies could be disaggregated into private decisions. Under a school voucher system, for example, parents dissatisfied with the kind of education their children receive need never complain or join with other parents to protest. They can simply choose to send their children to a different and more satisfactory school.

There is an undercurrent in twentieth-century American politics that flows through movements and measures strikingly at odds with one another. The postwar conservatives who backed the Administrative Procedure Act and the Great Society liberals who launched the War on Poverty will never be mistaken for ideological soul mates. They are connected, however, by a shared political sensibility that ties them not only to each other but also to the Progressives who preceded them and the Reagan-Bush conservatives who followed. The link between the two is a tendency to individualize democracy—an inclination to provide citizens with personal access to politics, policymaking, and administration and, by so doing, to reduce the frequency and the need for collective action.

Personal democracy lowers the political barriers that citizens used to breach only by collective assault. Freedom-of-information policies, sunshine laws, mandatory public hearings, public-notice-and-comment requirements, quotas for "citizen" representation on boards and committees, public agency "hotlines," and policies of choice—all these and other arrangements besides permit citizens to play politics alone. Yet the principal effect of these apparently benign arrangements for personal democracy is to shrink the role of citizens in American politics. Organizational entrepreneurs and elites who once mobilized followers in order to earn a place among the government's power holders and policymakers now discover that they can achieve similar or better results through litigation or that, by claiming to speak on behalf of a diffuse and otherwise voiceless constituency, they can qualify as "stakeholders" whose presence is essential to the legitimacy of federal policy.

When popular mobilization ceases to be a favored strategy among leaders, citizens are left to their own devices—of which there is no shortage these days. But these devices generally lend themselves only to an attenuated kind of citizenship, and they seldom result in political mobilization for collective ends. More frequently the outcome is individual action for improved service or personalized treatment. One alternative for citizens is community activism designed not to raise political issues or reshape public policy but to produce public goods and services directly—cleaning up the environment, for example, or serving meals in a homeless shelter. This dimension of personal democracy may be personally rewarding and certainly helpful to needy people or the local community at large, but it does not represent an exercise of political democracy. A nation of citizens, once illuminated by democratic purpose, has disintegrated into a thousand points of light.

Chapter 2

The Rise and Fall of the Citizen

FOR MORE THAN two centuries, the survival of Western governments depended not just on the consent of the governed but on their active and willing cooperation. By contributing to the administrative, coercive, and extractive capabilities of their countries, the governed elevated themselves from mere subjecthood to the dignity of citizenship. They made their entrance disruptively in the eighteenth century with the revolutionary bang of the shot heard round the world. In time, however, they brought a welcome stability to national politics. They represented the foundation of public order and the energy source for functioning government.

In return for their services, citizens received a variety of benefits, perhaps most notably the right to vote. The history of suffrage is often written to suggest that the opportunity to participate in national politics was wrung from unwilling rulers after bitter popular struggles. Yet, as E. E. Schattschneider observed, the difficulty with which voting rights were secured in the United States and elsewhere has often been overstated.[1] Political elites learned that accepting the extension of suffrage was worthwhile even though it seemed to pose a risk to their own power. By integrating citizens into the political order, elites enhanced the state's ability to wage war, raise revenues, and administer the government. In the eighteenth century, governments usually resisted demands for suffrage expansion. By the nineteenth and twentieth centuries, however, Western regimes had come to see popular voting rights in a more favorable light.

The tacit exchange of service for benefits drew citizens further and more fully into political life. Citizen administrators supplied much of the energy for vigorous political party organizations. Expansion of the government's revenue base to include tens of millions of ordinary citizens also expanded the power of the representative institutions. These institutions encouraged popular cooperation with tax collectors and moderated conflicts about the distribution of tax burdens. Reliance upon citizen soldiers expanded the boundaries of participation as those asked to fight demanded the right to vote.

Today, at the start of a new millennium, however, Western governments' reliance on the support and cooperation of citizens has diminished, and the scope of popular participation has narrowed. Today's public authorities manage to raise armies, collect taxes, and implement policies without widespread citizen involvement. These changes have enabled political elites to reduce their dependence upon popular political participation and to secure and exercise power by means other than mass politics. The era of the modern citizen, which began with a bang, is quietly slipping away.

In some respects, the symptoms of this change are most marked in America. The democratic exceptionalism of the Tocquevillian republic stands in stark contrast to the democratic demobilization of contemporary politics. The presidential election of 2000 is emblematic of the new order. In the most competitive and closely fought contest in generations, only a bare 50 percent of the electorate bothered to go to the polls, and the ordeal ended in a judicial determination that the counting of votes was not decisive in any case. Like the litigious contestants of 2000, contemporary political elites have substantially marginalized the American mass electorate and have come to rely more and more upon courts and bureaucracies to get what they want.

The essential and original claim of American exceptionalism was not just that we were different from other nations but that we had a different way of being a nation. America was a community of political belief, not of blood and soil. Political scientist Hans Morgenthau—no sentimentalist—detected something almost spiritual at the core of the country. Unlike other nations, America did not, he argued, gradually arrive at a conception of its national mission by reflecting retrospectively on the course of its history. "The rule that action precedes reflection in the discovery of the national purpose suffers but one complete exception. The United

States," Morgenthau wrote, "is the only nation that has reversed the sequence. The awareness of its purpose was not an afterthought. The United States was founded with a particular purpose in mind."[2]

John Winthrop provided a classic illustration of the anticipatory purposefulness that Morgenthau saw in American politics. In the middle of the Atlantic, on the deck of the *Arbella,* Winthrop—soon to be the first governor of the Massachusetts Bay Colony—preached a sermon to his fellow travelers, who would soon become the first citizens of that colony. His subject was the purpose of their errand in the wilderness, an errand not yet begun. The purpose that Winthrop had in mind was, of course, religious as well as political, but it was also a universal purpose that spoke to all humankind and not to a narrow sect. In the most famous passage of his sermon he urged his shipmates to "consider that we shall be as a city on a hill, the eyes of all people are upon us." But in a less prominent place, before he reached the summit of his homily, Winthrop reflected on the nature of the religious bonds that would solidify the Puritan political community: "though we be absent from each other many miles . . . yet we ought to account ourselves knit together by this bond of love."[3]

From the outset, the American polity was no mere territorial community; it was not defined by spatial propinquity. It was a compact among fellow believers. And although the nation remained Anglo-American for centuries, it would eventually surrender much of its ethnic distinctiveness as well. America claimed to be a nation defined by shared and universally valid purpose or principle. Long after that purpose had ceased to be a Puritan one, it still retained something of its original religious resonance. To English journalist G. K. Chesterton, America was the nation with the soul of a church. In Gunnar Myrdal's formulation, Americans became the people of the Creed: they shared a set of beliefs that was supposed to set the nation's existence on a different plane than that of other nations, and although writers like Samuel Huntington and Louis Hartz have found much that was troublesome in the Creed, hardly anyone denied its power.[4]

But a political community organized around ideas might redefine or simply dissolve itself much more easily than one rooted in blood and soil. Though all nations may be imagined communities, some are more imaginary than others. In the Civil War, America showed that it could imagine itself out of existence, and though we face no such dramatic rupture today, the bonds of American citizenship are sufficiently exiguous that they can be redefined in ways that drastically change the role and political attachments of the American people.

The exceptionalist vision of Americans as a people united only by democratic purpose may have been a patriotic conceit, but in the nineteenth-century Republic there was very little else to hold the citizens together as a nation. Even coercive efforts to preserve the country, like the Civil War, could scarcely have succeeded without an army of volunteers devoted to the cause of the Union. In an earlier departure from the exceptionalist vision, President Jefferson acquired the territory of Louisiana without first securing the consent of its inhabitants. They were citizens by purchase, not by principled belief. But the very fact that the government's hold over its new territorial acquisition was so tenuous made national authorities especially deferential to the inhabitants and heavily reliant on their willingness not only to transfer their loyalties from Paris or Madrid to Washington but to take on the work of governing. To facilitate such cooperation, the government agreed that courts in the most heavily populated section of the Louisiana Purchase would follow the continental civil code rather than the English common law.[5] They still do.

Nineteenth-century American citizens helped to perform the work of government and in return gained a voice in government. Of course, the United States was not the only nation that employed citizens to perform the tasks of government. What distinguished the United States from European regimes of the nineteenth century was the exceptional extent of its reliance on citizen government. The framers of the American Constitution were hardly radical democrats, but they felt compelled to provide for popular political participation in order to ensure that the new regime would have citizens' backing. They had no choice. More than forty years after they completed their deliberations, Alexis de Tocqueville reported that he had found nothing in America that a European would regard as government.[6] There was no professional civil service surviving from an earlier era of royal administration. There was scarcely any standing army. The country's territory extended to remote regions in which the only government was what the citizens provided themselves. It was no wonder that American government was exceptional for its attentiveness to citizen sensibilities and for its professed dedication to the creed of popular sovereignty. The United States was more democratic than other states of the time partly because it was exceptionally dependent on the good will, cooperation, and work of its people.

The Rise and Fall of the Citizen Administrator

Early-nineteenth-century America was certainly no bureaucratic state. Without a corps of professional civil servants to bring the government to bear on its people, early American administration had to rely heavily upon the people themselves. America's nineteenth-century administrators might have been lacking in expertise, but they possessed other essentials of public administration, namely, loyalty and public standing. Indeed, even European states with technically proficient bureaucrats had long recognized that expertise by itself was insufficient. Two more fundamental attributes were also vital. First, administrators had to be loyal to the government they were supposed to serve, and, second, they had to be capable of securing public compliance with government policy.

In early-modern Europe, meeting these two conditions was often far more difficult than securing competent administrators. In England and France, for example, the clergy provided a ready source of trained and reasonably competent administrators. Wolsey in sixteenth-century England and Mazarin and Richelieu in seventeenth-century France were prominent figures in this administrative tradition. These cardinals, in turn, recruited bishops and priests to flesh out the administrative structures of emergent nation-states. As the case of Thomas Becket suggests, however, kings could not always rely upon the loyalty of their clerical servants, particularly when princes and popes vied for secular power.

In early modern Spain, kings sought to avoid subordination to the church by drawing upon the exceptionally talented Jewish community as a source of managerial and financial acumen. As a result, particularly in Castile, many of the highest administrative positions were frequently held by *conversos,* Jews who had nominally accepted the Catholic faith in order to be legally eligible for government service. The *conversos* were vigorously loyal to the Crown. The king was their only protector in a hostile society that still regarded them as Jews. But it was precisely this anti-Semitic hostility that undermined public compliance with the dictates of a government managed by *conversos.* Dissident forces, charging that the regime had been subverted by Jews, insisted that its legitimacy was forfeit.[7]

The American solution to the twin problems of administrative loyalty and popular compliance was patronage. It was not an American invention. England had known patronage at least since the Tudors, who had met the problem of compliance by recruiting members of the local gentry as administrators, in the hope that the respect these worthies commanded in their communities might rub off on the government they served. The existing social hierarchy provided an armature to support administrative authority. And, since the appointees could expect to retain their posts only so long as their sponsors were in power, they had a tangible stake in the political survival of their patrons and a strong incentive to political loyalty. Patronage and public administration have been partners since the beginnings of modern state bureaucracies, and patronage was not necessarily inconsistent with effective government. Political leaders had good reason to choose the most competent of their retainers. Still, in eighteenth-century England, "no aspiring office holder could obtain a place without proper political connections or an obliging relative in high places."[8]

In the United States, as political scientist Martin Shefter points out, political patronage was far more extensive than in most European states because mass-based political parties emerged in this country long before there was a professional civil service. Because America possessed strong parties and no civil service tradition, government jobs were freely available for distribution as patronage.[9] The parties did not hesitate to exploit this resource. Patronage became an American system of government—the spoils system. The Jacksonians are charged with introducing the system to reward their political friends and build a party machine at the expense of the public treasury. The charge is not unfounded. But patronage served other purposes too, as it had for the Tudors. After the Jacksonians' 1828 victory, they faced not only their supporters' demand for government jobs but also an executive branch staffed by holdovers from the Adams administration, staffers who might sabotage their efforts to set a new course for the federal government. The remedy was a proscription of public employees associated with the prior government, and their replacement by loyal Jackson partisans.[10]

Jackson brushed aside concerns about the competence of the new partisan administrators, declaring that public administration required no special capabilities: "The duties of all public officers are, or at least admit of being made, so plain and simple that men of intelligence may readily qualify themselves for their performance; and I cannot but believe that more is lost by the long continuance of men in office than is generally to be gained by their experience."[11]

Under Andrew Jackson, between 10 and 20 percent of the government's administrative personnel were removed to make room for supporters of the new regime. Although the numbers were not as large as charged by Old Hickory's antagonists, the Jacksonians established the principle that the loyalty of public servants was to be ensured through the appointment of a new administration's partisan supporters. In 1840, when the Whig candidate, William Henry Harrison, captured the White House for the first time, the new cabinet met and resolved to replace Democratic appointees with loyal Whig supporters. Within a year, nearly twenty-three hundred Democrats had been removed to make way for the new president's adherents. When the Democrats returned to office in 1844, they replaced thousands of Whig appointees with their own men.

Patronage helped to guarantee not only the loyalty of government functionaries but also their ability to secure citizen compliance with government policy. In the United States, the problem of compliance was considerably more acute than it had been in England. The American government was weak, and its power did not extend very far into the country, particularly after the Louisiana Purchase opened vast new lands to settlement. By the 1820s, frontier squatters routinely ignored federal land law and imposed their own property settlements through armed violence and intimidation. Settlers who held their land under grants from the French or Spanish government might be less than fully loyal to Washington. In the South, doctrines of states rights and, eventually, of nullification challenged the authority of a federal government lacking the military force to impose its will on a recalcitrant population. Civil servants had to do more than administer. They had to win the loyalty of a people and shore up the legitimacy of the government that they served.

Unlike the Tudors, America's democratic rulers could not appoint members of a landed gentry to administrative posts in order to capitalize on the respect that they commanded among their less prestigious neighbors. Outside the South, there was no landed gentry, and hierarchies of status had always been much weaker in America than in Europe. By the 1820s, economic and political change had further eroded the institutions that supported distinctions of rank and privilege. But political parties were growing stronger, and the local leaders who ran them were prime candidates for federal employment. A party politician who enjoyed popularity among his neighbors (rather than aristocratic rank) and commanded their votes (if not their deference) might also command their compliance with federal law and "win the good will and affections of the people for the government."[12]

For the remainder of the nineteenth century and into the early years of the twentieth, patronage employees provided successive governments with a generally loyal body of administrators whose own retention in office was linked to the success of the politicians they served. By courting the voters, patronage employees also helped to build support for the regime they served. They provided citizens with a host of particularized benefits ranging from social services to legal assistance and employment. At times, these citizen administrators were able to secure popular compliance when coercion would probably have failed. During the Civil War, the efforts of Republican patronage workers helped to win acceptance of military conscription, assisted in the sale of government securities, and bolstered tax collection. The North's superior party and patronage organization played a largely unheralded role in the Union victory.

Citizen administrators not only helped to preserve the national government but also adapted its practices to local circumstances, local needs, and local political considerations. Harold Gosnell's classic study of machine politics in Chicago during the 1920s and 1930s shows how administrators reshaped government programs to fit the needs of individual citizens. Patronage workers helped constituents qualify for veterans' pensions, obtain citizenship for relatives, and secure government housing assistance through the Home Owners' Loan Corporation. They helped the sick to get public medical services, helped immigrant entrepreneurs secure permits needed for small businesses, showed them how to meet (or evade) complicated building and zoning codes, and helped their delinquent children to navigate the criminal justice system.[13]

From the perspective of the cosmopolitan upper classes of the late nineteenth century, this particularistic style of administration represented corruption and political favoritism, and perhaps they were correct. But at least some later observers offered a more benign analysis of patronage politics and the party machines that it supported. "In our prevailingly impersonal society," wrote sociologist Robert Merton, "the machine, through its local agents, fulfills the important social function of humanizing and personalizing all manner of assistance to those in need," a welcome alternative to "the cold bureaucratic dispensation of limited aid" by official welfare agencies.[14] Today's customer-friendly bureaucrats may have been trained to dispense services and assistance with more personal warmth than their predecessors. Their jobs, however, do not depend on loyalty to the party in power, and they have no role in the political mobilization of their clients. Public administration may continue to be an instrument of democracy, but it has largely abandoned its role as a functioning part of the democratic order itself.

The citizen administrator was the backbone of the political party organizations that were instrumental in expanding popular participation during the nineteenth century. Unlike their contemporary counterparts, they had a stake in expanding popular political participation because it was the basis upon which their own power and position rested. The government's reliance upon citizen administrators linked the state to mass participation. Using hundreds of thousands of patronage employees as their campaign workers, American political parties during the nineteenth century were capable of prodigious feats of electoral mobilization. In some regions, party machines maintained levels of voter turnout approaching 90 percent. During the critical 1896 presidential election, Republican party workers brought more than 25 percent of the Republican voters from every state in the union to walk past candidate William McKinley's home in rural Ohio as part of McKinley's "front porch" campaign.[15] Citizen administrators worked directly to enlarge and elaborate the universe of popular politics.

Progressives fought to replace these short-term and decidedly amateur administrators with professional bureaucrats whose chief loyalty would be to the state rather than to parties and fellow partisans. Accordingly, Progressives supported extension of the merit system in which an autonomous civil service commission selected government workers on the basis of competitive examinations rather than political loyalty and service.

Progressives insisted on the separation of administration from politics.[16] In his professorial phase, Woodrow Wilson himself pronounced the orthodoxy. Administration was a science or technology that aimed to achieve public objectives with greatest efficiency. But the administrators had no business helping to define those objectives. That was the job of politics. Administrators were politically neutral experts who served everyone and no one. They were pledged to the public interest rather than to the partisan purposes of the current administration.[17] The divorce of administration from politics also detached public bureaucracy from the popular base on which it had formerly rested. This separation, however, also implied the creation of a professionally staffed bureaucracy that would permit governments to function without having to mobilize popular support or win citizen compliance.

To ensure that government employees would be insulated as much as possible from popular political currents, academics and intellectuals linked to the Progressive movement invented "personnel administration." Its original principles called for military-like position-classification schemes; efficiency reports and evaluations; the idea of public service as a lifetime career; the circulation of bureaucrats among regions or localities; regulations governing salary, benefits, and promotions; and retirement and pension plans.[18] The techniques of personnel administration were designed to permit the work of government employees to be directed from the top down and to prevent those employees from being influenced by shifts in popular sentiment or by local attachments. Government would be able to rely upon this permanent civil service to escape its historic dependence upon short-term citizen administrators.

Many of the basic principles of personnel administration were adopted by the federal government in response to the report of the Keep Commission, appointed by President Theodore Roosevelt in 1905 to recommend improvements in federal administrative practices.[19] Roosevelt's successor, William Howard Taft, created the Commission on Economy and Efficiency, which supplemented the Keep Commission's work by elaborating principles of position classification and employee efficiency evaluation.[20] As they hoped, the Progressives had begun the separation of government from popular political mobilization. By the mid–twentieth century, patronage survived only in a few redoubts like Cook County, Illinois. The machinery of government was in the hands of professionals rather than citizen administrators. Later, even civil servants began to give way to the employees of private firms that contracted to perform the government's work[21]—one further step removed from the public will that endowed the state with its authority.

Taxation: From Voluntary Compliance to Automaticity

Revenue was as necessary to government as reliable administrators. In early-modern Europe, erratic tax systems made for fiscal instability and impeded the development of strong nation-states. Rulers generally depended upon income from their own lands, contributions from a usually reluctant nobility, and loans from financiers. Not only were these revenue sources unreliable, but they made rulers heavily dependent upon the noble estates and the wealthy financiers who controlled their fiscal destinies. Beginning in the sixteenth century, European monarchs introduced new revenue-raising devices designed to produce money more reliably, and without the political inconvenience of dependence on powerful barons or bankers. In France, for example, successive regimes sought to tax crops, acreage, and commerce, and at times they resorted to the sale of government offices and the confiscation of church properties. After taking control of Brandenburg-Prussia in the fifteenth century, the Hohenzollerns replaced the preexisting feudal revenue system with taxes on property and beer production. The effectiveness of the new measures was limited. In England, successive Tudor kings sought to introduce a variety of direct taxes but were unable to seize the purse strings from Parliament. Throughout Europe, a patchwork of customs duties and excise taxes also were introduced. These were often so inefficient that collection costs exceeded the revenues that accrued to the government.[22]

Beginning in the eighteenth century, European governments broadened the revenue base to the public at large. In addition to imposing income and poll taxes, states started to sell securities in denominations small enough that ordinary citizens, not just bankers and financiers, might purchase them. These new mechanisms produced a steady and substantial flow of royal revenue and diminished royal dependence on the crown's most powerful subjects. But in broadening the base for revenue collection, the state also broadened the population whose loyalty and support it had to cultivate. With expanded taxation came demands for expanded representation and citizen participation, and increased stature for the representative institutions. In most instances, the end result was an expansion of governmental power. But in trying to expand their revenue bases, some regimes unleashed forces beyond their control—in France, a revolution.

The United States began life as a nation with the sort of broadly based revenue system that European kingdoms reached only after centuries of trial and error. Local, state, and federal governments relied heavily upon ordinary citizens for their financial needs from the earliest days of the Republic. Even before the American Revolution, the governments of the thirteen colonies had already established mechanisms to expand their revenue bases. Colonial property taxes weighed most heavily upon farmers, whose property could be easily evaluated. In addition, most colonies also levied poll taxes. In colonial Massachusetts, for example, a person was valued at £20 and taxed at a rate of a penny per pound.[23]

The combination of property and poll taxes extended the reach of colonial taxpayers, but these taxes gave common citizens a substantial measure of political influence. Although most colonial legislatures were dominated by relatively small elites, ordinary taxpayers could threaten not to pay their taxes. Organized tax resistance was relatively common during the colonial period, and colonial governments lacked the military force to deal with it. They were compelled, as a result, to pay attention to the views of farmers, tradesmen, and small-property owners who might not command the prestige to hold seats in colonial legislatures but had the capacity to deprive the government of badly needed revenues. Tax resistance in Pennsylvania, for example, forced the colony's government to develop a more equitable system of property taxation in the early eighteenth century. After the Revolution, Shays' Rebellion in 1787 and the 1794 Whiskey Rebellion carried on the colonial tradition of taxpayer recalcitrance.

To avoid provoking their testy taxpayers, the more imaginative among the colonial governments sought to raise cash by issuing interest-bearing certificates of indebtedness in small denominations. Eventually, these came to circulate as paper money. According to Margaret Myers, colonial Massachusetts was the first government in modern history to issue paper money.[24] In the aftermath of King William's War (1689–1697), the colonial government was bankrupt and unable to borrow money. The government also lacked the coercive mechanisms needed to enforce tax increases in the face of what was certain to be substantial popular resistance. In 1690, the colony printed £7,000 in interest-bearing, redeemable certificates of indebtedness with which to fulfill its obligations. During the ensuing decades, new issues brought the total value of certificates in circulation to £194,000.

The smallest denomination of these Massachusetts certificates was £50, which limited their circulation. In the 1720s, however, New York issued interest-bearing £25 notes, and Pennsylvania produced £12 notes. These small notes made a large fraction of those involved in the cash economy de facto holders of government bonds. By the 1730s, most of the colonies had begun to circulate certificates of indebtedness in ever smaller denominations. For example, beginning in 1750, Maryland began to issue $1, $2, $4, and $6 notes. By the time of the Revolution, debt certificates, denominated in both pounds and dollars, were commonly used as paper money and had actually replaced coin as the country's primary medium of exchange. One contemporary observer estimated that by 1776, paper money constituted nearly 60 percent of the £12 million in circulation.[25]

Reliance upon widely distributed certificates of indebtedness was one of the factors that forced colonial governments to pay attention to the views of ordinary citizens. If a government lost public confidence, its notes would no longer be accepted and its ability to meet its obligations would be threatened. For example, the pacifist sentiments of its Quaker citizens compelled the government of Pennsylvania to pledge that none of its paper money issues would be used for any form of military expenditure.

After the Revolution and the construction of the federal government in 1789, the states continued to rely upon broadly based property and poll taxes as their major revenue sources. Initially, the federal government financed its limited activities through tariffs and customs duties, supplemented by moderate borrowing in national and international credit markets. During the Civil War, however, the need for revenues increased so dramatically that the government could not secure sufficient funds from the traditional sources—domestic banks and financiers. European investors, for their part, had no confidence that the Union would prevail on the battlefield and were reluctant to purchase U.S. securities.[26]

The federal government therefore turned to new forms of revenue extraction, including excise taxes on manufactured goods, a tax on incomes, bond sales to small investors, and the issue of a variety of legal tender notes, some interest bearing and some not, in small denominations. All these revenue devices depended upon a measure of popular acceptance and left the government financially dependent upon popular confidence to meet the Union's military expenses, which ultimately totaled more than $4 billion. By the end of the war, excise and income taxes had produced more than $1.2 billion in revenues. A moderately progressive income tax was enacted in 1862. A levy of 3 percent was imposed on all incomes below $10,000, with the rate rising to 5 percent on incomes above that level. In 1864 and 1865, the income tax act was amended, eventually providing for rates of 5 percent on incomes below $5,000 and 10 percent for those earning more than that amount.[27]

A third major revenue instrument introduced during the Civil War was the sale of government bonds to small investors. In 1862, Treasury Secretary Salmon P. Chase invited Ohio Republican banker Jay Cooke to attempt to place $500 million in government bonds that could not be sold to domestic banks or foreign investors. Cooke developed a plan to market these securities to ordinary citizens who had never before purchased government bonds. He thought he could appeal to the patriotism of ordinary Americans, and he believed that widespread ownership of government bonds would give large numbers of ordinary citizens a greater concern for their nation's welfare.[28] Cooke established a network of twenty-five hundred sales agents throughout the North and used the press to promote the notion that purchasing government securities was both a patriotic duty and a wise investment. In every community, Republican party organizations worked hand in hand with Cooke's sales agents, providing what historian Eric McKitrick calls the "continual affirmation of purpose" needed to sustain popular support and the regime's finances through four long years of war.[29] By 1863, all the bonds had been sold, and most were in the hands of private citizens rather than financial institutions.

A final revenue instrument introduced during the war was the issue of $450 million in legal tender notes. Some of these so-called greenbacks bore interest, and others could be redeemed for twenty-year government bonds. The bulk of the greenbacks, however, were unredeemable "fiat money." Issued in the form of payment on existing government debt, the greenbacks constituted an interest-free loan from the general public to the government. After the war, the constitutionality of federally issued paper money was challenged and, eventually, upheld by the Supreme Court.[30]

The revenue instruments devised during the Civil War became important parts of the national government's revenue-collection efforts during the ensuing decades. The income tax was declared unconstitutional by the Supreme Court in 1895 and then reinstated by the Sixteenth Amendment in 1913. During the late nineteenth and early twentieth centuries, business and financial interests, along with the Republican party that spoke for them, opposed the income tax and advocated financing the federal government through the sale of large-denomination bonds. Bondholders, unlike taxpayers, derived private profit from financing the operations of the federal government, and a government sustained by bonds tended to be attentive to the institutions and people who bought bonds.

Populists, most Democrats, and some liberal Republicans, in contrast, supported the income tax, especially one with a progressive rate structure. It made the government financially dependent upon the great mass of ordinary Americans and shifted influence away from the banks, financiers, and elite bondholders, who accrued interest and political influence at the same time.[31] If federal borrowing was required, Populists and most Democrats favored bonds in small denominations that could be purchased by ordinary citizens rather than fat cats.

The debate between the proponents of alternative modes of public finance came to a head during World War I, when the Wilson administration overcame congressional opposition and moved to raise a large part of the war's expenses through increased taxation. In his April 1917 message to a special session of Congress, the president said it was the government's duty to "protect our people . . . against the hardships and evils . . . that would be produced by vast loans."[32] As a result, the financing of World War I was at least partially consistent with the Democratic and Populist perspective. First, the income tax played an important role in financing American participation in World War I. A tax on incomes that by 1918 reached 6 percent on the first $4,000 in income and 12 percent on the remainder generated nearly one-third of the $33 billion in military and related costs incurred by the United States during the war. The remainder of the expense of the war was financed by corporate taxes, excise taxes, and, especially, government borrowing.[33]

Using marketing techniques similar to those devised by Jay Cooke during the Civil War, the government urged Americans, through "borrow and buy" campaigns, to participate in what were designated "Liberty Loans" and "Victory Loans." Four Liberty and Victory Loan campaigns generated an astonishing $22 billion for the war effort. Bonds were sold in denominations as low as $50, and purchase on an installment plan was allowed. The Liberty and Victory Loan campaigns were conducted by the War Loan Organization, which was organized into sales, speaking, and publicity bureaus. The entire sales network was staffed by tens of thousands of ordinary citizens who volunteered to work in coordination with local banks. Another $1 billion was raised by the sale of thrift stamps, war savings certificates, and small bonds in schools, post offices, and factories to those sufficiently patriotic but too impecunious to participate in the Liberty Loan drive. Stamps cost as little as twenty-five cents each. A sheet of sixteen thrift stamps could be exchanged for an interest-bearing $5 bond. Stamps and savings certificates were also sold by an army of civilian volunteers.[34]

Despite this resemblance to Civil War–era bond sales, the government did not rely entirely upon the patriotic ardor of ordinary citizens to market its securities. With the creation of the Federal Reserve System in 1913 and the designation of the Federal Reserve as the Treasury's fiscal agent in 1915, the United States government had greatly increased its borrowing capabilities. To support wartime financing, the Federal Reserve established a preferential discount rate on loans to member banks secured by government obligations. Funds borrowed by the banks were, in turn, used to promote installment loans to the public for the purchase of war bonds. In essence, the Federal Reserve System provided the economy with enough money to ensure that the bond sales would be a success.[35] Patriotism was bolstered by institutional innovation and a carefully conceived economic policy. Ordinary citizens played an important role in financing World War I, but the emergence of the Federal Reserve marked the advent of a new era in which institutional regularity would gradually replace reliance upon popular enthusiasm in public finance.

Taxes and borrowing rose once more during the Great Depression and even more dramatically after the nation entered World War II in 1941. World War II marked a watershed in government finance. First, the Revenue Act of 1942 substantially broadened the nation's tax base, increasing the number of households subject to the income tax from 13 million to 28 million. By 1944, tax rates began at 3 percent on incomes between $500 and $2,000, rose to 20 percent for incomes above $2,000 and climbed steeply to reach a nominal rate of 91 percent on income higher than $200,000.[36]

The second important innovation associated with the war was the enactment of the Current Tax Payment Act of 1943. Before 1943, federal income taxes were to be paid quarterly in the year after the income was received. This system depended heavily upon the honesty, good will, and foresight of individual taxpayers. Under the terms of the 1943 act, however, employers were required to withhold 20 percent of wages and salaries and to remit these to the government as the income was earned.

The 1943 Current Tax Payment Act partially freed the government from its historic dependence upon the support and integrity of the individual taxpayer. The act made the collection of income taxes automatic and involuntary from the perspective of the taxpayer and, together with higher rates, increased federal income tax revenues from slightly more than $1 billion in 1940 to just under $20 billion by 1944. While making greater demands on citizens, the Treasury thus reduced its dependence upon citizen compliance.

World War II also brought a great enhancement of the government's capacity to market and manage debt. The savings bond program was one element in this expansion. During the course of the war, some $50 billion in U.S. savings bonds were sold to individual citizens. Patriotic appeals organized by the War Finance Division of the Treasury Department and backed by mailings of more than 650 million pieces of advertising encouraged workers to enroll in the payroll savings plan. Under this scheme, workers agreed to have approximately 10 percent of their income automatically deducted from their paychecks and invested in savings bonds. Like taxation, the purchase of government securities became an automatic process requiring no continuing citizen effort. By the end of the war, nearly 28 million workers were participating in the plan, resulting in automatic monthly bond purchases of roughly $500 million.

Savings bonds sold to ordinary workers accounted for approximately one-third of the funds borrowed by the U.S. Treasury during World War II. The remainder, some $135 billion, was raised by marketing securities to individual investors, corporations, and banks. As was the case during World War I, government bond drives were marked by a great deal of patriotic hoopla, often centered around appeals by film stars, war heroes, and other celebrities. At the same time, however, the actual machinery for marketing government securities had become much less reliant upon the patriotism of individual citizens than had been the case during World War I.

As before, the Federal Reserve System served as the Treasury's sales agent for securities. The scope and character of Federal Reserve activities, however, changed substantially during World War II. Beginning in the 1920s, the Federal Reserve system had initiated open market operations, through which it regulated the supply of money by buying and selling government securities. When necessary, it could also print money to finance its bond purchases. In 1942, the twelve Federal Reserve banks began a policy of purchasing, at a fixed rates, all government securities offered to them. The fact that government securities could be sold to the Fed at this support price made them totally liquid and the equivalent of interest-bearing money. This policy assured the success of all government bond sales by giving banks and investors every reason to purchase government securities, since they could be easily resold at guaranteed prices.[37] In the process, however, the Fed also diminished the government's dependence upon the patriotism and support of individual citizens to finance its enormous wartime borrowing needs.

Broadly based taxes and small-denomination securities once allowed the federal government to finance its survival without subordinating itself to powerful financial interests. And by distributing its taxes and bonds into the hands of so many of its citizens, the government acquired a tangible incentive to fulfill the promise of democracy. To collect its taxes and sell its bonds, it needed widespread popular compliance and support, which could be sustained only if government remained attentive to public sentiment and values. Hence the historic relationship between taxation and representation. Even before this principle became a cause of revolution, the colonial governments of British America were sensitive to the possibilities of tax resistance. They resorted to debt instruments as a way to circumvent the need for tax compliance, only to find that they had created another kind of dependence upon popular support.

The tax system itself reflected the government's concern about its credibility with the public at large. The principle of progressivity, enshrined in American tax law since the Revenue Act of 1862, was a concession to the popular sense of justice. According to tax historian Sidney Ratner, progressivity accompanied the extension of new and relatively high rates of taxation to citizens with small incomes.[38] In principle, at least, the handful of wealthy Americans had to be taxed at even higher rates in order to convince tens of millions of their less prosperous fellow citizens that the tax system was fair and that they should comply with its demands.

The progressivity of the income tax has been weakened significantly since the 1980s—one more sign, perhaps, that the government's fiscal reliance on the good will of ordinary citizens is waning. But it was not only the great mass of ordinary citizens who lost influence as a result of changes in the methods of tax collection and the marketing of government securities. The distribution of authority within the government has changed as well. From colonial times onward, legislatures gained in political stature because the executive could not levy taxes without their acquiescence. During the Reagan and Bush administrations, however, budget deficits coupled with adamant Republican resistance to any tax increases undercut the fiscal powers of Congress and shifted control of the economy to the Treasury and the Federal Reserve.[39] For the government of the United States, as for most other regimes, the historic problem of revenue collection has been to persuade millions of citizens to pay taxes and purchase government securities. Dependence upon a broad base of taxpayers and modest investors increased governments' dependence upon popular confidence. These "democratic" measures of public finance paid for America's independence, its survival, and its victories in two world wars—but to a diminishing extent as time passed.

U.S. savings bonds, the democratic foundation of government finance, have now become occasional birthday presents for grandchildren. They account for less than 1 percent of national debt. The federal tax system has expanded on the collection techniques devised to minimize its dependence on taxpayer cooperation. Of the $2 trillion in federal tax revenues collected every year, about one-half are generated by the personal income tax; and employer withholding, which accounts for approximately 75 percent of this sum, is remitted to the Treasury without any positive act of support or compliance on the part of the individual taxpayers. Another $500 billion is withheld from employees' paychecks for old-age, disability, and unemployment insurance. As one tax expert noted recently, "Taxpayers who receive only wage, interest and dividend income . . . have virtually no opportunities not to comply with tax requirements."[40] Employers withhold income tax on wages and report it to the Internal Revenue Service on 1099 forms. Computers allow the IRS to match 100 percent of these reports to individuals' tax returns. For those who receive nonsalary income, the IRS examines the millions of third-party information returns disclosing financial transactions that banks, brokers, and businesses are required to file each year. These information returns are matched by computers to the incomes reported by taxpayers.

In short, the government collects revenues from millions of ordinary citizens without having to worry much about whether they are willing to pay. Tax avoidance has not disappeared, but unpaid taxes represent a very small percentage of the nation's overall tax obligation. Those few Americans who resist taxation are easily managed through bureaucratic intimidation and the criminal justice system, without calling out the militia—a far cry from the time of Daniel Shays. So too is the financing of government debt, which is no longer a matter of small-denomination bonds and securities peddled with patriotic zeal by thousands of volunteers to millions of citizens. Today it is a quiet matter of bond auctions at Federal Reserve banks with only a few dozen representatives of financial institutions in attendance.

Once, citizens in general played a large and active role in public finance and earned the government's deference as a consequence. But the gradual development of new arrangements for collecting taxes and financing public debt has reduced government's financial dependence on citizens, and it has diminished citizenship in the process. How little the government depends upon citizens' cooperation for its revenues became manifest in October 2001. Some members of Congress proposed that the Treasury issue war bonds to help finance the nation's war against terrorism and to provide Americans with an outlet for their patriotic sentiments in the wake of terrorist attacks. The Bush administration was cool to the idea. An administration spokesman said it would be better if Americans "put their money to work for the nation" by shopping rather than purchasing securities.[41]

The End of the Citizen Soldier

Along with administration and raising revenue, a third essential requisite for the modern state is the ability to defend itself militarily. Here too the role of ordinary citizens, once critical to national survival, is now much diminished.

England's yeoman archers were a formidable presence on medieval battlefields, but the era of the citizen soldier began only at the end of the eighteenth century. Before that time, wars were typically fought by armies of professional soldiers who campaigned for pay and booty. Armies were small by contemporary standards. The eighteenth-century Prussian army, for example, one of the most powerful in Europe, consisted of only 80,000 men.[42] For major campaigns, kings commonly filled out their forces by recruiting mercenary troops. But mercenaries were mere hirelings. Occasionally loyal to their entrepreneurial captains, but seldom to the regime that employed them, they sometimes switched sides in the middle of campaigns. Their commanders tended to regard battle casualties as a capital loss inconsistent with good business practice, a policy powerfully supported by their troops.

These military practices were defeated in battle by the *levee en masse* of the French Revolution. In 1793 it produced 300,000 volunteers and conscripts to defend France and the Revolution. Though scarcely trained and poorly equipped, the French troops fought with an ardor born of devotion to a cause. Under Napoleon, the French nation's call to its people produced an army of 1.3 million. Its battlefield triumphs converted France from a kingdom to an empire and demonstrated that popular support could be transformed into military power.

For the rest of the nineteenth century, other European governments tried to convince their own subjects to emulate the élan and self-sacrifice of the French troops. Universal military service became the European norm, along with nationalist indoctrination, which was soon extended from soldiers to children by universal compulsory schooling. In time, the expansion of military service led to the development of national pension systems, initially introduced to reward former soldiers and their immediate dependents. And finally there was the right to vote. Proponents of suffrage expansion argued that the franchise would give subjects a sense of ownership in the state and inspire them to fight for their country. A Swedish slogan of the nineteenth century captured the essential connection: "One man, one gun, one vote." Modern warfare transformed politically voiceless subjects into citizens.

World War I was associated with a great wave of suffrage expansion in Europe and North America as governments sought to mobilize support for the war effort.[43] In Canada, for example, under the Wartimes Election Act, women with relatives serving in the armed services were given the right to vote for the duration of the war. The government apparently believed that a woman with a vote would have reason to urge her husband, son, or brother to make whatever sacrifice was needed for victory.[44]

While most of Europe still relied on mercenaries and professional soldiers, the British colonies in North America were already fielding armies of ordinary citizens. England had urgent missions for its own professional troops elsewhere and consistently urged the thirteen colonies to provide for their own defense against the French in Canada, the Indians on the frontier, and the Spanish in the South and West. The militia forces organized for these purposes would eventually defeat Britain itself and create a new nation.

Colonial militiamen made up the bulk of Washington's Continental Army, but their short tours of duty reduced their military effectiveness. Like their French Revolutionary contemporaries, however, the militia's enthusiasm for the cause often made up for what they lacked in training and discipline. The colonies' part-time soldiers had other virtues as well. When they returned home, they performed the vital service of holding their communities to the patriot cause, often by intimidation or violence, so that the Continental Army had continuing access to its recruitment base and to most of the food produced in the colonies.[45]

Once independent, the United States continued to rely primarily on militiamen so as to avoid the costs and political risks that a large professional army entailed for a fledgling democracy. The federal Militia Acts of 1792 and 1795 provided for the enrollment of able-bodied, free white men between the ages of eighteen and forty-five in the state militias and authorized the president to call the state militias to national service for a period not to exceed three months in any one year. The statutes carried no penalties for failing to enroll in the militia; nevertheless, thousands of Americans signed up and received some measure of military training.[46] The militia produced politicians as well as soldiers. Like Abraham Lincoln, many aspiring officeholders without wealth or social standing brought themselves to the attention of fellow citizens through militia service.

Virtually all the American soldiers who fought in the War of 1812 were militiamen. The vast majority served for six months or less, and their military performance was spotty. In some instances, rival units refused to cooperate with one another, and battles were lost because militiamen decided to return home in midcampaign. But militia forces led by able officers like General William Henry Harrison of Kentucky, General Jacob Brown of New York, and, of course, Andrew Jackson were able to defeat larger, well-trained British forces, thus confirming the American conviction that citizen soldiers could outfight professionals.

After the War of 1812, the organized state militias gave way to local volunteer units that drilled on weekends and paraded in fancy uniforms on patriotic occasions.[47] But some saw military action in civil disturbances, during which they often performed effectively. One volunteer regiment in New York City put down major riots in 1834, 1836, and 1837. On the frontier, volunteer units were responsible for much of the violence against Native Americans, and during the Mexican-American War, they accounted for more than 70 percent of the troops mustered. Despite many casualties, primarily from disease and malnutrition, volunteers and militiamen fought well throughout the twenty-one months of the war and distinguished themselves at Buena Vista. Congress was so pleased with the military performance of the volunteers that it slashed the size of the regular army from 30,000 to 12,000 men at the war's conclusion, calculating that volunteers would always be available to serve the nation's military needs.

At the outbreak of the Civil War, both the Federal and Confederate governments called the state militias into service. In 1861, President Lincoln asked the states to send 75,000 soldiers to serve for three months under officers appointed by the state governors. As the war continued, the president called for more troops to be raised by the states. The Civil War's bloody consumption of manpower, however, soon outran the supply of state volunteers. In July 1862, facing severe manpower shortfalls, Congress took the unprecedented step of directing the states to draft soldiers to fill their quotas. In 1863, for the first time, the national government, rather than the states and communities, sought to mobilize citizen soldiers. Congress enacted a conscription law summoning young men directly into the military service of the United States. Those ordered to report were permitted to hire substitutes. Only some 160,000 draftees and substitutes ever served in the Union army, but many tens of thousands of men volunteered in preference to being drafted. Counting militiamen, conscripts, volunteers, and "involuntary volunteers," more than 2 million citizen soldiers fought in the Union army and another million on the Confederate side.

In the aftermath of the Civil War, the Southern states were initially prohibited from organizing militia units. Once Republicans took control of the Southern state governments, however, Congress authorized the formation of new state militia units. Composed largely of African American enlisted men and white officers—often carpetbaggers—these units were disparaged by Southern whites as "black and tan" militias.[48] Acting outside the law, the whites formed their own militia companies, generally composed of Confederate veterans. These units engaged in a campaign of terror and intimidation against African American militiamen, killing many of their leaders. In the closing days of Reconstruction, the official and extralegal militias fought a number of pitched battles, with casualties on both sides, before the South's Republican regimes crumbled.[49]

Beginning in the 1870s, the states reorganized their militia units and renamed them the National Guard. By 1900, state guard units had enrolled a total of 114,000 men. Five states supported entire divisions, twenty-five supported brigades, and the others supported at least one regiment apiece. Despite the word "national," the guard units were controlled by the states and were used by the state governors primarily to suppress civil disorder. Between the end of Reconstruction and the beginning of World War I, governors summoned the guard units more than five hundred times to end race riots, quell religious disputes, and intervene in political conflicts. During the great period of strikes and labor unrest between the 1870s and 1890s, the guard was often used to protect industrial property and disperse strikers. Though guardsmen were citizen soldiers drawn from all classes of society, the officers were almost invariably members of the well-to-do classes who had little sympathy for strikers. As a result, the National Guard became notorious for its use of violence against labor protestors. During the 1894 Pullman strike, for example, the Second Illinois Regiment fired into a crowd, killing more than twenty strikers and wounding many more.

The association of the National Guard with strikebreaking and violence led to demands that it be reorganized or even disbanded—demands supported by the officer corps of the regular army, which saw the guard as a rival and resented the system of political promotions that made untrained civilians colonels and generals. But it was the Spanish-American War that first undermined the guard's autonomy. At the war's start, Congress passed the Volunteer Act, which created regiments of *national* volunteers who would, after training, become units of the regular army. They would make up part of the expeditionary force. The guard would defend the coast.

After some political maneuver, however, the act was amended so that state National Guard units could volunteer en masse for combat duty while retaining their identities. A number of guard units entered the service through this route, but most saw their identities diluted as the regular army required them to add new men, usually from outside their home states, to bring units up to regulation strength. The Volunteer Act also gave the president, rather than the state governors, the power to appoint all general officers and their staffs. As a result, the National Guard units came to be more fully integrated within the army. Most of the Americans who served during the war were citizen soldiers. More than 233,000 volunteers entered federal service, as compared to a regular army of slightly more than 30,000 men. Nevertheless, citizen soldiers had been subordinated to the professionals.

After the war, the 1903 Dick Act formalized the subordination of the guard to the national army. The act declared that the National Guard constituted the organized militia of the United States rather than merely a congeries of state forces. The administration and organization of all state guard units was required to conform to that of the regular army, and the guard was to be issued arms and equipment by the federal government. The president was authorized to summon state guard units for federal service for a period of up to nine months. Under the act, once a unit entered the federal service it lost its identity as a state force and became part of the regular army's volunteer forces. In essence, during periods of military necessity, the guard would serve as a recruitment base for volunteers who would then become integrated into the United States Army.

The nationalization of the guard advanced further with the National Defense Act of 1916. It allowed states to retain their responsibility for training guard units, and the guard continued to be available to governors for in civil emergencies. In time of war, however, guardsmen could be drafted into the federal service for the duration. The president was given the authority to appoint all commissioned officers and noncommissioned officers for men so drafted. At the same time, the act began the creation of today's military reserves by authorizing the establishment of a force consisting of soldiers who had completed a tour of active duty. These were to be former regular army soldiers with no ties to the states or to the National Guard. This subordination of the guard and the creation of the prototype for the modern military reserves clearly signaled a declining role for the citizen soldier in the United States.

The American army that fought in World War I was primarily composed of draftees. More than 24 million men registered under the 1917 Selective Service Act, and nearly 3 million were drafted. Another 700,000 young Americans volunteered for service, and 370,000 soldiers were drawn from the National Guard. Guardsmen were drafted by Wilson in August 1917 as individuals, which formally severed their ties with the states. Most guard units were merged with other units and lost their identities and community ties. In July 1918, the army chief of staff, General Peyton March, completed the integration of the guard into the regular army in his General Order 73, which declared, "This country has but one army, the army of the United States."[50] Guardsmen were prohibited from attaching any state insignia to their uniforms. Henceforth, "U.S." was to be the only indication of an American soldier's civic affiliation. The community-based militias that had won independence and crushed secession had given way to a nationally conscripted military force—an army of strangers.

At the same time, however, the federal government sought the support of local communities to reduce anticipated political opposition to conscription. To this end, the actual task of inducted draftees was entrusted to forty-six hundred local boards of citizen volunteers. Additional citizens' committees gave medical and legal advice and assisted inductees until they reported for duty.[51] As a result, the creation of the World War I army was based on a mix of national recruiting drives aimed at stimulating patriotism, and local administration designed to elicit community cooperation for the war effort.

Like World War I, World War II was fought by an army of conscripted and volunteer citizen soldiers with state guard units providing only a small fraction the nation's forces. Congress enacted the first peacetime draft in American history in 1940. During the next five years, 10 million men were inducted into the armed forces, and another 5 million were given deferments for work in war industries. Another 5 million Americans, including more than 300,000 women, volunteered for service, prompted by the same mix of patriotism and anticipation of conscription that produced the original *levee en masse.* Community boards once again took on the work of conscription and the goal of cultivating grassroots support for the Selective Service System.

Postwar legislation, however, further diminished the status of community-based military units and the role of citizen soldiers themselves. The 1952 Armed Forces Reserve Act created a Ready Reserve consisting of all members of the Army and Air National Guards as well as all those with unfulfilled reserve obligations. The act not only reduced the distinction between the National Guard and the reserves but also virtually converted the National Guard from a state force into another component of the national reserve forces.

During the two major postwar conflicts, the wars in Korea and Vietnam, reserve and National Guard forces played virtually no role. Fewer than 2 percent of the soldiers who fought in Korea were drawn from the guard and reserves. In the case of Vietnam, President Johnson decided that sending draftees to fight in an unpopular war might arouse less political resistance than sending reservists—many of them family men with strong community ties.[52] Popular opposition to the war, however, spilled over into widespread draft resistance—one factor contributing to the conversion of the American military into an all-volunteer professional force. Military planners would later argue that the technical complexity of the new weapon systems required a highly trained, professional army rather than a force composed of short-term conscripts. By the time large numbers of reservists were once again called to duty, this time in the 1990 Persian Gulf War, they were mainly former members of the standing military rather than true citizen soldiers.

Community-based units of citizen soldiers have finally disappeared from the nation's military. Some experts, in fact, argue that new weapon systems will make massed troops obsolete.[53] Future wars, they assert, will be fought by computers and "smart" weapons. The American-led NATO attack on Serbia in 1999 seemed to foreshadow a new era of war without casualties. The campaign depended entirely upon "smart" missiles and bombs launched from ships and aircraft that generally remained out of the range of enemy fire. President Clinton made no appeals for citizen sacrifice and assured the American people that none of their soldiers would be hurt in the fighting. The American military effort in Afghanistan in 2001–2002 similarly depended mainly upon advanced technology and devastating air power; few Americans were actually sent into dangerous situations.

Citizens once entered the nation's service accompanied by their friends and neighbors, tied to one another and to particular parts of the country. They were not solitary conscripts who stood alone in the face of military authority. They were in a position to make demands and to command respect. Not surprisingly, the government's reliance upon citizen soldiers was closely associated with the expansion of voting rights and with the construction of the nation's public welfare system. Theda Skocpol has shown that the system of veterans' pensions established after the Civil War may have anticipated the development of America's welfare state. At its peak, not long after the turn of the century, Civil War pensions provided support not only to veterans but to their widows as well.[54]

Militiamen called to place their lives at the service of the nation thought themselves just as entitled to vote as those who risked only property. The revolutionary militia was known as a breeding ground for radical democrats. In 1776, the Philadelphia Committee of Privates, an organization of Pennsylvania militiamen, advised voters, "Let no man represent you disposed to form any rank above that of Freeman."[55] The sentiments of armed militia men could not be ignored in the suffrage debates that followed the success of the revolutionary cause. Throughout the colonies, citizen soldiers pressed for and helped to win expanded voting rights. Organizations of state militiamen demanded an end to property restrictions on the suffrage on the ground that those asked to fight should not be barred from voting. In Maryland, groups of armed militiamen went to the polls in 1776 demanding to vote whether or not they could meet the state's existing property requirements for voters. In some instances, those denied the right to vote threatened to refuse to continue to fight. The result in Maryland and other states was a general expansion of the suffrage during the revolutionary period, an expansion designed to accommodate the demands of those Americans being asked to fight. The War of 1812 led to suffrage reforms in a number of states on the argument that "men who were good enough to fight were good enough to vote."[56] Women's suffrage in the United States, as in England and Canada, was partially brought about by World war I, on the basis of the notion that women were more likely to support the war effort if they possessed the right to vote.[57] Most recently, the Twenty-Sixth Amendment, lowering the voting age to eighteen, was designed in part to bolster support among young men who were then being conscripted for service in the Vietnam War. It may have been the last feeble gesture acknowledging that soldiering and citizenship went hand in hand.

The Decline and Fall of the Citizen

No antidemocratic onslaught will be found responsible for the decline and fall of the American citizen. Behind the general political demobilization of the past several decades stand mostly good intentions—even democratic ones. The diminution of citizenship has, in many cases, followed as an unforeseen consequence of efforts to improve the effectiveness and responsiveness of government. Several generations of military reformers—beginning with General George Washington—viewed the citizen soldier as inferior to the well-trained and well-disciplined professional fighting man. General Emory Upton, one of the army's most influential strategists during the late nineteenth century, was assigned to study military tactics and formations in Europe and Asia. Upton's great work, *The Military Policy of the United States,* published in 1904, was designed to show that professional military forces under centralized bureaucratic control were inherently superior to armies based upon citizen soldiers.[58] Upton's work influenced the views of the American officer corps for the next half century.

Practices designed to make the nation's government and economy operate more smoothly have diminished the space in which citizenship can operate. Civil service reform, income-tax withholding, and the open-market operations of the Federal Reserve System were all compellingly reasonable innovations. All reduced the government's reliance upon the active and collective cooperation of its people.

In making citizens expendable, the government did not exclude them. But it included them on new terms. Beginning with the Progressive reformers of the late nineteenth century, collective participation in politics was gradually replaced by individual access. Initiative, referendum, recall, and the direct election of U.S. senators seemed straightforward advances in the inexorable progress of mass democracy that was born in revolution and grew along with the country itself. But the Progressive ideal emphasized the solitary and independent citizen, the self-mobilizing citizen. Progressive democracy attempted to dispense with the party organizations that had been the chief vehicles for the collective mobilization of the public. Collective mobilization gradually evolved into the selective mobilization of personal democracy. The administrative, financial, and military needs of the government no longer required the political engagement of the general population.

The declining dependence of the government upon the allegiance of its citizens marks the end of the political era that began with the French and American Revolutions. Governments can fight wars, collect revenues, and administer programs without having to rely much upon the collective and active support of millions of ordinary people. Indeed, in some respects, enthusiastic citizens have come to be seen as a hindrance rather than a help. In recent military conflicts such as the Kosovo War and even the Persian Gulf War, the U.S. government deliberately avoided stirring up popular enthusiasm because doing so would have made it more difficult to limit the wars' objectives to the narrow ones deemed consistent with America's interests.

Americans do not seem to be in immediate danger of losing the formal rights they won in an earlier political epoch. The vestigial organs of citizenship can survive long after their original purposes have evaporated. The Roman Senate, after all, survived long after the death of the Republic that gave it meaning and even after the collapse of the Western Empire that had given it ritualized recognition. Today, the institutions of popular democracy persist and continue to command the obligatory respect of politicians and officials. But they are being displaced by the institutions of personal democracy, and a critical dimension of citizenship is disappearing. To an increasing extent, ordinary citizens deal with government one by one, and forfeit the influence that they once enjoyed as members of a mobilized public.

Chapter 3

Elections without Voters

AS LONG AS national security, public finance, and government administration depended upon the cooperation and active support of citizens,
political authority flowed from democratic elections. Triumph at the
polls was not just proof of popularity. It was a test of the capacity to
govern—both an endorsement of the victor's policies and an indication
that citizen administrators, citizen soldiers, citizen taxpayers, and bondholders were prepared to cooperate in carrying them out. The federal
government's early and extensive reliance on its people was a factor in its
early realization of full white manhood suffrage. Reliance on the citizenry also meant that electoral competition was the principal means
through which nineteenth-century political elites settled their policy differences on everything from internal improvements to tariffs.

The reliance of nineteenth-century elites on voter mobilization and
countermobilization drove electoral turnout to heights never achieved
since. By the 1890s, almost 80 percent of the eligible voters went to the
polls in the average presidential election, and turnout approached 70 percent for midterm congressional races. In some areas outside the South,
more than 90 percent of the electorate regularly exercised their voting
rights.[1]

In spite of twenty-first-century communications technology, today's
elections barely turn out a majority of the eligible voters even in presidential contests. Part of the explanation—perhaps the most important

part—is that political elites have found ways to achieve their policy objectives without mobilizing voters. Rather than take issues to the electorate for resolution, today's contending elites attempt to outdo their opponents by litigating, by manipulating administrative procedures, or by the use of mechanisms like privatization, vouchers, or bureaucratic adjudication that remove policy to arenas beyond the reach of their rivals. In the process, the millions of citizens who might once have been called to the aid of their parties now remain passive bystanders. Yesterday's actors have become today's audience—spectators and customers rather than citizens.

Mobilization and Its Alternatives

The age of the citizen soldier was the era of "militaristic" political campaigns.[2] Well-organized political parties mobilized their troops in virtually every constituency. Voters in each precinct were "drilled" by party "captains" who in turn received support and direction from a disciplined and well-financed party organization. A rabidly partisan press disseminated news that sometimes amounted to little more than propaganda.[3] On election day, hundreds of thousands of party workers marched from house to house, handing out leaflets, urging voters to the polls, and occasionally offering financial inducements to help voters make up their minds.[4] Millions of citizens attended campaign rallies, listened to speeches, and marched in parades. Playing electoral politics was the national pastime.[5]

It was not, however, the only game in town. Even in the nineteenth century, politicians occasionally achieved their ends by means other than mobilizing voters. Slavery, for example, was too big an issue for electoral resolution. Shortly after it was settled, the country went through its first impeachment crisis, and not long after that, criminal indictments and prosecutions orchestrated by political reformers undid the Whiskey and Tweed Rings. Even in elections, extralegal violence played a role, and in the South it helped to restrict the size of the electorate.[6] Nevertheless, all-out voter mobilization in national elections was a central strategy for forces seeking to control the government and influence national policy.

The nineteenth-century pattern of mass mobilization has little in common with the conduct of American politics today. For the last generation, voter turnout in the United States has averaged slightly more than 50 percent in presidential contests. Fewer than 49 percent of those eligible actually voted in the 1996 presidential election, the lowest electoral turnout since 1924. In midterm congressional elections, more than two-thirds of eligible voters stay home. The averages, however, conceal sharp differences in political participation. Affluent and well-educated Americans continue to vote at nineteenth-century levels. Except among the young, presidential election turnout among college graduates remains close to 80 percent. Less affluent and less well educated Americans, in contrast, have been politically marginalized. Among eligible voters with less than a high school education, for instance, turnout has dropped from nearly 50 percent in the early 1970s to barely 30 percent today.[7]

Competing political elites obviously continue to appeal for votes. Parties and candidates may have spent as much as $2 billion dollars competing for popular support in the 1996 national, state, and local races.[8] Much of this money, however, is typically spent on television spots during the final month of the campaign. These ads are aimed primarily at middle-class Americans who are already registered and likely to vote. Sophisticated polling techniques allow candidates to target narrow slices of this truncated and already attentive audience with political advertising tailored to their interests.[9] The development of direct-mail tactics, computerized databases, the new possibilities for campaigning on the Internet—all make targeted or "customized" campaigning a political growth industry.[10]

In sharp contrast with the nineteenth-century pattern, today neither party makes much effort to mobilize the tens of millions of poorer and less well educated Americans who are not currently part of the electorate.[11] On the contrary, many candidates deliberately depress turnout by engaging in "negative" campaigning, which disparages the opposition and is designed to discourage both nonvoters and their opponents' established supporters from going to the polls.[12] Many Americans claim that negative campaigning and smear tactics have made them too disgusted to participate in politics.[13] Only the occasional political outsider like Minnesota governor Jesse Ventura makes any real effort to bring nonvoters into the electorate.[14] Neither of the major parties supports electoral reforms such as the elimination of voter registration requirements or a shift from weekday to weekend voting. Both practices are standard in Western Europe, and the European experience suggests that these two changes alone would appreciably boost electoral turnout.

More than 60 million Americans entitled to vote in presidential elections neglect to do so. The parties' apparent indifference to this enormous reservoir of potential voters is especially curious in view of the bitter conflicts that divided them in the last third of the twentieth century and the inconclusive outcomes of recent electoral contests. The vast sums spent on holding the loyalties of current voters have failed to give either party a decisive political edge. Divided government and political stalemate seem more acceptable to party elites than an effort to shift the political balance by activating the politically inert.

Party divisions in Congress, as evinced by patterns of roll-call voting, have achieved levels of polarization unseen since the nineteenth century, and partisan struggles between Congress and the White House are pursued with a ferocity that is virtually without precedent in American history. Democratic Congresses drove Republican Richard Nixon from office and sought to do the same to Ronald Reagan. A Republican Congress impeached, but failed to convict, Democratic president Bill Clinton. Yet these titanic battles of national politics have not induced either party to engage the interest of the unmobilized voters. The battles provoke scarcely a ripple of political activity beyond the Washington Beltway, and participation continues to decline.

The conjunction of elite combat and popular disengagement defies a well-established generalization of political science. The generalization says that high levels of elite conflict will promote mass participation as contending forces engage in competitive efforts to mobilize political support. Writing during the 1950s, E. E. Schattschneider argued that popular mobilization was most likely to be initiated by the losers in elite struggles, losers who hoped to change the outcome by "expanding the scope of conflict" and enlarging the universe of participants.[15] French political scientist Maurice Duverger asserted that mass mobilization was most likely to be initiated by elites representing groups in the lower reaches of the social hierarchy, where potential voters are most numerous. Politically upscale competitors resort to all-out mobilization in response. Duverger called it "contagion from the left."[16]

American political practices were generally consistent with this model until the last third of the twentieth century. The Jeffersonians, Jacksonians, and Republicans all expanded the suffrage and brought new groups into the political process in an effort to overwhelm their opponents at the polls. During the 1930s, the New Dealers sought to solidify their political power by increasing participation on the part of working-class and ethnic voters. As recently as the 1960s, liberal Democrats tried to fend off the Republicans and overpower conservative forces within their own party by passing the Voting Rights Act to enfranchise millions of African Americans in the South and by securing passage of the Twenty-Sixth Amendment, which gave the vote to young people.

Recently, however, American politics seems to have departed from the democratic patterns of the past. An ongoing presidential impeachment battle failed to drive turnout above one-third of the voters in the 1998 congressional elections. In fact, the contending parties deliberately refrained from mobilizing the politically inactive. "I don't think we ought to play to that crowd," said Representative John Lindner of Georgia, chairman of the House Republican campaign committee, when asked if the GOP should seek to bring new voters to the polls in 1998.[17] Such reluctance may have been understandable for Republicans because the relatively low incomes and educational levels of nonvoters mark them as potential Democrats. But Democrats are no less reluctant. In 1984, Walter Mondale's campaign advisers told him that the idea of mobilizing new voters was "backward thinking."[18] Democrats refrained from engaging in large-scale voter registration efforts even though the polls indicated that among Americans registered and likely to vote, Mondale faced nearly certain defeat at the hands of Ronald Reagan.

Schattschneider, Duverger, and other theorists of democratic mobilization may have failed to give sufficient weight to elite apprehensions about expanding the universe of participants. Even in an era of scientific opinion polling, the political leanings and partisan loyalties of new participants are always uncertain. Democrats in the 1960s, for example, pushed for the vote for eighteen-year-olds, only to discover that, on balance, young voters helped the Republicans in the 1970s and 1980s.

Even if new participants remain loyal to the political party that mobilized them, they are likely to bring with them new aspirants for the party's leadership positions. Party leaders who attempt to recruit political outsiders may wind up watching their success from the sidelines. The popular forces brought into politics by the Jeffersonians, for example, ultimately displaced their patrons and transformed Jeffersonian republicanism into Jacksonian democracy. Expanding the population of participants is a risky strategy seldom undertaken lightly. Lord Derby famously called the expansion of Britain's electorate under the Reform Bill of 1867 a "leap into the dark."

Today, both political parties seem more afraid of the dark than ever. Republicans are concerned that an expansion of the electorate might lead to an influx of poor and minority voters, who are unlikely converts to the GOP. Some Republican conservatives, in fact, hold that ordinary Americans have succumbed to a moral and intellectual paralysis that renders them unfit to participate in governing the nation. This was the explanation advanced by some right-wing intellectuals and commentators to explain why most Americans seemed insufficiently outraged by President Clinton's conduct to support the GOP's campaign to impeach him.[19] The people were no longer good enough for democracy.

An expansion of the electorate might be expected to benefit the Democrats. But the influx of tens of millions of new voters would represent a substantial risk for current Democratic officeholders. Even if these new voters remained loyal to the Democratic party as an institution, they might not support the party's current leadership. Some liberal interests allied with the Democrats—upper-middle-class environmentalists, public interest lawyers, and antismoking activists, for example—might lose influence in a more fully mobilized electoral environment.[20] Liberal activists may have understandable misgivings about increased participation among working- and lower-middle-class whites, whom they see as opponents of abortion rights and affirmative action and proponents of school prayer and unrestricted handgun ownership.[21]

Elites, of course, have always been wary of popular participation. The crucial difference between today's elites and those of the past is not that politicians have overcome their fear of the dark but that they have found the means to avoid the dark altogether. When citizens were essential to governance, political leaders were compelled to mobilize them. It was the only way to govern. But when the cooperation of citizen soldiers, citizen administrators, and citizen taxpayers became expendable, it was easy to dispense with citizen voters as well. Contemporary leaders can pursue their goals by means that do not require them to take the risks inherent in old-fashioned democratic mobilization.

Almost all American politicians publicly deplore the nation's low levels of voter turnout. But even modest efforts to boost voter turnout inspire little support in Washington. The so-called Motor Voter Act, for example, signed into law by President Clinton in 1993, was bitterly opposed by most Republicans.[22] Congressional Democrats, for their part, were willing to delete those portions of the bill that were most likely to maximize registration among the poor, such as the provision for automatic registration of all eligible clients at welfare offices. Many Democrats had actually been happy to see a previous version of the act vetoed by President Bush in 1992. At any rate, the Motor Voter Act has had little effect upon the size or composition of the electorate. Thus far, few of the citizens registered under the act have actually gone to the polls to cast their ballots. In 1996, the percentage of newly registered voters who appeared at the polls actually dropped.[23] Political mobilization requires more than the distribution of voter registration forms. Candidates and parties must make political warfare, as they did in the era of "militaristic" campaigning.

The Rise and Fall of the American Electorate

A quarter century before the American Revolution, a sizeable percentage of white males living in the colonies (and even a few black men) had the right to vote. As in Britain, the suffrage was usually limited to freeholders. The minimum value of the freehold required in order to vote varied from one colony to the next, and in Virginia it was acreage rather than assessed value that made a man a member of the electorate.

In crowded Britain, substantial landownership was limited to a privileged few, and the freehold requirement disenfranchised most men. But it was relatively easy to become a freeholder in the colonies, where population was sparse and land was plentiful. The inflationary effects of the colonies' reliance on paper money added to the pool of eligible voters by elevating the nominal value of their real estate. By the time of the Revolution, between 50 and 75 percent of the colonies' white males satisfied the freehold requirement.[24]

Easy access to landownership was not the only contributor to the expansion of America's pre-Revolutionary electorate. Colonial governments, as we have seen, counted on broad support from their taxpayers and militiamen and were in no position to deny the vote to the citizens who defended and financed them. After the Revolution, the new national government's dependence upon popular acquiescence shaped the framers' discussion of voting rights at the Constitutional Convention. Though many of the delegates expressed misgivings about the "excessive democracy" found in states with liberal voting requirements, the framers regarded popular participation as an indispensable source of authority and stability for the new government they were creating. They could not impose limits on the suffrage more restrictive than those already in place at the state level. Delegate Elbridge Gerry, noted for his mistrust of popular influence, conceded that widespread citizen participation would be necessary in order to ensure the widespread support needed for a strong and stable central government.[25]

In the end, most delegates were convinced that popular participation would increase the power of the national government relative to the states and would give citizens sufficient confidence in the new regime so that it could function effectively. The new Constitution provided that citizens eligible to vote for members of the lower house of their states' legislatures would also be eligible to vote for members of the U.S. House of Representatives. Though the Constitution retained the property restrictions then in effect, the result was nevertheless fairly widespread white manhood suffrage.

Property restrictions on voting were gradually abandoned by most states, beginning with Maryland in 1802 and South Carolina in 1810. Both the Jeffersonians and Jacksonians sought an expanded suffrage to enfranchise their numerous but impecunious supporters. Jefferson himself asserted that all men who paid taxes or served in the militia should have the right to vote. The Jeffersonians were especially prone to make this argument in the North, where their Federalist opponents held power. Under Jeffersonian pressure, property requirements were reduced or dropped altogether in Connecticut, Massachusetts, and New York during the second decade of the nineteenth century.

During the Revolution itself, the property and freehold requirements that restricted the right to vote had come under severe attack. Men of military age demanded the right to vote as a condition for accepting the risks and hardships of military service. The issue of suffrage reform was therefore linked to the more general question of independence. Advocates of independence supported extension of the right to vote because they recognized that soldiers with voting rights would have a personal stake in the success of the revolution. Politicians with pro-British sympathies opposed the elimination of the various property restrictions that limited voting rights.[26] For its part, the Continental Congress sought to encourage the martial spirit and loyalty of state militiamen by recommending that all noncommissioned militia officers be elected by their men.

After the war, veterans and their political supporters demanded expansion of the suffrage as a reward for their wartime sacrifices. "The soldier is as much entitled to vote as the Captain of the company or the Colonel of the regiment," thundered the Fredericktown, Maryland, *Hornet.*[27] Some opponents of suffrage reform argued that military service was its own reward and that the true burden of the war actually had been borne by the civilians, who had been required to "pay heavy taxes to support you in the field, endure all that anxiety which the patriot feels for his suffering country . . . [and had not the] . . . privilege of shining in the heroic page."[28] Members of one Pennsylvania militia company answered this argument forcefully by appearing at the polls fully armed. They were allowed to cast ballots.[29]

In the late 1790s, anticipation of possible American involvement in a war against the French revolutionary regime led to another wave of suffrage expansion. In Maryland, for example, prominent state legislator Michael Taney introduced a bill in 1797 establishing universal white manhood suffrage. Taney pointed out that Maryland militiamen might soon be called up for service. He urged the legislature to avert the difficulties encountered during the Revolution, when the state had been compelled to expand the suffrage because its militiamen had been reluctant to fight unless they were given the right to vote.[30] A number of states substituted tax-paying requirements for the freehold restriction, thus achieving nearly universal white male suffrage.

The need to summon militiamen to service during the War of 1812 and, again, during Dorr's Rebellion of 1842, led to the further lowering of property and freehold requirements in the northeastern states.[31] In the

South, ironically, the institution of slavery helped to bring about suffrage reform for poor whites. The maintenance of citizen patrols to pursue runaway slaves and the frequent summons of the militia to confront the dreaded threat of servile insurrection compelled Southern states to expand the suffrage to whites too poor to own slaves themselves.[32] During the 1820s, unenfranchised members of the militia in Virginia and North Carolina demanded the right to vote as a condition for serving in slave patrols. By 1829, several southern states had begun systematically to enfranchise white men of military age to bolster white unity and to enhance the security of the slave system.

By the closing decades of the nineteenth century, virtually all white males in the United States had the right to vote. Women, of course, remained outside the electorate until 1920, and African Americans in the South were expelled from it after the end of Reconstruction. Immediately after the Civil War, African Americans voters ensured Republican control of the South while the disenfranchisement of ex-Confederates prevented Democrats from challenging that control.[33] After the compromise of 1876, however, white southerners regained the right to vote and used it, along with violence and economic coercion, to drive black voters out of the electorate, thereby destroying the Republican party in the South.[34] Black voting rights were not fully restored in the South until the enactment of the 1965 Voting Rights Act nearly a century later.

Despite the exclusion of women and blacks, late-nineteenth-century America was the world's most democratic nation. In Europe, voting rights were hedged by restrictions, and even voters were not fully mobilized. In the United States, not only did white males hold the right to vote, but most of them exercised it.[35]

Demobilization: The Legacy of Progressivism

The nineteenth-century era of electoral mobilization ended with the rise of Progressivism. Like the Constitution's framers, the Progressives spoke for an upper class that hoped to construct a powerful and active government, one with the capacity to expand the nation's economy, regulate social relations, and advance the national interest on the world stage. But the framers had believed that building a strong state would require them to tolerate and even encourage widespread popular participation. The Progressives regarded mass mobilization as an impediment to effective government. Rather than broadening the government's receptivity to popular activism, the Progressives narrowed it. They weakened the party system, disfranchised millions of immigrant and working-class voters through voter registration requirements, and contributed to the development of bureaucratic institutions whose authority was based on expertise, not popular support.

The Progressive inventory of antiparty reforms is a familiar one. The Australian ballot reform took away the parties' traditional privilege of printing and distributing ballots and encouraged split-ticket voting. The introduction of nonpartisan local elections eroded grassroots party organization. The extension of civil service systems for administrative appointments stripped party organizations of much patronage and reduced their resources for recruiting workers and adherents. The introduction of the direct primary diminished party leaders' control over candidate nominations. Although these reforms hardly destroyed party organizations, they did diminish the political vitality of the parties and enhance the power of the institutions controlled by the upper middle classes—newspapers, civic associations, chambers of commerce, and the municipal research bureaus that were the forerunners of today's think tanks.[36]

Another major Progressive Era reform was the introduction of personal registration requirements for voting. They drove millions of potential voters from the electorate and continue to depress voter turnout in the United States today. U.S. voting turnout declined sharply between 1890 and 1910 as laws were adopted across much of the nation requiring eligible individuals to appear personally at a registrar's office prior to election day to prove their eligibility and register to vote. The nominal purpose of registration rules was to discourage corruption and fraud in the conduct of elections. To many Progressives, however, the term "corruption" was a code for the sorts of politics practiced in America's large cities, where political machines had organized immigrant and ethnic populations. Progressives not only objected to the corruption that was unquestionably an aspect of party politics during this era but also opposed the growing political power of the big-city parties and their working-class and immigrant supporters as a corruption of the democracy envisioned by the founders.

Personal registration rules imposed a new burden upon potential voters and altered the format of American elections. Under the registration systems adopted after 1890, it became the duty of individual voters to secure their own eligibility. This duty could prove to be a significant burden. During a personal appearance before the registrar, would-be voters were required to furnish proof of identity, residence, and citizenship. The inconvenience of registration varied from state to state, but usually voters were allowed to register only during business hours on weekdays. Many potential voters could not afford to lose a day's pay in order to register.

Moreover, voters were usually required to register well before the next election, in some cases up to several months earlier. Finally, since most personal registration laws included a periodic purge of the election rolls, ostensibly to keep them up to date, voters often were required to re-register to maintain their eligibility. All of these hurdles represented barriers to participation in the electoral process.[37]

Subsequent changes in state laws, as well as the 1993 Motor Voter Act, have considerably diminished the difficulty of registering. Nevertheless, any registration rule has the effect of depressing voter turnout, especially among the poor and uneducated. Registering to vote requires a greater degree of political interest and involvement than the act of voting itself. To vote, a citizen need only be concerned with a particular election campaign. To register weeks or months prior to the election, however, a potential voter must have a more general or abstract interest in the political process rather than merely a specific interest in the campaign at hand.[38]

Abstract interest in politics is largely a product of education. Those with relatively little schooling may be stirred by the events and issues of a particular campaign, but by election day, it is usually too late to register. It is largely for this reason that voter participation in the United States is highly correlated with education and, thus, with income, race, and social class background. Registration rules continue to deter poorer, less educated voters. They can still be brought to the polls, but only by special efforts that contemporary parties and candidates are usually unwilling or unable to undertake. For reasons already noted, candidates prefer media campaigns aimed at actual rather than potential voters.

In addition to narrowing the electoral base of government, the Progressives also restricted the recruitment pool for public service. They aimed to eliminate the citizen administrators who had arrived at their government jobs by way of service in political party organizations. Progressives were determined to replace these short-term and decidedly amateur administrators with professional bureaucrats whose chief loyalty would be to the state itself rather than to any group outside it. They supported the "merit" system, under which an autonomous civil service commission selected administrative employees on the basis of competitive examinations rather than political connections.

The system assumed that politics could be separated from administration.[39] Administrators, in other words, should be politically neutral experts or technicians, the efficient servants of a larger public interest rather than of the factional biases of the party in power.[40] The bureaucratic ideology of the Progressives allowed that the party in power might have a role in defining the public interest, but the professionally staffed bureaucracy would no longer have a role in mobilizing popular support for the government or its policies. Divorcing administration from political mobilization detached the state's executive apparatus from the popular base upon which it had once rested.

The emergence of personnel administration during the Progressive Era helped to ensure that government employees would be insulated as much as possible from popular political currents. As noted in Chapter 2, personnel administration included a system of position classifications; efficiency evaluations; the idea of public service as a career; and rules governing salary, benefits, promotions, and pensions.[41] These instruments of personnel administration helped to detach government workers from shifts in popular sentiment so that their labors could be directed from within the government itself. Public servants would now constitute a civil service of quasi-permanent career officials rather than short-term patronage workers whose sympathies and supporters lay outside the state itself.

Many of the basic principles of personnel administration were developed by President Theodore Roosevelt's 1905 Keep Commission.[42] As we saw above, Roosevelt's successor, President Taft, created the Commission on Economy and Efficiency, which supplemented the Keep Commission's work by elaborating principles of job classification and standards of workplace efficiency.[43] The Progressives had begun to detach the institutions of public administration from those of public mobilization.

But they were not altogether successful. The administrative reforms advocated by the Roosevelt and Taft commissions were not fully adopted by Congress and the states. Congress, through its powers of legislative oversight and such practices as senatorial courtesy, maintained its capacity to intervene politically in administration. And at the state level, many party machines resisted civil service and other Progressive reforms well into the twentieth century.

More generally, while the Progressives were able to lay a foundation for state autonomy, they failed to create political institutions that could operate without mobilizing mass support. They engineered new institutions that foreshadowed such independence—the Federal Trade Commission, the Federal Reserve Board and an increasingly powerful Interstate Commerce Commission. All of these institutions expanded the federal government's capacity to take the initiative in regulating the economy and society. They also created new channels of access to power that bypassed the arena of popular politics—advisory commissions and legislative reference and municipal research bureaus that gave business and professional elites direct access to the executive institutions of government.[44]

But recruiting soldiers, raising revenues, and administering programs still took substantial popular backing. Woodrow Wilson required a massive public relations effort and the services of an advertising agency to bolster popular support for the fiscal and personal sacrifices Americans were required to make during World War I.[45] At the same time, the absence of widespread popular political support weakened the new administrative agencies created during the Progressive Era and helped open them to rapid colonization by the interests they nominally regulated.[46]

The political possibilities opened by the Progressives would not be fully exploited for several decades. In the meantime, however, the advocates of active government returned to the strategy of popular mobilization. It was the principal reliance of the New Deal and the civil rights movement that emerged after World War II.

Partial Remobilization: The New Deal

In the 1930s, Franklin Roosevelt and his liberal allies sought to reverse the course that had been charted by the Progressives and to mobilize new constituencies that would support his domestic policy initiatives, some of which originated in the unfinished business on the Progressive agenda. In the aftermath of the 1932 national elections, Franklin Roosevelt and his party found themselves in control of the White House and both houses of Congress for the first time in two decades. Democratic victory, however, was a result of the economic crisis brought about by the Great Depression. The bulk of the nation's wealth as well as some of its most powerful institutions—private and public—remained in the hands of the New Deal's conservative opponents. Democratic electoral success in 1932 might not survive the crisis that caused it or bring any lasting change in the distribution of political power.

The New Dealers saw a strategy of popular mobilization as a way to add durability to their momentary triumph over an opposition that had privileged access to the courts, the federal bureaucracy, most major corporations, universities, major law firms, and the national news media. Accordingly, the Roosevelt administration sought to establish or strengthen party organizations and to build ties to labor unions capable of bringing blue-collar workers and their families to the polls. This effort brought a substantial number of new voters into the electorate and helped to make the Democrats the nation's majority party for the next thirty-five years.[47]

As it responded to the nation's economic emergency, Roosevelt's administration established a number of major domestic spending programs that would energize the Democratic party's electoral machinery and attach millions of new voters to the New Deal coalition. In states and cities where established Democratic party organizations were willing to give their allegiance to the new president, the administration used them as the conduits for the millions of dollars distributed to citizens under the aegis of such new federal initiatives as the Civil Works Administration, the Federal Emergency Relief Administration, the Works Progress Administration, the Civilian Conservation Corps, and the National Youth Administration. Over the course of the thirties, nearly half of all American families would draw assistance from one or another of these programs, and by controlling the distribution of that assistance, Democratic machines in cities like Chicago and Pittsburgh were able to enroll millions of new voters. Most of the party's new adherents were drawn from the ranks of the unemployed and willingly gave their political support to the party organizations that provided them with crucial jobs or emergency relief funds.

In states and localities where established Democratic organizations were controlled by the president's enemies, Roosevelt channeled relief funds to insurgent Democratic factions and encouraged attempts to seize control of the party machinery. In Michigan and Minnesota, for example, insurgents loyal to the president were able to take control of state party organizations and, with the help of federal relief funds, mobilize large numbers of new Democratic voters.[48] In other states, such as New York, factional struggles between Democratic supporters and opponents of the Roosevelt administration weakened the Democratic party and reduced its effectiveness as an instrument for popular mobilization.[49] The chief beneficiary of New Deal patronage here was Republican-Fusion mayor Fiorello La Guardia.

Not only party organizations but also labor unions were enlisted in the New Deal campaign to mobilize new blocs of voters, especially unions affiliated with the newly created Congress of Industrial Organizations (CIO). Roosevelt supported the Wagner Act, through which the government guaranteed labor's right to organize—a guarantee badly needed by the CIO's industrial unions, which had been locked in mortal combat with America's manufacturers. In response, the CIO gave all-out support to the Democratic party. The CIO and its constituent unions contributed nearly $2 million to Roosevelt's 1936 campaign for reelection. Where local Democratic party organizations were weak or nonexistent, the CIO in effect became the Democratic party, organizing meetings and rallies, mounting registration drives, and delivering voters to the polls.[50]

By 1944, the CIO Political Action Committee, which organized tens of thousands of union members to work on behalf of Democratic candidates, had become a central part of the national Democratic party's campaign apparatus. Thanks to local party machines and labor unions, the Roosevelt administration was able to expand voter turnout in the North and to begin the process of permanently attaching millions of new voters to the Democratic party. Presidential election turnout outside the South rose from less than 57 percent of eligible voters in 1928 to more than 73 percent by 1940. A large percentage of new voters were unemployed and had received some form of relief under the auspices of New Deal programs. The overwhelming majority of these supported the Democrats. According to an August 1936 Gallup poll, an astonishing 82 percent of Americans receiving some form of federal relief planned to vote for Roosevelt. Millions of the voters mobilized by the Roosevelt administration during this period became permanently attached to the Democratic party coalition and provided the Democrats with a stable base of support that, for a generation, would contribute to Democratic control of America's political institutions.[51]

Democratic efforts to organize and mobilize new voters during the 1930s were confined to the North. Roosevelt believed that retaining the support of the southern wing of the Democratic party was essential to the success of his legislative agenda and his continued tenure in the White House. He did not challenge either the political establishment of the former Confederacy or the region's segregationist order. Since the administration of most New Deal programs was decentralized, southern state governments shaped them to suit their racial customs. Benefits under the new Aid for Families with Dependent Children Program, for example, rarely went to black recipients in the southern states.[52] To appease southern landowners, agricultural labor was exempted from federal minimum wage and labor legislation.

Though they were potentially Democratic voters, most blacks and a large number of poor whites living in the South were disenfranchised by electoral systems that included poll taxes, literacy tests, and, in the case of blacks, the threat of violence against those who sought to vote. The South had the lowest voter turnout in the nation—only 18 percent, for example, in the 1924 presidential election. Unlike their northern counterparts, who faced Republican competition, the Democratic leaders of the one-party South had no interest in boosting voter turnout. Most viewed voter mobilization as a threat to their power and resisted all efforts to expand the southern electorate. Roosevelt refrained from interfering with these regional arrangements, and after World War II, the Truman administration followed pretty much same course. Truman, for example, helped to thwart the CIO's "Operation Dixie," an ambitious effort to use veteran union organizers to expand both union membership and voting rights among southern black workers and sharecroppers. The administration feared that the reaction of the Democratic party's southern, "Dixiecrat" wing would destroy the Democratic coalition and ruin the president's chances for reelection in 1948.[53]

In the North, Roosevelt's political efforts produced a Democratic coalition similar in its general outlines to that of a European social democratic party. It included members of the middle-class intellectual, professional, and quasi-professional strata; unionized workers; and the poor. Some segments of the business community supported particular Democratic programs or saw the New Deal as an acceptable alternative to more radical economic and social changes. The Democratic coalition also included immigrant-stock voters and virtually the entire African American population. As this coalition developed, it provided the mass base of support for the agenda of social reform and economic regulation associated with the latter part of Roosevelt's first term.

New Deal mobilization efforts in the 1934 midterm congressional elections increased the size of the Democratic majorities in both houses of Congress. With the backing provided by this reinforced mandate, Roosevelt embarked on the so-called Second New Deal. It included the enactment of the Wagner Act, the Social Security Act, the Banking Act of 1935, the Public Utility Holding Company Act (Wheeler-Rayburn Act), and the Revenue Act of 1935. The last of these measures, dubbed the "Soak the Rich" tax act, increased federal income tax rates and began the modern-day expansion of the national government's revenue base. The Democratic congressional landslide of 1934, powered by a flood of new voters in such states as New York and Pennsylvania, swept aside or at least temporarily disheartened Roosevelt's foes in both political parties and opened the way for his new legislative program.[54]

Though the New Deal mobilization effort was impressive, it was incomplete and temporary. The two forces upon which Roosevelt had relied, organized labor and urban political machines, both lost political potency after World War II. Labor was internally divided by struggles between radical and moderate unionists.[55] New technologies challenged the machine's domination of the electoral process. The use of the new broadcast media permitted political candidates to run successfully for office without organization support.[56] By the 1950s, voter turnout in the North had returned to pre–New Deal levels.

The possibilities for political change—much less social democracy—during the New Deal era were even more sharply constrained by the place of the South in the Democratic party. The South as a region benefited from New Deal social and agricultural programs. Southern conservatives, however, opposed a number of the administration's tax and regulatory initiatives, were deeply suspicious of the influence of liberal and labor forces in the Democratic coalition, and were determined to protect the southern apartheid system. The congressional seniority system placed many southerners in the key leadership posts of both House and Senate, posts from which they could hinder New Deal initiatives and prevent any social or racial reforms from penetrating their region.

In 1939, southern Democrats and conservative Republicans joined forces in a conservative coalition that slashed relief expenditures, cut business taxes, launched an investigation of the National Labor Relations Board, and eliminated the Federal Theatre Project. Over the next thirty years, this coalition worked to prevent liberal social and economic measures from being enacted. Conservative Republicans supported southern autonomy on matters of race. The southerners worked with the Republicans to prevent labor and liberals from bringing about the economic and social reforms they sought. During the 1940s, 1950s, and early 1960s this conservative coalition was quite successful, for example, in blocking national health insurance proposals initiated by Presidents Truman and Kennedy while simultaneously preventing the enactment of the significant civil rights bills proposed in 1944, 1946, 1950, 1960, and 1963.[57] Roosevelt's determination to conciliate white southern Democrats by overlooking the denial of voting rights to black southerners meant that the New Deal and its ideological successors would be unable to overcome the local and parochial elites who opposed their political goals.[58] During the 1960s, however, black civil rights leaders and their various white allies sought to rectify this mistake.

The 1960s: Civil Rights, the Vietnam War, and the Great Society

Popular electoral mobilization sparked by the civil rights movement undermined the power of the conservative coalition. In Alabama, the Montgomery bus boycott of 1955 focused national attention on a wave of African American protest that would rock the South for a decade. At first, national leaders of the Democratic party remained faithful to Roosevelt's strategy of preserving party unity by avoiding confrontation with the white South on the issue of race. In his 1956 presidential campaign, for example, Democratic candidate Adlai Stevenson asserted that the resolution of racial conflicts should be left to the individual states.

But the civil rights struggle won the support of northern liberals as the campaign of protest escalated. Televised images of southern law enforcement officers savagely beating peaceful demonstrators convinced large numbers of northerners that support for the cause of black civil rights was a moral imperative. For their part, a number of northern

Democratic politicians began to calculate that their own political interests might be served by supporting at least some of the demands of civil rights protestors.

Because of the great postwar migration of African Americans from the rural South to northern cities, blacks now constituted a significant voting bloc in a number of key northern states. John F. Kennedy campaigned for black support in 1960 at the risk of antagonizing white southerners, and black urban voters helped to produce his narrow presidential victory, giving him 82 percent of their votes—an increase of more than 20 percentage points over Stevenson's showing in 1956. Without this strong African American support, Kennedy would have lost the electoral votes of New York, Illinois, Pennsylvania, New Jersey, and Michigan, and the presidential election itself. Once in office, Kennedy acknowledged the loyalty of black voters by issuing a series of executive orders attacking discrimination in transportation, housing, employment, and education.

Northern Democrats had little to lose and much to gain by supporting the civil rights cause. On the one hand, they might win favor with their increasingly numerous black constituents. On the other hand, by aligning themselves with southern blacks, northern Democrats could shift the balance of power within their party by undermining the white southerners, who had long enjoyed disproportionate influence in the Democratic coalition.

Initially, the goals of the civil rights movement matched its label. It concentrated on civil rather than political rights—chiefly public accommodations and employment.[59] In 1961, however, the Kennedy administration pressed civil rights leaders to shift their focus to voting rights.[60] The administration believed that an emphasis on voting rights would be less confrontational than the full-scale ground assault against the South's system of racial separation in restaurants, swimming pools, and transportation.[61] Kennedy also calculated that moving the battle to the polling place would increase black Democratic votes in the South and offset defections among whites, improving the president's prospects in the 1964 presidential election.[62] Kennedy therefore supported the initiative that became the Twenty-Fourth Amendment, outlawing the poll taxes used in the South to disenfranchise blacks as well as many poor whites.[63] Some civil rights leaders viewed the Kennedy administration's focus on voting rights as an effort "to cool the militancy" of the protest movement.[64] Most, however, were willing to accept the federal protection and subsidies offered by Kennedy for voter registration drives.

Other politicians and interest groups had reasons of their own for supporting the expansion of voting rights in the South. Upper-middle-class liberal activists with ties to universities, foundations, philanthropic institutions, and the media had played a significant role in the Democratic party since the Roosevelt administration; and, with the increasing political and economic importance of the institutions to which they were linked, they played even larger roles in the Kennedy and Johnson administrations.

These liberal activists had consistently exercised greater influence at the national level and in the White House than on Capitol Hill or in state and local governments. The postwar liberals strongly favored expanding the power of the federal government and of the presidency at the expense of Congress and state and local governments. Liberal activists had been the brain trust behind Roosevelt's New Deal and the intellectual force behind Truman's Fair Deal. In the 1960s, liberals continued to support the idea of a powerful national government, led by a vigorous chief executive, that would initiate national programs to regulate the economy, protect the environment, and provide a variety of social services.[65]

The alliance of Dixiecrats and conservative Republicans had posed the major obstacle to realization of the liberal agenda. During the 1940s and 1950s, this coalition went on the offensive, initiating a series of investigations whose chief political aim was to discredit liberals and liberal institutions by linking them to the threat of international Communism.[66] To this end, the House Un-American Activities Committee (HUAC) probed supposed Communist influence in such liberal bastions as labor unions, the film and broadcast industries, the news media, philanthropic institutions, and the universities. HUAC investigations led to criminal sentences for a number of witnesses who refused to testify before the panel. Others saw their careers ruined by unsubstantiated allegations linking them to Communist organizations.

In general, HUAC was used by successive chairmen, including southern Democrats like Martin Dies of Texas and John Rankin of Mississippi, as well as arch conservatives like J. Parnell Thomas of New Jersey, to attack liberal Democrats. Meanwhile, in the Senate, Joseph McCarthy (R.-Wisconsin) conducted probes of Communist infiltration of such institutions as the State Department, in which liberal Republicans played significant roles. McCarthy was backed by the midwestern, conservative Taft wing of the Republican party. Taft and his allies saw McCarthy's probes as a useful means of discrediting the more liberal Eastern Establishment wing of the GOP, which had aligned itself with the New Deal and often supported liberal Democratic programs.[67]

The emergence of the civil rights movement provided liberal forces with an unexpected opportunity to turn the tables on their conservative foes. Extension of voting rights to African Americans in the South could produce several million black voters to undermine the Dixiecrat politicians aligned with the conservative coalition. This strategy promised liberals a measure of revenge against the forces that had only recently sought to portray them as Communist sympathizers. More important, enfeebling the Dixiecrats would open the way for implementation of the liberal agenda that the conservative coalition had blocked for more than two decades.

Liberals were joined in their support for the expansion of black voting rights by important segments of the American business community. Many national corporations were anxious to stop the turmoil of civil rights demonstrations and boycotts and were happy to join the Kennedy administration in encouraging black protestors to "work within the system"—seeking to achieve their ends by voting rather than demonstrating.[68] Firms with international markets were anxious to end the embarrassment abroad caused by worldwide exposure to scenes of southern police officers enforcing racial subordination by brutalizing peaceful civil rights protestors.[69]

The national news media also had a stake in supporting the campaign for black voting rights. The morality plays enacted on the streets by civil rights organizations were irresistible to television networks in search of dramatic, "visual" news. Electronic journalists just learning the uses of their medium discovered new possibilities for shaping as well as reporting the news. In Little Rock and elsewhere, a few of them helped to stage the set-pieces that became national emblems of a renewed determination to resolve the peculiar American dilemma.[70]

At the same time, civil rights leaders like Dr. Martin Luther King learned to use television to gain the sympathy of northern audiences for their cause.[71] His movement's struggle to win voting rights for black southerners captivated the networks and electrified their viewers. Segregationists unwittingly played the role scripted for them by the civil rights movement, though occasionally they overacted. The murder of three voter registration workers in Mississippi during the Freedom Summer of 1964 appalled the nation and turned the networks' klieg lights on county courthouses and black churches in the Deep South.[72] They finally converged on Selma, the seat of Dallas County, Alabama.

Martin Luther King targeted Selma for a concerted campaign of protest activity partly because the disenfranchisement of African Americans in Dallas County was so starkly obvious. Though they made up 58 percent of the county's population, only 2 percent of the county's registered voters were black. A sustained voter registration drive between 1962 and 1964 had produced only 795 new black registrants. The county government responded to even these meager gains by instituting new registration standards—devices transparently designed to keep black residents off the voting rolls—requiring new registrants to be able to read and interpret passages from the state and federal constitutions and to provide a certificate of "good character" from an already registered voter.[73]

Selma had been chosen, however, not only because it had an outrageous record of discrimination against would-be black voters but also because Dr. King was confident that state and county political leaders would respond to peaceful protests with violence, and in the process imprint themselves on the collective consciousness of a national television audience as the irrationally brutal oppressors of defenseless crusaders ready to sacrifice themselves for freedom and democracy. Whatever the voting rights campaign may have been on the streets of Selma, on television it was a clear-cut struggle of good against evil.[74] Alabama and Dallas County authorities played their assigned roles convincingly. Before a full array of network cameras, Alabama state troopers launched a vicious attack against protestors on the Raymond Pettus Bridge, leaving forty demonstrators seriously injured in what the national news media dubbed "bloody Sunday."[75]

From the perspective of protest leaders and the national media, Dallas County sheriff Jim Clark might have been sent by central casting to play his part in the drama. Clark displayed a violent temper on camera and off, wore a "Never!" button in his lapel, and armed his deputies with electric cattle prods. Clark's extravagant cruelty unwittingly contributed so much to the cause of African American voting rights that the protestors made him an honorary member of Dr. King's Southern Christian Leadership Conference (SCLC) as well as the Student Nonviolent Coordinating Committee (SNCC) and the National Association for the Advancement of Colored People (NAACP).[76] The previous year, Birmingham, Alabama, police commissioner, Eugene T. "Bull" Connor had been similarly helpful to Dr. King's efforts when, in full view of network television cameras, he arrested King and unleashed his deputies against peaceful demonstrators.[77]

The drama and passion generated by television coverage of the Selma protests helped to create the setting for passage of the 1965 Voting Rights Act. The 1964 Democratic landslide had added significantly to the strength of northern Democrats in both houses of Congress. This allowed President Johnson to secure congressional passage of sweeping voting rights legislation that substantially increased African American voter registration in the South. Under the terms of the 1965 Voting Rights Act, federal officials took control of voter registration in those states and localities that had previously acted to deny voting rights to blacks. Millions of black southerners became voters as a result.

The overwhelming majority of these new voters, of course, gave their support to the Democratic party. At the same time, large numbers of white southerners expressed their opposition to the national Democratic party's civil rights policies by shifting their support to the GOP—first in national presidential contests and later in state and local races as well. As a result, Democratic party organizations in the southern states, institutions that had been controlled by conservative whites since Reconstruction, became increasingly dependent upon the support of African Americans. In such states as Alabama, Mississippi, and South Carolina, blacks quickly came to make up more than a third of the electorate and to account for at least half the votes received by Democratic candidates in statewide races. No southern Democrat could hope to be elected to statewide office without overwhelming black support.

Forced to confront this new electoral reality, some Democratic politicians, like Senators Jesse Helms and Strom Thurmond, joined their white constituents by moving into the Republican camp. One—George Wallace of Alabama—led a third-party revolt. Other southerners adjusted their rhetoric and behavior to court black support. This strategy required southern Democrats to abandon their alliance with Republican conservatives and to support the national party on social welfare and civil rights issues.[78] As a result, the political potency of the conservative coalition, which for so long had thwarted American liberals, began to wane.

Its passing briefly created the climate for an efflorescence of liberal politics. During his first full term in office, President Johnson led congressional Democrats toward his vision of a "Great Society," whose key components were embodied in a sweeping legislative program that included the enactment of a comprehensive War on Poverty, Medicare, Medicaid, the 1965 Elementary and Secondary Education Act, the 1965 Voting Rights Act, the 1966 Civil Rights Act, and the 1968 Fair Housing Act. Liberals hoped that in alliance with newly mobilized African Americans, they would be able to sustain the political momentum for further domestic social reform. But even as Democrats enacted President Johnson's ambitious legislative agenda, the Democratic coalition was confronting serious internal divisions created, in part, by the party's own efforts to attract and mobilize an African American constituency.

Though proposed as an assault on poverty in general, the Great Society's economic opportunity initiatives served as vehicles for racial protest in northern cities. The targets of protest frequently included urban political party organizations and labor organizations—mainstays of the New

Deal coalition and the political bedrock beneath Lyndon Johnson's landslide victory of 1964. The community action agencies that served as local outposts of the War on Poverty represented potential competition for the patronage-consuming parties of big-city politics. The parties could distribute government-sponsored jobs, and they often did so in the form of jobs with nonprofit corporations beyond the limits of local government and outside the orbits of established political organizations. Even if local political leaders managed to take control of the antipoverty agency, as Mayor Daley did in Chicago, the effort was likely to ignite or intensify the underlying struggle between Democratic stalwarts and black insurgents.[79] Political allies that had helped to return Democrats to the White House in 1960 now turned against one another in combat.

Organized labor was soon engaged as well. Job training and employment programs undertaken under the aegis of the War on Poverty created new competitors in the labor market, and affirmative action policies threatened to displace union members from slots in city government and the building trades, slots that they had long regarded as theirs to occupy and bequeath to family members. The "street-level bureaucrats" of municipal government struggled to maintain authority over a restive and resentful clientele that consisted, increasingly, of culturally alien Latinos and African Americans.[80]

Until disrupted by the combined forces of the civil rights movement and the War on Poverty, unions, urban party organizations, and local real estate interests had found common ground in "executive centered coalitions" centered on entrepreneurial mayors and cemented together by federally subsidized urban redevelopment programs that assured profits to developers, work for construction unions, lower taxes for homeowners, and secure jobs in the municipal civil service for the lower-middle-class and upwardly mobile members of the working class.[81] For black city residents, these local urban renewal initiatives seemed little more than campaigns of "Negro removal" designed to banish them from the fringes of central business districts, where their presence posed a threat to commercial property values. Now they struck back.

They had allies. White liberals—academics, foundation officials, social welfare professionals—had participated in the design of the War on Poverty, but in local politics, their social reform objectives confronted many of the same obstacles that confronted black activists. They denounced municipal bureaucracies and party machines as "insensitive" to the needs of the black community; construction trade unions, as racist; and neighborhood resistance to racial balance in the schools, as segregationist. Its southern base overturned by the civil rights struggle, the Democratic party's foundations in the North were now shaken as the underlying racial schism within its ranks rumbled to the surface. The emerging pattern of alliances and animosities in the Democratic party was characterized at the time as a coalition of the top and bottom against the middle—upper-middle-class white professionals allied with blacks in opposition to lower-middle- and working-class whites.[82]

These divisions were hardened by the Vietnam War. During the early years of American military involvement in Southeast Asia, President Johnson sought to minimize tensions within his party by restricting increases in military expenditures in order to avoid draining resources from the domestic programs supported by white liberals and black activists. America, he argued, could afford guns and the Great Society at the same time. His effort to sustain consensus among Democrats was one consideration in his choice of gradual escalation in Vietnam rather than a massive military effort from the beginning.[83]

As escalation followed escalation, however, federal funds flowed away from the War on Poverty to the war in Vietnam. The antipoverty initiatives were also undermined by resurgent conservative forces in Congress. The price of their support for White House policy in Vietnam was a federal retreat from social engineering at home. Liberals—including members of Johnson's own cabinet, such as Secretary of Health, Education, and Welfare John Gardner and Labor Secretary Willard Wirtz—saw the Vietnam War as an immediate threat to the programs and institutions to which they were committed. It was both an assault on liberal conscience and on the policies that reflected liberal power.[84]

Thousands of liberal Democrats turned away from the Democratic president to join the student radicals who had been campaigning against the war since its early stages. They sought not only to end the war but also to reverse the massive diversion of funds and political energy from the movement for social reform that had seemed so promising at the dawn of Johnson's Great Society.[85] Among their student allies on college campuses, resistance to military conscription had already reached epidemic levels. The war was a more immediate threat to them than to their elders. But their educational status made it possible for many of them to avoid Vietnam. Higher education, in fact, was one common attribute among the antiwar forces, both old and young. Blue-collar "Middle America," in contrast, provided disproportionate support for the American war effort in Vietnam—and many of the soldiers who fought there.

The conflict over the war exacerbated social class divisions within the Democratic party, divisions that had been exposed by the struggle over civil rights. Blue-collar Democrats resented what they saw as an effort by a small but well-educated and relatively affluent stratum to impose its own social and cultural values on the remainder of society. Alabama governor George Wallace expressed the anger of working-class Americans when he exhorted them to resist the efforts of "pointy-headed intellectuals," "pot smokers," and "Harvard professors on bicycles" to come into their communities and tell them how to live. Working-class Americans, for the most part, were also angered by the lack of patriotism exhibited by the sons of privilege who found ways to avoid the draft while their own sons were sent to fight. The echoes of these conflicts of the 1960s can be heard clearly today in arguments about "family values" and even in continuing recriminations about the past drug use and military records of some prominent politicians.

For their part, many middle-class Democrats viewed members of the white working class as racists and jingoists. After a mob of New York City construction workers wearing yellow safety helmets attacked and beat student antiwar protestors, the term "hard hat" became synonymous with working-class thuggery in the lexicon of liberal Democrats. "Archie Bunker," the white, working-class lead character of a television situation comedy enormously popular among viewers of the period, was depicted as a bigoted, neo-Fascist dolt.[86]

The collapse of the conservative coalition initially seemed to offer liberal Democrats an opportunity to extend the New Deal agenda of social reform beyond the 1960s. By the end of the decade, however, the opportunity had been forfeited. Widening class and racial divisions within the Democratic party destroyed the prospects for a grand alliance of races and classes that would have united college-educated liberals with their would-be working-class allies both black and white. Millions of working-class whites in the North and South abandoned the Democratic party to support George Wallace's independent presidential bid in 1968 and at least briefly joined the Republican camp to vote for Richard Nixon in 1972. Nixon's hard hat supporters were the forerunners of the "Reagan Democrats," who would help to elect a Republican president in 1980 and 1984.

The Democratic party faced a choice at the start of the 1970s—whether to attempt a revival of the New Deal electoral coalition that included organized labor and the white working class or whether to work out their political destiny without the party's traditional blue-collar base. In the national political arena, the first strategy was most closely associated with the presidential campaign of Robert Kennedy and the second with what came to be called the "New Politics." Kennedy's electoral strategy included efforts to continue the remobilization of the electorate begun by the New Deal and the civil rights movement, taking advantage of the possibilities opened by the enfranchisement of millions of African Americans in the South. His strategy envisioned a significant expansion of the electorate. The postmaterial forces of the New Politics, however, had little affinity for the working-class wing of the Democratic party and no inclination to mobilize them in elections.

Electoral Mobilization or New Politics?

Before John Kennedy's assassination, his younger brother Robert had not been a popular political figure. Liberal Democrats remembered Robert as an aide to Senator Joseph McCarthy during the anti-Communist witch hunts of the early 1950s. Organized labor recollected his aggressive investigation of links between organized crime and the labor movement as staff attorney for the McClellan Committee.[87] The business community recalled his pugnacious tactics toward prominent steel industry executives during the 1962 conflict between the Kennedy administration and the steel industry over steel price increases. Finally, many African American leaders resented his apparent lack of enthusiasm for the civil rights cause when he was attorney general during the early 1960s. Kennedy had authorized the FBI to place wiretaps on the phones of Dr. Martin Luther King and his close aide, Stanley Levison—an action that infuriated the entire civil rights leadership when it became known.[88]

After John Kennedy's death, however, Robert Kennedy benefited from the nationwide torrent of grief and emotional support for the Kennedy family. Popular sympathy for the brother of the martyred president helped Robert Kennedy defeat Republican incumbent Kenneth Keating to win election to the U.S. Senate from the state of New York in 1964. But Robert Kennedy had to work for his victory, and, sympathy notwithstanding, he still had political handicaps to overcome. Though he won the election by a comfortable 719,000-vote margin, President Lyndon Johnson, who led the ticket, carried New York by a 2.7 million vote margin. Thus, nearly 2 million New Yorkers who cast their ballots for the Democratic presidential candidate in 1964 made the decision not to support Robert Kennedy.[89]

After his election to the Senate, Kennedy undertook a major effort to expand his political base in preparation for a future presidential run. He moved first to build a secure bastion of support on the Democratic party's liberal left. Kennedy proved to be a gifted politician, able to stake out positions in support of previously neglected causes that would subsequently prove to be extremely popular among Democratic liberals. He was among the early supporters of Cesar Chavez in his efforts to organize migrant farmworkers in California.[90] Kennedy's presence on the picket lines alongside Mexican American farmworkers did much to enhance the senator's image among liberals while at least partially erasing the memory of Kennedy's service for McCarthy and his approval of the King wiretaps. Kennedy was also among the first national politicians to take a position on Native American rights. He toured reservations, spoke out on behalf of Native Americans and Eskimos, and became the Senate's champion of expanding funding for the education of Native Americans.

To enhance his standing among African Americans, Kennedy courted the support of both mainstream civil right leaders and more radical activists. He promoted expansion of funding for social programs including the community action programs that were popular among local black and white political activists because they provided a channel of federal funding for community organizations. Kennedy proposed a variety of programs designed to create private-sector jobs in the ghetto. He traveled to South Africa in 1966, where he met with Albert Luthuli a Nobel Prize–winning writer who had been banned by the government. Kennedy received a great deal of media coverage in the United States for speaking out against South Africa's apartheid system. Gradually, civil rights leaders like Martin Luther King, John Lewis, Willie Brown, and Roy Wilkins began to believe that Kennedy's commitment to their cause was sincere. At the same time, even more-radical blacks like Floyd McKissick were drawn into the Kennedy circle through regular meetings and, at least in McKissick's case, financial support from the Kennedy family.[91]

During the 1968 Democratic primaries, Kennedy campaigned vigorously in black areas and won the overwhelming support of black voters. According to news accounts, Kennedy's campaign swings through African American neighborhoods often radiated the ecstatic aura of religious revivals, his candidacy borne upward by wildly enthusiastic crowds. In Indiana, Kennedy captured nearly 90 percent of the African American vote. In Nebraska, nearly 85 percent of the black voters in the Omaha area backed Kennedy. In the District of Columbia, Kennedy carried two-thirds of the black vote. In California, blacks and Mexican Americans were Kennedy's core constituency. Rival politicians generally ceded the black vote to Kennedy, believing there was little point to competing against him for African American support. Eugene McCarthy, for example, refrained from campaigning in Harlem because, he said, there was "No need to stir up the blacks and minorities. They were Bobby's people and I saw no point in wasting time campaigning there."[92]

Kennedy also saw disaffected young people as a potential supporters. He gave scores of speeches on college campuses and solicited the advice of such leaders of youth protest as Tom Hayden, president of Students for a Democratic Society, and New Left spokesman, Staughton Lynd. Hayden wrote, "the only politician who expressed an interest in what I was doing was Robert Kennedy";[93] and he subsequently worked for Kennedy in the

1968 California Democratic primary. Kennedy's most important appeal for the support of radical young people was, of course, opposition to the Vietnam War. Kennedy broke with the Johnson administration in 1965, calling for the creation of a coalition government in Vietnam. Between 1965 and 1967, Kennedy avoided taking strong positions on the issue of the war. In the aftermath of the 1968 Tet offensive, however, he began to make a series of strong speeches to enthusiastic student audiences, condemning the war on moral grounds and calling for an end to the fighting. Kennedy was sufficiently successful in attracting the support of young people to cause some radical youth leaders like Abbie Hoffman to worry that he threatened their positions of prominence. Until Kennedy's assassination, the ranks of Hoffman's Youth International Party thinned as members rushed off to work for the Kennedy campaign.[94]

While Kennedy worked to build a solid political base on the left, he was also eager to retain the backing of traditional Democratic supporters, including labor, farmers, ethnic groups, and machine politicians. As he began his campaign, Kennedy's relations with all these groups were unsettled or just uncertain. Elements of organized labor were troubled by Kennedy's prosecution of Jimmy Hoffa and other officials of the Teamsters Union. But Kennedy developed close ties with leaders of other unions—Walter Reuther of the United Auto Workers and Cesar Chavez and his farmworkers, as well as the leaders of newly unionized workers like the Indiana steel haulers. The link with Chavez helped Kennedy to win nearly 95 percent of the Mexican American vote on the way to his victory in the California primary. Where Kennedy was unable to win over the top national union leadership, he courted local union leaders, lower-ranking national staff, and the rank and file. Young Kennedy staffers attended union conventions, where they made a point of meeting rank and filers. Kennedy himself joined striking workers on the picket lines. Circumventing labor's leaders paid off. By April 1968, polls showed Kennedy leading both McCarthy and Humphrey among union members, notwithstanding their leaders' endorsements of Humphrey and the vigorous efforts of the AFL-CIO's Committee on Public Education to mobilize union support for the vice president.[95]

Kennedy also cultivated the support of a second traditional Democratic constituency—members of white urban ethnic groups whose ardor for the party had cooled because of its stand on civil rights. Many white, working-class voters believed that the Democrats favored black aspirations at their expense. Kennedy was convinced that he could forge a coalition between blacks and urban ethnics based on their common economic concerns, much as Franklin Roosevelt had done. He campaigned energetically in ethnic areas of primary states like Indiana and focused his messages on the importance of New Deal and Great Society social programs that were popular among working-class whites, as well as blacks.

News accounts of the period indicated that Kennedy had been enormously successful in winning white ethnic support. In reporting the results of the Indiana primary, the *New York Times* asserted that Kennedy had managed to win over working-class ethnic whites in Gary as well as rural whites, thus commanding the support of whites who had previously backed Alabama governor George Wallace. One commentator called Kennedy "the last liberal politician who could communicate with white, working class America." Another said, "Kennedy could do the miraculous: attract the support of desperate blacks and white working class people."[96]

A close analysis of Kennedy's vote in the 1968 primaries suggests that initial observers overestimated the extent of white ethnic support for the New York senator. In the Indiana primary, Kennedy actually lost six out of seven white precincts in Gary and was able to capture urban areas only because of his overwhelming support from black voters. Nevertheless, Kennedy did well among Indiana's Polish voters and Nebraska's German voters, and he scored significantly ahead of all candidates among Catholic voters in national polls. After his death, many of these working-class voters would become "Nixon Democrats" and then "Reagan Democrats."

The precise extent of Kennedy's success among white ethnics may be less significant than his vigorous effort to get their support. He was convinced that he could win their backing and was ecstatic over news accounts suggesting that he had succeeded. After the Indiana primary, Kennedy told his aides, "I've proved I can really be a leader of a broad spectrum. I can be a bridge between blacks and whites without stepping back from my positions." In a similar spirit, Kennedy courted the nation's farmers without much hope of making significant inroads in the farm belt. But Kennedy scored significant victories in both the Nebraska and South Dakota Democratic primaries, capturing absolute majorities in both of these farm states. Kennedy was a liberal politician who sought to build a broad electoral coalition of younger, middle-class whites, working-class whites, and poor blacks. When accused by journalists of demagoguery for his often emotional appeals to voters, Kennedy replied that such appeals were needed to build a broad base of popular support. "I have to win through the people. Otherwise I'm not going to win," he said.[97]

The New Politics Matures

Robert Kennedy's assassination in 1968 also meant the death of his electoral strategy. Many liberal activists were no longer willing to make common cause with the labor leaders and machine politicians who had dominated Democratic party politics for decades. They were estranged from these traditional Democrats by attitudes on race or the Vietnam War or both. Liberals cemented alliances with African Americans by their support of affirmative action policies, and constructed their own version of affirmative action within the Democratic party, in order to assure the representation of women and minority groups at national conventions. The McGovern-Fraser rules, adopted at the 1972 convention, effectively imposed race, gender, and age quotas on state delegations and outlawed winner-take-all presidential primaries, which were often controlled by party leaders. States were required to select convention delegates through open caucus procedures or primaries based on proportional representation. The reforms strengthened liberal activists and racial minorities within the party while weakening party politicians and labor leaders.[98]

The ability to mobilize an electoral constituency was now only one way to earn admission to party councils. It was also possible to gain entry by "symbolizing" a constituency through one's racial identity or gender. A similar practice was later embraced at Republican conventions, where the televised image of cultural diversity served as surrogate for the experience of diversity itself.

In the New Politics of the 1970s, such imaginary political constituencies achieved an institutional embodiment in the formation of public interest groups. Public participation in public interest groups was actually quite limited. These groups relied on access to administrative agencies and litigation to achieve their ends rather than on popular mobilization in elections. Liberal and (later) conservative activists established hundreds of interest groups, public interest law firms, and think tanks to further such goals as environmental quality, the elimination of nuclear weapons, consumer protection, auto safety, and individual liberty.[99] Common Cause, the Sierra Club, the various organizations formed by consumer activist Ralph Nader—all sought to distinguish themselves from traditional interest groups by claiming to serve broad public interests rather than the narrower demands advanced by more traditional pressure groups on behalf of business corporations, organized labor, or other producer groups.[100] Financial support for public interest groups came from the Ford Foundation, which provided tens of millions of dollars through its Fund for the Republic; and moral support came from the mass media, which rarely questioned the claims of public interest groups to speak for the public interest.

By speaking for the interest of everyone in general, public interest groups distanced themselves from anyone in particular. It followed that they had to exercise political influence by means other than the mobilization of a definable public constituency. To this end, the practitioners of the New Politics pursued an agenda of regulatory and bureaucratic reform, including an expansion of the role of the courts in the administrative process, an agenda that enabled them to advance the public interest without having to rouse the public itself.

One expedient was to urge the delegation of governmental tasks and public funds to nongovernmental institutions likely to be staffed by fellow practitioners of the New Politics—nonprofit social service agencies, legal services clinics, public interest law firms, and the like.[101] At the same time, public interest groups and their allies sought to enhance their access to the regulatory activities of the federal government. Consumer advocates and environmentalists, in particular, were able to increase their influence in the regulatory process through sunshine laws, by subjecting federal agencies to close judicial supervision, by providing for the representation of public interest groups in the administrative process, and by using their access to the media to launch exposés attacking administrative practices to which they objected.[102]

Once created, new federal regulatory agencies like the Consumer Product Safety Commission, the Environmental Protection Agency, and the Occupational Safety and Health Administration extended the domain of the New Politics. Indeed, the executives of the new regulatory programs created between 1966 and 1976 were often recruited from the public interest lobby, just as the executives of traditional regulatory agencies were often drawn from the industries that they were supposed to regulate.[103]

The courts presented the partisans of the New Politics with access to another kind of influence that did not depend upon the mobilization of popular constituencies, and these partisans generally sought to subject federal programs and agencies to tighter supervision by the judiciary. During the long struggle for civil rights, liberals had learned that judges could be critically important allies when popularly elected legislatures were controlled by hostile forces. Public interest groups and their friends in Congress now supported a lowering of the requirements for standing, a virtual elimination of the political questions doctrine, the expansion of class action suits, and an enriched range of judicial remedies. Moreover, many consumer and environmental statutes, such as the Endangered Species Act, contained " citizen-suit" provisions that enabled public interest groups to use the courts to enforce the statutes' provisions without having to seek administrative remedies. Groups could finance such litigation by means of fee-shifting provisions that allowed them to collect attorneys' fees and court costs when they prevailed.[104]

Party reform, public interest groups, new regulatory programs and procedures, and the use of litigation all created a political platform for the New Politics that did not rest to a significant degree on the mobilization of the electorate. Ideological justification for their nondemocratic approach to reform was provided by liberal scholars who argued for essential democratic values that could not be left to the vagaries of majority rule.[105]

Having established their political influence in the absence of comprehensive electoral mobilization, the liberal heirs of the New Politics were understandably reluctant to place it at risk by issuing appeals for mass activism. They were likely to flourish politically in a low-turnout environment. Today, tens of thousands of political activists affiliated with public interest groups, nonprofit organizations, and the quasi-public institutions of the domestic state form the backbone of the Democratic party's electoral effort. For these groups, expanded participation would now represent a threat to their influence over the party rather than an opportunity for increased political power.

Political conservatives were not at all inclined to seize the initiative in popular mobilization. They rarely are.[106] In some respects, they imitated the public-interest-group model pioneered by liberals. Litigation was a specialty. Through Judicial Watch, the Washington Legal Foundation, and the Federalist Society, they employed the courts to torment elected officeholders. Republicans did welcome new constituencies to their party—southern whites, the Christian Coalition, the National Rifle Association, and the National Federation of Independent Business.[107] These groups, however, including the Christian Coalition and its predecessor, the Moral Majority, generally appealed to middle-class Americans who already participated in politics. Republicans did little or nothing in the 1980s and 1990s to bring new voters into the electorate.

Historically conservative parties have tried to protect their own congeries of interest groups, courts, and media that have helped corporate interests to exercise political power. When liberal forces opted to follow the path of the New Politics, they eliminated the possibility of electoral expansion resulting from what Duverger called contagion from the left and virtually guaranteed that popular political participation would be marginalized.

The combination of New Politics and conservatism's resurgence has created a highly stratified political process. Those citizens whose resources and education enable them to take advantage of the of the new opportunities for personal access to politics benefit from the ability to communicate their views to policymakers. But tens of millions of Americans are barely involved in the political process, which has produced what political scientists Sidney Verba, Kay Schlozman, and Henry Brady call "representational distortion."[108] These are the citizens who have become mere "customers" for the programs and services designed by their political betters.

Chapter 4

The Old Patronage and the New

FOR MOST OF the nineteenth century, American parties were led by political managers whose chief goal was electoral success. They were pragmatic—or perhaps just unprincipled—willing to embrace almost any issue or policy that promised to bring victory at the polls. The patronage-seeking campaign organizations that they led were working prototypes for the vote-maximizing model of party competition introduced by Anthony Downs in the 1950s and still central to rational choice theory today.[1]

Though the party managers were no ideologues, the politics of their era was anything but issueless. They orchestrated history-shaping debates about slavery, tariffs, internal improvements, public lands, railroads, banks, and monetary policy. The very opportunism of the party politicians meant that they were ready and willing to exploit new issues that might expand the legions of their faithful. Their aim was to outmobilize the opposition and ride the election returns to the seats of power in Washington.

But the electoral surge that was sustained by party building and party competition in the nineteenth century receded steadily during the twentieth. The political organizations that had energized the electorate were battered by Progressive reformers, a coalition of issue-oriented professionals and business leaders determined to overthrow America's version of party government. Lacking the capacity to outmobilize the party managers, the Progressives sought to influence policy by non-electoral means.[2] They created privileged avenues of access to the courts and the bureaucracy, avenues that allowed them to achieve their political ends while bypassing the elections, in which mass-based parties held the advantage.[3] But the Progressives also restructured elections themselves to improve their success in waging popular politics. Their principal innovation was the party primary, which weakened the party bosses' ability to handpick candidates. And, like the nonpartisan elections that the Progressives also championed, the direct primary was a contest in which the candidates were not distinguished by the party labels that they carried, which thus deprived many rank-and-file loyalists of the vital cue that told them how to mark their ballots. The primary was the sort of election that appealed to voters guided not by party identification but by issues, ideologies, and policy preferences. It was an election for well-informed and well-educated voters—in short, for people like the Progressives themselves.

Weaker parties meant declining turnout, but only until the Depression and the New Deal expanded the electorate with thousands of new voters driven to political action, first by desperation and later by an electoral coalition that was the artful construction of Franklin Roosevelt. As pragmatic as any nineteenth-century boss, Roosevelt assembled his forces around the mission of restoring economic prosperity. To the Democrats' traditional base among white southerners, he added strength among northern labor, African Americans, and liberal intellectuals. It was an improbable alliance, a creature of crisis; and even during the New Deal itself, there were signs of the internal strains that would eventually break it apart. To satisfy southern conservatives in Congress, for example, New Deal social welfare policy was reshaped so as to exclude African Americans from eligibility for most benefits.[4]

The political managers who inherited the New Deal coalition displayed almost as much ideological flexibility as the party leaders of the nineteenth century. They had to. But their exploitation of national issues was constrained by a distinctive political vulnerability. There were some issues that had to be avoided because they would fracture the disparate Democratic congregation. They would haunt the Democrats even in the hour of their greatest success.

In 1964, the New Deal coalition achieved its most decisive victory since Roosevelt's own reelection triumph in 1936, but the Democratic landslide of 1964 set the stage for the coalition's eventual fragmentation. The landslide meant that every section of the discordant Democratic chorus now had a strong voice in government. The party's family quarrels would now be carried on at a higher volume than ever before and, because they would be fought out among the bearers of public authority, with greater likelihood of internal injury. But in 1964, the party's ideological breadth made it seem invincible.

In Barry Goldwater, the Democrats faced a candidate whose commitment to ideology seemed stronger than his determination to get elected. His decisive defeat may have concealed the extent to which his campaign transformed American politics. It was not just that control of the Republican party's nominating process had passed from the Eastern Establishment to ideological conservatives from the West and Midwest. Goldwater may also have signaled a broader change in the character of American parties and politics. He was a right-wing harbinger of the New Politics that would soon derange the New Deal coalition. Goldwater and his followers made ideological correctness a test for political standing within the Republican party. By the 1970s, the Democrats would be doing the same, and they occupied such far-flung ideological real estate that the consequences proved even more fractious for them than for the GOP.

By the late 1960s, moreover, Republican strategists had become adept at exploiting "wedge issues"—contentious subjects that set Democrats against Democrats. The Nixon administration's promotion of affirmative action in the construction trades under the "Philadelphia Plan" fanned animosities between labor unions and blacks. During the war in Vietnam, issues of patriotism could be manipulated to alienate ideological liberals from blue-collar hard hats. And the pursuit of the "Southern Strategy" would eventually shift the political allegiances of an entire region, along with the political balance in Washington.

Within the Democratic party, the cleavages opened by the civil rights movement, the Vietnam War, and Republican strategy triggered a general struggle for control of the party's machinery as well as its soul. The pragmatic heirs of Roosevelt's New Deal squared off against the proponents of the New Politics, who were in many respects the political descendants of the Progressive reformers. They sought to refashion the political party to suit well-educated and ideologically motivated activists like themselves. Among other things, they reconstituted the Democratic party's nominating process through the so-called McGovern-Fraser rules, which increased the influence of liberal activists by guaranteeing representation for women and minorities at the party's national convention.[5] Mobilizing popular support was now only one of the ways to gain access to the Democrats' presidential nominating process.

The struggle to control that process was an echo—only much louder—of the one that had made Goldwater the Republican presidential candidate in 1964. Pragmatic political managers lost influence in both parties, replaced by issue-oriented leaders and their followers. Pundit

William Schneider, writing in 1987, looked back with a sense of loss to the days when "a political party was a big tent, with room inside for all kinds of people. The Democratic party included southern white racists, blacks, urban bosses, and liberal reformers." The Democratic and Republican parties alike had been converted from big tents into narrow citadels that accommodated the favored few who could pass the appropriate ideological "litmus tests."[6] Political victory had been redefined. Winning elections was no longer the point. It was only one of several means for parties to advance their programs, policies, and principles. In fact, as noted in Chapter 3, the new party elites sometimes regarded an aroused electorate as a potential threat and frequently opted to pursue their goals by means other than full-scale mobilization of the voters.

As the electoral exertions of the two parties weakened in the 1960s and 1970s, many observers thought they were witnessing the "decline of parties" in American politics.[7] But there is now a dawning recognition that political parties did not so much decline as change in character and focus.[8] Once oriented almost exclusively to electoral struggle, parties began to develop other approaches to politics that did not require the maintenance and mobilization of a large popular support base. Instead, they developed a capacity to engage in what might be called "institutional mobilization." Each party established a network of outposts in interest groups, think tanks, the news media, public agencies, nonprofits, and other private institutions. Today parties carry on their struggles by calling up their institutional reserves—a process Benjamin Ginsberg and Martin Shefter have called "politics by other means"—with only peripheral engagement of ordinary citizens.[9] The Watergate affair, the Iran-Contra controversy, the Clinton impeachment process, and the Florida post-election struggle of 2000 are all cases in point. To the extent that the parties do involve the general public in their battles, they typically employ what political scientist Steven Schier has labeled the "activation" strategy. This strategy targets tried, true, and politically reliable citizens rather than the unpredictable public at large.[10] Competition at the grassroots has given way to a battle of mailing lists, phone banks, fax machines, and the Internet. In effect, the two parties repeatedly round up the usual suspects and set them in motion. The unknown public at large is rarely uninvited.

Institutional Mobilization

The Democratic and Republican parties have staked out their respective institutional territories in government and politics. The Democrats are entrenched in the social and regulatory agencies of the domestic state; in the not-for-profit, public, and quasi-public institutions connected to one another by the so-called grants economy; and in a host of public interest groups and important segments of the news media. The Republicans have built a support base in the nation's military and national security apparatus, among corporate contractors and private-sector interest groups, in religious organizations, and in a complex of conservative newspapers, magazines, think tanks, and radio stations. This competitive entrenchment has at least partially replaced voter mobilization as a means of securing political power in the United States and is one of the reasons that high levels of partisan conflict can coexist with low levels of voter participation.

The Democratic party began building its institutional base during the New Deal, but the growth of this base continued thereafter, especially during the years of Lyndon Johnson's Great Society. The core of the Democratic institutional party lies in the social, regulatory, and grant programs created, in large part, by Democratic presidents and congresses. To administer these programs, they created or expanded such agencies as the Department of Health and Human Services, the Department of Labor, the Department of Education, the Office of Economic Opportunity, and the Environmental Protection Agency (EPA). These national agencies are programmatically linked to state and local bureaucracies which are nourished in large part by federal grants. These subnational governments have grown far more sharply during the past forty years than the federal government itself.[11] Other grants-in-aid support nonprofit organizations that administer national social programs. These institutions and programs are generally staffed by Democrats, promoted by Democrats, and defended by Democrats in the Capitol and White House.

Federal social welfare and regulatory agencies serve as centers of influence for the Democratic party in several ways. Federal domestic agencies create strong ties between the Democratic party and the millions of Americans who work in the public sector and the millions more who benefit from social programs such as Medicare. These agencies and programs also link the Democrats to nonprofit institutions such as universities, to private social welfare organizations, and to other nonprofit groups that receive federal grants and contracts. Planned Parenthood, for example, receives roughly one-third of its $500 million annual budget from federal grants and Medicaid reimbursements. AARP gets tens of millions of government dollars each year as a provider of federally sponsored services to the elderly. Other institutions, including museums, art galleries, and universities, also receive hundreds of millions of dollars in federal grants and contracts from agencies linked to the Democratic party. The liberal Democratic affinities of artists, academics, and intellectuals may be reinforced by the material benefits that they receive, directly and indirectly, from the federal treasury.[12]

The Democratic entrenchment in domestic agencies gives the party substantial influence over policy implementation even when Republicans control the presidency and Congress. A majority of the career employees of federal social welfare and regulatory agencies are Democratic loyalists.[13] The reason for this is quite simple. Public agencies that administer health care, education, and welfare programs quite properly seek to hire staff members who are committed to agency objectives. Public servants who support a positive role for government in social policy and economic regulation are more likely to be Democrats than Republicans. Democratic career employees, in turn, usually cooperate with Democrats in Congress to maintain the programs to which they have shared commitments. With the support of congressional Democrats, agencies that administer federal social welfare and regulatory programs often resist efforts by Republican presidents to redirect or limit their activities. For example, when the Reagan administration sought to reorient EPA policies, it encountered stiff opposition from the agency's staff. Agency employees leaked information to Congress and to the media designed to discredit Reagan's EPA chief, Anne Burford Gorsuch. After a series of congressional investigations, Gorsuch was forced to resign, and Reagan appointed a new EPA head whose views were more acceptable to the career staff.

The institutional confederation that undergirds the Democratic party today is the product of the New Deal and the Great Society. Its Republican counterpart took root in the military and national security apparatus that mushroomed during World War II and hardened during the Cold War that followed. It soon embraced a huge quasi-governmental defense contracting industry. In fact, it was precisely the convergence of the public- and private-sector elements of this defense establishment that prompted Republican Dwight Eisenhower to voice his apprehensions about the military-industrial complex not long before he left the White House. It was no coincidence that the Republican surge of the 1980s was accompanied by a parallel surge in the national security budget. The Reagan administration sponsored the largest peacetime military buildup in the nation's history. Annual military expenditures in constant 1982 dollars increased by more than 40 percent from $171 billion at the end of the Carter administration to $242 billion by President Reagan's second term.[14] Although the Democratic opposition in Congress limited further increases to the annual rate of inflation, the enormous military buildup of the first Reagan administration had vastly expanded the base upon which those increases were calculated.

The Republicans have not yet developed a network of nonprofit social service agencies to match those in the Democratic coalition of institutional supporters, but they are trying. The conservative promotion of "faith-based" social policy promises to convert one of the most important Republican constituencies into a beneficiary of the new patronage. The organizations known collectively as the religious right have several hundred thousand members, chapters in every state, and hundreds of full-time staffers. They stand ready to lobby, litigate, or contest low-turnout congressional and local elections when issues of abortion, public morality, or church-state relations are at stake. If President George W. Bush has his way, these organizations will also become eligible to function as federally financed providers of social services. Secular social welfare and public interest groups with Democratic affinities may soon find themselves competing for federal funds with "spiritual" counterparts sponsored by a Republican administration. African American churches that currently help to mobilize Democratic voters might be politically neutralized if they became the beneficiaries of conservative social policy. Religious conviction is one of the few remaining sources of widespread grassroots activism in American politics. If sectarian charity becomes an annex of the Republican party, Democrats will surely attack this partnership as a transgression of the constitutional injunction against the government's establishment of religion. There is also the possibility that religious groups financed by government will become less dependent on the offerings of their members, less responsive to their grassroots constituencies, and less interested in turning out the faithful.

The New Patronage

America's political parties have changed because government has changed. Before the New Deal, the government did not amount to much, and it was even less substantial before the Progressives instituted regulatory programs designed to rein in capitalist monopolies and protect the public against the perils of urbanism and industrialism. Below the cabinet level, civilian bureaucrats oversaw the sale of public lands, the delivery of the mails, and the collection of customs. As a rule, they did not make or influence policy; instead, they helped to sustain the party organizations that elected the people who did make policy. Their jobs were valuable chiefly as patronage. Bureaucrats were cogs in the machines that solicited public support for elected officials, and once elected, the officials gave them their patronage jobs.

Party patronage is not dead. It has evolved to accommodate the conditions of political life under a new bureaucratic state. Today's parties employ a new patronage, not so much to contest elections as to influence directly the making and implementation of public policy. That is why today's parties seem so much less interested in popular mobilization than those of the past. Party elites and their institutional allies can often get what they want from government without stirring up the public. In fact, federal grants enable some organizations to sustain themselves without appealing for popular support.

The new patronage is also distinctive because so many of its beneficiaries are not government employees. Even under the regime of old patronage, private-sector contractors were among the leading beneficiaries. Since World War II, however, the number of beneficiaries of federal grants and contracts has increased much more rapidly than the number employees of the federal government itself. In some agencies—the Department of Energy is a prime example—the workforce employed by private contractors far outnumbers the personnel employed directly by the agency.

The emergence of the new patronage has also changed the terms of political combat in the United States. Parties attempt to get what they want through institutional colonization and mobilization. They also try to disable the institutional base of the opposition party—its patronage network. During the 1990s, for example, Republicans attacked the Democratic emplacements in social welfare and regulatory bureaucracies by calling for regulatory reforms that would have weakened a number of agencies. They also demanded the elimination of several agencies identified with Democratic interests, including the Corporation for Public Broadcasting, the Legal Services Corporation, and the National Endowment for the Arts. In an effort to "defund the left,"[15] conservatives campaigned for the termination of a variety of federal grant programs. Through devolution, they attempted to dismantle national social programs by transferring their authority to the states. The Republicans' aim was shared by Presidents Nixon and Reagan, both of whom fielded "New Federalism" initiatives to break up a Washington bureaucracy that seemed hostile to Republican chief executives.[16] The GOP failed to achieve significant regulatory reform, and it eliminated no agencies or programs. In 1996, however, federal public assistance programs were devolved to the states and converted from open-ended entitlements into capped block grants. This shift from federal to state responsibility for welfare reflected the GOP's conviction that federal social service bureaucracies had become Democratic dependencies, and the Republicans succeeded not only in transferring bureaucratic authority for welfare to the states but also in putting some distance between the social welfare programs and the liberal interest groups that lobbied for them in Washington.[17]

The Democrats have attempted to launch similar attacks on the institutional base of the Republicans. When the Democrats gained the White House in 1993, they attacked the military and national security sectors. President Clinton proposed substantial cuts in defense spending. Moreover, Clinton and some congressional Democrats sharply criticized the military for closing its eyes to the sexual abuse of women in the ranks and for prohibiting the recruitment and retention of gay and lesbian personnel. In some respects, the 1993 congressional investigation of the so-called Tailhook affair and the conflict regarding gays in the military may be seen as efforts by Democrats to stigmatize and delegitimize an institution that had become an important Republican bastion. In October 1993, Clinton's navy secretary, John Dalton, cited sexual harassment at the annual Tailhook Association convention both in demanding the resignation of the chief of naval operations (CNO) and in instituting disciplinary proceedings against a dozen admirals and U.S. Marine Corps generals.

The attempted decapitation of the navy's chain of command (the secretary of defense ultimately refused to fire the CNO) was announced just one day after the Pentagon had indicated that it would delay implementing the "don't ask, don't tell" compromise concerning gays and lesbians in the military that it had negotiated with the Clinton administration. The Pentagon attributed this delay to the technical difficulty of informing base commanders of the new regulations. Other incidents also bespoke the hostility between the military and the Clinton administration. For example, in 1993 a White House staffer refused to respond to a greeting from Lt. General Barry McCaffrey, an aide to General Colin Powell, saying, "I don't talk to the military."[18] Later that same year, when Powell, then chairman of the Joint Chiefs of Staff, introduced former Republican defense secretary Dick Cheney at a Pentagon function, he saluted and called Cheney "Boss." The entire room, filled with military officers, erupted into loud and sustained cheering at this suggestion that the wrong people were now in power.

By themselves, these incidents may have made little difference, but they show that Republican officials tend to develop close ties with military personnel as officers rise through the ranks. Republican defense secretaries typically recruit their assistants from the military rather than from civilian institutions (Colin Powell had served as assistant to Secretary of Defense Caspar Weinberger); they also rely heavily upon the Pentagon's Joint Staff (the uniformed staff of the Joint Chiefs) for policy planning. In contrast, Democratic defense secretaries recruit their assistants mainly from congressional staffs and university faculties. These civilian officials regard the Joint Staff with suspicion, and the military brass, in turn, is disdainful of inexperienced civilians. Even Republican members of Congress have come to rely upon military officers to augment their personal and committee staffs. The armed services are happy to cement their alliance with the GOP by providing such assistance. In 1994, former Democratic congresswoman Pat Schroeder of Colorado caused a minor furor by denouncing this practice, which has, nevertheless, continued.[19]

Just as the officials of the EPA appealed to congressional Democrats for support when they were saddled with a hostile director, so the military sought the support of congressional Republicans in its conflicts with the Clinton administration. Within the first few months of the Clinton presidency, the military launched an attack against Defense Secretary Les Aspin's civilian staff assistants. Acting on a complaint from career officers, the Pentagon's inspector general charged that two of Aspin's senior deputies had violated government ethics rules while awaiting Senate confirmation. These charges infuriated members of the Senate Armed Services Committee, who compelled the White House to withdraw the nominations.

A year later, Aspin himself was forced to resign after military officers leaked information to Congress and the media suggesting that Aspin's decision not to send heavy tanks to support American troops in Somalia had led to needless American casualties there. The military's triumph over the White House was so complete that Clinton was forced to name an officer, Admiral Bobby Inman, to replace Aspin. At the televised announcement of Inman's appointment, Clinton stood in grim silence as Inman told the press that his interview with Clinton had left him with a "comfort level" regarding Clinton's qualities as commander in chief sufficient to allow him to work with the president. Ultimately, Inman withdrew his name for personal reasons, but Clinton replaced him with William Perry, an appointee acceptable to Republicans and to the military.

In his second term, Clinton appointed William Cohen, a former Republican senator, to head the Department of Defense, in a sense acknowledging that this institution belongs to the GOP. But Cohen's appointment did not end hostility between the uniformed services and the White House. In 1999, for example, the U.S. Army all but explicitly defied the president's order to send its Apache attack helicopters into action against Serbian tanks in Kosovo. The army did not believe in the mission or trust Clinton's strategy and offered one reason after another to delay deployment of the helicopters. In fact, army brass waited until the conflict was over before declaring the helicopters to be fully ready for combat.[20]

The Battle for the Bench

Though the two major parties have been able to secure a variety of institutional strongholds, the federal judiciary is one institution of unquestioned strategic value that remains contested territory. From World War II through the 1960s, the federal courts were generally aligned with liberal Democrats on issues of civil rights and civil liberties. With the support of liberal Democrats, the federal courts expanded their role in the political process and their power in American society. The Supreme Court, for example, significantly relaxed the rules governing justiciability— the conditions under which the courts will hear a case—increasing the range of issues and parties subject to judicial remedies. The Court has also broadened the arsenal of remedies and forms of relief that courts can employ. In some cases, for instance, the courts have taken control of the day-to-day operations of school systems and state prisons to assure that their orders are fully implemented (see Chapter 7).

Given the liberal activism of the judiciary, groups identified with liberal causes took up litigation as one of their principal political weapons. Civil rights groups used the courts to launch successful assaults on southern school systems, state and local governments, and legislative districting schemes. Environmental groups used the courts to block construction of highways, dams, and other public projects that not only damaged the environment but also provided money to their political opponents. Women's groups used the federal courts to overturn state laws restricting abortion as well as statutes discriminating against women in the labor market. Congress contributed to the tide of liberal litigation when it empowered public interest groups to challenge the decisions of executive agencies in the courts and to collect their legal expenses if they won.

Successive Republican presidents sought to counter this alliance between Democrats and the federal courts by using their appointment powers to place more conservatives on the federal bench. Against the backdrop of expanded judicial power, this effort led to years of harsh interparty struggles over judicial nominations. Presidents Nixon, Reagan, and Bush sought to appoint conservative jurists to the federal bench while Democratic congresses fought to thwart those efforts. During the Nixon administration, for example, congressional Democrats blocked the confirmations of two conservative judges, Clement Haynsworth and G. Harold Carswell.

Democrats fought unsuccessfully to prevent President Reagan from elevating William Rehnquist to chief justice. Reagan's efforts to place Judge Robert Bork on the high court, however, encountered fierce resistance. Democrats and liberal interest groups organized fund-raising drives and sponsored television advertising in the largest public campaign in the nation's history designed to defeat a judicial nominee. The administration's opponents on the Senate Judiciary Committee sought to discredit Bork in nationally televised hearings. In the end, Democrats defeated the Bork nomination. Later, Democrats forced Reagan Supreme Court nominee Douglas Ginsburg to withdraw his name by revealing that Ginsburg had been seen smoking marijuana while on the faculty of the Harvard Law School.

In 1991, President George Bush nominated Clarence Thomas, a prominent black conservative, to replace Justice Thurgood Marshall. Thomas's nomination sparked one of the most bitter struggles in recent American political history. In their efforts to prevent Thomas's confirmation, Democrats were able to persuade Anita Hill, a University of Oklahoma law professor, to testify that Thomas had sexually harassed her when she worked for him at the Equal Employment Opportunity Commission and, previously, at the Department of Education. At the end of the controversial hearings, Thomas was confirmed in the Senate by a narrow vote, but the shadow cast by the confirmation process undermined his subsequent influence on the Court.

During the Nixon, Reagan, and Bush years, congressional Democrats sought to limit the impact of Republican presidents upon the federal judiciary. In the Clinton years, the tables were turned as the GOP fought to prevent a Democratic president from exercising substantial influence over the composition of the federal bench. Clinton named two Democratic moderates, Ruth Ginsburg and Stephen Breyer, to the Supreme Court and sought to name a number of liberal Democrats to the district and appellate courts. Senate Republicans, however, blocked many of Clinton's nominees, especially after 1994, when the GOP took control of the Senate Judiciary Committee. Republicans adopted the tactic of simply bottling up nominees in committee and refusing to bring the names before the Congress for confirmation. Liberal Democrats such as Messiah Jackson of Pennsylvania and Richard Paez and Marsha Berzon of California remained in political limbo for a number of years.[21] Though Paez and Berzon were eventually confirmed, a number of other nominations were withdrawn, and Clinton's impact on the federal courts was diminished as a result.

Institutional Struggle

The rancorous partisan warfare that now erupts in the formerly decorous judicial appointment process is symptomatic of a recent change in American politics. The parties vie for power not so much through the competitive mobilization for voters as by exploiting their control of institutions in and around government and by disrupting the institutions controlled by the opposition. In the 1970s and 1980s, when the Republicans usually controlled the White House, they sought consistently to enhance the powers of the president in relation Congress, which was almost as regularly controlled by the Democrats. President Nixon, for example, impounded billions of dollars appropriated by Congress and sought, through various reorganization schemes, to bring executive agencies under closer White House control while severing their ties to Congress. Presidents Reagan and Bush created and tolerated huge budget deficits in part because they precluded any congressional policy initiatives that called for new spending. Reagan and Bush also sought to disempower the Democrats in Congress and the government regulators allied with them by centralizing control over administrative rule making in the Office of Management and Budget. In addition, Reagan and his staff surreptitiously violated legislative restrictions on presidential conduct embodied in the War Powers Act—a congressional measure intended to curb presidential authority.

There were many others such measures. Congressional Democrats sought to strengthen the Congress while reducing the powers and prerogatives of the presidency. Through the 1974 Congressional Budget and Impoundment Act, for example, Congress countered Nixon's challenge to its fiscal authority. In addition to the War Powers Act, congressional Democrats also drafted the Foreign Commitments Resolution and the Arms Export Control Act, both designed to restrict presidential authority in foreign policy. Democrats used the investigative powers of the legislature to discredit Republican presidents and the administrative officials who served them. The Watergate and Iran-Contra investigations were the most important of these offensives. The first drove a President from office and temporarily crippled his party. The effects of the second were not so dramatic, but the Iran-Contra investigation seriously injured the Reagan administration. Democrats charged that the administration had covertly sold arms to Iran and used the proceeds to provide illegal funding for Nicaraguan Contra forces, in violation of the Boland Amendment, which prohibited such assistance. In the aftermath of televised congressional hearings in which many of the Democratic allegations were substantiated, Reagan was compelled to appoint a national security adviser, a Central Intelligence Agency director, and a White House chief of staff acceptable to Democrats in Congress. Iran-Contra also halted the advance of the president's conservative agenda. The "Reagan revolution" had been stopped in its tracks.

As in the Iran-Contra case, the substitution of institutional warfare for electoral competition frequently produces no clear winners. The intention is to distract or preoccupy the opposition sufficiently to paralyze its capacity to make policy. When parties pursue politics in this way—and both parties do—the result can be stalemate.

After winning control of Congress in 1994, Republicans used its investigatory power to inquire into allegations that the Clinton administration had sought to use confidential FBI files for political purposes. Then congressional Republicans conducted a probe of allegedly illegal fund-raising activities in the 1996 Clinton-Gore campaign. There would also be investigations of the dismissal of employees in the White House travel office.

The criminal justice system is an alternative to congressional investigation as an arena for combat between the legislative and executive branches. Since the early 1970s, the number of federal indictments against national, state, and local officials has increased more than tenfold, to more than a thousand per year. Many of those indicted have been lower-level civil servants, but large numbers have been prominent political figures, including more than a dozen members of Congress and high-ranking federal administrators.[22] During the Reagan and Bush administrations, a substantial number of top Republicans in the executive branch were the targets of criminal prosecutions stemming from allegations or investigations initiated by Democrats. These included former defense secretary Caspar Weinberger, former assistant secretary of state Elliott Abrams, presidential aides Michael Deaver and Lynn Nofziger, Labor Secretary Raymond Donovan, and national security official Oliver North. Before leaving office in 1992, President Bush pardoned Weinberger and Abrams, asserting that their prosecutions were the result of inappropriate efforts by Democrats to criminalize policy disputes.

During the Clinton administration, a number of prominent Democrats became the targets of criminal prosecutions sparked by allegations initiated by the Republicans. Early in Clinton's first term, the powerful chairman of the House Ways and Means Committee, Dan Rostenkowski (D-Illinois) was sent to federal prison after being convicted of corruption. Charges of improper conduct were later leveled at Agriculture Secretary Mike Espy, Transportation Secretary Henry Cisneros, Commerce Secretary Ron Brown, Interior Secretary Bruce Babbitt, and Labor Secretary Alexis Herman. Espy and Cisneros were forced to resign and were ultimately indicted on fraud and corruption charges. Ron Brown died in a plane crash before the investigation into his conduct was completed. Babbitt and Herman were both exonerated after lengthy investigations, though the exhaustive probes undermined their effectiveness in office. During the same period, Clinton himself became the target of an intensive probe that led to his impeachment, though not to his conviction of any criminal conduct.

Despite the large number and importance of cases involving official wrongdoing, there is little reason to believe that the actual incidence of official corruption or abuse of power has increased since the 1970s. Instead, the growing use of criminal sanctions against public officials has been closely linked to struggles for political power in the United States. The creation of the Office of the Independent Counsel in the aftermath of the Watergate scandal established formal machinery to investigate allegations of unethical conduct on the part of public officials. The 1999 expiration of the special counsel provision of the Ethics in Government Act changes the manner in which special counsels will be appointed but does not eliminate their future use in investigations of official conduct. The mechanism gives both parties a weapon with which to discredit—or at least immobilize—their opponents. It activates a squadron of investigators, accountants, and lawyers who are almost certain to find something embarrassing or questionable before they are finished.

Revelation, Investigation, Prosecution

Today's tactics of political combat—revelation, investigation, and prosecution (RIP)—have moved to the center stage once occupied by electoral mobilization. The acronym is a fitting political epitaph for the public officials who have become its targets. RIP was a repertoire of attack that emerged from the Watergate controversy and was refined by Democrats in Congress when the White House was under Republican control. During the Clinton administration, however, the roles were reversed, and congressional Republicans used the tactic against a Democratic White House.

In the first year of his presidency, Clinton advanced a health care proposal that would have achieved an enormous expansion of the Democratic party's institutional base, giving the Democrats control over a substantial portion of the nation's economy and making virtually every American a beneficiary of a Democratic program. Health care reform might have enhanced the popularity and power of the Democratic party in much the same way that Social Security had sixty years earlier.

Clinton's health care reform effort alarmed Republicans. Some Republican strategists like William Kristol, who had served as chief of staff for former vice president Dan Quayle, worked feverishly to mobilize GOP opposition to Clinton's proposal. Ultimately the plan was defeated by a coalition of corporate interests and the Republican party. But the combat experience convinced many Republicans that Clinton was a dangerous adversary, and they mounted an all-out campaign to neutralize him. Adding to the ferocity of the GOP attack, of course, was the rage of some social conservatives in the party about the president's stands on such issues as abortion, gun control, and gays in the military.

In 1993 and 1994, Republicans laid down a barrage of charges against Clinton and his wife, mainly related to their involvement in the failed Whitewater real estate development in Arkansas. Although they were able to embarrass and harass the Clintons, Republicans failed to disable the administration. In 1994, however, the GOP won both houses of Congress, gaining in the process control of the congressional authority to investigate and to secure appointment of independent counsels to investigate on its behalf. Now headed by Republicans, congressional committees immediately launched wide-ranging investigations of Clinton's conduct during his years as governor of Arkansas.

At the same time, congressional Republicans launched several independent counsels to search for wrongdoing by Clinton and his associates. The most important of these prosecutors, Kenneth Starr, was able to extend the scope of his investigation to include allegations that the president had had an affair with a White House intern, Monica Lewinsky, and that he later both perjured himself and suborned perjury on the part of the intern and others to prevent disclosure of his conduct. A month after Clinton was forced to appear before Starr's grand jury and acknowledge his affair with Lewinsky, the GOP-controlled House Judiciary Committee began impeachment proceedings. Clinton's impeachment was approved by the full House on a party-line vote. By another party-line vote, the Senate declined to convict. But Clinton's presidency had been devastated.

While the process spiraled to its conclusion, the Clinton administration was preoccupied with the president's defense. Clinton and his allies responded aggressively to every accusation and innuendo, leveling countercharges against his accusers and the special counsel's office, sometimes employing private detectives to collect damaging information about the president's adversaries.[23] Throughout the long struggle, the president was vigorously defended by the Democratic party. In January 1998, the Democratic National Committee established a damage control center to coordinate strategies, disseminate information, respond to charges, and generally seek to protect the president from new revelations and accusations.[24] Until Clinton's admissions of sexual misconduct compelled several prominent Democrats to distance themselves from him, not a single significant Democratic politician or interest group spoke against the president. Whatever their personal feelings about the president, most Democrats believed that the destruction of the Clinton administration would bring a renewed Republican effort to undermine the domestic social institutions fashioned by the Democratic party. Even the women's movement, which might have been expected to turn against a president who admitted having a sexual relationship with a young intern, decided that Clinton's support for abortion rights and federal funding for child care, as well as his record of appointing women to high office, outweighed his sexual indiscretions.

Just as Democrats had been able to undermine two Republican administrations through a process of revelation, investigation, and prosecution, the GOP had now wrecked a Democratic presidency. Both parties had developed and demonstrated the capacity to drive their opponents from office without mobilizing or even consulting the electorate, which seemed a mere vestigial organ of the American body politic.

The 2000 Presidential Selection

The new, peripheral status of the electorate was underlined by the Florida post-election struggle that finally made George W. Bush president. It was fought outside the electoral arena and without the participation of ordinary Americans. Instead, the decision was in the hands of the Florida legislature and the executive institutions of the Florida state government, and it was dominated by small groups of attorneys and political activists. Forty lawsuits were filed during the course of the dispute.[25] Together, the two campaigns ran up nearly $10 million in legal expenses during the month of litigation. This does not include the cost incurred by litigants who were not formally associated with either campaign. In most of the courtroom encounters, the Bush campaign prevailed. Despite two setbacks before the all-Democratic Florida Supreme Court, Bush attorneys won most circuit court cases and the penultimate clash before the U.S. Supreme Court, whose conservative majority seemed determined to prevent a Gore victory.

Bush defeated Gore not only because he prevailed in the courts but also because he and the Republicans were able to mobilize a powerful set of institutions that gradually wore down their Democratic foes. Democrats controlled the South Florida canvassing boards that tried to conduct manual recounts, but this advantage was trumped by GOP control of the governor's mansion and the secretary of state's office. In addition, the Republican-dominated Florida legislature was prepared to select Bush electors even if the Texas governor lost the court battle, and so gave the GOP an insurance policy against judicial defeat. Republicans also were better able to mobilize political activists and party notables to counter and, in some instances, intimidate Democratic workers on the ground in Florida.

Although both campaigns deployed their institutional resources, neither seemed especially interested in mobilizing popular support. Both sides sought to suppress large numbers of popular votes that had already been cast. Bush fought to block recounts that might have revealed additional votes while Gore allies worked to negate military ballots as well as thousands of absentee ballots in Seminole and Martin Counties.[26] The national news media insisted that the so-called battle for public opinion was every bit as important as the legal and institutional struggle. Perhaps they are prone to such claims because, as the principal line of communication between political elites and the public, the media's political status grows when leaders battle for public opinion. But there was little evidence of any such battle in Florida. Instead of communicating with the public directly, the candidates employed surrogates to carry their claims and counterclaims to the press. Neither candidate sought to mobilize public support. They ignored the calls of political activists like Reverend Jesse Jackson for mass demonstrations and protests. The two candidates' occasional public appearances were intended less to bolster popular enthusiasm than to strengthen the commitments of political allies and to induce contributors to keep their wallets open to finance the battle of maneuver between battalions of party attorneys. Although their public appearances were rare, both Al Gore and his running mate, Joe Lieberman, spent hours on the telephone each day contacting contributors. GOP fund-raisers were active throughout the nation as well. Gore, in fact, acknowledged the irrelevance of the mass public to the post-election dispute. In response to a television reporter's question about the role of public opinion, Gore said, "I'm quite sure that the polls don't matter in this, because it's a legal question."[27]

Media misinterpretation was also evident in self-congratulatory editorials that pointed with pride to the fact that an all-out battle between the nation's two major political parties was being resolved peacefully. There were no tanks or troops in the streets. On a typical day, fewer than a score of protestors stood outside the vice president's residence in Washington. The absence of political ferment, said the commentators, was a mark of the maturity of American democracy and the people's respect for the rule of law. The absence of tanks in the streets was surely a positive sign, but the muted expression of popular feeling about the post-election dispute, the slender ranks of the demonstrators, and the near absence of any popular political action or protest during the course of the battle for the presidency should not be seen as a symptom of America's political well-being. Quite the contrary. They were signs that most Americans were indifferent to the struggle in Florida. People assumed it would be quietly concluded, and, as the polls suggested, they were prepared to accept either outcome. Popular participation was limited and popular feeling was subdued not because of Americans' political maturity but because they knew that they had no role to play in the post-election controversy and did not feel strongly about it. Citizens at large had become politically irrelevant.

Virtual Citizenship

Though they were originally formed to contest elections, political parties today carry on a good part of their struggle without benefit of voters. Elections are still held. Parties still try to pile up more votes than the opposition. But partisan appeals are currently aimed at a narrow slice of the electorate—the reliable, predictable voters whose names, addresses, and affiliations have already been entered into the partisan databases. The mobilization of the electorate at large has been supplanted by electronic retrieval of the electorate at hand.[28] Even more restrictive than this electronic electorate is the small elite of Americans who have the resources, education, and access to exploit the new opportunities for political participation in America's new, personal democracy: litigation, bureaucratic consultation, and recognition as a stakeholder or advocate. These are the actors who play politics for real these days.

Current political circumstance does leave at least one place for ordinary citizens—on the answering end of public opinion polls. They get to play virtual politics, expressing their views "as if" a real political leader were actually listening to them. Politicians, interest groups, and government officials sponsor thousands of opinion surveys every year to test public sentiment on issues ranging from abortion to zootomy. Some pollsters have argued that precisely because opinion surveys capture the views of those who do not participate, the surveys provide a more scientific and accurate picture of public opinion than voting does. George Gallup, one of the founders of the modern polling industry, asserted that opinion polls, more than any other institution, "bridge the gap between the people and those responsible for making decisions in their name."[29] Polling, of course, has no official place in American democracy. The Constitution does not require public officials to follow poll results. During the entire Clinton impeachment process, the president's standing in the polls remained high—as did Richard Nixon's until the eve of his resignation. And, Gallup notwithstanding, the representation of public opinion provided by surveys does more to widen than to bridge the gap between the people and public decision-makers. The virtual representation provided by the polls renders public opinion less disruptive, more permissive, and more amenable to government and elite manipulation

In fact, little distinction is made between poll results and public opinion, but they are not the same thing at all. Public opinion can be articulated in ways that present a picture of the people's political thinking very different from the results of sample surveys.[30] Statements from leaders of interest groups, trade unions, and religious groups about their adherents' feelings are a common mechanism for expressing public opinion. The hundreds of thousands of letters written each year to newspaper editors and to members of Congress are vehicles for the expression of opinion. Protests, riots, and demonstrations express citizens' opinions. Government officials take note of all these manifestations of the public's mood. As corporate executive and political commentator Chester Barnard once noted, before the invention of polling, legislators "read the local newspapers, toured their districts and talked with voters, received letters from the home state and entertained delegations which claimed to speak for large and important blocks of voters."[31] These alternatives to polling survive today. But when poll results differ from other expressions of public opinion, the polls almost always carry more credibility than the competition. The labor leader whose account of rank-and-file sentiment differs from poll results is not likely to be taken seriously. Nor is the politician who claims that his or her policy positions are more popular than the polls show. In 1999, for example, Republican congressional leaders claimed that the public opinion disclosed by letters and phone calls supported their efforts to impeach and convict President Bill Clinton, even though national opinion polls indicated that the public opposed Clinton's removal from office. Virtually every commentator took the polls to be correct and accused Republicans of disregarding true popular sentiment.

This presumption in favor of the accuracy of opinion polls stems from their apparent scientific neutrality. Survey analysis is modeled on the methods of the natural sciences and conveys an impression of technical sophistication and objectivity.[32] The polls, moreover, can claim to offer a more reliable and representative view of popular opinion than any alternative. People who claim to speak for groups frequently do not. The distribution of opinion reflected in letters to newspapers and government officials is clearly unrepresentative. Demonstrators are always a tiny, skewed segment of the public. Scientific samplings of public opinion provide a corrective for false or biased representations of popular sentiment.

Polling, however, is both more and less than a scientific measure of public sentiment. The substitution of polling for other methods of gauging the public's views profoundly affects what is perceived to be public opinion. Polling is what statisticians call an "obtrusive measure."[33] Surveys do not simply measure continuities and changes in a naturally occurring phenomenon. The polls also define how individual opinions are to be aggregated. In opinion surveys, for example, the views of well-informed people usually carry no more weight than those of the clueless. Pollsters also choose the topics for which public opinion will be tested. In other words, the data reported by the polls are not "pure" public opinion but the product of an interaction between the opinion holders and the opinion seekers. As surveys measure opinion, they also form opinion.

Polling changes the character of public opinion in at least three important ways.[34] First, polling subsidizes the cost of asserting opinions. In the absence of polling, the cost and effort required to organize and communicate an opinion are normally borne by those who hold the opinion. Someone wishing to express a view about abortion, for example, might write a letter, deliver a speech, contribute to an organization, or attend a rally. Polls, however, organize and publicize opinion without requiring the opinion holders to exert themselves in any significant way. The great majority of those whose views are supposedly captured in a survey are never actually interviewed. A survey claiming to reflect the opinions of 250 million Americans is typically based upon interviews with only two or three thousand randomly sampled respondents.[35] The remainder are statistically or "virtually" represented. They need not even have endured the nuisance of an interview.

This displacement of costs from the opinion holder to the polling agency has important consequences for the character of the opinions likely to be expressed. In general, one's willingness to bear the costs of asserting political opinions is closely tied to the intensity of those opinions. If you have strong feelings about an issue, you are more likely to invest the time and energy needed to make your views known than are others who hold less intense views. One never hears, for example, of a march on the Capitol by citizens who are undecided about abortion. As the example suggests, people with strongly held views are also more likely than their less zealous fellow citizens to be found at the extremes of opinion on any given question.[36] When the costs of expressing opinions are borne by opinion holders, the views heard are likely to be both intensely held and relatively extreme.

Polls undermine this relationship between public expression and the intensity of opinion. The assertion of opinion through surveys requires almost no effort on the part of opinion holders. The views of those who care hardly at all about an issue count just as much as the opinions of those who care deeply. For this reason, the distribution of opinion reported in surveys is typically both less intense and less extreme than the public opinion that concerned citizens would have expressed on their own.[37] In opinion polls, the voices of Americans with strongly held views are drowned out by the indistinct murmur of the apathetic mass public.

This is not an entirely bad thing. The polls may make it more difficult for activists at the ideological extremes to claim widespread popular support when they do not have it.[38] Presidential candidate Pat Buchanan, for example, presented himself as spokesman for "brigades" of true conservatives in 1996 and 2000, but surveys indicated that his right-wing, isolationist views commanded the support of only 2 percent of the American public.

The polls, however, also enable governments and politicians to claim that they represent true public opinion even in the face of manifest public discontent. President Richard Nixon, for example, claimed to be governing on behalf of the "silent majority" of Americans who did not join protest marches to demand changes in American race relations and an end to the Vietnam War. The administration invoked a silent majority that spoke only through the polls to counter the political weight and credibility of the hundreds of thousands of noisy Americans—citizens who felt strongly enough to take action on controversial issues. The administration preferred to govern on behalf of this silent majority precisely because of its silence. It was silent because it had no particular views on controversial issues and therefore imposed no particular constraints upon the government's conduct. Poll results provided the administration with an excuse to ignore people who actually had opinions.

Polling transforms opinion in a second way—by treating it as an attribute of individual citizens rather than a property of groups. Before politicians sponsored polls, their information about the attitudes of ordinary Americans often came from the leaders of associations and groups. Those interested in the views of working people, for example, might consult trade union officials. To find out about public sentiment in a town or county, a politician might inquire with one of its leading citizens. In the absence of contradictory evidence, the recognition of these leaders as knowledgeable informants about grassroots opinion enhanced their own political influence and may have bolstered the apparent political coherence and strength of the groups that they led. The leader spoke for the group as a unified force and, by doing so, increased the likelihood that others would regard it as such.

Opinion surveys, however, go directly to individual members of the public, bypassing the groups to which they belong and the people who lead them. Polling therefore tends to disclose disagreements among group members. This, too, is not all bad. Survey data may prevent the leaders of a group from accidentally or deliberately misrepresenting their members' views. For example, the views of political party convention delegates differ considerably from those of the average voter. Republican delegates tend to be much more conservative than GOP voters, and Democratic delegates are decidedly more liberal than typical Democrats in the electorate. The polls are a helpful reminder to party leaders that not all Democrats, say, would support the views articulated at the convention by gay rights activists,[39] and that not all Republicans share the beliefs of the leaders of the party's religious right.

At the same time, however, by undermining the ability of group leaders and activists to speak for their members, the polls can undermine a group's influence. In 1947, for example, organized labor bitterly opposed the enactment of the Taft-Hartley Act, which union leaders disparaged as the "slave-labor act." After President Truman vetoed the act, the presidents of major unions vowed to work for the defeat of any member of Congress who voted to override Truman's veto. While senators and representatives weighed their options, poll data showed that most union members—as opposed to the leadership—neither fully understood the Taft-Hartley Act nor saw it as the decisive consideration for their congressional voting preferences. These findings emboldened a number of legislators with large trade union constituencies to vote for the bill, and Truman's veto was overridden.[40] On the one hand, accurate information about the preferences of individual union members diminished the collective power of organized labor. On the other hand, if union members had had accurate information about the bill, the poll results might have been different, and Taft-Hartley might never have become law.

Political polling was introduced in the United States by Mugwumps, Progressives, and conservative elites as a way of reducing the collective power of their working-class opponents, who depended heavily upon coherent and disciplined organizations to make up for their members' individual lack of resources and influence.[41] The conservative *Chicago Tribune* was a major sponsor of polls in the 1890s, and the Hearst newspapers were avid promoters of polling in the early twentieth century. Today, of course, all political forces make extensive use of polling. The fact remains, however, that polling reduces the political weight of precisely those groups whose most important resource is their collective weight.

The third way that polling changes public opinion is by restricting the agenda of topics. Writers of letters to the editor generally choose the topics on which to express their views. The organizers of a protest march define the purpose of their action. But respondents in opinion polls express themselves on issues that have been selected by someone else. Opinions filtered through polls are not spontaneous expressions of the public's own concerns but rather a reaction to concerns chosen by the pollsters.

Polling, in other words, may offer a misleading impression of the public's political agenda. During the 2000 presidential campaign, for example, daily polls indicated enormous short-term swings in the relative standing of Al Gore and George W. Bush. On Monday, August 7, a USA Today/CNN poll indicated that Bush was leading Gore by nineteen points. On Tuesday, August 8, Bush's lead had dropped to two points in the same poll. By Saturday, however, his lead was back up to ten points.[42] These erratic bounces in public opinion probably indicated that the presidential election was not high on respondents' list of priorities, and, as a result, they did not have solid opinions to express. The election was more important to the pollsters than to the public.

Given the commercial character of the polling industry, differences between the polls' concerns and those of the general public are probably inevitable. Polls generally raise questions that are of interest to the purchasers of poll data—newspapers, political candidates, government agencies, business corporations, and public relations and advertising firms. These questions may or may not reflect citizens' own needs, hopes, and aspirations. Perhaps more important, polls are components in the modern technology of opinion shaping. Corporations poll to determine how to persuade customers to purchase their products. Candidates poll as part of a campaign to convince voters to support them. Governments poll as part of the process of ensuring popular cooperation, or, as the National Performance Review report might put it, to create less troublesome customers. Rather than communicating the opinions that citizens want political leaders to hear, polls tell elites what they want to learn about citizens' opinions. The end result is to change the public expression of opinion from an assertion of demand to a step in the process of persuasion. Polls are tools for the management of opinion.

From Electorate to Virtual Citizenry

Scarcely anyone today recommends a revival of the patronage-seeking parties of the nineteenth century, but hardly anybody seems satisfied with today's parties either. In America, it appears, political parties have never been able to get it right. Perhaps we should have paid more attention to the founders' warnings about the evils of faction.

The parties of the late nineteenth century were notable for turning out the voters in numbers that have never been surpassed. But to what purpose? The parties were ideologically amorphous, nonprogrammatic coalitions that embraced issues primarily to exploit them.

Today's parties, in contrast, occupy generally consistent and distinguishable positions on issues like abortion, social welfare, gay rights, taxation, the environment, and economic regulation. But as their positions have come into focus, they have pared down their popular followings to the reliable, mailing-list voters who have helped to make American elections invitation-only affairs for an electoral elect. For contemporary parties, the public at large is a statistical artifact of opinion polls, a virtual electorate whose scientifically sampled representatives express opinions only on issues that they are asked about, and often not even on those.

The parties of the past mobilized real citizens and ministered to the material wants of at least some of their followers. But to induce mass activism, they relied on workers who were paid in patronage. As a result, graft became the bad habit of American politics; and administrative competence, the forlorn hope of reformers who were generally unwelcome even in the big-tent parties of their time.

The parties of our time mobilize institutions, many of them staffed by specialists with policy expertise. Republicans can draw on a Pentagon full of military bureaucrats; Democrats, on the mandarins of social welfare and regulatory policy. These institutions are the embodiment of the "new patronage," sustained by weapons programs, grants, contracts, and government reimbursements. But in the age of institutional combat, one of the central war aims is to disable the institutional support network of the opposition. More often than not, major policy initiatives informed by expertise—health policy, for example—remain suspended in institutional stalemate.

At the end of the eighteenth century, America was the first nation with a mass electorate. In the middle of the nineteenth century, America was the first nation with strong mass-based political parties. At the end of the twentieth century, America became the first nation with a virtual citizenry. To be sure, millions of Americans not only continue to vote but also have unprecedented opportunities for political access through the media, the bureaucracy, and the courts. The American upper middle class practices what we have called personal democracy with great effect. Tens of millions of other Americans, however, live outside this political sphere. As we saw in Chapter 2, their services as soldiers and taxpayers are no longer needed. Opposing political parties have developed techniques through which to achieve their goals without mobilizing ordinary citizens for political struggle. The presence of citizens in the political process is increasingly a statistical matter of virtual representation through polling.

The views of these virtual citizens, so carefully monitored by the polls, have been robbed of the qualities that once made public opinion an important phenomenon. Those with strong views are submerged by the more apathetic. Groups and collectivities are atomized and their political weight is reduced. And, finally, consistent with their status as customers, they are polled to make them more amenable to persuasion. Confined to the political margins, these virtual citizens can watch political struggles in which they are not invited to participate.

Chapter 5

Disunited We Stand

AS ENGINES OF popular mobilization, American political parties gradually ran out of steam during the course of the twentieth century. But the work of animating the public continued under the auspices of other institutions that sought to profit from the power of numbers. To a considerable extent, political interest groups succeeded parties as the principal vehicles for aggregating and expressing popular sentiment, and for pressuring government to follow its dictates. By midcentury, political scientists had come to regard group politics as the essence of American politics.

Whether group politics was a good or a bad thing for popular democracy had been a matter much in dispute. To James Madison and his contemporaries, the evils of faction had seemed obvious. But Madison's remedy was counterintuitive: The best defense against the dangers posed by special interests was more special interests. In a republic as large as the United States, Madison reasoned, the despotic designs of one interest group would be checked by a multitude of other groups. In time, Madison's remedy came to be regarded as a virtue in its own right. Competition among interest groups seemed to be the functional equivalent of party competition. It was not only a guard against tyranny but also a mechanism of popular sovereignty. Competing groups would reach out for public support in order to advance their interests, and the victorious interests would be the ones able to assemble the broadest coalitions of adherents.[1]

The doctrine of interest-group democracy assumed that groups would stick to the strategy of grassroots mobilization. For political parties, it had been the only strategy because there was only one test of party success—winning elections. For political interest groups, however, winning the favor of an electoral majority was not the ultimate objective, and it was only one of many ways for groups to get what they wanted from government. To the extent that they employed other means to achieve their ends, their influence upon government might become distinctly undemocratic.

That was the prevailing verdict concerning interest groups until the late nineteenth century. "Factions" were cast as enemies of popular government. Their lobbyists interposed themselves between the electorate and its elected representatives, and if groups had any effect at all, it could only be to divert government from the will of the majority.

Interest groups took on a different appearance, however, when reformers of the Progressive Era began to argue that boss-ruled political parties had themselves betrayed the majority's best interests. It was then, says sociologist Elisabeth Clemens, that three groups ill-served by the major parties—women, farmers, and organized labor—sought to achieve their political destinies outside the framework of partisan politics. "What was novel in the late nineteenth century," writes Clemens, "was the intent *and* the organizational technologies to link `lobbying' to significant numbers of voters who would be guided by associational ties rather than partisan loyalty."[2]

Group politics had been reinvented as a vehicle of mass democracy, an alternative to the political parties of the time—parties that appealed not to the collective interests of the public but to private appetites for patronage, graft, and favor, or to the tribal loyalties of ethnic immigrants and native Protestants. Addressing policy issues, in other words, was not the only way to win elections. On the contrary, avoiding issues might be the best way to preserve party unity, especially in parties that spanned different sections, interests, and ideologies.[3]

Group politics, by contrast, was issue-based politics. It linked public opinion to public policy. That was the function of the so-called new lobby, whose emergence was described by E. Pendleton Herring in the late 1920s. It had eclipsed "the representatives of corporations, the patronage brokers, the `wire-pullers,' the crowd of old-style lobbyists." The wire pullers had been sidelined by the "spokesmen of organized groups"—groups, in other words, that claimed to speak for a grassroots constituency of dues-paying members. "These group representatives," wrote Herring,

> work in the open; they have nothing to hide; they know what they want; and they know how to get it. . . . The "old, sly, furtive, pussy-footed agents of special privilege trusts" have been pushed to one side. The great organized groups, which now in such large numbers maintain headquarters in the capital, constitute the lobby of today. They are the "third house of Congress," the assistant rulers, the "invisible government."[4]

"Lobbyist" had ceased to be simply a term of opprobrium. It was no longer reserved for the "old, sly, furtive, pussy-footed agents of special privilege trusts." New practitioners of group politics, supported by grassroots constituencies, promoted special interests in the open. Territory once occupied by the pussy-footed wire pullers was now theirs.

The new interest groups had also gained ground against political parties. The parties, according to Herring, were no longer sufficiently coherent to take positions on policy issues. Prohibition was a case in point. On the one hand, in New York City, Democrats were wets, but Democrats in rural Missouri were dries. Republicans, on the other hand, were wet in St. Louis but dry in rural New York. An institutional interest in self-preservation prevented parties from taking forthright positions on controversial issues. Since the political party had forfeited leadership in public policy, Herring argued, "nonpartisan associations of voters" had stepped forward in Washington to meet democracy's need for "means of expressing the opinions and beliefs held by the citizens."[5]

But these organizations could also help the government to meet needs of its own. Inviting interested groups to participate in the policy-making process was likely to enhance the efficacy and legitimacy of the policies that resulted. Charles Nagel, secretary of commerce and labor under President William Howard Taft, was one of the first public servants to perceive the possibilities—the positive political *convenience*—that interest groups might afford to government agencies. In 1912, with the approval of Taft, Nagel convened an assembly of seven hundred delegates sent to Washington as the representatives of the nation's commercial organizations. After being called to order by Secretary Nagel and addressed by President Taft, the delegates proceeded to create the Chamber of Commerce of the United States. It was a private organization formed with the encouragement of government and endowed with a quasi-official status. As Nagel told the delegates, "[It has] been suggested not only that you organize so as to have a common commercial opinion to submit to the government but that you get the sign of authority in the shape of a National Charter." This mark of authority, said Nagel, would "enable every officer of the government to say, `This is the recognized representative of commerce and industry in the United States.'"[6]

To public officials, in other words, the chamber's assent would henceforth mean that American business was on board, that public policy carried the corporate seal of approval. By conferring semiofficial status on an interest group, however, government agencies not only changed the relationship between public policy and private interest but also modified the relationship between interest groups and their constituencies. Pendleton Herring had traced the influence of interest groups to the popular support that they could command as instruments "for expressing the opinions and beliefs held by the citizens." But they could also derive power from their privileged access to government decision-making. They had become officially recognized "stakeholders." While their members' support gave them leverage with government, groups' partnership with government gave them leverage with their members. Citizen support was still an element in group influence, perhaps the most important element, but it was only one. Official recognition had become another.

The Chamber of Commerce, of course, was scarcely the voice of grassroots populism. Its members were businesses, not people, and the government's recognition of the chamber as its semiofficial "representative of commerce and industry" could hardly be said to have co-opted the organizational vanguard of a popular democratic movement.

The case was different, however, where American farmers were concerned. The Smith-Lever Act of 1914 gave the federal government's money and sanction to the agricultural extension movement, an enterprise pledged to increase the productivity and prosperity of the nation's farmers but originally financed in large part by banks, railroads, and agricultural implement companies. The corporate backers' concern for the farmers' productivity was secondary to their own interest in the profits that they could harvest from agricultural prosperity. Their concern stemmed in part from their determination to head off outbursts of rural populism that typically targeted banks, railroads, and implement manufacturers. Under the Smith-Lever Act, the Department of Agriculture added federal sponsorship and financial support to the extension movement. The county agents who transmitted the latest agricultural methods from the nation's land-grant colleges to its food producers became public officials, and they emerged as key figures in the formation of the agricultural interest groups that came together in the early 1920s as the American Farm Bureau Federation, the most aggressive voice of agriculture in national policymaking, but a voice that spoke for only some of the farmers. Even in the Department of Agriculture itself, some officials expressed doubt about the federation's representativeness. A few years after the passage of the Smith-Lever Act, Assistant Secretary Clarence Ousley worried that the federation failed to reach the poorer and more backward tenant farmers and sharecroppers and instead concentrated its attentions on prosperous and progressive commercial farmers.[7]

The federation's political influence may not have been fully representative of rural interests, but it carried the imprimatur of the Department of Agriculture and the state land-grant colleges. If its support among farmers was less than complete, this deficiency at the grassroots was easily offset by the federation's semiofficial status in Washington and the foundation of support that it commanded among the successful, go-ahead farmers who were converting agriculture into a business. In fact, the limited range of the federation's constituency might be counted as a political advantage. It enhanced the organization's ability to speak with one voice, which was precisely what most national policymakers wanted to hear.

Almost as soon as they established themselves in Washington, the groups that made up Pendleton Herring's new lobby learned that grassroots mobilization need not be the sole source of their political influence. Official recognition and access to policymaking were also vital political assets. Without them, interest-group leaders would find it difficult to make effective political use of the grassroots fervor that energized their organizations. Perhaps it was inevitable that institutional access and recognition would eventually become *substitutes* for grassroots support. Political scientist Theodore Lowi has propounded an "Iron Law of Decadence" that seems to govern the natural history of interest groups. Investments in organizational infrastructure and stable relations with public agencies inevitably divert some of the group's energies from the forceful representation of its constituency's interests to the maintenance of the group itself and its relationships with public authorities.[8]

Frances Piven and Richard Cloward make note of a similar phenomenon in *Poor People's Movements*. A movement's potential for disrupting the status quo begins to die as soon as its leaders turn their attention to the acquisition of resources needed to sustain the group. This secondary mission, according to Piven and Cloward, invariably turns leaders of lower-class insurgencies toward accommodation with the elites who control the resources.[9]

Activist women of the Progressive Era seem to have followed a similar trajectory. The National Congress of Mothers and its Department of Parent-Teacher Associations—a significant focus of female activism prior to the enfranchisement of women—simplified itself into the National Congress of Parents and Teachers during the 1920s, and control of the organization passed from grassroots participants to professional educators. The same transformation occurred in other crusades powered by women. The movement for mothers' pensions achieved victory in forty states, only to have the program pass out of the custody of activists and into the care of professional caseworkers. The Sheppard-Towner Infancy and Maternal Protection Act of 1921 was a monument to mobilized women, but not for long. Implementation of the program was the business of medical professionals, and grassroots support was not sufficient to sustain the program. It was killed by the Senate in 1929. Female suffrage itself diminished the intensity of grassroots mobilization. Having won the right to vote in 1920, women did not cease to be politically active, but their activism subsided into the more conventional and less strenuous rituals of electoral participation rather than erupting in protests, parades, and demonstrations. Even before the vote was won, says Elisabeth Clemens, the division between active leaders and passive followers was growing more pronounced in women's organizations, separating the general membership from a "more 'professional' activist core."[10]

How Government Helps Groups Win
What They Want without Mobilizing

Organizational maturation and success may help to distance interest group leaders from their followers. The distance, however, is not simply a function of institutional aging. It is also a reflection of the increasing availability of alternatives to democratic mobilization, mechanisms that interest groups can exploit in order to get what they want without developing or rousing a grassroots constituency.

Starting with the Interstate Commerce Commission (ICC) in 1887, the federal government constructed an entire family of institutions that served as venues for the pursuit of group interests without group mobilization. Independent regulatory commissions, though not an invention of the Progressive Era, became institutional embodiments of the Progressive faith in nonpartisan expertise. But by placing the regulatory commissions outside of partisan politics, the Progressives left them with little organized political support apart from the very groups that they were supposed to be regulating. That, at least, was the assessment of Marver Bernstein, writing from the vantage point of the 1950s. Regulatory legislation, he argued, rode a wave of popular indignation that usually receded soon after enactment, leaving the regulatory agency alone with its discretion but with no internal means to defend the exercise of that discretion.[11]

Extending Bernstein's argument in the 1960s, Murray Edelman contended that one of the chief functions of federal regulatory agencies was precisely to calm popular indignation, to reassure citizens that their interests were being defended against corporate profit-seekers, and to encourage public quiescence—even when regulators were allied with the corporate profit-seekers, and regulation failed to achieve its official objectives.[12] Government regulation, in this view, became a mechanism for popular demobilization.

In the United States, government regulation originated as a response to technological change and economic concentration. That much seems agreed.[13] Agreement ends, however, on the question of who was responsible for this response. On one side are those who trace the regulatory impulse to populist indignation. They see the roots of the ICC, for example, in the Granger movement that rose up from the plains to protest the discriminatory practices of railroads, their anticompetitive rate-fixing and pooling agreements. An opposing view holds that regulatory policy began with the very business interests that were supposed to be subject to regulation. Approaching one another from different disciplines and political dispositions, historian Gabriel Kolko and economist George Stigler have both argued that regulation originated in the interests of the regulated industries, because it protected them from the uncertainties, constraints, and costs of unregulated competition. Marver Bernstein's formulation might be regarded as a synthesis of the populist and elitist views: popular outrage provides the starting point for regulatory policy, but its implementation is heavily influenced by the regulated interests themselves.[14]

Among the backers of national railroad regulation in the 1880s, there were some who hoped that the creation of the ICC would give western farmers and small merchants a place to stand and fight the economic power of the giant railroads and the large shippers to whom they gave favored treatment. Without such a forum, argued Congressman William Hepburn of Iowa, the average freight customer was helpless: "He stands there alone, weak and poor and ignorant though he may be, with a ten-dollar case or a one-hundred dollar case. He must make his own case against a wealthy corporation. He must do that, too, without technical knowledge of the matters litigated. He has no witnesses who are better informed than himself." But the standard democratic remedy for those who stood alone, weak, and poor in the face of overwhelming power was to join forces with one another and to mobilize against their common enemy. The ICC, however, was supposed to reduce the need for such combinations. According to Congressman Robert LaFollette, it would give every citizen "the right to present his grievance and have his case tried without the attendant cost which now practically closes the courts to him."[15]

The expertise and impartiality of the independent commission, it was hoped, would help to even the odds for individual citizens who confronted the new corporate leviathans of the late nineteenth and early twentieth centuries. As a result, the existence of the commission might diminish the tendency toward mass mobilization along the lines of the Granger movement. Some early ventures at state-level regulation of railroads were self-consciously designed to move the issue out of state legislatures, which were exposed to mass agitation, and into administrative tribunals where quiet arbitration might take the bite out of agrarian protest while meeting the railroads' demands for flexible and responsive regulation unattainable under the strictures of black-letter law. Illinois, whose Railroad and Warehouse Commission provided a model for the ICC, originated in just such a compromise.[16]

In practice, however, institutional accomplishment failed at first to meet such expectations. The ICC, as political scientist Stephen Skowronek points out, initially lacked the capacity to create an enclave insulated from political pressure, an enclave where individual claims could be adjudicated independently by impartial experts. Congress had not endowed the commission with sufficiently clear or solid authority to defend the jurisdiction that it claimed, and what powers Congress had granted, the Supreme Court soon invalidated. The longstanding academic controversy about which interests created or captured the ICC obscures a more fundamental point. "The key to understanding the early regulatory effort," writes Skowronek, "is not to be found in the interests themselves but in the structure of the institutions they sought to influence." The nineteenth-century American state was too porous and politically insubstantial to achieve autonomy from the organized interest groups that sought to shape policy outcomes. The basic problem, according to Skowronek, was "how to formulate a coherent regulatory policy in a government that was open to all contending factions."[17]

The early experience of the ICC was symptomatic of a more general institutional regime under which even the courts themselves, though institutions of the state, acted to restrict state power in relation to private interests. It was, in Skowronek's phrase, a "state of courts and parties," and its weaknesses helped to account for the strength and diversity of the interests that mobilized to influence regulatory policy. Since the state was not strong enough to protect any particular interest, all interests had an incentive to mobilize in their own defense—or to seize the advantage. The most intensely held and best organized interests were most likely to get what they wanted.[18]

The loose-jointed institutional regime that encouraged interest-group mobilization did not survive far into the twentieth century. The powers of the ICC, for example, were sharply increased by the passage of the Hepburn Act in 1906. It established the commission's authority to set "reasonable" railroad rates in response to complaints from shippers. Four years later, the Mann-Elkins Act gave the commission the power to suspend proposed railroad rate increases and required that railroads assume the burden of proving that such rates were "reasonable." Commission rulings thus went into effect immediately, preempting court injunctions that might postpone implementation until the interminable possibilities for litigation had been exhausted.[19]

The commission used its new powers to disaggregate the politics of interest groups into an adjudication of individual cases. In the year before the passage of the Hepburn Act, shippers had mobilized on both sides of the railroad rate issue—some to lobby for more stringent regulation of rates, others to insist on the preservation of the status quo. As Richard Vietor has pointed out, they tended to choose sides based on the kind of railroad service available in the communities where they were located. Shippers in towns served by several competing railroads generally opposed new regulations. Railroad rate wars usually gave these firms a competitive advantage when it came to shipping costs. Where a single road monopolized the local railroad business, however, shippers tended to support more potent regulation by the commission. During 1905, when railroad rates were the subject of group mobilization and conflict, the commission received only 633 complaints from shippers. In 1907, after the Hepburn Act had taken effect, there were more than five thousand individual complaints.[20]

Change in the strength and character of a government institution created an alternative channel of adjudication that substituted case-by-case balancing of interests for collective mobilization and legislative resolution. It was true that the invigorated ICC provided an alternative, not just to pressure-group politics but to legal proceedings in the courts, where the task of proving that railroad rates were "unreasonable" had imposed an exasperating burden on dissatisfied shippers.[21] But it was precisely their frustration with the vicissitudes of the judicial process that had helped to turn farmers and merchants toward lobbying rather than litigating in the first place. The commission restored the quiet, case-by-case approach to resolving conflicts between shippers and railroads.

The courts also played a role in the creation of the Federal Trade Commission (FTC), one of the Progressive Era's most notable additions to the ranks of the independent regulatory commissions. The Supreme

Court's rulings in the American Tobacco and Standard Oil cases in 1911 interpreted the Sherman Anti-Trust Act as prohibiting only "unreasonable" restraints of trade. Monopoly, in other words, was not necessarily illegal. It could result legitimately from corporate efficiency and successful competition on the open market. Congress created the FTC, in part, to make the case-by-case determinations needed to distinguish the reasonable from the unreasonable monopolistic practices. But the law went further than this. The FTC was empowered to set standards defining the "unfair trade practices" that restricted competition unreasonably, and it could prosecute firms that violated such standards or issue cease-and-desist orders to prevent them from doing business in ways that the commission had proscribed.

The FTC's mission, as Alan Stone points out, was bedeviled by contradiction. It was supposed to preserve business competition, but by specifying what kinds of competition were "fair," it also restricted competition. By 1919, the commission was playing host to industry conferences designed to achieve "voluntary" agreements on fair trade standards, and the commission used its legal authority to impose sanctions on the firms that violated these standards.[22] In effect, the commission's exercise of its statutory powers enabled private trade associations to solve what rational choice theory identifies as the most critical problem for collective action—free riders who violate collective understandings in order to gain short-term advantages over their business competitors. The FTC punished them and thus reduced the interest groups' need to monitor and motivate their own members.

Another regulatory innovation of the Progressive Era—the Federal Reserve System—sharply curtailed the mobilizing efforts of organized interests. As we have already noted, the Fed gradually narrowed the base for government borrowing from the public at large to banks and financial institutions. In time, the introduction of central banking would also reduce the playing field for political mobilization on issues of currency and banking. For most of the nineteenth century, state and national politics had been animated by currency controversies. Goldbugs, greenbackers, and silverites contested elections, wrote pamphlets, and formed organizations.[23] Like the ICC, the Federal Reserve Board was not immediately able to establish an autonomous domain within its realm of interest-group politics. The regional structure of the Federal Reserve System and the power of state banks and banking regulators at first prevented the Fed from functioning as the central banks of Europe did.[24] But currency controversies had already begun to wane after the silverites lost the election of 1896 and Congress passed the Gold Standard Act of 1900, and the accretion of the Federal Reserve System's control over national monetary policy virtually guaranteed that the rhetoric of gold, silver, and paper would permanently fade from the American political vernacular.

Public Policy and Private Government

At the dawn of the New Deal, Pendleton Herring published a pair of articles titled "Special Interests and the Interstate Commerce Commission," demonstrating how fully the ICC had become engaged with the interests that it was supposed to be regulating. The commission benefited from these relationships at least as much as the special interests did. The number and complexity of the cases that came before the ICC had increased sharply since the days of the Hepburn Act. The commission and its staff, said Herring, were "confronted with tasks of huge proportions and handicapped by a lack of resources." It was, he said, "impossible for them to rely solely on their own expert knowledge." They had to "obtain necessary information by sympathetic contacts with those in possession of it." In 1893, for example, Congress had called on the commission to issue safety regulations for couplers and hand brakes. But the standards finally adopted in 1900 were the ones worked out by a private trade group, the Master Car Builders Association. In the 1920s, ICC staff and a delegation from the American Railway Association jointly arrived at specifications for automatic train control. The commission, however, brought something to these discussions that no private trade association could contribute. As one of the commissioners observed in a speech before the Railway Association, the agency put its coercive authority behind the regulations to apply them consistently and with "full force and effect."[25]

The ICC was not simply enforcing the interests of the railroads. The railroads had opposed most of the legislation under which they were regulated. But having lost the battle to escape regulation, wrote Herring, the railroads were determined to submit to rules that were "framed intelligently."[26] That was why they cooperated with the ICC. Cooperation, however, may have come more easily because the railroads could rely on the legal authority and administrative capacity of the ICC to assure that few if any railroads would be able to evade the costs of complying with the regulations, and thereby leave the carriers that followed the rules at a competitive disadvantage. That was how the commission contributed to the cooperative spirit of the railroad industry as a whole.

Cooperation prevailed even in rate disputes between shippers and carriers. To avoid the cost and inflexibility of formal proceedings, the commission had established the Bureau of Informal Cases and the Bureau of Traffic to settle complaints about railroad rate changes before they could burden the formal docket of the commission itself. The Bureau of Traffic arranged informal conferences among affected shippers and carriers; after discussion, the bureau would offer nonbinding opinions in the cases under negotiation. The Bureau of Informal Cases attempted to achieve similar settlements by correspondence with shippers and carriers. Interested parties who remained dissatisfied with the results of these negotiations were free to demand formal hearings before the ICC. But Herring suggested that they were unlikely to achieve more satisfying results by resorting to official procedures: "This is because the Commission, in deciding a formal case, must act in strict conformity with a statutory authorization which necessarily limits its freedom of action, and which may result in a decision less pleasing to both parties than would a compromise adjustment involving no direct order."[27]

Informal regulation by correspondence probably made the ICC accessible to small shippers and farmers who could not hire attorneys or travel to Washington for formal hearings. Because they were acting on their own, however, they may also have been inclined to accept settlements that they would have rejected as participants in organized interest groups. Informal proceedings offered a low-key alternative to collective mobilization and protest. They did not, however, immunize the ICC and its cooperative family of special interests against group conflict.

Congress, as Herring pointed out, was "a natural expansion chamber for the energies of the many interests concerned." Complainants or respondents who did not receive satisfaction from the commission could turn to their congressional representatives for solutions to their problems, and, one suspects, congressional representatives sometimes raided the commission's jurisdiction on their own initiative to stir up support in their constituencies. Occasionally, to back up their demands on behalf of farmers or business travelers or the geographic regions that they represented, legislators threatened to investigate the commission or to diminish its authority or jurisdiction. The railroad companies, for their part, were powerful enough to pressure the commission without relying on the intervention of Congress. They orchestrated public relations offensives to support their demands for rate increases, offensives that culminated in letter-writing campaigns aimed at the ICC. The commission professed to be unmoved. It was not guided by public opinion: "The statute does not authorize us to arrive at a decision with respect to the reasonableness of rates on the basis of preponderating views."[28]

The commission, in fact, had its own pressure group to champion its independence from "improper" outside influences. The Association of Practitioners before the Interstate Commerce Commission, formed in 1930, framed a code of ethics for the representatives of the shippers and carriers who had dealings with the ICC. The association was a response to the representatives' concern that they had been

> too lax in failing to support the Commission in its obvious wish that testimony, briefs, arguments, letters, telegrams, and other forms of appeal shall not be presented when they are remote from the issues contemplated by law, and which can only be described as clamorous appeal for class or sectional recognition. We have by our own course of conduct accentuated the looseness of the Commission's system of pleading and practice with the tendency to convert what ought to be law suits into something like town hall meetings, and I regret to say, at times, political gatherings.[29]

But politics could not be denied. The railroad industry was in trouble. It now faced competition from trucking companies, which threatened not only the nation's rail system but its system of railroad regulation as well. "Cross-subsidization" was essential to railroad rate policy. It meant that railroads could equalize their rates to shippers by using revenue from more profitable routes and cargoes to subsidize less profitable routes and cargoes. The truckers, unburdened by regulation, naturally sought the cream of the carrying trade and, in doing so, took the revenue that railroads needed to equalize their rates. Railroad regulators were as concerned about this loss as the railroads themselves because it threatened the principle of nondiscriminatory freight rates that was fundamental to the ICC's mission, and soon the problem was attracting attention at the highest levels of government. Even in the best of times, the financial collapse of the nation's railroads would have represented a shock to the country's economy. Against the background of the Depression, it was unthinkable. With the support of the ICC, the Roosevelt administration, the railroads, and the shippers who benefited from the ICC-enforced equalization of freight rates, Congress enacted the Motor Carrier Act of 1935. It brought the trucking industry under the regulatory umbrella of the ICC, chiefly for the purpose of bolstering the railroads' competitive position. Even some of the larger trucking companies backed the legislation because it helped to stabilize shipping rates in a chaotic new industry with relatively low entry costs.[30] But unlike the legislation that created the ICC, the act that added so significantly to the commission's jurisdiction was not a response to any groundswell of popular protest against abuses committed by the trucking industry.

Though the Motor Carrier Act was supported by a variety of organized interest groups, the interests that figured in its passage had been shaped in large part by the government itself as a result of its own regulatory policies. The ICC foreshadowed an entanglement of public policy and private interest that would become pervasive under the New Deal.

This entanglement resulted from the same political circumstances that were implicit in the formation of the regulatory authorities themselves. When Congress created regulatory commissions, it delegated a portion of its legislative discretion to an administrative agency, but Congress could not delegate its democratic legitimacy. Nobody elects bureaucrats, and this democratic deficiency creates two problems for bureaucratic regulation. First, the commission has to establish the legitimacy of decisions not specifically mandated by any statute, decisions that unelected bureaucrats make on their own discretion. The second and related practical problem is getting regulated industries to comply with these rulings. Outright defiance was not an uncommon response to the orders of federal regulators, and litigation was another instrument of intractability that could not only forestall the operation of regulatory authority but also restrict or overturn it. The solution was to incorporate the regulated groups themselves into the regulatory process. As Theodore Lowi points out, "direct interest-group participation in government became synonymous with self-government."[31] Direct participation seemed democratic and promised to be efficacious. Rulings made in consultation with interest groups might be expected to command the respect of the interests that the groups represented.

Until the Depression, this pattern of delegation, consultation, and legitimation had been confined, for the most part, to a handful of regulatory commissions. But Congress responded to the economic crisis of the 1930s by delegating its authority in wholesale lots to an alphabet soup of administrative agencies with broad discretion over industry, labor, agriculture, and finance.

Writing in the mid-1930s, Pendleton Herring observed that the proliferation of federal administrative agencies had been accompanied by an increase in the representation of interest groups in Washington. There was nothing new about this. He had noticed that the same connection between governmental expansion and interest-group activity had occurred in the 1920s. But now a special relationship had developed between New Deal bureaucrats and organized interests. It was not simply that bureaucracies needed the legitimating assent of interest groups more than Congress did. Bureaucracies also exhibit a higher degree of internal specialization than legislatures do. Administrators therefore found themselves dealing with narrowly limited groups, usually organized into formal associations that became "articulate forces in administration." Administrators and interest-group representatives developed close working relationships, and Herring noted that there was "a discernable tendency toward the systematizing of these relationships, toward according them legal recognition, and toward utilizing them in the routine of administration." These new arrangements for administrative consultation convinced Herring "that we are no longer content with the crude instrument of the ballot as a means of measuring consent, but are cognizant of more efficient methods of discovering the opinions of the governed." In fact, Herring envisioned the gradual development of "an administrative advisory body with a membership embracing all the interests falling within the jurisdiction of the federal government."[32]

Herring's congress of bureaucratic clientele groups would presumably overcome the narrowness of the interests that attached themselves to particular agencies. This body's more inclusive deliberations might diminish the likelihood that a clientele would "capture" its agency and undermine the independence and impartiality of the public servants who worked there.

Apprehension about the capture of public authority by private groups figures prominently in critiques of "interest-group liberalism." It is liberalism because it envisions a positive government, but it is a positive government that seeks legitimacy and compliance by ceding control of public policy to private interests. Government, in effect, becomes merely a broker in the business of group politics, and it seeks no higher public interest than the "average" interest that emerges from the balancing of special interests. But the result, according to the critics, is that public authorities undermine the very legitimacy that they are struggling to achieve. "Private government" loses the respect of its public. Policy bargains worked out among the most immediately affected interests rarely do justice to the more general interests of an indirectly affected public at large.[33]

But the operations of regulatory agencies like the ICC and the FTC suggest that interest-group democracy can also undermine the integrity of the interest groups themselves. First, to the extent that a private group "captures" public authority, the group may reduce the occasions on which it has recourse to its rank-and-file constituents. As a stakeholder or bureaucratic insider, the group already commands the attention of decision-makers. Second, to the extent that an organization can rely on the coercive authority of the state to police the free riders who would violate the group's collective interests, it can diminish its own efforts to monitor and motivate its members.

As Grant McConnell has observed, the internal "private government" of interest groups is rarely democratic.[34] But the tendency toward elitism is not simply the result of some iron law of oligarchy inherent in private associations. The internal functioning of private interest groups can be affected decisively by the structure of political institutions and the constitution of public authority. Government's accommodation of interest-group democracy provides organized interests with an alternative to the collective mobilization of popular democracy. The groups can get what their members presumably want without stirring up the members themselves. And the members, for their part, may be provided with alternative avenues for advancing their private interests. Within their narrowly restricted domains, the independent regulatory commissions substituted case-by-case adjudication for lobbying and legislating. In the process, they began to reshape the practice of citizenship.

Chapter 6

From Masses to Mailing Lists

INTEREST-GROUP LIBERALISM originated in a political discovery. Public agencies and private interest groups discovered that they could help to resolve one another's problems. For the agencies, there was the complex task of regulating modern industries, which would have become incomparably more complex had the industries been disorganized and uncooperative. In effect, interest groups helped to prepare their industries for regulation by organizing the members into coherent and articulate alliances. The inclusion of these alliances in the regulatory process assured a high degree of voluntary compliance. The agency, for its part, used its coercive power to enforce the regulations that emerged from its deliberations with the regulated interests. If most firms cooperated with regulations, the occasional free riders who attempted to sidestep the costs of compliance in order to gain unfair competitive advantage could be targeted for regulatory sanctions. Compliant firms might therefore have some confidence that their political agreeability would not place them at an economic disadvantage with respect to lawless competitors. Voluntarism and coercion were two ends of the same bargain.

The New Deal and Interest-Group Liberalism

In the New Deal's National Recovery Administration (NRA), interest-group liberalism reached its fullest expression.[1] The NRA was one of the programmatic landmarks of Franklin Roosevelt's first hundred days in the White House—a dramatic blueprint for national economic planning on a scale previously equaled only in wartime. Though the NRA would eventually aggravate the alienation of American business from the Roosevelt administration, it emerged, in part, as a concession to longstanding business demands for a relaxation of the antitrust restrictions in effect since the Sherman Anti-Trust Act of 1890.[2] Business groups, in consultation with NRA officials, drew up codes of fair competition for particular industries and trades. The NRA was responsible for enforcing these standards. Its prohibition of "predatory" practices would allow for the survival of firms and jobs that might otherwise succumb to cutthroat competition for the paying customers who had become so scarce in the 1930s. The reduction of competitive pressures would allow industry to pay higher wages to workers—or at least to avoid cutting wages in order to reduce prices or preserve a profit margin. The workers would use their augmented incomes to make consumer purchases, which would support business expansion, higher employment, and eventual recovery.[3]

That was the theory, though the National Industrial Recovery Act was drawn in such general terms and embraced so many compromises and improvisations that it was difficult to discern any particular theory in the legislation itself.[4] It was, however, a classic and unambiguous instance of private collective action supported by government coercion. To stabilize prices at levels sufficient to pay decent wages, the business firms in an industry would have to agree to restrict production. As Mancur Olson has pointed out, such restrictions are unlikely to survive on a voluntary basis.[5] Each firm has an interest in boosting output so as to take advantage of the artificially high prices sustained by production curbs. But if many firms succumb to this temptation, they will glut the market with goods and prices will fall. One solution is to substitute the coercive authority of government for the voluntary compliance of individual producers, and this is precisely what the government-sanctioned codes of the NRA were designed to accomplish—not only with respect to production quotas but also with respect to fair trade practices and labor practices.

In practice, however, the NRA appears to have met hardly any of the expectations with which it was invested. It did not raise real wages or bring cooperation to American industry. It did not live up to the theory of collective action.[6] In the short term at least, the NRA does not even seem to bear out our argument that government by private interest groups tends to reduce the political mobilization of the groups' members. General Hugh Johnson, the administrator of the NRA, initiated a campaign of mass mobilization around his agency's Blue Eagle emblem to rouse public support for the recovery program and to pressure business into compliance with the preliminary "blanket code" of the NRA—the standards that employers were supposed to follow until specific industry codes could be drafted and approved. In New York, a quarter of a million people marched up Fifth Avenue on behalf of the Blue Eagle while millions cheered from the sidewalks.[7] Not long after the cheering stopped, the NRA triggered a different kind of political activism. The agency's operations exacerbated both group and class conflict and, as a result, contributed to political mobilization in general, but especially to the mobilization of American labor.

Like farmers and women's rights activists, labor was one of those late-nineteenth-century interest groups that generally operated outside the framework of partisan politics. But at the national level, at least, labor did not become part of Pendleton Herring's "new lobby." It rarely lobbied at all. Under Samuel Gompers, the American Federation of Labor pursued an official policy of "pure and simple trade unionism." Whatever workers gained, they won through collective bargaining in the workplace, not by political mobilization. Long experience had demonstrated that labor's hard-won legislative victories were frequently overturned by the courts, and in any case securing benefits for workers through government institutions would only divide their loyalties between their trade unions and their political champions.[8] It seemed best to forswear political organization in favor of labor organization and collective bargaining.

Organized labor's political isolation ended decisively with the New Deal, but not because unions formed a significant part of the coalition that elected Franklin Roosevelt and a Democratic Congress. In fact, labor's role in making Roosevelt president was negligible. Union membership had fallen throughout the 1920s, and labor leaders played scarcely any part at all in shaping the legislation of the early New Deal.[9] Instead, it was New Deal legislation that enhanced and redefined the political role of labor, and helped to mobilize the workers.

Organized labor would emerge from the New Deal not just as one powerful interest group among others but as an interest with a strong ties to grassroots support and a distinctive tendency to rely upon the politics of mobilization. Unions are mass membership organizations, and as Lawrence Flood argues, they "are among the very few American institutions expected to practice democracy."[10] The Landrum-Griffin Act of 1959—designed in part to curb the dictatorial power of union bosses— was a reaffirmation of this democratic expectation, though also a measure of labor's failure to meet it. If measured by the standards of other interest groups, however, unions actually do exhibit a distinctive propensity for democratic mobilization. According to political scientist Ken Kolman, organized labor is more likely than most other interest groups to rely on such "outside lobbying" tactics as letter-writing campaigns and protest demonstrations.[11] In this respect, at least, unions seem to be misfits in a demobilized democracy. But the commitment to mobilization has weakened over time, and its political effectiveness may have diminished as well.

The political mobilization of labor was a direct result of federal legislation—first the National Industrial Recovery Act (NIRA) of 1933 and, later, the Wagner Act. For unions, the critical provision of the NIRA was Section 7(a), which said that each industry code of fair competition drawn up under the auspices of the NRA would contain a guarantee that employees had the right to bargain collectively and to be free from employer interference in choosing and organizing a union to represent them. (Codes were also required to prohibit yellow-dog contracts, by which nonmembership in a union was made a condition of employment. Compulsory membership in company unions was also prohibited.)

To Depression-era observers, the explanation for 7(a) seemed self-evident: "In view of the special encouragement given in the act to self-organization by employers, all labor, and especially organized labor, would have been put into an ugly, resentful mood, if not given equivalent rights and opportunities."[12] If the NRA gave business a vacation from antitrust prosecution so that corporations could achieve industry-wide coordination, unions could not be denied a similar respite from the antilabor injunctions of the courts so that they could create parallel organizations of workers. In fact, the Norris-LaGuardia Act of 1932 had already taken a step in this direction by prohibiting federal courts from issuing restraining orders against unions in most labor disputes. If capitalists could create corporations, workers should be able to organize unions free from the interference of their employers or the judiciary.[13] Section 7(a) and the later Wagner Act were intended to form a more perfect pluralism that allowed labor and business to engage in collective bargaining and interest-group politics on roughly equal footing.

Today it is generally agreed that organized labor was insufficiently powerful in 1933 to extract such favorable terms from the Roosevelt administration, and the explanation for Section 7(a) has become a focus of uncertainty and argument. Conflicting interpretations are even more at odds in the case of the Wagner Act, whose more staunchly prolabor provisions succeeded Section 7(a) after the Supreme Court's 1935 decision in the *Schechter v. United States* case shut down the National Recovery Administration. The Wagner Act also created an enforcement mechanism—the National Labor Relations Board (NLRB)—far more formidable than its NRA predecessor. If organized labor lacked the power to impose

Section 7(a) on the national recovery program, then its role in shaping and passing the Wagner Act is even more questionable.

One thing seems reasonably clear. The architects of New Deal labor policy did not fully anticipate its consequences. In general, their vision of labor relations had been formed in a Progressive tradition "that had grown increasingly skeptical of the rule of law and increasingly interested in nonlegal modes of conflict resolution." They shared the Progressive dream of "a new era of social cooperation."[14] Senator Robert F. Wagner was convinced that court injunctions and company unions could not provide the foundation for this cooperative regime. Speaking to his Senate colleagues in 1932 in support of the Norris-LaGuardia Bill, he argued that workers should be free to form unions of their own. Statesmanship, he said, demanded that workers be encouraged "to take this road of organized action to responsibility, to self-mastery, to human liberty, and national greatness. We can convert the relation of master and servant into an equal and cooperative partnership, shouldering alike the responsibilities of management and sharing alike in the rewards of increasing production."[15]

Urgent circumstance as well as Progressive ideology may have shaped the New Deal's determination to create a "cooperative partnership" between capital and labor. A wave of strikes and worker protests crested in 1934–1935. Political scientist Michael Goldfield has argued that the Wagner Act was a response to this disruption—an attempt to replace class conflict with the negotiated peace of collective bargaining. David Plotke offers a somewhat different explanation for the Wagner Act. The abandonment of the NIRA after the *Schechter* decision and the disappearance of Section 7(a) "seemed to create a dangerous vacuum." It was filled by a surge of strikes—some of them "citywide strikes with a political dimension." Progressive ideas and the reformers who articulated them contributed to the shape of the Wagner Act, but a mass uprising of organized and unorganized labor created the circumstances for its passage.[16] It was the shop-floor manifestation of the same popular mobilization that produced the highest voter turnout of the twentieth century in the presidential election of 1936.

Political scientist Frances Piven and sociologist Richard Cloward argue not only that the Wagner Act was a response to disruptions created by workers but that by encouraging labor organization instead of labor insurgency, the legislation deprived workers of their most potent weapon. Senator Wagner had been right when he argued that giving workers the freedom to organize would make them more "responsible." To become organized, labor had to arrive at a modus vivendi with the status quo and the elites who controlled it. Labor organization, paradoxically, meant the political demobilization of workers. It meant the substitution of interest-group bargaining for mass insurgency.[17]

There is some support for the contention that a mass mobilization of workers created the conditions for the passage of the Wagner Act. Leon Keyserling, Senator Wagner's aide and one of the bill's chief draftsman, later recalled that the legislation had been powered by insecurity about social order and the hope that the bill's framework for collective bargaining would help to "prevent revolution."[18] But if the New Deal's labor legislation was a response to disruption, it was also a cause of disruption. Both Section 7(a) and the Wagner Act contributed—at least temporarily —to an intensification of sit-down strikes and protests as workers across the country tried out their rights under the new regime in labor law.[19] The cooperative order envisioned in the NIRA had backfired, not simply because the Section 7(a) and the Wagner Act encouraged labor-management conflict but because conflict that might ordinarily have been confined to the private sector was now politicized.[20]

The Labor Question: Movement or Interest?

The NLRB was to become a means for the political containment of this conflict. But converting group mobilization and strife into routine adjudication would be more difficult for the NLRB than it had been for the Interstate Commerce Commission (ICC). The NLRB was different from other independent regulatory commissions. Most of them were responsible for regulating politically well organized corporations on behalf of politically diffuse consumers. The NLRB's job was to make decisions of intense interest to two well-organized constituencies often locked in fierce struggle with each other.[21] From the time of its creation to the implementation of the 1947 Taft-Hartley Act, the NLRB was a focus of business-labor conflict. Over a period of one year, 1939–1940, the board was the subject of three hostile congressional investigations.[22]

Taft-Hartley trimmed the powers of the NLRB, prohibited the closed shop, and made unions subject to sanctions for unfair labor practices, ostensibly to protect the rights of individual workers. But business conservatives could not achieve sufficient unity for further rollbacks of the Wagner Act, and organized labor could not muster the strength to overturn the most objectionable provisions of Taft-Hartley. The result was peace, not the peace of labor-management cooperation envisioned by the Progressives but the peace of stalemate. Although the legislative deadlock did not end political contention between business and unions, it transferred some of their sparring from Congress to less conspicuous decision-making processes in the executive branch—to the NLRB and the president who appointed its members.[23]

Organized labor found a strategic point of political access in the presidential nominating process, but the exploitation of this opening did not entail much political mobilization of the rank-and-file unionists. National union leaders and AFL-CIO president George Meany worked the proverbial smoke-filled rooms pressuring delegations from states heavy with union members to support labor's presidential choices. Behind a screen of political neutrality, says Taylor Dark, national labor leaders "enjoyed a high degree of autonomy" in the politics of nomination "both from their own membership and from other leaders in the union organization. In fact, a strong union president could endorse a candidate without undertaking any serious process of internal consultation."[24]

With New Deal support, rank-and-file insurgents and sit-down strikers had laid the foundation for the postwar labor movement, and the postwar New Deal coalition incorporated the leaders of organized labor. But the rank and file had become largely silent partners in this alliance. Occasionally labor leaders would blunt their own members' wage demands or steer them away from striking in order to maintain access to the White House, where presidents—both Republican and Democratic—sought the help of union barons in averting labor strife and inflationary wage increases that might damage the economy along with their party's electoral prospects. In return, labor leaders got a voice in NLRB appointments and in shaping national policy, along with occasional White House support in maneuvering legislation through Congress, where labor lobbyists mobilized to achieve its passage. During the Johnson administration, for example, civil rights legislation, the Poverty Program, and Medicare all benefited from union backing. But measures that might have contributed directly to the strength and membership of labor organizations made no headway. Repeal of a critical provision of the Taft-Hartley Act that prohibited the closed shop was a low-priority item on the Johnson legislative agenda, and intensive lobbying by the National Right to Work Committee prevented congressional repeal of closed-shop provisions in 1966.[25]

The success of union-supported social welfare measures may actually have undermined rank-and-file support for unions. In the first place, opinion surveys from the 1950s to the 1980s consistently showed that union members were less supportive of labor leaders' political activities on behalf of social legislation than of their collective bargaining efforts. Leaders were generally more liberal and more firmly attached to the Democratic party than their followers were.[26] Second, to the extent that union members benefited from government social policies, unions were likely to lose importance as guardians of members' welfare.

The political demobilization of union members was not just a by-product of their leaders' use of "insider" lobbying at the Democratic convention, at the White House, and in Congress. Collective bargaining itself tended to mute the voices from the assembly line. Marxist analysis holds that the union-management contract displaces conflict from the shop floor to "a framework of negotiation" that *"generates a common interest* between union and company, based on the survival and growth of the enterprise." The contract, according to this view, is "the principal instrument of class collaboration between trade unions and corporations."[27] Exponents of liberal pluralism arrive at similar conclusions. According to sociologist Daniel Bell, "the trade union operating in a given market environment, becomes an ally of 'it's' industry." The union becomes "a buffer between management and rank-and-file resentments" and "often takes over the task of disciplining the men, when management cannot."[28]

Management itself grew less confrontational as the process of unionization, overseen by the NLRB, spread from one company to another. Labor relations became a routine function of the firm, and employers came to regard unions as convenient institutions through which they could deal with their workers.[29] Managers who accepted labor organizations and collective bargaining were relatively unlikely to engage in conduct that workers would regard as threatening or provocative, and were therefore less likely to trigger rank-and-file mobilization in the workplace.

Even in the face of threat or provocation, workers were restrained from reactive mobilization by the Supreme Court's reinterpretation of labor law and its implementation by the NLRB. The shift in legal doctrine began as a practical adjustment to the extraordinary national needs of World War II. Labor and management voluntarily agreed to suspend all strikes and lockouts in order to maintain wartime production, and the National War Labor Board not only encouraged both sides to include arbitration clauses in labor-management contracts but also ordered arbitration in cases where no such clause existed.

When the war was over, government support for private arbitration continued. It seemed an appropriate means to cope with the outburst of strikes that occurred once war's end closed the brief era of labor-management peace. In a series of decisions made during the 1950s, the NLRB and the Supreme Court both established a policy of deference toward the outcomes of private arbitration. Unless there were evidence of procedural unfairness or irregularity, the board and the Court would accept the results of private arbitration without examining the evidence or the reasoning that produced those results.

The NLRB began by ruling that it would not accept jurisdiction in complaints of unfair labor practices that had already been resolved by "fair and regular" arbitration. The board later extended this doctrine to complaints that were scheduled for arbitration and, later still, to cases in which arbitration was not scheduled but only a possibility. The Supreme Court declared its support for private arbitration partly to sidestep the consequences of a provision of the Taft-Hartley Act that gave the federal courts jurisdiction in the enforcement of collective bargaining agreements. The Court opted for private arbitration to avert a potential avalanche of labor relations cases that would have overwhelmed the federal judiciary. It reasoned that Taft-Hartley revealed a congressional intent to encourage the inclusion of no-strike provisions in union contracts, and that the no-strike pledge was the union's quid pro quo for the employer's agreement to submit disputes to arbitration. Congress, the Court argued, had therefore called on the judiciary to support a national labor policy based on private arbitration. In later decisions, the Court held that even when the agreement to arbitrate was uncertain, the doubt should be resolved in favor of a commitment to arbitration, and that an employer's agreement to submit grievances to arbitration bound employees to an "implied" no-strike pledge even if no such promise appeared in the contract.[30]

Under Section 7(a) and the Wagner Act, government had politicized labor-management disputes and encouraged the mobilization of workers. After World War II, by incremental steps taken in relatively obscure decisions, government not only privatized the settlement of workplace grievances but also effectively prevented workers from mobilizing to protest them. If the workers' contract contained or even implied an agreement to submit disputes to private arbitration, their employer could counter a walkout with a federal injunction forcing them back to work because their grievance might be subject to arbitration, and arbitration implied an agreement not to strike.

The demobilization of the rank and file was not complete or inevitable. One study of CIO contracts from the mid-1930s to the mid-1950s shows that Communist-led labor organizations were less likely than non-Communist unions to cede control of the workplace to management.[31] The former encouraged their members to contest the employer's authority on the shop floor. But the Taft-Hartley Act required all union leaders to file non-Communist affidavits if their unions were to have access to the protections of the NLRB, and Communist-led unions had been expelled from the CIO by 1949. A subsequent ruling by the NLRB dissolved contracts between the expelled unions and employers and declared that affiliates remaining in the AFL or CIO were free to raid the memberships of the proscribed organizations.[32]

The anti-Communist purge probably eased labor's entry into the mainstream of American politics, where, by the late 1960s, it had become the organizational mainstay of the Democratic party.[33] Recognizing its dependence on the Wagner Act and its vulnerability to antilabor legislation like Taft-Hartley, unions had decisively forsaken Samuel Gompers's firm policy of noninvolvement in partisan politics.

Unions may also have turned to politics as a remedy for a steady erosion of their grassroots base. Though union membership remained roughly stable in absolute terms until the 1990s, it had been shrinking as a percentage of the workforce since the mid-1950s. By the 1970s, the relative decline could no longer be ignored as a temporary contraction. At about the same time, reforms recommended by the Democratic party's McGovern-Fraser Commission threatened the role of union power-brokers at national party conventions and undermined labor unity in electoral politics. Angered by new rules that moved the nominating process from hotel suites to primaries and guaranteed convention representation for women and minorities, George Meany's AFL-CIO boycotted the 1972 presidential election, refusing to endorse any candidate, though some AFL-CIO affiliates made endorsements of their own.[34]

Anxiety about the political status of labor may have contributed to the unions' first major legislative offensives since their attempt to repeal the Taft-Hartley prohibition of the closed shop almost ten years earlier. In 1975, labor lobbyists persuaded Congress to overturn a 1951 Supreme Court decision that banned picketing of an entire construction project when a union had a dispute with only one subcontractor on the site. President Ford, however, vetoed the bill. In 1977, with a Democratic president in the White House, labor confidently pushed for passage of the same bill, but it was narrowly defeated in the House. And in 1978, a comprehensive Labor Law Reform Bill, endorsed by President Carter, cleared the House only to succumb to a Senate filibuster. The legislation had been designed in part to reverse the decline of organized labor by simplifying the procedures for union representational elections, by increasing NLRB membership to speed up the processing of unfair labor practice complaints, and by stiffening employer penalties for unfair labor practices while indemnifying the workers who were hurt by them.[35]

Labor had suffered legislative defeats before, and they had been more severe than these. Had it not been for the antimajoritarian features of the legislative process, in fact, organized labor would have won both of its labor law reforms. It had been frustrated in one case by a presidential veto and in the other by a Senate filibuster. Taft-Hartley had been a much more decisive and jarring setback, and it had occurred at a time when the proportion of union members in the workforce was approaching its peak. Labor's near victories of the late 1970s, however, occurred after unionism had passed its apogee, when its share of workers was clearly contracting. Although unions' representation in the workforce was declining, their financial resources had continued to grow, and these funds made possible both an expansion of union lobbying staffs in Washington and a boost in their political contributions.[36]

Union political influence was no mere reflex of union membership. In fact, it may have been a substitute for membership. Perhaps this is why research finds that union political activity increases as a union's organizing efforts decline. The size of union lobbying forces and political action committee (PAC) contributions are negatively associated with the extent of union efforts to recruit new members. A union turns to political activity, in other words, when it has ceased trying to expand its membership base.[37]

According to Terry Moe, labor's new political assertiveness of the late 1970s inaugurated a period of instability and conflict in the politics of labor relations. The election of Ronald Reagan accentuated this conflict. There was no room on Reagan's ideological agenda for a continuation of the union-business accommodation orchestrated by the NLRB. American businesses themselves, citing low-wage foreign competition, were ready to roll back wages and unionism at home—or to export union jobs to the same low-wage countries whose products competed with theirs. Reagan appointed as NLRB chairman an antiunion ideologist and right-to-work activist not even supported by most corporate labor relations executives. With the cooperation of other Reagan appointees, he reversed twenty-nine NLRB precedents during his first two years in office. According to *Business Week,* the decisions of the NLRB under Reagan gave employers a "green light to at least try to bash unions."[38]

In adversity, the AFL-CIO found the determination to achieve political unity and restore its former influence over the Democratic party's presidential nomination in 1984. The federation's president, Lane Kirkland, reasoned that an early endorsement by the AFL-CIO would prevent its member unions from scattering their political commitments across the field of candidates. Such an early commitment to a candidate would also preclude consultation with labor's rank and file about their political preferences, which were unlikely to have crystallized so early in the presidential election cycle.

The executives of all ninety-nine unions in the AFL-CIO endorsed Walter Mondale for the Democratic presidential nomination almost five months before the first primary. The significance of this decision obviously depended on the federation's ability to deliver the labor vote to its candidate. Delivery had been one of organized labor's longstanding political problems. Substantial numbers of union members fail to vote or, worse yet, vote for candidates opposed by labor leadership.[39] Internal problems help to explain organized labor's difficulties in mobilizing the union vote. Union leaders not only had no time to consult their followers but also were wary of grassroots mobilization. "Internal union dynamics," notes historian Taylor Dark, "which sustained the leadership in power, was often predicated on a quiescent membership that did not challenge the status quo. A mobilized membership could make new demands on the established leaders, possibly threatening their incumbency."[40]

Labor's mobilization nevertheless got much of the credit for Mondale's nomination in 1984. Its failure to secure his election was counted as a sign that labor had lost its grip on its own rank and file. Among union households, Ronald Reagan received 43.2 percent of the voters. But Taylor Dark points out that Mondale did slightly better in union households than Jimmy Carter in 1980 and much better than George McGovern in 1972, and that the percentage difference in the Democratic vote between union and nonunion households was the highest since 1964. Unlike Mondale, of course, neither Carter nor McGovern had the benefit of an early and unanimous AFL-CIO endorsement, and in 1964 union members accounted for more than 30 percent of the workforce. By 1984, the figure had fallen to less than 19 percent.[41] In order to equal past feats of political mobilization, today's unions must turn out a significantly larger share of their members.

One widely held view, in fact, holds that labor has lost influence in American national politics, not just because membership has dropped but also because employer resistance to unionization has stiffened, because public policy has become less supportive, and because unions themselves have become less aggressive in organizing the unorganized.[42] In spite of changes in the size and circumstances of organized labor, there are signs that its political power survived Reaganism largely intact. Even as the political system seemed to veer sharply to the right, labor could count several legislative successes. Two measures strongly supported by unions—a family and parental leave bill and an increase in federal subsidies for child care—passed both houses of Congress only to be vetoed by President Bush. A law requiring that employees receive sixty days' notice of layoffs or plant closings had been passed earlier over President Reagan's veto.[43]

With the election of President Clinton, labor regained regular access to the White House and eliminated the presidential veto as an obstacle to prolabor legislation. Clinton's appointments to the NLRB reversed the antiunion course that the board had pursued under Reagan and Bush.[44] But the Clinton legislative agenda sent mixed signals to organized labor. On the one hand, the president's resolute support of the North American Free Trade Agreement (NAFTA) antagonized unions whose members' jobs might be threatened by competition with Mexican workers. On the other hand, the president's health care reform initiative responded to one of organized labor's longstanding policy objectives. But rank-and-file animosity toward Clinton roused by NAFTA kept unions from rushing to support the president's health care proposal. "Union leaders," as political scientist Tracy Roof points out, "may have been able to go home, change hats, and come back to work to push Clinton's health care bill, but many of the activists were not so forgiving. The labor effort on Clinton's health care reform initiative started late because many of the supportive unions had to give people time to cool off."[45]

The AFL-CIO had failed to achieve its legislative goals when it opposed the President on NAFTA. It failed again when it supported him on health care reform. Then came the congressional elections of 1994 and the Republican Contract with America. The lengthening train of political defeats moved some of the most powerful unions in the AFL-CIO to press for the retirement of President Lane Kirkland and led to his replacement by an insurgent candidate, John Sweeney, president of the Service Employees International Union.

Sweeney's election reflected a leftward shift that carried the labor movement against the conservative tide of American politics. The composition of organized labor had changed. Politically liberal public-employee unions and teacher unions had grown, and so had their representation at AFL-CIO conventions. Blue-collar craft and industrial unions had lost both membership and delegates. President Sweeney himself joined the Democratic Socialists of America and declared his intention to make labor a movement once again and not just an interest. The AFL-CIO would turn away from insider lobbying and checkbook politics in favor of rank-and-file mobilization. It would renew its commitment to organizing the unorganized and restore its membership base.

In fact, however, the AFL-CIO opened its checkbook wider than ever in preparation for the election of 1996. Its goal was to take the House of Representatives back from the Republicans, who had claimed it with much celebration in 1994. Democratic House candidates were even more financially dependent on labor's money in 1996 than they had been in 1994. Unions accounted for 47.6 percent of Democratic candidates' PAC contributions in 1996 compared to 35.8 percent in 1994.[46] (In addition, the AFL-CIO ran its own ad campaign in the districts of targeted Republican freshmen. The ads succeeded, by one estimate, in decreasing the Republican congressional vote by an average of 4 percent.)[47]

According to Tracy Roof, labor's millions brought results even before they were spent. In anticipation of labor's mobilization for the 1996 elections, apprehensive Republican members of Congress defected from the party line to vote for a labor-endorsed increase in the minimum wage and against an exemption for small business. But notwithstanding Sweeney's populist rhetoric, there was no clear-cut increase in turnout among union voters in 1996, and though Republicans lost seats in the House, they remained in control of Congress. In the low-turnout congressional elections of 1998, union households did account for a larger share of the voters than in the presidential elections of 1992 and 1996[48]—demonstrating, perhaps, that labor's electoral impact increases as turnout declines—but it was still not enough to put Democrats in control of the House.

In the 2000 presidential campaign, President Sweeney intensified the AFL-CIO commitment to grassroots mobilization but also increased its campaign contributions. Sweeney insisted, however, that labor's comparative advantage in politics was its access to people, not money. The AFL-CIO could never match the political expenditures of corporations. "But we have people power and an ability to communicate with people one-on-one. They have to try to buy that kind of voter contact." Labor's strategy for 2000 would abandon its television ad campaign of 1996 and concentrate instead on a direct effort to organize its members and get out the vote.[49]

Taylor Dark concedes that "many political operatives and members of Congress are convinced that union political money remains a more important resource for many unions than their members votes." Organized labor's ability to win the votes of its own members is still open to question. AFL-CIO studies show that television ads are much less effective in mobilizing union voters than are personal contacts with union officers and members. But shop stewards and business agents are reluctant to engage in activities unrelated to such collective bargaining responsibilities as the processing of grievances. According to Dark, "the institutional incentives that shape union leaders' quest to retain power within their organizations have often made them hesitant to take advantage of the more open, plebiscitarian aspects of the political system. Such mobilization can threaten the status of leaders who depend on an unaccountable bureaucratic machine to maintain organizational control."[50] Political mobilization can also be a political inconvenience that handcuffs labor's lobbyists in Washington. As Tracy Roof points out, "Insider bargaining gives an organization the ability to compromise and yield to political necessity, whereas grassroots mobilization can potentially build up the support of a group's membership for a particular legislative path."[51]

Finally, a successful voter mobilization strategy for labor demands that it reverse the contraction of the membership base from which it draws its electoral support. The "New Voice" leadership of the AFL-CIO elected in 1995 has stepped up its organizing efforts, but the results thus far are insufficient to maintain organized labor's share of the workforce, much less expand it. To increase the unionized percentage of the American labor force by one percentage point, the AFL-CIO would have to recruit about 1.5 million new members. But in 1996, the federation's unions won less than half of the representation elections overseen by the NLRB and added, at most, 69,111 new members. The actual growth was probably much less than this. After winning a representation election, a union must negotiate a contract with the employer before the employees begin to pay union dues. Unions succeed in gaining first contracts for only about half of the bargaining units in which they win elections. And the calculation of union growth must take account not only of representation elections but also of decertification elections, of which there were 435 in 1996. Unions lost most of these elections and, along with them, most of the 25,011 workers who were employed in the bargaining units where unions were decertified.[52]

Figures such as these contribute, understandably, to a preoccupation with the diminished stature of organized labor in American society. But this preoccupation tends to obscure one critical consideration concerning the relationship between union size and union power. Even in its reduced state, the AFL-CIO, with more than 13 million dues-paying members, is one of the largest organizations in American society. It lags behind the 33-million-member AARP and falls slightly below the Southern Baptist Convention. But its membership is between four and five times that of the National Rifle Association. If mass membership could be readily converted into power, organized labor would tower over most other interest groups like Gulliver among the Lilliputians. Perhaps the most telling feature of labor's political experience has been its ability to exercise power *without* mobilizing its membership. And perhaps its recent struggles to hold its own politically indicate that the power of numbers is no longer the potent political resource that it was when labor emerged from the Great Depression to become a senior partner in the New Deal coalition.

The Advocacy Explosion

Numbers still count. The civil rights movement's march on Washington in 1963 was not just the occasion for Martin Luther King's impassioned eloquence but an opportunity for the movement to show the nation that it was too big to ignore. Interest groups have been imitating its example ever since. But the example is a curious one. In the first place, many of the movement's most fervent supporters were not registered to vote—an obvious handicap in any attempt to deploy the power of numbers in politics, and one for which the movement sought a remedy—the Voting Rights Act of 1965. Second, the made-for-television drama of civil disobedience demonstrations in the streets was paired with a law-governed campaign of litigation. In fact, the two strategies were frequently linked. Civil disobedience often provided the occasion for courtroom offensives against racial segregation.

Litigation and demonstrations had something else in common with each other. Both were the tactics of political outsiders whose access to democratically constituted political institutions was impaired by popular prejudice and exclusion from many of the nation's polling places. The civil rights movement was therefore handicapped in most efforts to lobby legislative bodies as though it were a conventional interest group with an electoral base. The movement attempted to overcome this weakness by taking its fight to the battlegrounds that were most accessible to its democratically disadvantaged constituents—the courts and the streets.

This double-barreled strategy elicited a twofold policy response in Washington that echoed the movement's own dual character. On the legalistic side there was the Civil Rights Act of 1964. It defined a set of rights that were enforceable in the courts or by civil rights agencies like the Equal Employment Opportunity Commission (EEOC)—a new addition to the ranks of government regulatory bureaucracies. Less obviously connected to the civil rights movement, but no less responsive to it, were the Poverty Program and the Model Cities Program. Their emphasis on "maximum feasible participation," community action, and community development encouraged the political mobilization of poor people in general and African Americans in particular.[53]

Though receptive to the objectives of the civil rights movement, the federal government's response was structured so as to disaggregate and privatize black political demands and disperse the African American political offensive. The Community Action Program, for example, was a national initiative aimed at localities, and the resources that it offered for organization and mobilization were designed to encourage local, not national, activism. In short, Washington's antipoverty response to the civil rights movement was designed to get its people off the government's back, or at least to redirect the movement's forces from national to local government. National political leaders wanted the civil rights activists to go home not just because they were disruptive and demanding but because for Democratic leaders in particular, they represented a threat to party cohesiveness. The New Deal coalition had become an increasingly precarious alliance of southern whites, northern blacks, and blue-collar union members. The political apprehensions of the Democrats were reflected in President Johnson's mandate to the designers of the Community Action Program—that they should "do something for Negroes fast without in the process alarming whites.[54]

In practice, "maximum feasible participation" created much less disturbance than anticipated, imagined, or remembered. Notwithstanding War on Poverty atrocity stories about the infiltration and capture of community action agencies by subversive revolutionaries, black nationalists, or violent gangs, most local poverty programs posed little threat to the established order and remained on peaceful terms with the institutions of local government. Often they were controlled by local government, and such control was an explicit condition of the Model Cities Program. To some critics, in fact, the idea of the government's mobilizing the poor to make demands of the government seemed faintly ridiculous or positively pernicious. That was why independent organizer Saul Alinsky denounced the Poverty Program as "political pornography." In the end, "maximum feasible participation" turned out to be minimal.[55]

Guaranteed representation for the poor in local agencies of the Community Action and Model Cities Programs reduced the need for the programs' constituents to mobilize as a group in order to achieve access to decision-making. In the absence of such a constituency-forming experience, it was unclear whether the selected representatives of the poor spoke for anyone but themselves. In some cities, it was true, representatives of the poor were chosen by election rather than by city hall appointment. But the electorate in this case was relatively unaccustomed to political participation. Turnout was generally very low, and campaigns were issueless. There was nothing unexpected about this. The rationale for the Community Action Program itself presupposed that the poor suffered from a sense of powerlessness and would not become politically active without strenuous encouragement. In fact, Community Action probably made less sense as an antipoverty program than as a citizenship program for poor people.

Even on these terms, however, the program was not uniformly successful, and not just because of low participation rates. Representatives of the poor frequently advanced highly particularistic demands designed to benefit themselves or the handful of friends and neighbors who had elected them. Others articulated no demands at all, and still others abandoned their representative roles in order to accept paid positions as staff members in local community action agencies. But the personalized politics of poverty did not prevail everywhere. Political scientists David Greenstone and Paul Peterson found that where poor neighborhoods were already well-organized, community representatives tended to speak for the substantive interests of poor people in general. These representatives, however, were usually not poor people themselves, but members of an activist elite distinguished by its concern for community control of community institutions, a concern that was not shared by most of their low-income constituents.[56]

The Community Action Program represented a less-than-successful attempt to convert poor minority-group members into an influential interest group in local politics. Titles VI and VII the Civil Rights Act offered legalistic rather than political remedies to many of the same people. Unlike the solutions promised by the War on Poverty, they did not call for the collective mobilization of the poor, just individual complaints and lawsuits. Title VI prohibited the practice of racial discrimination in activities supported by federal grants and contracts. Title VII prohibited employment discrimination and created the EEOC as the principal federal agency to address racial bias in workplaces.

The EEOC's enforcement powers were far more limited than those of other federal regulatory agencies. Until 1972, in fact, the commission was authorized only to secure voluntary compliance with fair employment practices. It could do so through conciliation proceedings between complainants and employers, or by suggesting general guidelines that would enable employers to avoid discriminatory practices prohibited by the Civil Rights Act. The EEOC could also recommend cases to the Justice Department for prosecution. Only in 1972 did the commission acquire the authority to initiate suits itself.[57]

The new power did not significantly enhance the commission's effectiveness in combating job discrimination. It was hamstrung because it attacked the problem case by case, taking action only in response to a particular employee's charge of bias. One critic has pointed out that the commission's approach tends "to focus on isolated incidents of discrimination. Discrimination occurs, however, not in isolation but in systematic practices. Although sometimes these practices are addressed by class action lawsuits, individuals do not usually have the information or resources to identify these practices and litigate against them." In fact, victims of discrimination may not even be aware of the bias that denies them a job. Because their employment applications have been turned down, they have no opportunity to compare themselves to the people hired by a firm and no way to discover whether their qualifications match those of the people who work there. Individual complaints, in other words, do not provide effective points of attack against discriminatory practices, and the attempts of EEOC staff members to expand individual cases into more comprehensive investigations of employer practices only prolonged the processing of each case and created an enormous backlog at the commission. Processing delays meant lost evidence and led to "huge back-pay claims which employers were loathe to pay."[58]

Rather than fight discrimination a case at a time, the EEOC might have made more progress toward equal employment opportunity by addressing the practices that produce racially disparate outcomes in the job market. That, at least, has been the suggestion of some of its critics. During the Carter administration, in fact, when Eleanor Holmes Norton chaired the commission, it actually shifted toward a strategy that employed class action suits aimed at discriminatory practices instead of individual cases of discrimination. But the EEOC's effort to focus on the institutional mechanisms of discrimination was hindered by its enormous waiting list of unresolved cases. The commission's accumulation of unfinished business, which had stabilized at a backlog of about 100,000 cases by the mid-1990s, created a bureaucratic climate that emphasized administrative management at least as much as the defeat of discrimination. In any case, the EEOC's effort to shift its aim to larger targets was abruptly abandoned during the Reagan administration after Clarence Thomas became chair of the commission and limited the agency's attention to individual cases in which there were "identified victims." By the time of the Clinton administration, the EEOC was still trying to deal with its case backlog, though the new chair of the commission, appointed in 1994 after a two-year hiatus, attempted to pick and choose among the unsettled cases so as to concentrate on the ones that seemed to promise the greatest impact on discrimination.[59]

In effect, enforcement of Title VII disassembled the movement against employment discrimination into a vast accumulation of private grievances. Title VI seemed to retain more of the collective character of the civil rights struggle. Federal agencies drafted general regulations specifying the discriminatory practices that would warrant a cut-off of federal funds to a contractor or grantee. The postwar expansion in federal aid to states and localities and in federal contracts with defense firms and other suppliers and service providers had extended the reach of such regulations across much of the society. Local public schools receiving federal education aid were among the first institutions to feel the force of the new rules. Within a remarkably short time, southern school segregation gave way before a joint assault of the U.S. Office of Education and the federal courts.[60]

The elevation of the Title VI regulations above the particularities of litigation was partly optical illusion. Just as the ICC had to worry about

the democratic legitimacy and political efficacy of its rulings and regulations, so the Title VI standards needed to be endowed with more political
gravity than mere administrative fiat could provide. The solution was to
model the regulations on standards established by federal court decisions. Civil rights lawyers who wanted to influence the regulations did so
by litigating in federal courts.[61]

After 1976, Congress provided attorneys with a substantially
strengthened incentive to litigate in civil rights cases. Plaintiffs in these
cases were rarely if ever wealthy. Unless a large organization like the
NAACP provided legal counsel, they could get their day in court only by
means of a contingency fee arrangement with a private attorney. But
many civil rights cases do not result in significant monetary compensation for plaintiffs, only injunctive relief, and hence no financial settlement from which to compensate civil rights lawyers. Since much civil
rights legislation presupposed enforcement by private plaintiffs as well as
public prosecution, Congress enacted the Civil Rights Attorney's Fees
Award Act in 1976. It was designed to give greater force to civil rights laws
by authorizing courts to require that defendants in civil rights cases pay
the plaintiffs' legal fees if the plaintiffs' attorneys succeeded in making
their case.[62] The law meant that civil rights lawyers no longer needed
large and well-financed organizations to underwrite their legal attacks on
racial discrimination. They no longer needed a constituency. If they
could win cases, they could win their fees and survive to file more suits.

The proliferation of fee-shifting statutes like the legislation enacted
for civil rights attorneys in 1976 may help to explain one of the most
remarkable things about the development of Title VI. Its applicability was
rapidly extended during the 1970s from the prohibition of racial discrimination in federally financed activities to the prohibition of discrimination on grounds of sex, disability, and age. There was a crucial difference
between these sweeping extensions of antidiscrimination policy and its
original concern with racial bias. "In each instance," says historian Hugh
Davis Graham, the expansion of antidiscrimination controls over the
recipients of federal grants and contracts "occurred with little grassroots
pressure from constituency movements, little attention in the media, and
little congressional debate." In other words, there was no collective mobilization of the kind that had contributed to the passage of the Civil
Rights Act of 1964. "Grassroots constituencies," Graham explains, "do
not understand the arcane workings of federal regulation."[63] But policy
entrepreneurs in Congress and their allies in advocacy groups did. So did
attorneys.

The arcana that placed federal regulation beyond the comprehension
of grassroots constituencies were the products of politics, administration,

and litigation. Title VI created a civil rights enforcement machine to which a variety of advocacy groups subsequently tried to hitch their interests. The fact that the machine was already functioning diminished the extent to which these groups had to mobilize their public constituencies, because the political and bureaucratic obstacles to be overcome were less formidable than the ones that had to be surmounted when civil rights forces inside and outside government constructed the antidiscrimination machine. Popular demands therefore played only a minor role in the extensions of Title VI to women, the people with disabilities, and the elderly. In effect, these new antidiscrimination initiatives grew out of the machinery of government itself, manipulated by an "issue network" of policy experts who knew the machinery because they had created it, operated it, lobbied it, or litigated against it.

Political scientist Hugh Heclo has pointed out that public policies now bring into being Washington-based "villages" of policy specialists attentive to the operation of particular public programs: "Everywhere extensive networks of village folk in the bureaucracy, Congress, and lobbying organizations share experiences, problems and readings on people and events."[64] To the residents of such villages, political executives and most members of Congress are mere tourists—although they are welcome contributors to local prosperity, they are not members of the policy network and are largely uninformed about the intricacies of village life.

The emergence of these policy-centered villages was just one development in new era of interest-group politics and public regulation. The most widely recognized accompaniments of this new era have been a sharp upsurge in the population of organized interest groups in Washington—the so-called "advocacy explosion"—and a shift in group interests and regulatory policy described (imperfectly) as a turn from "economic" toward "social" regulation. The ICC and the NLRB have been succeeded by new generation regulatory agencies and regulations concerned more with "quality-of-life" issues than with economic security. They deal with matters of environmental protection, consumer product safety, cigarette advertising, highway safety, and human rights. Interest-group concerns shifted in a similar direction. According to political scientist Jeffrey Berry, group politics has entered the era of postmaterialism.[65]

Postmaterialism's tangible embodiment was a proliferation of citizen groups or public interest groups in Washington. By the 1990s, according to political scientist Jack Walker, they constituted a larger proportion of national lobbying organizations than ever before, and more than half of them had been founded in the preceding twenty-five years. Their seedbed was the era of civil rights, and many drew inspiration from the movement itself. They belonged to a different species than older business and occupational groups like the Chamber of Commerce, the American Farm Bureau Federation, and the AFL-CIO. The Sierra Club, the Children's Defense Fund, the Environmental Defense Council, the Center for Science in the Public Interest, and the Fund for Animals all mobilize their supporters around interests other than those rooted in their jobs.

The concerns of these groups, as Jeffrey Berry acknowledges, are not exclusively nonmaterial. The National Organization for Women, for example, frequently addresses issues related to the employment opportunities and economic status of its constituency, but it articulates interests far more comprehensive than those defined by job and income. Perhaps the distinguishing feature of the new citizen groups is not the intangible character of their interests but the way in which their interests are defined. These groups strive to advance the interests of women, children, the elderly, consumers, or the disabled across a broad range of institutions, economic sectors, and situations. The concerns of animal rights groups, for example, extend from farms, zoos, and scientific laboratories to the cosmetics and fashion industries. In a sense, the interests of the new citizen groups are structured "horizontally," unlike the interests of the older groups, which were organized "vertically" on the basis of particular industries, institutions, or professions.[66] In this respect, the concerns of the new public interest groups resemble those of the civil rights movement, which addressed the costs and consequences of being black across the entire spectrum of the society. A similar comprehensiveness has been articulated explicitly by environmental groups, whose ecological ideology emphasizes the interconnectedness of air, water, flora, and fauna with one another and with human activities.

A powerful concern with democratic processes and open government also distinguishes the new public interest groups. Historian Richard Harris argues that this preoccupation is not just a legacy of the activist culture of the 1960s but a response to the enhanced role of regulatory agencies in policy formation. Breaking into bureaucratic agencies required that public interest groups establish a permanent presence in Washington—hence the advocacy explosion—and that administrative institutions and processes be restructured to give them at least as much access to policymaking as more traditional trade and industry organizations. Public interest groups had concluded that the ostensible aims of regulatory policy are sometimes subverted during the process of implementation when agencies, hidden behind a screen of legal and technical details, give way to the interests of the regulated groups. The reformers' solution was to open the regulatory process to citizen participation, so that public interests could be represented as vigorously as corporate interests. The reformers demanded that regulatory agencies make decisions in public, that they disclose information relevant to those decisions, and that citizens have direct access to the process of decision-making through public hearings or provisions for public comment. New public interest groups like Common Cause, founded in 1970, made it their principal business to promote such democratic practices in political parties and election campaigns as well as in public agencies.[67]

The struggle for participatory administration achieved some of its most notable victories during the 1970s, when a variety of regulatory statutes provided for direct citizen intervention in agency decision-making and allowed for citizen lawsuits to compel an agency to enforce particular safety or environmental standards. But the judicial system contributed even more to the range of opportunities for citizen intervention by extending conventional concepts of standing to sue so that citizens, like corporations subject to administrative regulation, could appeal bureaucratic decisions to the federal courts under the Administrative Procedure Act. An interest in environmental protection or scenic beauty now established the same basis for litigation as the threat of substantial private economic loss.[68]

With the exception of a few mass membership organizations like the National Wildlife Federation, the new generation of public interest groups mobilized hardly any citizens at all to support their insistence on citizen participation. Some of them had no arrangements for democratic participation or consultation with their own presumed constituents.[69] Even groups that legitimately claim mass memberships can count only handfuls of activists. Political scientist Michael McCann concludes that "the internal structures of power and initiative in most public interest groups are little more participatory than the state bureaucracies the activists openly criticize." In many groups, membership means little more than being on a mailing list. Members may never assemble to deliberate among themselves or to arrive at a collective expression of their common interests. AARP, the largest membership organization in the United States, could hardly be expected to convene its 33 million members for open discussion. The group, reports Theda Skocpol, "deals with masses of individual adherents through the mail."[70] Membership, in other words, is a personal rather than a collective experience.

In fact, the concentration of interest groups based in Washington now includes a sizeable population of organizations without any members at all. The advocacy explosion was powered by a determination to keep public authority under public scrutiny, to expose its accommodations with corporate elites, to unmask its commitments to growth, prosperity, and security as complacent acceptance of environmental perils and threats to consumer or worker safety. But the advocacy groups so forcefully demonstrating that the emperor had no clothes were organizations that had no bodies. "Many of these new groups," wrote historian Michael T. Hayes, "have no members at all, freeing them from the imperative of satisfying the policy preferences of a mass constituency. Among those groups with large nominal memberships, there is frequently little or no opportunity for members to influence group decision making." Using data on almost three thousand "social welfare" and "public affairs" organizations founded from the 1960s through the 1980s, Theda Skocpol finds that close to half of them have no members whatsoever. She sees the outlines of "a new civic America largely run by advocates and managers without members and marked by yawning gaps between immediate involvements and larger undertakings."[71]

Conventional assumptions about the nature of democratic politics make it difficult to understand the very existence of such memberless groups, much less their success in influencing public policy. Pendleton Herring's "new lobby" of the 1920s drew sustenance and strength from its membership base. Today's new lobby obviously depends on other sources. Private foundations figure prominently among them. In 1970, for example, in what Jeffrey Berry has described as a seminal move inaugurating the era of public interest groups, the Ford Foundation financed sixteen public interest law firms dedicated to increasing public representation in government decision-making.[72] A decade earlier, it had been the Ford Foundation that sponsored the first experimental community action projects that provided models for the War on Poverty. Now it helped to fashion a new paradigm in popular politics, one that emphasized the restructuring of government institutions rather than the mobilization of the disenfranchised. Once set in motion, the new law firms would be able to run on their own power, sustained by funds derived under one or another of the hundred or more fee-shifting statutes that paid plaintiffs' lawyers in public interest lawsuits. The law firms' example was followed by a host of interest groups without benefit of Ford Foundation grants, and some of the groups received funds from the federal government's own Legal Services Corporation. Litigation became the vital core of many Washington-based interest groups not just because it generated resources but because it represented a means for influencing government without having to mobilize a popular constituency—a crucial condition for groups without members. The use and impact of the litigation strategy is the subject of the next chapter.

Like the early public interest law firms, many of the new citizen groups in Washington are kept alive not by the support of citizen members but by government and foundation grants or large gifts from private patrons. During the Carter administration, for example, the Federal Trade

Commission and the Consumer Products Safety Commission financed the participation of citizen groups in agency proceedings.[73] One recent study finds that almost half of a sample of public interest groups receive at least 50 percent of their financial support from "patrons," such as foundations, corporations, government, or individual donors. These sources accounted for 44.7 percent of the funding for the entire sample of public interest groups. Membership dues supplied only 36 percent of the total. When dues are added to revenue from publications and conferences, constituent support draws approximately even with major gifts or grants from patrons.[74]

To the extent that their finances depend on government grants or tax-exempt contributions, public interest groups expose themselves to the attacks of their ideological opponents and political antagonists among businesses subject to the environmental or safety regulations for which the advocacy group is lobbying. The conservative campaign to "defund the left" is an attempt to exploit this vulnerability. It began under Ronald Reagan, who disparaged public interest litigators as "a bunch of ideological ambulance chasers," and it was revived under the Contract with America when Republican leaders of the 104th Congress targeted liberal advocacy groups—with the assistance of conservative advocacy groups like the Heritage Foundation, the Cato Institute, and the Washington Legal Foundation. It is difficult to confirm the claim that public interest groups received as much as one-third of their money from the federal government at the start of the Reagan administration, but there is no doubt that they depend on the tax-exempt status of the private contributions that they receive. Under the Internal Revenue Code, groups that lobby public authorities are not eligible for tax-exempt status, and Republican strategists believed that this provision could be used against many of the advocacy groups that campaigned for social and economic regulation. But it proved relatively easy for public interest groups to sidestep this and other attacks. Lobbying responsibilities could be assigned to a legally separate subsidiary of an organization. Foundations and private contributors stood ready to compensate advocacy groups that lost public funding. In fact, the Reagan administration's assault on environmental regulation actually resulted in increased membership and contributions for national environmental organizations. The emergence of conservative advocacy groups has also complicated conservative attempts to cut support for such organizations, because many of the institutional arrangements that support liberal groups also benefit conservative ones.[75]

Interest groups can survive without members because they have patrons. But what explains the influence of these groups, and why do so many "citizen" groups have so few citizens as members? The two questions are related. Members become expendable when advocacy groups can exercise influence without them. Power without popular support becomes a possibility through the use of litigation and because the interest-based policymaking associated with the classic model of group politics in the age of "iron triangles"—stable alliances of interest groups, government agencies, and congressional committees—has been replaced in part by policy formation based on expertise and ideas. Heclo's "village folk" are able to shape public policy because they know the neighborhood, not because they command legions of concerned citizens. Indeed, part of the Republican campaign to disarm liberal advocacy groups was to slash congressional committee staffs because they represented part of the liberal "knowledge base."[76] The new politics of policymaking attempts to open itself "to all those who have ideas and expertise rather than to those who assert interest and preferences."[77] Those admission requirements exclude the great mass of ordinary citizens.

But the requirements do not guarantee that people with ideas and expertise will actually be able to influence public policy. These talented activists gain considerable advantage if they show off their expertise and play up their ideas in Washington, where they can join the inhabitants of one of Heclo's villages. Simply being in Washington means that lobbyists and advocates can form personal relationships with members of congressional committee staffs or members of Congress themselves. They can stay in touch with administrators in regulatory agencies and with fellow activists in allied interest groups. Success in shaping complex regulatory or social welfare policies is the product of day-to-day contacts and the slow work of building a reputation for being knowledgeable, trustworthy, and smart. It is work that can be done only in Washington.[78] Like real estate, lobbying is in large part a matter of location, location, location, but the favored locations are almost all inside the Beltway.

Location carries an interest group to the threshold of power. Crossing the threshold is now much easier than it was before the public interest legislation of the 1970s opened bureaucratic decision-making to advocacy groups. The Federal Advisory Committee Act of 1972 is one of many relatively obscure statutes that significantly enhance interest-group access to the policy-shaping processes that operate deep within the executive branch. One of the law's purposes was to control the proliferation of formal advisory groups created by statute or by bureaucratic authority. But "worry that special interests had captured advisory committees and were thus exercising undue influence on public programs" was a concern of at least equal importance.[79]

The law addressed this concern by requiring that the membership of administrative advisory committees be "fairly balanced in terms of the points of view represented and the functions to be performed by the advisory committee." Committee meetings must be open to the public and announced in the *Federal Register* at least fifteen days before they occur. Advisory groups are also required to keep detailed minutes of all meetings, and those minutes must be available for public inspection along with copies of all reports issued, approved, or received by the committee. Members of the public who are interested in the deliberations of the committee are entitled "to attend, appear before, or file statements with any advisory committee." The legislation does allow committees to operate outside of public view in some circumstances, and the courts have not always ruled in favor of plaintiffs trying to use the law to gain access to advisory committees. But advocacy groups ranging from Public Citizen to the Center for Auto Safety to People for the Ethical Treatment of Animals have litigated under the law to challenge policymaking processes from which they believed they had been unjustly excluded.[80]

In principle, laws like the Federal Advisory Committee Act help to open government to all citizens. In practice, however, ordinary citizens do not comb the pages of the *Federal Register* looking for the scheduled meetings of the groups that advise government agencies, and very few know that they are legally entitled to attend these meetings. The potential attendance base is reduced further by the fact that most of the advisory committee meetings occur in Washington. In short, laws guaranteeing public access to government enable a small elite of advocacy groups in Washington to walk in on the workings of government without mobilizing support among the citizens outside government, thus reducing the incentives to engage in mobilization efforts or to maintain a mass membership.

At times, of course, interest groups must demonstrate, especially to elected policymakers, that a large segment of the public—preferably registered voters who are the policymaker's constituents—shares the group's interest. The usual show of support is an outpouring of letters, telephone calls, and (recently) faxes and e-mail messages aimed at public officeholders and endorsing the interest group's position. At one time, an organization might have called on its members to provide this show of support, or it might have launched a broad ground offensive to win grassroots backing from the public at large. Today it has other, more discriminating alternatives.

Political scientist Steven Schier distinguishes between political mobilization and political activation. On the one hand, mobilization was the traditional business of political parties—a general appeal designed to rouse a mass response across a broad range of the electorate. Activation, on the other hand, is the political equivalent of niche marketing. "Successful activation," says Schier, "turns mainly on accurate identification of the appropriate audience and the appropriate tone and content for that audience." Activation is the product of interest-group economics and modern technology. General mobilization is expensive and unpredictable. A massive propaganda campaign may succeed only in triggering countermobilization by the opposition. But even if a group's message reaches an entirely sympathetic audience, it is wasted noise unless the recipients are inclined to act on the message. Interest groups must therefore be able to target not just their likely supporters but also those supporters who are most likely to take political action on behalf of the group cause. Groups accordingly aim their messages at citizens with high levels of education, income, and political knowledge who have been politically active in the past. The strategy, in other words, does not expand the universe of political activists. It simply reinforces existing inequalities between the politically connected and the disengaged.[81]

Even organizations with mass memberships, like AARP, the National Federation of Independent Business, and the Sierra Club, stratify their members according to the likelihood that they will respond to the group's appeals. The Sierra Club, for example, has approximately 500,000 members, but only 15,000 receive its political newsletter, and only about 5,000 of these—the so-called core group—are regularly activated by the organization. They are the association's state and local officers along with a handful of volunteer activists who can be counted on to swing into action when the club calls. Such narrowly focused activation is not far removed from so-called grasstops lobbying, used by interest groups to activate the handful of powerful people likely to have especially close relationships with the political decision-makers who are the ultimate targets of group influence.[82]

Activation is one species of "outside lobbying," an attempt to influence public decision-makers indirectly, by provoking the public to which they presumably respond. Interest groups that engage in outside lobbying direct their efforts outside the government in order to get what they want from the insiders. But their appeals are frequently directed at audiences outside the interest group itself, at people with whom the organization has only a momentary connection. Indeed, the organization may hire an outside company to do its outside lobbying—a direct-mail specialist, a public relations firm, a political consultant, or even an Internet expert. In effect, outside lobbying can be an interest group's way of "outsourcing" membership. Instead of having to maintain a steady following, the organization calls up a temporary constituency when it needs one and thus frees itself to shift its ground when political circumstances war-rant. The constituency needed for this year's battle in Congress may not be suitable for fighting next year's bureaucratic regulation. Like the labor unions that opposed President Clinton on NAFTA but supported him on health care reform, organizations that rely on their own members for lob-bying the government may suffer from political flat-footedness. A group that employs outside lobbying—especially selective activation—may achieve greater political agility than one tied to a large membership base.

Questions arise, of course, about the authenticity of the public opin-ion elicited by outside lobbying. Reviewing a series of recent national lob-bying campaigns, Kenneth Goldman concludes that "little about mass participation in the United States is spontaneous. Rather, interest groups and lobbying firms inside the beltway are increasingly utilizing new and sophisticated techniques to water the grass roots outside the beltway." And what appears to be grass occasionally turns out to be Astroturf. According to Ken Kolman, "it is no secret in Washington today that grass-roots support during the time between elections can, in most cases, be bought. Consulting firms and lobbying specialists can frame an issue in such a way and communicate the issue's urgency to constituents so as to generate any plausible number of telephone calls or letters to members of Congress." Kolman adds that some commercially induced expressions of public opinion can be just as genuine as the spontaneous ones, but he cautions that "in the face of improving technological means to generate phony grass roots, it is vitally important that we come to terms with the ways groups can lead policymakers away from popular policies."[83]

Policymakers will almost certainly be misled if group leaders cannot maintain contact with their own constituencies. For the new public interest and advocacy groups, maintaining contact is apt to be a problem. Vertical connections between interest group leaders and their con-stituents tend to be scarce when groups define their interests "horizon-tally" across diffuse and largely disconnected members of society—consumers, women, the poor, the disabled, the elderly.

Interests defined vertically deal with limited slices of people's lives, often the occupational parts. Unions, industries, professions, and other job-based groupings were the narrow interests that matched up so conve-niently with the narrowly specialized bureaucratic agencies that Pendle-ton Herring wrote about in the 1920s and 1930s, when economic concerns dominated regulatory policy. The vertically defined constituen-cies often included structures of leadership or authority that linked elites to their followers, and these hierarchical relationships increased the like-lihood that leaders would be able to mobilize followers in politics.

Trade associations, labor unions, and professional organizations usually had an existence that preceded their transformation into political interest groups. Horizontally defined constituencies are usually called into being for the purpose of political action, and they have few if any preexisting organizational ties to knit them together. Leadership is usually self-defined. Hierarchies are weak or entirely absent. It is not difficult to understand why the leaders of the new advocacy groups attempt to advance their causes by means other than the mass mobilization of their presumed constituents, and when the group clientele is composed of children, animals, or the mentally ill, the neglect of mobilization strategies requires no explanation at all.

There may be exceptions to the more general pattern of demobilized democracy. In contemporary American politics, for example, the Christian right has been notable for its ability to mobilize a grassroots following. But the movement is also exceptional for its institutional structure. Unlike many other advocacy groups, the fundamentalist right was organized around a network of preexisting church congregations, with their own leader-follower relationships. Though the interests of the Christian right were as comprehensively defined as those of other advocacy groups, it is organizationally distinctive.

The decline of mass political participation in the United States is not simply a consequence of the decay of civil society brought on by television, suburbanization, and the decline of the family. It is in large part a product of state development and of changes in the way political elites define political interests. Beginning with the development of its regulatory capacity after the start of the twentieth century, American government multiplied the mechanisms by which organized interests could achieve their ends without mobilizing their grassroots constituents. Government also multiplied the opportunities for groups to support themselves without relying upon membership contributions.

Mobilization is an exercise of leadership that also imperils leadership, and for a large class of contemporary political interest groups, membership mobilization is difficult or impossible, because they have no members or because their members have only a dues-paying relationship with the organization and no relationships at all with one another. In effect, they have "hired" the organization to be politically active on their behalf. Largely disconnected from their fellow members, they are in no position to become politically active on their *own* behalf. They are disconnected not because society is falling apart but because the interests that they want to advance are those of a large, diffuse, and largely disorganized constituency.

Chapter 7

The Jurisprudence
of Personal Democracy

LONG BEFORE baseball became the national pastime, litigation was practically an American folkway, a popular expedient for resolving private disputes. Americans are still an exceptionally litigious people. Today, however, they resort to lawsuits not merely to settle private differences but to shape public policy, and in this they are aided and abetted by the federal courts themselves.

In the past, judicial self-restraint and a majoritarian political culture deterred unelected judges from substituting their views for those of elected officials.[1] The repeated exercise of judicial activism has eroded such restraint, and the majoritarian spirit of popular democracy has given way to a new personal democracy that exalts the individual citizen's access to the policy process. It is a regime made to order for government by lawsuit. Federal statutes and judicial rulings now enable individual plaintiffs to raise policy questions for resolution by the courts, and the result is that courts have moved from the outskirts to the heart of the policymaking process, where the president and Congress once reigned supreme. These changes have also contributed to a decline of collective mobilization—a decline that is characteristic of personal democracy—because they enable individual litigants to influence public policy without enlisting a larger public to support their claims. They need only mobilize their attorneys.[2]

The Expanding Role of the Courts

In the 1950s and 1960s the expansion of judicial policymaking generally served liberal political objectives—civil rights for racial minorities, civil liberties for individual dissenters. But there is nothing inherently liberal about judicial policymaking. By the end of the 1980s, in fact, federal courts had demonstrated that judicial activism could just as easily serve conservative ends,[3] and in 2000, they demonstrated that it could appoint a conservative president.

The expansion of judicial authority has been championed at times by left, right, and center because litigation, though expensive and uncertain, is far less arduous and risky than the effort to achieve political ends through the mobilization of a popular constituency. In 1988, for example, liberals in Congress supported the Act to Improve the Administration of Justice, which, by limiting the Supreme Court's mandatory jurisdiction to a handful of cases per year, gave the high court almost complete discretion to select cases it deemed important.[4] Environmental groups used the courts to block the construction of highways, dams, and other public projects that threatened not just to damage the environment but to generate material resources that enriched their political rivals. In response to these and other liberal legal offensives, wealthy conservatives and corporations financed organizations like the Pacific Legal Foundation, the National Legal Center for the Public Interest, and the Washington Legal Foundation. These organizations have exploited the litigation option on behalf of crime victims, private property owners who oppose government regulation of land use, and plaintiffs in "reverse discrimination" cases who claim to have suffered as a result of affirmative action programs or legislative redistricting.[5]

But the courts themselves have probably done the most to enhance the political attractiveness of the litigation option. Since the 1960s the Supreme Court has relaxed the rules governing justiciability—the circumstances under which the courts will accept a case for adjudication. The Court, for example, has liberalized the doctrine of standing so that it can hear challenges to the actions of administrative agencies, enable associations to appear as representatives of their members, and permit taxpayers' suits in which First Amendment issues are involved.[6] It has also amended the Rules of Civil Procedure to facilitate class action suits. The class action is a legal device that permits a court to combine the claims of many individuals and to treat those individuals as a class during a lawsuit.[7] In the past, a class could be almost any aggregation of plaintiffs deemed by a court to share a common interest. Recent rules have narrowed the standards for the certification of classes. In 1996, for example, congressional Republicans enacted a prohibition against class actions brought by advocates for immigrants against the Immigration and Naturalization Service (INS) and by Legal Services lawyers on behalf of indigents. For more privileged classes, however, class litigation remains an important political tool.[8]

While increasing opportunities for class action suits, the Supreme Court has also effectively rescinded the abstention doctrine, under which federal courts declined to hear cases not yet resolved by the state courts. It has relaxed the rules governing determinations of mootness and has in practice abandoned the political questions doctrine, which once kept the courts out of policy disputes. Stretching the legal concept of justiciability has broadened the range of issues subject to judicial settlement and allowed a wider range of litigants access to the courts.

But the courts have also made a wider range of remedies available to those litigants. In the past, for example, a federal court might have ruled that a government agency had violated a plaintiff's rights and then have ordered the agency to devise appropriate remedies. Today's federal courts can issue detailed decrees specifying how the agency must conduct its business in the future. Suits challenging conditions in state prisons, for example, have generated an extensive array of court orders detailing the living space, recreational programs, and counseling services that must be provided to all prisoners. Judges have also made use of special masters, under the control of the court, to intervene in the day-to-day operations of institutional defendants such as the Boston school system, the Alabama state prison system, and the Baltimore Housing Authority. In short, the federal judiciary can now offer to private litigants remedies that were once provided to the public at large only through the executive and legislative branches.[9]

The legislative branch itself has encouraged a shift in interest-group politics from lobbying to litigation. In Title II of the 1964 Civil Rights Act, for example, Congress designated the plaintiffs who filed suit under the act as "private attorneys general" because they were contributing to the enforcement of federal law, and the legislation made them eligible to collect attorneys' fees from defendants if they prevailed at trial. This fee-shifting provision was endorsed by the Supreme Court in 1968.[10] In 1976, Congress passed the Civil Rights Attorneys' Fee Awards Act, which allowed for the recovery of attorneys' fees for actions brought under all civil rights laws enacted since 1876. The 1990 Americans with Disabilities Act protects persons with disabilities from discrimination in employment and requires that public services be accessible to them. The legislation created a cause of action that opened the way for extensive litigation by groups championing the rights of the disabled. Likewise, the 1991 Civil Rights Act, which prohibited job discrimination against women as well as minorities, opened the federal courts to litigants claiming to have been the victims of gender bias.

A number of regulatory statutes enacted during the 1970s contain citizen-suit provisions that gave public interest groups the right to challenge the decisions of executive agencies in environmental and consumer fraud cases. Virtually every federal environmental statute authorizes individual citizens and groups to sue private parties for failure to comply with the provisions of federal statutes and regulations and to collect legal fees and expenses if they succeed. Such citizen enforcers act not so much as injured parties seeking to redress a wrong done to them but as private attorneys general serving a public interest.[11] By the mid-1980s, more than 150 federal statutes contained fee-shifting provisions.[12] The Supreme Court has limited the standing of private attorneys general by ruling that litigants must have a demonstrable stake in the outcome of the case and that the remedy sought must be within the court's power to grant.[13] Nevertheless, citizen suits continue to be important mechanisms through which public interest groups can simultaneously achieve policy goals and finance their operations.[14]

Their success was noted and imitated by a coalition of small business groups that won the right to collect attorneys' fees for some cases in which small firms were defending themselves against government regulations. The Equal Access to Justice Act of 1980 allows for the collection of attorneys' fees when individual citizens or business firms successfully defend themselves against "overreaching government actions." Though intended to protect small businesses from the ravages of giant regulatory bureaucracies, the act is often used by trade associations representing giant industrial corporations.[15]

In 2001, the Supreme Court placed restrictions on fee shifting in its 5-4 decision in *Buckhannon v. West Virginia*.[16] The state of West Virginia had voluntarily dropped its opposition to the plaintiff's case after months of litigation. Buckhannon had therefore prevailed only informally, but not as the result of a court decision. For this reason, according to a majority of the Supreme Court, the plaintiff was not entitled to a fee award covering legal expenses. Although some public interest lawyers asserted that this decision would render fee-shifting statutes meaningless, most believed that plaintiffs' attorneys could get around *Buckhannon* by simply demanding damages in addition to equitable relief; by doing so, they prevented their cases from being mooted by the voluntary actions of defendants and, in the process, preserved statutory fee awards, notwithstanding *Buckhannon*.[17]

Taken together, these statutory and jurisprudential changes have opened the way for groups and even citizens acting alone to use the courts to achieve policy goals that might once have required collective political action, if they could have been achieved at all. Litigation has played a significant role in the development of important public policies regarding employment discrimination and voting rights, consumer and worker protection, women's rights, protection of the environment, the rights of the disabled, and the exercise of religion freedom.[18] On issues like racial segregation and women's rights, the federal courts have taken action that we now recognize as essential to democratic fairness but that went far beyond what could have been won at the time in the arena of popular politics.[19] These are victories of principle for which the judiciary is revered.

On the other side, however, opening the courts to organized interests presents at least three major problems. First, litigation allows narrowly defined groups to imprint their interests on national policy without having to create broader coalitions of support or even to defend their positions against the full range of alternative claims that would be more likely to arise in legislative proceedings. Second, litigation often allows advocacy groups to achieve their objectives without mobilizing or even taking account of the needs and preferences of the groups they claim to represent. Third, the expanded importance of litigation as a political tactic has further increased the authority of the judiciary—the least democratic and publicly accountable of America's governmental institutions. This increase comes at the expense of the legislative branch, which, for all its flaws, is still far more representative and democratic than the judiciary exalted behind its bench.

Litigation and the "Cabals of the Few"

Conflicts fought out and resolved before a judge recall the government of lofty lawgivers that James Madison warned against in *Federalist No. 10*. According to Madison, a polity that relies on "enlightened statesmen" to solve its problems is less likely to achieve the public good than one that makes its decisions through the open clash of a multitude of interests in a representative assembly. In other words, Madison's cure for the evils of faction was more factionalism. Free and open debate among as many groups as possible would moderate the influence of any one faction and encourage compromise and coalition formation while frustrating the "cabals of the few."

Courts sometimes permit the few to impose their interests on the public without resorting to the secrecy or machinations of cabals. By comparison with legislative policymaking, judicial proceedings usually permit the active presentation of only a few viewpoints. Interests that might be powerfully articulated in congressional debates or committee hearings may not even have standing to speak in a courtroom.[20] In court, what might have been a cabal of the few finds a political venue where it can show itself in public without shame and acquire the respectability of legal recognition. Collusion can occur almost anywhere in the political process—as in the famous iron triangles that once dominated policymaking in agriculture, military procurement, and other arenas of interest-group politics.[21] But the narrow scope of judicial decision-making actually lends itself to collusive outcomes. Litigating interests often find some common ground that satisfies their needs at the expense of broader interests not represented at trial. Courts can make collusion constitutional.

Collusive Settlements: Taxation through Litigation

Consider, for example, the so-called tobacco settlement among the cigarette manufacturers, most state attorneys general, and a collection of tort lawyers. The settlement appears to satisfy the interests of these participants as well as those of several powerful lobbying groups. The settlement, however, amounts to a new tax upon tobacco, not mandated by any representative body, that will be paid by smokers who had no representation in court. At the same time, the settlement largely ignores and in some respects actually undermines the public's interest in reducing its exposure to tobacco products.

Although the health risks of cigarettes and other tobacco products were known or suspected as early as the 1920s, no smoker ever filed a successful suit for health damages against any tobacco company until the 1990s. There were many unsuccessful suits. In 1984, a plaintiff finally won a jury verdict against a cigarette manufacturer, the Liggett Group, only to see the verdict overturned on appeal.[22]

The tobacco industry followed a litigation strategy designed to exhaust plaintiffs' resources and energies and to discourage trial lawyers from even undertaking cases. The companies consistently refused to compromise or settle any case and appealed every adverse decision to the limit of the law. Plaintiffs' attorneys were compelled to deal with masses of pretrial motions that could have taken years to resolve. The tactic discouraged attorneys from accepting tobacco cases on contingency fees, because they had to face years of legal costs before they could hope to recover anything from a favorable verdict. And a favorable verdict would be followed by years of appeals and retrials, forcing most attorneys to conclude that the costs of filing suit were not justified by the hope of gain in the remote future. Few if any plaintiffs could afford to initiate and fund such proceedings from their own resources.

Between the 1950s and the 1990s, however, a number of developments eroded the tobacco manufacturers' legal position. First, whereas the 1964 surgeon general's report had identified tobacco as a dangerous substance, the 1988 report classified nicotine as an addictive drug. In many instances before 1988, juries had found that plaintiffs knew the risks they ran by smoking but continued to smoke anyway and, therefore, assumed responsibility for the damage that they did themselves. But if nicotine was an addictive drug, then the plaintiffs had been deprived of the power to choose, and the cigarette companies could be held liable for the damages that smokers suffered.[23]

The legal exposure of the tobacco companies increased in 1994, when a paralegal employee at a Louisville law firm retained by Brown & Williamson secretly copied nearly ten thousand pages of the tobacco company's internal documents and memoranda relating to the health risks of smoking. The employee, Merrell Williams, mailed the material to Stanton Glantz, a University of California professor active in the campaign against cigarette smoking, and he quickly made the documents public.[24] The purloined B & W documents revealed that the company had known since the early 1950s that its product caused cancer and other serious diseases. Moreover, twenty-five years before the surgeon general's 1988 report labeling nicotine an addictive drug, the industry's own studies had shown that nicotine was highly addictive. They had also shown that secondhand smoke posed a serious health risk to nonsmokers. Not long afterward, the industry had established a research arm, the Tobacco Industry Research Committee, whose purpose was to prepare nominally scientific studies designed to cast doubt upon publicly available scientific evidence about the hazards of smoking. Knowing that nicotine was an addictive drug, B & W had actually increased nicotine levels in its products in order to make it more difficult for smokers to give up cigarettes.

In the wake of the Williams revelations, a number of prominent plaintiffs' lawyers pooled their financial resources to counter the tobacco companies' legal tactics. They filed several new individual and class action suits on behalf of plaintiffs suffering from smoking-related illnesses. Attorneys could now show that at least one manufacturer, knowing its product to be both dangerous and addictive, deliberately deceived and manipulated its customers without regard for their health or for the health of others exposed to their smoke. Confronted with the evidence, juries awarding substantial damages to several of the plaintiffs.[25] In the meantime, more than forty state attorneys general filed suit against the tobacco companies seeking to recover funds the states claimed to have spent on the treatment of tobacco-linked illnesses among their residents.[26] These suits were followed by others filed by municipalities, union health funds, and insurers seeking to recover similar costs.[27]

Initially, the tobacco companies mounted a vigorous defense against these suits. In 1997, however, the Liggett Group, one of the smallest of the tobacco companies, sought to settle with the state attorneys general. Liggett had been financially weakened by a failed takeover attempt and, near bankruptcy, could not afford the continuing cost of the various suits against the industry. The deal negotiated between Liggett required the company to pay the states $25 million and 25 percent of its pretax income for the next twenty-five years, and to cooperate in suits against the other tobacco companies. The states agreed to help protect Liggett against other damage suits. Consistent with its agreement, Liggett turned over documents implicating the entire tobacco industry in the manipulation of nicotine levels to encourage addiction and in the use of cigarette advertising aimed at snaring teenage smokers. The plaintiffs' attorneys now had a "smoking gun" to use against the industry as a whole.[28]

This smoking gun induced other tobacco companies to begin negotiations with the state attorneys general. In exchange for a multibillion-dollar payment to the states to reimburse them for the costs of treating smokers' illnesses through Medicaid, the industry sought state support for federal legislation that would limit their liability to both individual and class damage suits. An agreement to this effect was reached between the companies and the attorneys general in June 1997. It called for more than $300 billion in payments to the states over twenty-five years. Congress, however, refused to enact the legislation that the industry and states requested. Once the struggle between the industry and its antagonists became a congressional matter, a variety of previously unheard interests voiced their grievances.[29] Antismoking groups thought the bill did not go far enough to reduce cigarette sales. Liberal interest groups saw an opportunity to secure new federal funds for social programs through penalties or taxes levied on tobacco. Conservative forces jumped into the fray to block these efforts. The national media subjected the entire matter to intensive scrutiny. A bill introduced by Senator John McCain in 1998 would have settled all state suits, capped the tobacco manufacturers' civil liability, and compelled the industry to pay more than $500 billion over a twenty-five year period to the federal and state treasuries. Two parties to the original agreement were unhappy with the results of expanding the conflict to take account of broader interests. In particular, the tobacco companies thought the price they were now being asked to pay was too high, whereas trial lawyers representing various plaintiffs in cases against the industry opposed the proposed cap on civil liability for smoking-related damages. After the trial lawyers succeeded in securing the elimination of the liability caps, a vigorous lobbying campaign by the industry defeated the bill.[30]

Once the McCain bill had been torpedoed, the industry, the state attorneys general, and the trial lawyers returned to court—an arena where they were far less likely to confront the interests that had unraveled their legislative plans in Congress. A lawsuit against the industry by the state of Washington led to secret talks in November 1998, involving most of the other states. These talks produced a settlement among the industry, the trial lawyers, and the forty-six attorneys general who had cases pending against the tobacco companies. The remaining four states accepted the general settlement several months later. Under its terms, the companies agreed to pay more than $230 billion to the states over the next twenty-five years, with each state's share determined by formula. The plaintiffs' attorneys in the case stood to receive fees ranging from 9.3 percent of Massachusetts's share to an astonishing 35 percent of Mississippi's, depending upon arbitrators' rulings.[31] The total fees to plaintiffs' attorneys are likely to total $15 billion over the next twenty-five years.[32]

The tobacco manufacturers agreed to the settlement for two reasons. First, they regarded the states as their most dangerous adversaries and feared numerous multibillion-dollar judgments that would have to be paid not from future earnings but immediately, thus bankrupting most of the companies.[33] In fact, the settlement actually gave the industry's most dreaded foes a stake—a $240 billion stake—in the tobacco manufacturers' survival and profitability. The industry calculated that the state governments, the trial lawyers, and others receiving money under the tobacco settlement would now feel compelled to oppose any step that would prevent smokers from buying more cigarettes.[34]

The new tobacco coalitions helped defeat the Clinton administration's efforts in June 2000 to impose more-severe financial penalties and restrictions on the industry.[35] The next month, a consortium of industry lobbyists, state officials, and plaintiffs' lawyers rallied to the industry's defense in response to a Florida jury's decision to impose $150 billion in punitive damages upon the tobacco companies because they had knowingly caused injury to hundreds of thousands of smokers in the state. The companies immediately appealed the verdict. Appeals were expected to last for years, and most legal experts doubted that the decision would be upheld. But until they were decided, Florida law would have required the tobacco companies to post an appeal bond equal to the $150 billion awarded at trial—except that the industry and its new allies in state government had already pushed a bill through the Florida legislature limiting to $100 million the amount that a defendant in a lawsuit had to post to appeal a verdict.[36] Having become beneficiaries of the tobacco industry, state governments and plaintiffs' lawyers were eager to keep it alive and profitable.

For the cigarette companies, the tobacco settlement was both protection against bankruptcy and a means for recruiting political reinforcements, for which they had to accept a relatively small price increase for cigarettes, ranging from twenty-five to forty cents per pack. To guard against the possibility that new companies, not part of the settlement, would attempt to undercut this increased price, the settlement required the participating states to enact laws imposing severe tax burdens on cigarette sales by new tobacco companies.[37] A state that fails to levy this taxes can lose its cut of the tobacco windfall.

Despite heavy taxes, a number of off-brand cigarettes such as Smokin' Joes and Old Smoothies have entered the market and are being sold at prices as little as one-third the cost of the major brands. This development, which threatens tobacco revenues, has upset state governments and led them to look for ways of keeping the upstarts out of the marketplace. "I am disturbed by the proliferation of little companies," said Oklahoma attorney general W. A. Edmondson.[38] Six states have gone to court to try to compel the small companies to pay tens of millions of dollars into escrow accounts to cover the potential costs of future state claims against them. This requirement would effectively put many of the poorly capitalized small companies out of business.

The 1998 tobacco settlement yielded tangible rewards for the tobacco companies, state governments, and some trial lawyers. Most of its costs fell on smokers, generally members of the lower middle class and the working class whose addiction to nicotine makes them a captive market, a fact now acknowledged by all parties to the agreement. The revenues generated by the tobacco settlement may enable some states to reduce or stabilize tax burdens that fall disproportionately on middle- and upper-middle-class taxpayers. For the next twenty-five years these taxpayers will be subsidized by their tobacco-addicted and generally less prosperous fellow citizens.

The more general public interest in curbing the use of tobacco products also suffers. With the exception of an ill-defined pledge to reduce smoking by young people, the settlement devotes only a few million dollars to antismoking efforts. For the most part, the states are simply adding their settlement windfalls to their general revenues. According to one study, only 5 percent of the tobacco settlement revenues received by the states thus far have been used to fund antismoking programs. Indeed, the amount of tobacco money spent by the states on antismoking programs barely exceeds the amount that states spend to subsidize tobacco growers.[39] Some of the trial lawyers are using their newfound fortunes to purchase sports teams and, perhaps, to bankroll a future assault on some other industry that endangers the public, and then protect that industry's profitability to assure that it pays off its court judgments.[40] The states, though they originally filed suit to cover the cost of medical treatment for tobacco-linked illnesses, no longer have any reason to reduce tobacco consumption and every reason to maintain it. They now occupy positions similar to those of national tobacco monopolies in Europe and Asia where governments resist antismoking campaigns.

The tobacco settlement is a case of taxation without representation. It is a narrowly focused and collusive bargain, forged in litigation and validated in court proceedings that were closed to some of the most directly affected interests.

Zones of Interest: Endangered Species versus Endangered Interests

Occasionally, judicial proceedings enable a cabal of the few to dominate not just a particular policy outcome but an entire policy regime. Although Congress is not immune to such manipulation, the courts have an inherent susceptibility to "capture" by a narrow but intensely motivated coalition.[41] Like administrative agencies, but unlike Congress or the presidency, the judiciary lacks a popular political base. Like many bureaucratic agencies, the courts tend to be drawn into long-term alliances with organized groups that can provide them with the political support necessary to enforce their will against the resistance of other institutions, both public and private.[42]

Twenty years of litigation under the Endangered Species Act (ESA) of 1973 illustrate the syndrome. The ESA protects wildlife at risk of extinction. The agency chiefly responsible for administering the act is the U.S. Fish and Wildlife Service (USFWS), which is under the authority of the secretary of the interior, though marine species fall under the authority of the secretary of commerce working through the National Marine Fisheries Service. On behalf of the interior secretary, the USFWS indicates which species are threatened and designates their "critical habitats." But the ESA requires that economic impacts be taken into account when critical habitats are designated. The secretary of the interior may amend a critical habitat proposal if the economic costs of blocking its development outweigh the benefits, so long as this does not result in a species' extinction.[43] Once a species and its critical habitat are properly designated, the act requires that federal agencies refrain from undertaking actions that may have an adverse impact upon them. Any agency that believes its actions might have such an impact is required to seek a written "Biological Opinion" from the USFWS. Agencies are generally prohibited from proceeding with actions likely to jeopardize the species or its habitat. The act also provides for the reintroduction of an endangered species into its historic habitat if is not currently found there.

The ESA allows for enforcement by citizen suits. "Any person" may ask a federal court to enjoin alleged violations of the act or compel the secretary to perform duties required by the act. Citizen suits have become one of the chief enforcement mechanisms under the ESA. But, in practice, "any person" has not meant individual citizens. The "persons" have usually been environmental interest groups, such as Defenders of Wildlife and the Sierra Club, able to initiate federal suits because they can cover the initial expenses with foundation grants or membership dues. If the action succeeds, they can recover their legal expenses through the fee-shifting provisions of the ESA. Given their commitment to environmental protection, these groups invariably argue in favor of the strictest interpretations of the ESA and generally view the claims of property owners, logging companies, land developers, water users, and even federal agencies whose interests might bring them into conflict with wildlife preservation as secondary if not completely irrelevant. Thus, "any person" has come to mean that judicial enforcement of the ESA is initiated by committed environmental activists.

Of course, the statutory declaration that any person can file suit under the act might be interpreted as a grant of legal standing to mining companies, loggers, property developers, and other interests affected by the protection of endangered species. But a number of federal courts sympathetic to the environmentalists' cause—including the Ninth Circuit Court of Appeals, which oversees much of the West—chose to interpret the law differently.[44] One of the key legal decisions defining the term "any person" was the Supreme Court's opinion in *TVA v. Hill*. The Court ruled that economic interests should not weigh as heavily under the ESA as environmental ones.[45] In the Hill case, the Court enjoined the Tennessee Valley Authority from completing a dam upon which it had already spent more than $100 million. A citizen suit brought by an environmental group had charged that the dam would destroy the habitat of a three-inch fish called the snail darter. The Court ruled that the trend toward species extinction must be reversed, "whatever the cost." In short, the costs that environmental protection imposed on companies and communities were not to be taken into account.

Other federal courts ruled that the citizen-suit provisions of the ESA were available only to environmental groups. These rulings extended the so-called zones of interest test of prudential standing initially developed by the Supreme Court in a case involving data-processing services. The test requires that plaintiffs seeking judicial review under a statute providing for citizen suits must show that their interests fall within the "zone of interests" protected by the statute.[46] In a number of cases, federal district and appellate courts held that claims by purely economic interests asserting that they were suffering harm from enforcement of the ESA did not fall within the zone of interests protected by the act, and the courts therefore denied these interests standing to bring suit under the law.[47] This limitation became even more important when the Court extended the scope of the ESA to include the actions of private individuals. Though the act had been aimed at the operations of government agencies, the Court, in response to citizen suits filed by environmental groups, held that ESA's prohibitions against harming an endangered species also applied to the actions of private persons on private land.[48] In this particular case, a group of landowners, loggers, and families dependent upon forest product industries were prevented from developing private lands because of an alleged threat to the critical habitat of the red-cockaded woodpecker and the northern spotted owl.[49]

Another group of private citizens who ran afoul of the ESA consisted of cattle and sheep ranchers in Idaho, New Mexico, Montana, and Wyoming. In 1995, under pressure from environmental groups to obey the act's mandate to reintroduce endangered species into their historic habitats, the USFWS began releasing populations of wolves imported from Mexico and Canada into several national parks where they had not existed for many decades.[50] The wolves soon began leaving the parks and attacking livestock and dogs on ranches in surrounding areas. Local ranchers discovered they had little or no legal redress. The act's citizen-suit provisions were not available to them, and under federal law, the government is not liable for the actions of wild animals even when the government itself placed the animals in a position to do harm.[51]

Ranchers responded with their own "shoot, shovel, and shut up" solution to the wolf problem. They killed the animals and buried the carcasses where they were unlikely to be found by federal authorities. One of the ranchers, however, a Montana man named Chad McKittrick, was caught and sentenced to six months in federal prison for killing a gray wolf in Red Lodge, Montana. The wolf was part of a pack of Canadian wolves that had been brought to Yellowstone National Park by the USFWS. McKittrick's attorney argued that the gray wolf was certainly not an endangered species in Canada—where the wolves are apparently thriving—and had not even been listed under the ESA as an endangered animal. But the Ninth Circuit Court of Appeals, relying on a novel argument advanced by attorneys for environmental groups, held that the Canadian gray wolf had become endangered the moment USFWS workers transported it across the border from its home in Canada and that the wolf was therefore protected under the statute.[52]

Although environmental interests dominated the courts, their influence in Congress was challenged by the various economic and political interests the courts were not willing to hear. After the Supreme Court's *TVA v. Hill* decision declaring environmental concerns to have priority "whatever the cost," Congress amended the ESA to create the Endangered Species Committee, nicknamed the "God Squad," empowered to grant exemptions from the ESA when a national or regional public interest or economic concern outweighed the need to preserve an endangered species. The God Squad, however, seldom granted such exemptions, and commercial and property interests continued to press for relaxation or even outright elimination of the ESA. A number of bills loosening ESA rules were introduced during the 1990s, and President George Bush called the ESA a "broken law that must not stand."[53]

By 1997, the Republican-controlled Congress, responding to a militant new interest—the property-rights movement based in the West— began to draft legislative proposals designed to water down ESA restrictions on private development and land use.[54] In July 2000, the USFWS responded to Congressional pressure by proposing rule changes that would allow federal agents, but not ranchers, to kill gray wolves that posed a threat to livestock,[55] and the Clinton administration urged the use of procedures that minimized the impact of the ESA upon private landowners. In what might be seen as a parting shot at the ranchers, however, the USFWS proposed returning grizzly bears, a species somewhat more formidable than gray wolves, to a spot along the border between Idaho and Montana.[56]

The Supreme Court may actually have diminished the congressional threat to the survival of the ESA by issuing a decision unfavorable to environmental groups in 1997. In *Bennett v. Spear*,[57] the Court ruled that commercial and other interests could use the ESA's citizen-suit provisions to claim that their property rights were being violated by aggressive enforcement of the ESA. In other words, ranchers concerned about the reintroduction of wolves, or developers accused of encroaching upon an endangered bird's critical habitat, could now bring suit to charge that the act was being overenforced. By including property owners and business firms within the zone of interests covered by the ESA, the *Bennett* decision may have saved the act from extinction.[58]

The decision also marked the end of a twenty-year period in which the federal courts seemed to be captives of environmental organizations determined to protect species at all costs. The courts ruled that economic interests could not be taken into account under the act, applied the ESA to private landowners, and refused to grant property owners standing under the act's citizen-suit provisions even though the language of the act stated that "any person" was entitled to a day in court. The interests excluded from court found a hearing in Congress, just as Madison would have predicted, and it was Congress whose institutional influence was largely responsible for breaking the judicial monopoly of the environmentalists.

Using Litigation to Settle Scores

In addition to the dangers of collusion and capture, judicial proceedings also suffer from a third institutional shortcoming. An interest too narrowly defined to be confident of success against its rivals in congressional or electoral politics may find that the courts offer a more congenial forum for its purposes. In court, a narrowly defined interest needs only to convince a judge of the virtues of its position. It need not prevail against the opponents and rivals it would have to confront in the free play of American politics. The judiciary can be a great equalizer. It has protected the politically helpless and defended the rights of the weak, but it can also bestow profit on the privileged when they cannot secure it democratically or competitively. One of the more unseemly examples of this phenomenon is what might be called "competitor litigation," in which firms use the courts to challenge and defeat rivals whom they could not best in competitive markets or democratic politics.

A case in point is the breakup of the American Telephone and Telegraph Company (AT&T), which resulted from the settlement of a Justice Department suit against the company and was completed in January 1984. The outcome was, in large part, the work of MCI and other new firms trying to enter the telecommunications market in the 1960s and 1970s.[59] AT&T's rivals were not able to defeat it in the marketplace, nor were they successful in persuading Congress to enact legislation favorable to their interests. Having struck out in politics and the market, MCI and the others went to court, alleging that AT&T and its operating companies represented a conspiracy to preserve monopoly power against newcomers in the telecommunications field.

In 1974, MCI was able to convince the Justice Department attorneys, eager to demonstrate the department's commitment to the then prevailing notions of the public interest, to charge AT&T with a variety of monopolistic practices in violation of the Sherman Act and other federal antimonopoly statutes. During the lengthy trial that ensued, MCI officials provided hours of testimony and thousands of pages of documents that it had obtained from AT&T during prior litigation, and helped the government to secure the services of expert witnesses against AT&T. Ultimately, AT&T was compelled to accept its own dismemberment. MCI had succeeded through litigation in bringing about a result it had not been able to achieve in more public venues.

The Justice Department's ongoing antitrust case against the Microsoft Corporation is not substantially different from its action against AT&T. Microsoft is currently appealing a federal court finding that the company engages in illegal monopolistic practices—the basis for U.S. District Judge Thomas Penfield Jackson's June 2000 order that the company be split into two independent firms. Microsoft founder Bill Gates has frequently asserted that the antitrust case was actually the work of the company's competitors, and there is evidence that he may be correct.

The Justice Department's case was initiated after the department received a 222-page report titled "White Paper Regarding the Recent Anticompetitive Practices of the Microsoft Corporation." The white paper was written in the summer of 1996 by attorneys for Netscape Communications, Microsoft's chief competitor in the market for Internet browsers.[60] The paper detailed Microsoft's allegedly illicit business practices. Netscape sent copies of its white paper to the Justice Department and to the attorneys general of a number of states. The company also sought to interest members of Congress in its problems but failed to win significant legislative backing. The Justice Department, however, was interested. The legal and economic theories of the Netscape white paper—even its language—would turn up in the Justice Department brief against Microsoft two years later.

Netscape could not force the Justice Department to take up its cause, but it did introduce ambitious federal prosecutors to a case big enough to make their reputations, along with much of the legal ammunition needed to make it succeed. It was Netscape, not the Justice Department, that first conceived of the idea of an antitrust suit against Microsoft. Former Netscape general counsel Roberta Katz said that prior to Netscape's intervention, the Justice Department "did not understand the Internet or software" and "had a lot of learning to do." Katz added, "My whole approach was to get to the point where they really understood what was going on."[61] In addition to the accusations against Microsoft, the Netscape document contained materials that Netscape had received from other computer companies, materials suggesting that Microsoft had violated a 1996 consent decree in which it promised not to compel users of its Windows software to feature its Explorer browser over Netscape's Navigator browser.

Netscape also sent copies of its white paper to the heads of a small number of other firms involved in the computer and software businesses in an effort to enlist them in the legal campaign against Microsoft. Subsequently, several of these companies, including Time Warner, Disney, Sabre, Palm, Sun Microsystems, and America Online, provided information and testimony to the Justice Department. Apple Computer and several others produced their own anti-Microsoft white papers, detailing allegations of illegal practices by the software giant.

Microsoft responded to its legal defeat by mounting a huge public relations and lobbying campaign aimed at swaying popular and congressional opinion. Part of this effort involved the common ploy of creating or funding "citizens' groups" that lobbied on Microsoft's behalf and sponsored advertisements and press releases criticizing the Justice Department's case against Microsoft. Judging that Microsoft's campaign was having some success, rival software companies moved to discredit these groups by publicly revealing their ties to Microsoft. To this end, Microsoft's rivals engaged in various forms of corporate espionage. For example, laptop computers containing information about Microsoft's contributions to a group calling itself Citizens for a Sound Economy had been stolen from the group's offices. This group had inspired pro-Microsoft op-ed pieces in newspapers and urged Congress to block funds for the Justice Department's antitrust case.[62] Subsequently, information obtained from the laptops became the basis for a number of newspaper articles exposing Microsoft's propaganda campaign. In a similar vein, the Independent Institute, a group that sponsored pro-Microsoft newspaper ads in June 1999, reported that laptop computers were stolen from its offices. The computers contained information indicating that Microsoft had paid for the ads. The information was later given to the *New York Times* by "a Microsoft adversary associated with the computer industry," an adversary that the *Times* refused to name.[63]

In June 2000, the *Wall Street Journal* reported that one of Microsoft's rivals, Oracle Corporation, had hired Washington private investigator Terry Lenzner to collect information about Microsoft and its allies that might be useful to the government's case.[64] Lenzner, a veteran of so-called opposition research, specialized in locating the skeletons in people's closets—or their garbage. He had previously attracted attention for his efforts to obtain information that might discredit the various women who made allegations of sexual improprieties against President Bill Clinton. One pro-Microsoft lobbying group, the Association for Competitive Technology, charged that after leasing space in its office building, Lenzner's employees had twice sought to purchase the association's trash from night cleaning crews—a practice known as "dumpster diving." Lenzner refused to comment, but critics noted that the tactic was remarkably similar to one the detective had characterized in a 1998 magazine profile as a "very creative" means of securing information.

Tough tactics are common in competitive markets, as they are in adversary proceedings at law. But market rivalries have traditionally been resolved through competition, not litigation. Within the narrow confines of the courtroom, Microsoft's competitors were able to accomplish what they had failed to achieve on the broader playing fields of the Congress and the market. It is by no means clear just how the public interest is served by processes that permit economic rivals to short-circuit the market and use the federal courts to do business on their behalf.[65]

Mobilization and Representation

Economic, social, and political interests often prefer litigation precisely because by litigating, as legal scholar Stephen Yeazell puts it, they can "dispense with the costs of creating an organization."[66] Litigation, of course, has its limitations. Political scientist Gerald Rosenberg suggests that the courtroom accomplishments of groups battling for civil rights, women's rights, the environment, and criminal-law reform were relatively ineffective, despite decades of litigation.[67] But such assessments overlook two vital considerations. First, they fail to take account of the extent to which litigating groups can prosper even though they make little progress toward their declared social or political objectives. Some advocacy groups flourish when their causes seem most threatened. Others prosper more by litigating than by succeeding. A second and more serious problem is that the advocates are often self-appointed. Those who claim to speak for particular social goals or to serve as the agents of deserving groups speak mainly for themselves.[68] "Pseudo-representation" is not unique to the courts, but the judiciary is probably most susceptible to it. Advocacy groups that campaign to elect their friends to public office or lobby to achieve their ends by legislation are usually forced to mobilize large numbers of supporters if they hope to be successful. The existence of an organized body of followers, in turn, operates as a check upon group leaders. Elite venality or departure from the group's agenda may result in membership disaffection and, ultimately, challenges to the leadership's authority. The history of the American labor movement, for example, is replete with examples of reformers charging entrenched union leaders with corruption and malfeasance, and campaigning for their dismissal—sometimes successfully.[69]

In the courts, however, group effectiveness need not be diminished merely because interested parties have not bothered to organize a substantial following. Most class action and other mass tort attorneys, for example, indicate that they see no particular reason for actually mobilizing the classes they claim to represent.[70] In fact, as we have already seen, one of the attractions of litigation is that it allows narrowly focused groups to take on more broadly based rivals and to do so on roughly equal terms. Having little actual incentive to organize a following, groups that pursue litigation will usually refrain from political mobilization. It would only expose their relative weakness. Some groups have even dispensed with the popular followings they built before deciding to shift their energies from the legislating to litigation.[71] Political organization and mobilization are difficult and costly endeavors that, among other things, may require leaders to share the spoils of victory with their erstwhile supporters.[72] Political and economic interests are typically unwilling to bear these costs if they can achieve their goals without incurring them.[73]

Pseudo-representation becomes an acute problem in the courts because interests that turn to litigation in place of other forms of political action speak—or at least claim to speak—for a constituency that has no tangible existence except, perhaps, as a list of signatures collected by attorneys in the course of class litigation. Citizens who become part of a court-certified class have little actual control over the litigation launched on their behalf.[74] Under some circumstances, in fact, plaintiffs cannot opt out of a class even if they are dissatisfied with the representation they have received.[75] Law professors Jonathan Macey and Geoffrey Miller argue that in most of these cases the plaintiffs are merely names on paper and the attorney is an entrepreneur exercising plenary control over the case.[76] Where the beneficiaries of litigation are presumed rather than formally defined, say breathers of polluted air or victims of school segregation, constituents have even less control over the actions of their self-proclaimed representatives.[77] Lacking any concrete existence, these hypothetical classes also lack any concrete impact upon the conduct of their legal champions.[78]

Policymaking through Litigation: The Class Action

One form of litigation through which a few parties purport to represent the interests of large, unorganized constituencies is the class action suit. Class actions are provided for by Rule 23 of the Federal Rules of Civil Procedure as adopted by the Supreme Court in 1966. Rule 23 allows the common claims of an entire class to be adjudicated in a single proceeding and permits the class to be represented by a common attorney or group of attorneys.[79] From the perspective of the courts, class actions promote efficiency by allowing he courts to consolidate what might otherwise blossom into hundreds or even thousands of almost identical cases. From the plaintiffs' perspective, class actions can be desirable because they provide an avenue for making claims that, individually, might be too small to justify the costs of litigation but, in combination with other similar claims, allow them to seek redress for damages they believe they have suffered.

Perhaps most important, say proponents of class action, is the opportunity it offers to reinforce the regulatory efforts of the government by deputizing private parties to orchestrate collective litigation to right social wrongs that the state has failed to address.[80] Class action suits filed against the manufacturers of defective products or dealers in shady securities serve a public interest that public authorities may have overlooked. When the Supreme Court eased class action rules in 1966, for example, many liberals envisioned civil rights attorneys using this instrument to strengthen enforcement of the new civil rights laws. Citizen-initiated class actions have their counterparts in the administrative practices common in early modern Europe by which princes contracted with private tax farmers, bounty hunters, condottieri, and privateers like Sir Francis Drake to compensate for the state's own inability to collect taxes, bring criminals to justice, and wage war on land or the high seas. Modern states abandoned these practices in favor of state bureaucracies specializing in tax collection, law enforcement, and war making. Private government proved to be inefficient, prone to abuse, and, ultimately, incompatible with popular sovereignty.[81] As economists might say, the agency costs associated with tax farmers, mercenaries, and privateers were too high.

Reliance on private parties to advance the state's regulatory interests through class litigation turns out to be prone to similar abuses, and it may also be incompatible with popular sovereignty. Class actions rarely arise because some group of citizens recognize a common grievance and join together to seek a legal remedy. Instead, these cases are usually initiated by entrepreneurial attorneys who ferret out potential violations of the law and then track down the potential plaintiffs who may have suffered injury because of these violations.[82]

Such entrepreneurial activity is common throughout politics. Groups protesting abortion or marching against capital punishment or lobbying for more Medicare spending do not arise spontaneously. Entrepreneurial politicians form and sustain interest groups. Unlike the parties to a class action suit, however, the members of an interest group can argue with their leaders or even fire them. In 1965, for example, the membership of the Student Nonviolent Coordinating Committee (SNCC) decided that one of its founding leaders, John Lewis, was insufficiently radical and deposed him in favor of the more militant Stokely Carmichael, thus changing the course of the civil rights movement.[83] When leaders of organized interest groups get out of step with their followers, they place their jobs at risk.

Class action attorneys need have no such worries. They do not need to mobilize a following, only a lead, or representative, plaintiff and usually, though not always, the formal consent of other members of the supposedly aggrieved group to speak for their interests. The lead plaintiff is often supplied by the law firm itself. For example, John Coffee notes that a Mr. Harry Lewis, who possessed an uncommonly broad securities portfolio, served as the named plaintiff in several hundred securities cases.[84] Some of these quasi-professional lead plaintiffs have financial arrangements with the firm bringing the case. In other words, it is not the client who retains the attorneys, but the attorneys who hire the client.

The other members of the class usually consist of people who have been identified as potential victims of the abuse in question. Attorneys typically solicit these would-be plaintiffs by direct mail or through third parties such as medical clinics.[85] Once the class members sign consent forms giving the law firm permission to represent them in the case, they are unlikely to hear anything further from their advocates until they receive notice of settlement. Not all members of a certified class must give their consent to be represented. For purposes of settlement, a class may include potential future claimants whose injury may not yet have manifested itself. Examples might include smokers or persons exposed to asbestos who have not yet suffered any harm. These prospective plaintiffs may be bound by a settlement to which they have not explicitly consented,[86] and because the defendant, not the nominal client, pays the attorneys' fees, the plaintiffs have no leverage over the attorneys who claim to represent them.

Since the plaintiffs in class action suits have little or no actual control over the attorneys who represent them, the stage is set for attorneys to pursue their own interests, which may differ not only from those of their clients but also from the interest of the public at large. According to Coffee, for example, collusive or sweetheart deals between attorneys and defendants at the expense of plaintiffs are a serious problem in class litigation.[87] Such deals typically involve an agreement between the plaintiffs' attorneys and the defendant to a settlement that involves a high fee for the attorneys and a low damage recovery for the plaintiffs. One example is the so-called coupon, or in-kind, settlement, in which the plaintiffs' attorneys receive cash and the actual plaintiffs receive coupons allowing them a discount on future purchases of the allegedly defective product.[88] In one such case, each purchaser of an allegedly defective General Motors pickup truck received a coupon worth $1,000 toward the purchase of a similar truck. The attorneys bringing the suit received nearly $10 million in cash. In a similar case, the class plaintiffs in a suit regarding price fixing by domestic airlines received discount coupons on future air travel. The attorneys were paid $14 million. In most coupon settlements, only a small percentage of the coupons were ever used, which further reduces the cost of the settlement to the defendants.

But even these coupon-winning plaintiffs fared better than the nominal victors in a suit alleging that the Ford Bronco II had an unfortunate tendency to roll over. The vehicle's owners received no pecuniary compensation but were awarded a package of benefits that included a flashlight, a safe-driving video, and a road atlas. Their attorneys accepted $4 million in cash.[89] Even worse were the putative clients of a law firm that built a lucrative practice suing banks over the handling of mortgage escrow accounts on behalf of the mortgagees. In several cases, the firm reached settlements in which the banks agreed to pay the plaintiffs' lawyers with funds drawn directly from the plaintiffs' escrow accounts, leaving the nominal beneficiaries of the litigation poorer than they had been before.[90]

According to Coffee, collusion grows out of the very structure of the class action process.[91] Clients have no control over their attorneys. Attorneys' fees are usually determined by the "lodestar" formula on the basis of the amount of time spent on the case, giving attorneys an incentive to settle quickly once they have reached the maximum number of billable hours a court is likely to allow. Moreover, challenges to settlements are difficult to mount. Although in recent years, courts have refused to allow several clearly collusive settlements,[92] in general, courts have their own incentives to accept settlements at face value and seldom interfere with an agreement that seems to satisfy the plaintiff and the defendant.[93]

Even these settlements might be acceptable if class litigation actually augmented the government's administrative and regulatory capacities. Though individual plaintiffs may receive little, the cumulative cost of many small awards may add up to serious punishment for the defendant and a deterrent to future misconduct by others. But the relationship between class litigation and the public interest is problematic. Like the tax farmers, condottieri, and bounty hunters who preceded them, the plaintiffs' attorneys are untrustworthy servants of public authority because they are in a position to substitute their private interests for those of the state and the public. Bounty hunters tended to employ excessive and indiscriminate violence. Mercenaries often displayed insufficient zeal against the enemy, sometimes accepting bribes to leave the field of battle. Tax farmers squeezed and angered the populace but took such a large share of what they collected that little was left for the public coffers.

In a similar manner, plaintiffs' attorneys can substitute their private pecuniary interests for the public's administrative and regulatory interests.[94] Like bounty hunters, class action attorneys tend toward excessive enforcement of certain types of regulations. In particular, they tend to piggyback on the government's existing law enforcement efforts, using them as a guide to the selection of cases that are easy to win.[95] In antitrust law, for example, plaintiffs' attorneys are likely to follow in the wake of some earlier proceeding by a government agency, such as the Federal Trade Commission, or a criminal action brought by the Justice Department. Prior governmental action produces a mountain of documentary evidence at no cost to class action attorneys, and if the government's enforcement efforts succeeded in court, similar private suits are likely to succeed as well. It follows that class action attorneys have an incentive to engage in redundant overenforcement of regulations to which the government is already devoting considerable attention, and the efforts of "private attorneys general" might be directed more usefully elsewhere.

At the same time, like Renaissance condottieri, plaintiffs' attorneys often accept bribes from the nominal enemy to leave the field of battle. As noted above, collusive arrangements are common in the realm of class litigation. Class action attorneys, who have little allegiance to their clients and almost no contact with them, may work out settlements that actually enhance the capacity of defendants to continue the harmful activity in which they were engaged. The tobacco settlement is a case in point. The public's interest in reducing the damage produced by tobacco use was subordinated to the interests of trial lawyers and others who put themselves in a position to profit from the continuing sale of cigarettes.

Finally, like tax farmers, plaintiffs' attorneys harass and infuriate tax payers while keeping for themselves the lion's share of what they take in. One case in point is the infamous Agent Orange product liability case. The defendants, consisting of various chemical companies, were charged with responsibility for a number of illnesses suffered by Vietnam veterans allegedly exposed to a chemical defoliant known as Agent Orange. The defendants spent more than $100 million preparing for trial before finally agreeing to a settlement. The settlement called for payments of approximately $10 million to the plaintiffs' attorneys. A large percentage of this fee went to a group of "investor attorneys" who helped finance the suit but performed no actual legal work.[96] And what did these modern-day tax farmers recover for the public? Each plaintiff received a

$12,000 disability benefit and a $3,400 death benefit. The costs of collection and the fees paid to the collectors left little to distribute to the ostensible beneficiaries of the process.

Unlike collective political action, class action litigation sidesteps the costs of mobilizing a popular constituency and shortchanges the constituents. The class is not an organized group but often the invention of entrepreneurial lawyers, and it has little influence over its legal representatives. These pseudo-representatives are, as a result, free to pursue their own interests at the expense of the formally defined but actually nonexistent group for whom they speak in court. The class that benefits most from class action litigation is composed disproportionately of attorneys.

The Private Attorney General

The problems raised by litigation on behalf of court-certified classes can arise when private attorneys general present themselves to the courts as representatives of abstract interests like "the environment" or diffuse groups such as "the poor." Though the cases are sometimes filed as class actions, the legal representatives of these amorphous claimants scarcely ever ask their supposed clients' permission to speak for them in court, and as a result these "clients" have even less control over their representation than the unfortunate coupon winners in class action suits. Where attorneys are fighting on behalf of abstract goals, as legal scholar Marshall Breger observes, the cause is the true client, not the human beings who happen to serve as its symbolic embodiment.[97]

The term "private attorney general" has been applied by the courts to plaintiffs who are given a cause of action by the state not to seek redress for individual injuries but to facilitate the enforcement of public policies.[98] The first mention of the term came in the 1943 case of *Associated Industries v. Ickes*.[99] It turned on a challenge to a provision of the 1937 Bituminous Coal Act that authorized "any person aggrieved by an order issued by the Bituminous Coal Commission . . . to seek judicial review of the Commission's decision." Judge Jerome Frank of the Federal Circuit Court of Appeals asserted that Congress could enact a statute "conferring on any non-official person, or on a designated group of non-official persons, authority to bring a suit . . . even if the sole purpose is to vindicate the public interest. Such persons, so authorized, are, so to speak, private Attorney Generals [*sic*]."[100]

Today, private attorneys general receive statutory recognition in a variety of federal laws including the civil rights acts, the citizen-suit provisions of environmental statutes, and such diverse pieces of legislation as the Federal Election Campaign Act, the Federal Trade Commission Act, the Natural Gas Act, the Toxic Substances Control Act, the Federal Power Act, the Federal Communications Act, and the Violence against Women Act.[101] An individual or, more often, an advocacy group serving as a private attorney general is conceived to be a principled advocate for a particular public goal.[102] Litigation by a private attorney general is a form of political action aimed at law enforcement and the collective good rather than at the vindication of a particular private claim. In recent years, hundreds of federal court cases have involved advocates claiming to speak for broad public concerns.[103]

In most instances, those undertaking litigation under statutory citizen-suit provisions or similar causes of action are sincere spokespersons for civil rights or environmental quality or some other genuine public concern. Nevertheless, this form of political action through litigation raises a number of concerns. First, those presenting themselves in court as representatives of the poor, women, minorities, and other groups are always self-anointed. Unlike their public counterparts, private attorneys general are neither elected nor appointed by the duly elected representatives of the public they claim to represent. Unlike elected officials, private attorneys general seldom even present survey data showing that the principles they affirm in court are actually supported by members of the groups on whose behalf they are litigating. Discrepancies between the goals sought by advocates and the views of their nominal clients are inevitable. Since the client groups are often large, unorganized, and without clearly articulated interests, these differences are almost always resolved in favor of the advocates.

Harvard law professor Derrick Bell recounts one such case. In 1975, Bell was invited by representatives of black community groups in Boston to meet with them and attorneys for the NAACP Legal Defense Fund, who were planning the next phase of litigation in their effort to desegregate Boston's public schools. The NAACP lawyers were determined to bring about school desegregation through citywide busing of school children. This effort was opposed in the courts by the city administration and in the streets of Boston by violent protests on the part of whites in the working-class neighborhoods whose schools were to be desegregated. But Bell reports that black community groups did not support the NAACP's plans either. Black parents were less concerned with desegregation than with educational quality. They wanted to upgrade the quality of schools in black neighborhoods and to minimize busing to working-class white areas. Though the NAACP attorneys listened politely, according to Bell, they were unmoved. The NAACP, whose paramount goal was school desegregation, did not feel bound by the actual wishes of the black community in Boston, on whose behalf the fight was being waged.[104]

Because black parents in Boston were organized, they were able to communicate their views directly to federal judge W. Arthur Garrity, who adopted some of their positions despite the NAACP attorneys. In other instances, however, advocates using the courts to advance political goals have been able to ignore the wishes—and, perhaps, the real interests—of their unorganized, sometimes impoverished and voiceless clients. In a well-documented Pennsylvania case, for example, a small group of parents and guardians brought suit attacking conditions in the Pinehurst State School and Hospital for retarded children.[105] The lawyer who handled the case and some of the parents who brought the suit wanted to force deinstitutionalization of Pinehurst's patients, and they sought the closure of the institution and its replacement with community-based facilities. As the case developed, however, it turned out that the overwhelming majority of Pinehurst parents wanted to keep the facility open. Their opposition to deinstitutionalization was based on a variety of factors. Some parents may have seen Pinehurst as a safe place for severely retarded children. Others may have wondered whether community-based treatment would actually materialize. But the views of these parents were not taken into account. The lawyer strongly supported the principle of deinstitutionalization and took the position that the parents simply wished to avoid the embarrassment and difficulty of having their disabled children living at home. Accordingly, he argued successfully that the parents' interests were in conflict with those of the children whom he represented and should be disregarded by the court.[106]

Even when advocates accurately reflect the views of some members belonging to a large and diffuse group, they are almost certainly ignoring and misrepresenting the views of other members. Within any large group there inevitably exist significant differences of interest and outlook. It is absurd to claim that all women or all African Americans or all poor people agree on every significant topic that affects them. Once a group organizes and establishes agreed upon procedures for collective decision-making despite internal disagreements, its representatives may have a mandate to speak for the group. But private attorneys general representing large and diffuse groups almost never have such a mandate.[107]

At best, especially where groups are diffuse and issues complicated, those claiming to represent the interests of a group will reflect the views of only a fraction of the group's membership. In the absence of some accepted formula for aggregating preferences, this form of legal representation simply ignores the interests and opinions of many of the individuals for whose benefit the litigation has nominally been undertaken.

Aggregation of preferences through voting rules and mechanisms of representation is, of course, one of the most complex problems in political life.[108] In the case of private attorneys general, at least, the courts have solved the problem by ignoring it.[109]

But the problem does not go away. Advocates of bilingual education have pursued their cases despite the opposition of parents who saw proficiency in English as the necessary ticket for their children's success. Self-proclaimed advocates for people with mental disabilities have used the courts to demand deinstitutionalization over the opposition of some relatives who favored institutionally based treatment. Advocates for the homeless have pressed communities to build shelters, which many of the homeless shun.[110] In these and many other instances, those claiming to litigate on behalf of a needy group are using the courts to assert the interests of one segment of the group against those of others.

Even more problematic are those cases in which the interest being articulated in court is not that of a group but of an even more diffuse public at large. In such cases, the representative plaintiff is a mere stand-in for everybody in general and nobody in particular, and the attorneys are trying to gain the court's sanction for a particular conception of the public interest—their own, or the one held by their client-cum-everyman. The advantage of litigating on behalf of the public interest, of course, is that only a judge, and not the more numerous and various representatives of the public at large, needs to be convinced that some particular definition of the public interest deserves to be placed above others.

Advocates for recent interpretations of the public interest have succeeded in convincing judges—though not necessarily their fellow citizens—that protection of an endangered species takes precedence over all economic considerations, that parents have no right to object to the sex education materials presented to their children in the public schools, that power lines should not be allowed to interfere with scenic views, and that all forms of religious expression should be banned from public settings. The environment, education, aesthetics, and religion are important public concerns. But the particular positions taken by advocates in these cases are not the only plausible expressions of the public interest in these matters. These definitions of the public interest were made the government's definition in deliberations between a self-appointed advocate and a judge.

The absence of a true client for attorneys engaged in public interest litigation leads to still another concern. That absence means that the litigators are responsible only to themselves. Unfortunately, this arrangement sets the stage for conduct whose contribution to the public interest is highly questionable. One example of such an arrangement is a species of environmental litigation frequently undertaken by advocacy groups under the citizen-suit provisions of the Clean Water Act.[111] Like most environmental statutes, the Clean Water Act includes complex record-keeping requirements. The Environmental Protection Agency (EPA), which monitors compliance under the act, routinely reviews the records of firms subject to the requirements. Often EPA auditors find technical deficiencies in a firm's records and order the firm to take remedial action. Where the record-keeping defects are deemed willful or repetitive, the EPA may impose fines or take other actions. But in the case of minor infractions the agency usually declines to take further action.

These minor violations that the government has chosen not to pursue have provided several environmental groups with a steady source of funding for the past twenty years. The groups identify cases from EPA records obtained under the Freedom of Information Act and then bring suit in a federal court under the Clean Water Act to demand the imposition of fines and penalties where the EPA has already determined that these were not warranted. In practice, the penalties are seldom levied, because the advocacy groups agree to drop their suits in return for out-of-court payments that are lower than the potential fines. The money usually goes for the support of some environmental project sponsored by a group allied with the organization bringing the suit. In this case, litigation is little more than a form of extortion masquerading as legal action in the public interest. It is parasitic on the EPA's existing enforcement actions and so adds nothing to environmental law enforcement. Indeed, the advocacy groups involved are so busy stalking record-keeping violators that they seldom pursue other, more serious breaches of environmental law. All this is possible because in the absence of an actual client, these public interest litigators answer only to themselves.[112]

In another variation on the same theme, advocacy groups make widely publicized charges of wrongdoing, usually against some prosperous corporation. These charges are usually accompanied by actual or threatened litigation against the supposed malefactor. Negotiations follow, culminating in a settlement generally involving the creation of vague programs designed to correct the alleged abuse along with payments of various sorts to the advocacy group bringing the charges. This group then declares itself satisfied with the outcome, points to the corporation as a model of good citizenship, and begins the search for another case.

In 1999, for example, Reverend Jesse Jackson's Rainbow/Push Coalition helped mediate the settlement of a class action suit that had been filed against the Boeing Company by several thousand of its African

American workers, who charged that the company showed racial bias in its hiring, pay, and promotion practices. Reverend Jackson initially supported the workers' claims and widely publicized their cause as another example of racism in American industry. After a period of intense negotiation, however, Jackson announced that a favorable settlement had been reached. Under the terms of the agreement, the Boeing workers were to receive an average of $1,768 each.[113] The attorneys representing the workers collected $3.8 million. The Boeing Company agreed to make a $50,000 contribution to Rainbow/Push and to name a person who happened to be a Rainbow/Push board member to monitor the expenditure of several hundred thousand dollars in new antibias programs the company had agreed to create under the terms of the settlement. Outside the terms of the settlement, the company also directed multimillion-dollar contracts to two businesses connected with Rainbow/Push.[114] Boeing chairman Phil Condit and Reverend Jackson pronounced themselves well satisfied with the agreement. Though such settlements generally go unchallenged, a group of dissatisfied African American workers contested this one, claiming they had been betrayed. Attorneys for the dissidents raised pointed questions about the funds Boeing channeled to Jackson's organization. Asked directly by a federal judge whether he thought Jackson had engaged in fraudulent and collusive conduct, the attorney for the dissatisfied workers replied, "No Sir. We believe he was misled."[115]

Interestingly, Reverend Al Sharpton, a one-time Jackson protégé, recently threatened to stage sit-ins and boycotts against the Burger King corporation nominally on behalf of a black franchise holder who was then engaged in a dispute with the company. To Sharpton's dismay, Burger King called in Jesse Jackson, who urged Sharpton to halt his protests. It was later revealed that Jackson's organization had received a $500,000 donation from the company. Sharpton told a reporter, "It is very difficult for me—trained by Jesse Jackson to confront the corporate world—to now go in those same corporate suites, and they use the guy that taught me as their protection."[116]

Politicians who compete in elections or legislative bodies can also be "misled" into believing that their own interests coincide with the public interest. This is one reason for popular concern about the private financing of political campaigns. Large campaign contributions from the wealthy represent incursions of private interest into processes that are supposed to identify the interest of the public at large. The likelihood of self-dealing increases substantially, however, when private interests need not even undergo the formalities of democratic mobilization and consultation. The litigation conducted by private attorneys general and other self-appointed spokespersons is beyond the reach of these constraints.

The litigators need not campaign and have no constituencies. They are not formally accountable to anyone and are seldom compelled to answer to organized adherents or defend their conceptions of the public interest against the multitude of other conceptions likely to emerge in electoral or legislative debate. In the absence of these checks, it is relatively easy to succumb to the comfortable conviction that one's own interest and the public interest are one.

Judicial Power

The importance of litigation as a political tactic both reflects and reinforces the prominence of the judiciary as a decision-making institution in the United States. For two decades, the assertiveness of the courts has been the topic of considerable scholarly commentary.[117] Though familiar, the central point raised by critics of judicial assertiveness is still worth making. In a democracy, the legitimacy of policymaking by the courts rather than by elected officials is always open to question.

The federal courts are sheltered from public criticism of their policy-making role, not just by their undemocratic nature but by the recognition that they have often served as institutional defenders of individual rights and political equality. In fact, they have occasionally intervened to protect the democratic process itself. We should recall, however, that the courts' effectiveness as champions of democratic liberty has frequently been enhanced by other public institutions. In the advancement of civil rights, for example, the president and Congress both had roles to play along with the courts, and the principal force in the struggle was an organized, mobilized, and vibrant civil rights movement that fought for its cause in America's streets as well as its courtrooms—the prime example of mass mobilization in postwar American politics. Litigation accompanied a grassroots campaign of heroic proportions,[118] and this visible evidence of widespread citizen protest lent a democratic legitimacy to the courts' principled decisions. Litigation in this case was a by-product of democratic mobilization. More recently, however, litigation has become a substitute for democratic politics, whose chief beneficiaries are interests unwilling or unable to compete openly in the larger public forum. When self-appointed advocates attempt to make policy through litigation, personal democracy for the few takes precedence over popular democracy for the many.

Chapter 8

Movements without Members

THE IDEA THAT even the most humble citizens are capable of prodigious political feats has always possessed a certain romantic appeal in the literature of politics. Left to themselves, however, ordinary citizens usually lack the financial wherewithal, the organizational skills, and the political knowledge to make more than fleeting appearances on the political stage. They generally require considerable assistance from groups in possession of these resources to secure a more lasting place in the public forum. During the course of American and European history, competing elites brought ordinary folks into the political arena by building organizations and fashioning issues and policies that would appeal to their needs and interests. Elites, moreover, were compelled to broaden their appeals to take account of the views and interests of the common folk, whose political support they coveted. To acquire popular support for political struggle, elites were forced to offer to share the spoils of victory in the form of pledges and programs that would appeal to broad popular interests rather than their own more narrow concerns.

In recent decades, unfortunately, the elites that once activated and organized popular constituencies for political battle have found other ways to achieve their goals. They rely upon the courts, privileged access to the bureaucracy, and "insider" interest-group politics. Contemporary elites have found that they no longer need to engage in the arduous task of building popular followings. As a result, environmental groups have few members, civil rights groups field more attorneys than protestors, and national political parties engage in activation of the few rather than mobilization of the many. Even the 2000 presidential election was decided in the courts rather than the voting booth. This after a pitched battle involving small cadres of political activists rather than armies of voters was fought to decide Florida's electoral vote.

Today, even the most avowedly progressive political movements—movements that once might have been especially likely to mobilize popular followings in the name of political and social reform—pursue their ends through the courts and bureaucracies rather than in the arena of popular politics. As a result, the goals and aims of these movements are closely tied to the confined interests of their upper-middle-class leadership. Freed from the necessity of having to reach beyond their limited class base to accommodate broader constituencies, current reform movements often focus on the narrowly defined desires of affluent elites for comfort, status, and satisfaction of aesthetic needs rather than on the more fundamental material needs of their less fortunate compatriots. How else is one to characterize the "post-materialistic" or "quality of life" issues espoused by so many so-called citizens' groups?[1] To paraphrase Lenin's critique of the working class, left to its own devices, the bourgeoisie seem capable only of consumer consciousness. Three contemporary reform campaigns, the civil rights movement, the environmental movement, and the consumer movement, illustrate the point.

From Civil Rights to Affirmative Action

During the late 1950s and early 1960s, a coalition of African American ministers, intellectuals, and professionals, assisted by allies from the white upper middle class, mobilized a constituency of hundreds of thousands of blacks, including tens of thousands of young activists, on behalf of a broad civil rights agenda. The goals of the movement included voting rights, school desegregation, an end to housing and employment discrimination, and the eradication of what amounted to an apartheid system in public accommodations and transportation, as well as the creation of social programs to relieve poverty and enhance economic opportunities for blacks. This broad agenda served the needs of virtually all elements within the African American community and allowed the movement's leadership to build the strong and united mass base of support that would be needed for the long and perilous struggle ahead. Although the civil rights movement won some vitally important victories in the federal courts, most of its success stemmed from its strategy of mass mobilization.

This mobilization began with the 1955 Montgomery, Alabama, bus boycott led by Dr. Martin Luther King. During the decade that followed the boycott, Dr. King's Southern Christian Leadership Conference (SCLC) and other civil rights groups organized protests, demonstrations, and boycotts throughout the South. King's strategy emphasized nonviolence and passive resistance to the often brutal assaults launched by law enforcement officers and racist thugs who opposed desegregation efforts. A parallel strategy was employed by the Student Nonviolent Coordinating Committee (SNCC). The SNCC leadership organized thousands of black high school and college students in scores of southern cities and towns in a sit-in movement aimed at bringing about the desegregation of lunch counters, stores, movie theaters, and libraries. In a similar vein, beginning in May 1961, the Congress of Racial Equality (CORE) enlisted more than seventy thousand students, most of them black, as Freedom Riders. These students rode buses to more than one hundred southern cities to challenge segregated accommodations. Nearly four thousand Freedom Riders were arrested and thousands of others were subjected to intimidation and violence.

A strategy of nonviolent protest required the active participation of hundreds of thousands of marchers and demonstrators, and boycotts entailed action—or inaction—on the part of hundreds of thousands more. In addition to the activists in the South, millions of both black and white sympathizers in the North were sufficiently engaged by televised accounts of the protests and police violence to demand a response from national institutions and politicians. One indication of the success of this massive popular mobilization was the August 1963 march on Washington, D.C., organized by a coalition of civil rights groups. The march drew as many as 200,000 demonstrators to the capital to protest racial discrimination and press for the enactment of civil rights legislation then being debated in the Congress. The strategy of mass mobilization employed by the civil rights movement achieved a number of notable successes. Between 1957 and 1965, in response to the movement's efforts, Congress enacted several major pieces of civil rights legislation. For example, the 1957 Civil Rights Act established the U.S. Commission on Civil Rights, elevated the importance of the Civil Rights Division of the Justice Department and made it a federal crime to intimidate or threaten individuals attempting to exercise their right to vote.

Subsequently, the 1960 Civil Rights Act authorized the federal government to appoint referees to register voters wherever a "pattern or practice" of discrimination was found by a federal court. The omnibus 1964 Civil Rights Act prohibited discrimination in hotels, restaurants, theaters, and commercial conveyances. The 1964 act, moreover, empowered the attorney general to bring suit against segregated school districts and authorized the withholding of federal aid from segregated schools. The act also outlawed discrimination in employment practices and created the Equal Employment Opportunity Commission (EEOC) to enforce the law. The Voting Rights Act of 1965 empowered the attorney general to appoint federal voting examiners who would replace local registrars and ensure that African Americans would be allowed to register to vote in areas that had previously engaged in discriminatory electoral practices. These pieces of federal legislation, along with a number of federal court decisions dealing with racial discrimination, began the overthrow of the Jim Crow system that had arisen in large portions of the United States—in the North as well as the South—over the preceding century. At the same time, social programs enacted during the presidency of Lyndon Johnson, under the rubric of the Great Society, were aimed, in large measure, at alleviating the poverty of millions of African Americans.

After these initial victories, a number of strains emerged within the civil rights movement. The strategy of popular mobilization employed by Dr. King and the others activated and energized previously quiescent forces from the bottom rungs of the African American socioeconomic ladder. An unanticipated consequence of this process was the emergence of new, militant, activist cadres, who argued that the progress of the movement was much too slow to help the black masses. These new cadres created their own organizations—the Black Panther Party, for example—which rejected the integrationist and nonviolent philosophies theretofore espoused by the civil rights movement in favor of an agenda of black separatism and more forceful confrontation of the white power structure. These new organizations competed vigorously with the African American ministers and professionals who controlled the established civil rights groups for the allegiance of the black community. Even within existing civil rights groups, insurgents charged that the tactics employed by established leaders were insufficiently militant and sought to replace them with leaders committed to more emphatic forms of protest. For example, radical insurgents were able to take control of both the SNCC and CORE during the mid 1960s, leading both groups to adopt more militant stances.

The mobilization of new political forces accompanied by the emergence of militant black leaders contributed to the occurrence of increasingly violent forms of black political protest including serious rioting in the black neighborhoods of a number of major American cities between 1965 and 1967. The assassination of Dr. King in 1968 touched off another wave of violent protests and disturbances throughout the nation. The growing association of the civil rights movement with violence had a number of important consequences. Many of the movement's white sympathizers were alienated by this turn of events. This was especially evident among the movement's many Jewish supporters, who were hurt and offended by the anti-Semitism articulated by some black militants.[2] Black violence also provided some law enforcement agencies with a pretext for campaigns of violent repression. A number of Black Panther leaders, for example, were shot and even killed by police officers and federal agents under questionable circumstances. Black violence also provided ammunition for those white politicians who opposed the civil rights movement, allowing them to present themselves as champions of law and order rather than as proponents of segregation. This strategy played an important role in Republican campaigns after 1966. The promise to curb civil unrest helped Republicans increase their strength in Congress and helped Richard Nixon win the 1968 presidential election. Subsequently, the civil rights movement and its allies found that securing the enactment of significant legislation in the Congress became considerably more difficult, though some victories were achieved, such as the Equal Employment Opportunity Act of 1972.

Militant black groups were generally suppressed by the authorities or starved for funding. However, the threat posed by black militants to the established civil rights leadership and to white support for the movement led the mainstream civil rights organizations to abandon their campaign of mass mobilization. During the 1970s, the civil rights movement turned from a campaign of mass political mobilization to one that relied primarily upon litigation and the use of bureaucratic agencies such as the EEOC. The courts had always played an important part in the efforts of the movement, and the civil rights legislation enacted during the 1960s provided the movement with new causes of action under federal law, especially in the realms of voting rights and employment discrimination. Indeed, the 1972 Equal Employment Opportunity Act, the movement's most important Nixon-era victory, facilitated a litigation strategy by giving the EEOC authority to bring suit against persons or corporations engaging in employment discrimination.

The shift from a strategy of mobilization to a strategy of litigation and bureaucratic struggle had profound consequences for the character of the civil rights movement and the nature of its political objectives. The original agenda of the civil rights movement, consistent with its effort to build a broad base of support, included elements designed to appeal to virtually every segment of the black community. These included antipoverty and social programs for the poor as well as desegregation and voting rights legislation that would serve the interests of all African Americans. The end of the era of mass mobilization also brought a narrowing of the civil rights agenda from one that served the broad interests of the black community to one that served the somewhat narrower interests of the middle class and professional strata from which the movement's leadership was drawn. This new agenda, of course, was affirmative action.

From the late 1960s to the present, affirmative action has been the major focus of the mainstream civil rights organizations. Executive Order 11246, issued by President Lyndon Johnson in September 1965, required businesses holding federal contracts to search aggressively for qualified minority applicants through advertising or special recruitment efforts. Once identified, these applicants were to be considered, on a color-blind basis, along with white applicants. The same executive order created the Office of Federal Contract Compliance Programs (OFCCP) in the Labor Department to monitor contractors' conformity with this standard. Working closely with civil rights groups, the OFCCP quickly expanded its mandate to require federal contractors not only to search for qualified black applicants but also to ensure that blacks would be properly represented in their workforces.[3] This victory demonstrated to the middle-class leadership of the civil rights movement that it could achieve substantial gains for its own social stratum without being compelled to mobilize forces from the lower rungs of the black community's class structure.

Another important bureaucratic and legal victory for the civil rights movement came in 1967, when the EEOC interpreted Title VII of the 1964 Civil Rights Act to require large employers to collect and report data on the racial composition of their workforces. The data indicated that few African Americans held white-collar jobs. The commission responded by developing regulations placing the burden on employers to show that low levels of black representation, especially at the management level, were not the result of biased employment practices. Armed with the commission's data and findings, civil rights lawyers then began to bring cases against firms to force them to hire more African Americans, mainly for the semiprofessional, technical, white-collar, and administrative positions that were sought by middle-class blacks.

In subsequent years, affirmative action virtually supplanted all other goals of the civil rights movement and, as a result, became the cornerstone of the nation's civil rights policy. The OFCCP expanded its efforts to compel federal contractors to demonstrate that their workforces contained substantial numbers of minority employees. The EEOC increased its scrutiny of private and public employment practices. At the same time, other federal agencies began their own affirmative action programs. For example, in 1968, the Small Business Administration (SBA) initiated a program of set-asides guaranteeing that a percentage of federal contracts for small businesses would be reserved for firms owned by African Americans. In a similar vein, the 1977 Public Works Employment Act, which authorized $4 billion for local public works projects, required that at least 10 percent of the dollar value of the work be contracted or subcontracted to black-owned firms. Also, the Department of Health, Education, and Welfare issued regulations interpreting Title VI of the 1964 Civil Rights Act to give wide latitude to affirmative action admissions programs by colleges and universities.

In recent years, of course, affirmative action both in government contracting and college admissions has been subjected to intense attack from conservative quarters and has suffered a number of defeats in the federal courts as well.[4] Nevertheless, the continuation and expansion of affirmative action programs remains the chief goal of most civil rights organizations.[5] Whereas the original civil rights agenda offered benefits for all strata of the black community, affirmative action generally serves the interests of middle-class African Americans. It is the black middle class that is in the best position to benefit from preferences in admission to elite universities, from access to white-collar and managerial positions, and, especially, from set-asides for minority-owned businesses.[6] Partially as a result of the ability of the black middle class to take advantage of the affirmative action policies that were largely irrelevant to the needs of poor blacks, income disparities within the black community had increased sharply by the late 1980s.[7] Conceding this point, prominent African American social scientist Orlando Patterson recently argued that the middle-class slant of affirmative action programs should not be seen as a negative factor. "The argument that affirmative action has done almost nothing for the underclass and poor but favors middle-class workers, while correct, deliberately misleads," Patterson observes. "Affirmative action was never intended to help the poorest and least able members of the minority classes. . . . It is, by its very nature a top-down strategy. . . . For the underclass and working but chronically poor, an entirely different set of bottom-up strategies is called for."[8]

Patterson's argument is quite correct as far as it goes. Affirmative action is an effective mechanism for increasing the opportunities available to middle- and upper-working-class blacks. It might certainly be one important part of a larger package of programs and policies, including education, job creation, and antipoverty efforts designed to serve the needs of every stratum in the black community. These programs, however, have come to be more and more neglected by the civil rights movement. Once it abandoned its strategy of mass mobilization in favor of litigation and bureaucratic struggle, the civil rights movement also diminished its efforts on behalf of the larger black community. Affirmative action for the middle class became the movement's chief preoccupation. In the absence of a need for mass mobilization, the middle-class and professional strata that led the movement have found little reason to pursue a bottom-up policy goal. Instead, working through the courts and the bureaucracy, these leaders have come to focus upon a goal that serves the narrowly defined interests of their own social stratum.

From Saving the Environment to NIMBY

The history of the American environmental movement in important ways parallels that of the civil rights movement. The modern environmental movement began during the 1960s, sparked by rising levels of air pollution in urban areas and such environmental disasters as the death of virtually all plant and animal life in Lake Erie, a massive oil spill in the Santa Barbara Channel, and a fire on the heavily polluted Cuyahoga River in the center of downtown Cleveland, Ohio.[9] A number of books calling attention to environmental problems—such as Rachel Carson's work, *Silent Spring,* on the devastating impact of pesticide use—also played an important role in increasing public awareness of environmental issues.

Growing public concern about the environment led to the creation of several new organizations dedicated to improving environmental quality and reenergized some of the older organizations that had been established as part of the turn-of-the-century conservation movement. The largest organizations, centered in Washington, D.C., included the Sierra Club, the National Wildlife Federation, the National Audubon Society, the Natural Resources Defense Council, the Wilderness Society, and Friends of the Earth.[10] Later, these were joined by other groups including Greenpeace and the Defenders of Wildlife. In addition to the national organizations, a number of energetic local groups also formed during this period. These included the Campaign against Pollution (CAP) in Chicago and the Group against Smog and Pollution (GASP) in Pittsburgh.[11]

Though the majority of active environmentalists were drawn from the middle and upper middle classes, at its inception the environmental movement was definitely a citizens' movement, attracting the support and participation of millions of ordinary Americans with some representation from every social stratum, including members of minority groups. A survey conducted in 1980 found that more than 15 million Americans considered themselves "environmentally active." Activities included becoming involved in environmental groups and campaigns, writing letters to newspapers and politicians protesting environmental degradation, participating in demonstrations, and making financial contributions to environmental causes. The latter amounted to roughly a half billion dollars a year donated by citizens to environmental groups.[12] In some respects, the culmination of citizen activism was Earth Day 1970, organized by a coalition of environmental forces along with such politicians as Wisconsin senator Gaylord Nelson. Earth Day was celebrated by an estimated 20 million Americans who participated in rallies and activities throughout the nation including a huge demonstration on the Mall in Washington, D.C.[13] Consistent with its sizeable citizen base, the environmental movement presented a broad agenda of goals including restoring air, water, and soil quality, restricting the use of chemical pesticides, limiting population growth, controlling hazardous wastes, cleaning up toxic waste sites, protecting plant and animal life endangered by industrial and commercial development, creating renewable energy sources, and protecting employees from workplace hazards and consumers from dangerous products.

Environmental activism helped bring about the enactment of a number of major pieces of legislation during the 1970s designed to address many of the movement's concerns. These included the Clean Air Act of 1970, the Occupational Safety and Health Act of 1970, the Water Pollution Control Act of 1972, the Maritime Protection Act of 1972, the 1972 Federal Insecticide, Fungicide, and Rodenticide Act, the Marine Mammal Protection Act of 1972, the 1973 Endangered Species Act, the Safe Drinking Water Act of 1974, the 1976 Toxic Substances Control Act, the Resource Conservation and Recovery Act of 1976, the 1977 Clean Water Act, and the 1980 Comprehensive Environmental Response, Compensation, and Liability Act (also known as Superfund).[14] It is noteworthy that several of these statutes were enacted during the Nixon administration, which is not remembered as particularly sensitive to environmental concerns. In fact, the enormous scope of environmental activism convinced Nixon and other Republicans that it would be politically expedient to support environmental goals. Indeed, in his 1970 State of the Union address, Richard Nixon called upon Americans to "make peace with nature" and repair "the damage we have done to our air, to our land, and to our water." Journalists called the environment "Nixon's new issue."[15]

The need to administer new environmental programs led to the creation of a substantial environmental bureaucracy in Washington and the state capitals.[16] New federal offices and agencies established during the 1970s included the Environmental Protection Agency, the Occupational Safety and Health Administration, the Council on Environmental Quality, and the Consumer Product Safety Commission. Older federal agencies, such as the Fish and Wildlife Service, took on new environmental tasks. In addition, established federal agencies developed offices to deal with their responsibilities under environmental statutes. For example, the Justice Department created its Environment and Natural Resources Division, and the Department of Energy established an office to study alternative-energy programs. Most states and a number of municipalities also created agencies designed to deal with environmental issues.

In the wake of these successes, the tactics of the environmental movement underwent a significant transformation. First, as we saw in Chapter 7, all the new environmental statutes contained citizen-suit provisions that, in effect, invited environmental groups to use the courts to enforce and expand environmental law. Several environmental groups— including the Natural Resources Defense Fund, and the Sierra Club, through its Legal Defense Fund—had already embarked upon an active program of environmental litigation. Now the others followed suit, expanding their legal staffs and developing active court dockets.[17] Environmentalists welcomed their new statutory opportunities for litigation. They believed the courts would provide an arena in which the economic power of business and other antienvironmental forces could be more easily defeated than in the Congress. The director of the Sierra Club's Legal Defense Fund said environmental litigation "means power for people who don't have economic power. Its one way to fight the political fight."[18]

At the same time that the environmental movement expanded its presence in the courts, it also moved to take advantage of the new environmental offices and agencies created during the 1970s. Environmentalists sought and won appointment to the staffs of the agencies as well as to the various advisory groups that became components of the agencies' rule-making processes. As recognized stakeholders in the environmental policy arena, environmental groups were routinely asked for their comments on proposed regulations as well as their testimony in congressional hearings. During the Carter administration, a number of well-known environmental leaders—such as Joseph Browder of the Environmental Policy Center and Gus Speth and John Bryson, cofounders of the Natural Resources Defense Council—were appointed to federal posts.[19] The extent to which the environmental movement had become part of the government became even more evident during the organization of the first Clinton administration in 1993. Dozens of leaders and staffers from Washington environmental groups were appointed to posts in the new administration. For example, Rafe Pomerance of the World Resources Institute was appointed to an international environmental post at the State Department. Wilderness Society president George Frampton was named to head the Fish and Wildlife Service. Audubon Society lobbyist Brookes Yaeger took a post in the Interior Department. "I can't tell you how wonderful it is," said one environmental official, "to walk down the hall in the White House or a government agency and be greeted by your first name."[20] The movement, it seemed, had successfully stormed the bastions of political power.

Access to the courts and the bureaucracy changed the character of the environmental movement. As national environmental organizations shifted their focus to litigation and bureaucratic infighting, most of them reduced their grassroots recruiting and organizing efforts, becoming staff organizations rather than membership groups. Indeed, during the 1980s and 1990s, membership in the major environmental groups fell sharply, as did financial support from ordinary citizens. Most environmental organizations came to depend heavily on the proceeds from litigation and on grant support from foundations and national corporations for financial sustenance.[21] Financial support from business led to charges that some environmentalists had "tended to develop an all-too-cozy relationship with the industries they set out to battle."[22]

Collusion with business interests, however, was not the most serious problem that developed in the wake of the changes taking place in the environmental movement. When the movement relied upon a broad base of citizen support, as we saw, it also worked on behalf of a broad agenda of environmental issues. As the movement's base narrowed, so did its agenda. Currently, mainstream environmental groups focus upon natural resources, wilderness preservation, and endangered species. Although important, these issues are mainly of concern to a relative small number of upper-middle-class Americans whose material and physical well-being is sufficiently secure to allow them to focus upon the welfare of gray wolves and the aesthetics of wilderness preservation. A host of other environmental problems, particularly those affecting primarily lower-middle-class, working-class, and minority communities have not been major items on the agendas of established environmental groups. These concerns include toxic waste disposal, public health, and the distribution of environmental risks.[23]

The failure of established environmental groups to address major environmental problems has exacerbated what is known as the NIMBY, or "not in my backyard," problem. In many different parts of America, ad hoc local citizens' groups have mobilized against what they have regarded as potential environmental hazards in their own communities. Very often, these have involved efforts by private concerns and public agencies to site hazardous waste disposal facilities in working-class or poor communities presumably deemed to lack the political clout needed to offer serious opposition to the plan. Often enough, this calculation is correct, and the facility is built without significant community opposition. In some instances, however, local residents, perhaps helped by itinerant political activists, are able to mount serious opposition to the disposal of hazardous wastes in their own backyards. In recent years, California seems to have witnessed a number of such NIMBY battles, sometimes involving thousands of ordinary citizens and, on several occasions, forcing governments and corporations to retreat from their siting plans.[24] The ad hoc citizens' coalitions that engage in these fights are often criticized for selfishly seeking to push hazardous sites from their own neighborhoods into the backyards of perhaps even more powerless groups. There is certainly merit to this criticism. These battles would be better fought and resolved on a national rather than a local basis. Yet, the NIMBY phenomenon also shows the potential for grassroots environmental action. Ordinary citizens are willing to engage in political action on behalf of environmental goals that are relevant to their own lives and communities. The mainstream environmental movement, however, has chosen a form of political action that does not entail citizen mobilization. The movement seems to prefer the corridors of power in Washington to the gritty barrios of East Los Angeles. This choice of tactics, in turn, has left the environmental movement free to pursue goals that serve the needs and interests of a relatively small group of elites rather than the concerns of broader popular strata.

Can the Citizen Be Brought Back In?

In the abstract, the factors that induce groups to refrain from pursuing a policy of popular mobilization could easily be changed. The nation might impose strict limits on class action suits and modify or even eliminate citizen-suit provisions in regulatory statutes. These small legislative and juridical changes would have the major consequence of increasing the difficulty of legislating through litigation. This, in turn, might help induce competing interests to mobilize and organize popular followings in support of their legislative agendas rather than deploy staffs of attorneys to achieve their political goals through the courts. A strategy of mobilization and legislation would increase the likelihood that such a group would be compelled to develop a broad agenda rather than pursue narrow and selfish goals.

In a similar vein, we might suggest substantial modification of the various bureaucratic processes, discussed in Chapter 5, that allow political forces direct access to policymaking processes and absolve them of the arduous labor of creating and maintaining popular followings. Though it may seem paradoxical to argue that more-open administrative procedures are inimical to democratic processes, in an important respect they are.

Again, elites that do not need to build popular followings are not likely to do so, and the result is that non-elites are left out of the political process.

As to the "privatization" advocated by some politicians and management gurus, this, as we have seen, often represents a thin cover for the private use of public power. Fannie Mae and the other government-sponsored enterprises, for example, are private institutions that wield public power without being subject to even a modicum of accountability in the political arena. This is a recipe for continuing marginalization of the popular political arena. One could certainly suggest that these practices should be curtailed rather than encouraged.

The notion, however, that what might be true in principle could actually be realized in practice is rather unrealistic. Established political elites have no interest in changing the processes through which they maintain privileged access to power. For example, note the resistance to any significant change in the current system of campaign finance. Those who hold power under a particular set of rules and procedures seldom welcome their modification. It might seem, of course, that new or emergent groups and forces lacking "insider" access to the courts and bureaucracy might engage in old-fashioned popular mobilization to achieve their political goals. Perhaps Ross Perot's independent political campaign in 1992, Ralph Nader's Green Party campaign of 2000, and even the recent series of protests against the World Bank's policies are examples of such efforts. In recent years, however, most insurgent groups have shown a clear understanding of the new politics of personal democracy. These groups have launched campaigns seeking direct access to the courts and to governmental agencies without investing much effort at all in popular mobilization. One example of a set of political forces that from the very beginning abjured citizen mobilization in favor of an immediate strategy of litigation, lobbying, and burrowing into the bureaucracy is the consumer movement.

The contemporary consumer movement was born during the 1960s partly in response to a series of books and news stories highlighting defective products and deceptive business practices. For example, Jessica Mitford's 1963 volume, *The American Way of Death,* exposed fraudulent practices in the funeral industry. In a similar vein, Ralph Nader's *Unsafe at Any Speed,* published in 1965, asserted that a then popular automobile, the Chevrolet Corvair, suffered from design flaws that had led to several fatal accidents. The revelation that General Motors, the Corvair's manufacturer, had engaged in clandestine efforts to discredit Nader only increased the author's prominence and provided more publicity for his allegations. During the same period, a number of highly publicized product safety cases, including the 1960 thalidomide scare, raised additional questions about consumer product safety. Thalidomide was a European tranquilizer linked to birth defects when used by pregnant women.

A number of new organizations were formed and several established groups reenergized in response to the publicity surrounding consumer issues. These included Ralph Nader's Public Citizen, the National Consumers League, the Consumer Federation of America, Consumers Union, the Center for Auto Safety, the Center for Science in the Public Interest, and a host of others. During the late 1960s and the 1970s, consumer groups used media exposés and lobbying campaigns to bring about the enactment of several important pieces of consumer rights and safety legislation. These included the 1968 Truth in Lending Act, the 1972 Consumer Product Safety Act, the 1974 Fair Credit Billing Act, and the 1976 Toxic Substances Control Act.[25]

The large number of groups associated with consumerism hides the fact that most of these groups never had many actual members. They were what John McCarthy and Mayer Zald call "professional social movements" led by a small, full-time staff and purporting to speak for largely unorganized and imagined constituencies.[26] Michael Pertschuk, former chairman of the Federal Trade Commission, argued that the term "movement" misdescribed the character of consumerism. According to Pertschuk, consumer advocacy has been the product of a small number of groups and Washington policy entrepreneurs rather than the result of a grassroots effort.[27] Rather than undertake an effort to build a strong membership base and engage in popular politics aimed at expanding consumer legislation, consumer groups focused their attention on gaining access to the courts and the executive branch. Even when they sought legislation, one of the primary goals of consumer groups was to bring about the enactment of laws that would contain citizen-suit provisions and new causes of action for litigation.

Consumer groups also fought tenaciously for the development of bureaucratic procedures that would open rule-making processes to small groups of policy entrepreneurs. As noted in Chapter 5, the Administrative Procedure Act requires that all interested parties be given an opportunity to comment on proposed federal regulations before these are adopted by any executive agency. Since the 1960s, consumer activists have made full use of this statutory provision to present testimony and file petitions during agency rule-making processes. Indeed, consumer activists sought to go beyond this general right to create an even more favorable environment for intervention into bureaucratic processes that concerned them. During the 1970s, Ralph Nader and other consumer activists fought for the creation of what they called the "Agency for Consumer Advocacy," which would have had the power to intervene in other agencies' rule-making processes on behalf of consumer interests.

Though the idea of a consumer advocacy agency was narrowly defeated in Congress, the 1972 Consumer Product Safety Act did establish a new government agency, the Consumer Product Safety Commission (CPSC), with broad power to recall dangerous products and to issue industry-wide regulations governing product safety.[28] Over the years, the CPSC has been a vehicle through which consumer activists have exercised significant power in the marketplace. CPSC regulations affecting product design and safety have forced manufacturers to negotiate with consumer forces and to make major design changes. For example, CPSC standards have affected the flammability of apparel, the packaging of pharmaceutical products, the design of children's toys and furniture, the characteristics of lawn mowers, and the manufacture of a host of other products used throughout the American economy. Under the law, consumer groups enjoy broad access to CPSC rule-making processes and regularly and successfully petition the agency with regard to new regulatory activity. In many respects, consumer activists set the CPSC's regulatory agenda.

Early in their history, consumer organizations also developed powerful legal arms such as Public Citizen's Litigation Group. In the 1980s, the Litigation Group won several important court decisions limiting Congress's power to overrule regulatory actions by administrative agencies.[29] Having gained access to the regulatory process, consumer groups strongly opposed allowing mere politicians the power to undo their work. In addition, consumer groups have made extensive use of litigation to challenge unfavorable regulatory decisions. The threat of litigation also forced a number of agencies, including the Food and Drug Administration, the Federal Trade Commission, the Department of Transportation, and the National Highway Transportation Safety Administration to give consumer activists greater representation in their own rule-making processes.

The consumer movement has achieved a number of notable successes. As in the case of a number of other movements, however, the absence of a mobilized popular base has narrowed the movement's agenda to issues of interest mainly to the upper-middle-class stratum that staffs and bankrolls the movement and for whom "consumption" is a major life activity. Perusal of recent issues of *Consumer Reports,* a magazine published by the Consumers Union to offer advice on products and services, tells the story. The March 2001 issue, for example, helps consumers choose among competing $700 large-screen color television sets, select among alternative $1,500 home gyms, and decide in which mutual funds to invest. In a similar vein, the January 2001 issue, featuring a photo of a $35,000 Mercedes sport-utility vehicle on its cover, offers advice on auto leases and $400 digital cameras. The editors seem unaware that most Americans have not reached a sufficiently exalted level of consumption to benefit from the advice being offered to them. In the 1960s and 1970s, consumer activists, like their progressive counterparts in the movements we have examined, built a movement without members that relied mainly upon litigation and bureaucratic processes to achieve its ends. This strategy virtually guaranteed that those ends would be very narrowly focused.

Chapter 9

Privatizing the Public

WRITING IN THE early 1950s, political scientists Robert Dahl and Charles Lindblom saw their society uplifted by a tidal surge of innovation in "social techniques." Technological progress, they argued, was not simply a matter of machines and the energy sources that powered them. There was also a technology of organization and politics, and its advancement was "increasing possibilities for rational social reform through the improvement of techniques." But movement toward rational reform through social innovation was also undermining the ideological categories that helped ordinary citizens to make sense of the political world. As governments developed their versatility by incorporating new social techniques into public policies, they dissolved the boundaries between capitalism and socialism, public and private, coercion and persuasion. Most policies turned out to be ideological hybrids or half-breeds that combined "techniques" drawn from disparate systems of political thought.

In fact, ideology itself seemed to be receding as a guide to political thinking and action. Like other observers of America during the 1950s, Dahl and Lindblom anticipated if not an end to ideology, then at least its demotion to a smaller, secondary role in politics. Policy, they wrote, "is technique-minded, and it is becoming increasingly difficult . . . to argue policy in terms of the mythical grand alternatives."[1]

With Daniel Bell, they looked favorably on a "middle way," guided by considerations of effectiveness, efficiency, and feasibility, not the all-

or-nothing temperament of the ideologue. The formula for any new utopia, said Bell, would have "to specify *where* one wants to go, *how* to get there, the costs of the enterprise, and some realization of, and justification for the determination of *who* is to pay."[2] It would have to be a decidedly practical utopia. It would have to make compromises.

The determination to be reasonable did not necessarily exalt rationality. In fact, the elevation of technique was accompanied by a new respect for the shortcomings of human calculation. Exhaustive, synoptic rationality was unattainable—just like the cloudy utopias of the ideologues—and expecting public decision-makers to achieve such austere precision in the messy work of government was unreasonable. Optimizing would have to give way to "satisficing"—settling for the outcome that was good enough rather than the best conceivable.[3]

But postwar receptiveness to new social techniques in public policy also suggested ways of expanding the modest attainments of human reason. Humans could pool their capacities for reasoned decision-making in social arrangements designed to expand the power of calculation and implementation. For example, although unable as individual consumers to determine the optimum allocation of economic resources, humans acting collectively through competitive markets could reach economically efficient distributions. Public policies could create their own quasi-markets as mechanisms of implementation and so turn the invisible hand of the private sector to the service of public purposes. Likewise, a lone decision-maker might not have all the information needed to define public welfare, nor the selflessness to pursue it, but if citizens were given the opportunity to express their preferences, the collective result might approximate the public interest. And if citizens could not be kept continuously on hand to vote for their conceptions of the general will, they could be represented by competing leaders or interest groups who struck bargains that reflected the balance of citizen sentiment. Taken together, the price system, bargaining, and democracy (or polyarchy) offered a powerful armory of devices that could be put to work on behalf of rational social reform.

Hierarchy, the command-and-control technique associated with government bureaucracy, also had its uses, but those uses were offset by a certain bureaucratic flat-footedness. Hierarchy imposed enormous demands on the information and calculation capabilities of top decision-makers. In practice, it was true that the limited vision and insight of top-level executives could be supplemented by the implementation skills of lower-level functionaries, but those subordinates, especially if they were skilled specialists, could resist changes mandated by their superiors. Hierarchy, therefore, might be hostile to innovation. In general, the shortcomings of hierarchy could be overcome only by moderating its top-down discipline with more loose-jointed policy mechanisms like the price system or bargaining that encouraged experimentation and compromise.[4]

Dahl and Lindblom conceded that the demands of warfare might make hierarchical coordination and coercion essential, but it was the experience of war, paradoxically, that helped to accelerate the abandonment of bureaucratic hierarchy. World War II had been the finest hour not just for the country's armed forces but for its government contractors, set to their tasks by a combination of bargaining and competitive bidding. The reliance on private organizations was especially pronounced in the case of the scientific research needed to develop the new weapons and detection systems that revolutionized warfare. These private contractors and grantees had their antecedents in the nongovernmental research organizations of the Progressive Era, like the Brookings Institution, the Russell Sage Foundation, and the National Bureau of Economic Research, all of which provided scarce expertise to government agencies. The wartime scientific establishment that succeeded these institutions begat the Rand Corporation and a host of other think tanks and laboratories nourished by the taxpayers to perform the work of government in peacetime. Government agencies themselves sometimes became little more than holding companies funneling funds to outside contractors. The work done by many of these contractors could often have been performed just as easily by government employees, but personnel ceilings in public agencies and hostility to public bureaucracy made private contracting the only feasible means to advance government agencies' missions.[5]

A longstanding fusion of public and private organization set the stage for the transfer of private-sector "techniques" to the conduct of public business. This was the kind of technology transfer strenuously promoted in the recent movement to "reinvent" government. Its advocates urged that government should become more "market-oriented"—not a big switch for an institution that was already doing much of its work through the market. Nor was it difficult to see how citizens might be reinvented as customers. After all, in its many contracts for goods and services, the government itself was already a customer.[6] The spirit of public entrepreneurship, reinvented as the latest thing in paradigm shifts, had actually been born from more than half a century of government improvisation with "social techniques." It was only on the eve of the Clinton administration, however, that the spirit of reinvention became fully self-conscious and unabashedly celebratory.

Critics wondered whether the administration's emphasis on producing results was consistent with the rule of law, which sharply limited the means that government could use to attain its ends, or whether "customer satisfaction" was the same as public accountability.[7] Behind the guiding maxims of reinvention, however, there was a single powerful premise: Hierarchy did not work, but flexibility did. In a democratic society, the proposition was hardly open to question. Hierarchy meant inequality; it meant authority exercised from the top down, rigidity, subservience, not thinking for oneself. Yet one of the political curiosities of the age is that the abandonment of hierarchy as a principle of government organization and public policy has progressed in tandem with a decline in the democratic mobilization of citizens. Perhaps by becoming less hierarchical, the government increased the points of access that individual citizens could exploit on their own without resorting to collective action. Or perhaps there was something about the abandonment of hierarchy that actually frustrated mobilization.

Long before the reinventors caught Washington's ear, two Hoover Commissions insisted that a starkly defined bureaucratic hierarchy was essential to government accountability. Unity of command and clear lines of authority helped to fix responsibility for public policy—a vital prerequisite for democratic control. Theodore Lowi, in the late 1960s, made a similar point about a congressional tendency to transfer discretion in wholesale lots to the agencies of the executive branch without specifying how that discretion was supposed to be exercised. It was difficult to hold anyone responsible for the results, and ambiguously defined policy invited special interests to shape it in the image of their own private wants. Abandoning the public elitism of bureaucratic hierarchy, with its clear assignment of responsibility, might make government the servant of private elites. But the campaign to make government less government-like could also make the collective mobilization of non-elites less likely.

According to Dahl and Lindblom, hierarchy works through "direct" rather than "indirect" controls. In policies that operate hierarchically, public decision-makers directly inform their bureaucratic subordinates or the public in general what they are supposed to do and (usually) why. Indirect controls are less obtrusive. They get people to do what the government wants not by telling them directly but by changing the incentives or environmental influences that shape their conduct. The essential difference is that direct controls require policymakers to state publicly what they want to accomplish; indirect controls do not. Indeed, indirect controls may even prevent decision-makers from declaring their objectives, because those ends are to be defined through the market, or bargaining, or consultation with citizens.

Public policies that articulate no particular purposes may represent a convenience for political elites because agreement comes more easily when the decision-makers need not arrive at the same understanding of what they are agreeing to. Conflict is limited, as is the inclination to mobilize constituencies. By themselves, diffuse policies may not inhibit popular participation. Vague promises, after all, have been known to win elections. But nonhierarchical policies are also disaggregated policies—decentralized, privatized, or atomized into thousands of market transactions—and while disaggregated policies may be highly effective as "social techniques," they are not conducive to widespread collective mobilization. Daniel Patrick Moynihan recognized this demobilizing potential inherent in disaggregated, market-based policies when he spearheaded the Nixon administration's welfare reform efforts at the beginning of the 1970s:

> An assertion came forth, labeled conservative but in historical terms almost classically liberal, that government administration did not work while the market did. . . . The assertion turned on the issue of incentives, the idea being that the incentive structure of the market was vastly the more powerful. A further argument which may be adduced on behalf of the new conservatism is that diffusing responsibility for social outcomes tends to retard the rise of social distrust when the promised or presumed outcome does not occur.[8]

In other words, the market mechanism is a powerful instrument of public policy that is unlikely to stir up the public. It obscures accountability and disarticulates collective purposes. In dissolving the "mythical grand alternatives" of ideology, the new, nonhierarchical techniques of the public policy specialists also dimmed the rallying cries that helped to make public policy a vehicle for popular mobilization. Privatization, decentralization, and the market are patterns for structuring public policy without a public.

Privatization

Privatization is one way of putting the market to work for government. It introduces competitive bidding into public programs and thereby avoids the supposed inefficiencies of government's monopoly on public services. But privatization is not just a way to get the most for the taxpayer's dollar. It is also an instrument for achieving privileged access to power; and once achieved, that power is sometimes exercised to impose additional costs on American taxpayers.

In the United States, privatization rarely means the outright sale of public assets to private purchasers. There have been exceptions—the sale of public lands to settlers and land transfers as a subsidy to railroads and, more recently, the sale of the government's interest in Conrail. In most cases, however, privatization refers to the use of nongovernmental organizations to run government programs. Today almost every federal agency relies heavily on private contractors. Whereas the federal government directly employs fewer than 2 million civilian workers, one recent study estimates that more than 12 million Americans are employed by a "shadow government" of private corporations, universities, research laboratories, foundations, and state and municipal governments that hold government contracts, receive federal grants, or are required to carry out federal mandates.[9] Many federal agencies have responded to presidential and congressional efforts to "downsize" their workforces by replacing civil service workers with contract employees. Between 1984 and 1996, for example, the Department of Education, in response to presidential directives, reduced its civil service workforce by 6 percent. During the same period, however, the agency's contract workforce increased 129 percent.[10] In this case, at least, downsizing actually meant growth.

A number of federal agencies could barely function without the support of this shadow government. The Department of Energy, for example, employs fewer than 17,000 actual civil servants but relies upon an army of 150,000 contract employees who work for private sector and not-for-profit entities with DOE contracts.[11] Increasingly, however, even the monitoring of contractors is being contracted out to private auditing and accounting firms.

The government's use of nongovernmental organizations to administer its programs is intended to promote a number of public interests. Private-sector firms, on the one hand, radiate a capitalist halo of competitive spirit, efficiency, flexibility, and discipline.[12] Voluntary and not-for-profit agencies, on the other hand, are supposed to bring a sense of mission to their missions.[13] Both are viewed as an antidotes to the tired, bureaucratic inertia of "big government."[14]

Though privatization is a governmental practice of long standing, it has lately become the objective of a coherent political movement energized, in part, by ideological emissaries from Thatcherite Britain. Some of the movement's determination to transfer public functions to private contractors rises from the conviction that many government programs are not responses to the demands of aroused constituencies but products of bureaucratic empire-building designed to enhance the status, job security, or income of self-interested functionaries. Personal democracy's unmobilized public is therefore a given in the privatizers' belief system. What government does, it does for its own reasons, not in response to popular sentiment. But the privatizers are also aware that the mere elimination of public services might provoke public resistance to privatization proposals. According to President Reagan's Commission on Privatization, "if privatization consists simply of eliminating government programs and cutting off benefits, change may come at a slow pace. If privatization consists, however, of forming and recognizing new private rights for the beneficiaries of existing programs, the pace of privatization could accelerate."[15] The substitution of private rights for public benefits would, of course, change the nature of the public itself. It would become a mere aggregation of private customers rather than citizens.

When the private organizations serving these customers are profit-seeking companies, an overriding preoccupation with the bottom line may divert them from the public purposes of the benefits that they sell. These organizations do not see themselves as providing citizens with assistance to which they are entitled by virtue of their membership in the American political community. They are simply selling a product to customers to whom they have no obligation beyond the exchange of a fee for a service. These customers need feel no connection with one another. They are buying alone, to paraphrase Robert Putnam. Detaching them from their government also separates them from their political community and may reduce their sense of commitment to public authority itself. As customers of a private service-provider, after all, they have only an indirect business relationship with government.

Not-for-profit organizations generally have a high level of commitment to the programs they administer and are less likely than for-profit firms to place revenue considerations ahead of service provision. But nonprofit organizations have their own social and political goals. A mandate from the government often allows such groups to use public power and resources to achieve what are essentially private aims. When nongovernmental organizations, whether for-profit or nonprofit, are used as vehicles for government programs, the danger is that they will displace the public agenda with one of their own.

Finally, whether privatization devolves government functions to profit-seeking or nonprofit organizations, its effect may be the political demobilization of would-be activists. A government contract can bring influence over public policy that might otherwise have been generated by rousing a public constituency. For nonprofit groups, in fact, a contract can make the mobilization of support unnecessary. The organization now has a source of income that does not come from grassroots adherents, and its agenda of responsibilities now includes tasks other than agitation. As social service provider, moreover, the nonprofit may also call for a new kind of activism from its members. Instead of assembling them for rallies, marches, protests, and letter-writing campaigns, it now recruits them as community service volunteers, who turn away from the frustrating mission of trying to influence the government to the more immediate gratifications of personal democracy—doing good directly. The new voluntarism, as political scientist David Wagner points out, represents "the encapsulation of oppositional groups within the landscape of social service and therapeutic endeavors."[16]

Government-Sponsored Enterprises: Public Power and Private Purpose

Perhaps the least understood vehicles of public policy are government-sponsored enterprises (GSEs). GSEs are privately owned, profit-making corporations created by the government to make credit available to borrowers and markets designated by Congress. Though federally chartered for specific purposes, the GSEs have boards of directors, sell shares on the open market, compete with other private firms, and try to reward their shareholders with dividends. Because the GSE is created by the government with a mission defined by Congress, it represents one of the most "public" vehicles of privatization. Its history demonstrates that even when private organizations are closely tied to government purposes, they can use their public powers to pursue private purposes of their own.

The best known of the GSEs are Fannie Mae (the Federal National Mortgage Corporation) and Freddie Mac (the Federal Home Loan Mortgage Corporation). The others are the Student Loan Marketing Association (known as Sallie Mae), the Farm Credit System (FCS), the Federal Home Loan Bank System (FHLBS), and the Federal Agricultural Credit Corporation (Farmer Mac). The GSEs are among the nation's largest banking institutions, collectively controlling assets of nearly $3 trillion. Fannie Mae alone is currently the nation's twenty-sixth largest business enterprise in terms of revenues, and it ranks third in total assets. Each of these six GSEs was originally established to overcome perceived flaws in credit markets.[17] The FCS, for example, was organized in 1916 to enhance the availability of credit in rural areas that were then isolated from the nation's financial centers.[18] Fannie Mae was chartered in 1938 as part of an effort to create a secondary market for residential mortgages, thus encouraging financially weak Depression-era banks to make loans available to home purchasers. Fannie Mae was a wholly owned government corporation until 1968, when it was converted into a GSE. Sallie Mae was established in 1972 to increase the supply of tuition loans to college students, a market that many commercial banks had avoided. Today, rather than compensate for perceived market failures, the GSEs operate to provide off-budget subsidies to specific groups favored by Congress.[19]

Though there are individual variations, the GSEs operate in similar ways. To begin with, GSEs raise money in the credit markets by issuing bonds and mortgage-backed securities. In principle, GSE bonds and securities, unlike Treasury bonds and other government bonds, are not backed by the formal promise of the United States government to repay investors. Because of the GSEs' quasi-governmental standing, however, investors treat their securities as though they were backed by the full faith and credit of the U.S. government. This perception allows the GSEs to borrow money at a rate only slightly higher than that paid by the U.S. Treasury itself and substantially below the rate paid by commercial institutions. GSEs also benefit from exemption from state and local taxes and from a variety of other valuable privileges normally enjoyed by federal agencies. According to Federal Reserve Board chairman Alan Greenspan, lower borrowing costs and tax exemptions are worth $6 billion per year to Fannie Mae and Freddie Mac alone.[20]

The GSEs use the funds that they borrow to make loans to private lending institutions that issue mortgages to home buyers, credit to farmers, and tuition loans to college students. These institutions borrow from the GSEs at a rate higher than the GSEs cost of funds, and the profit generated by this difference has provided a comfortable return for the GSEs and their investors. Fannie Mae, for example, produced a 25 percent return on equity in 1998 while Freddie Mac earned nearly 23 percent. The GSEs also provide primary lenders with a secondary market for their loan portfolios, further encouraging these lenders to extend credit to borrowers. By the end of 1999, Fannie Mae and Freddie Mac together owned single-family mortgage loans worth nearly $550 billion and representing 47 percent of all conventional single-family mortgages in the United States.[21]

Generally speaking, the GSEs have successfully carried out their primary mission of enhancing the availability of credit to defined classes of borrowers. But public purposes often get sidelined in private corporations, even those sponsored by government. To begin with, the GSEs are primarily responsible to their shareholders, not to the government; and they regard the president, Congress, and regulatory agencies as interlopers in their affairs.[22] The president appoints a minority block of directors to each GSE's board—five of eighteen directors in the case of Fannie Mae. But the duties of these presidentially appointed directors are unclear. Though the directors may seem to represent the public's interests, their fiduciary responsibility is actually to the shareholders rather than to the public at large. When public directors have sought to question a government corporation's practices, they have often been frozen out of decision-making processes and, in some instances, not even notified of board and committee meetings.[23] GSEs are less accountable to Congress than almost any other government-sponsored organization. In general, the most effective instrument of congressional control is the power of the purse. But the GSEs have purses of their own. They finance their own activities through the profits they earn on their operations.[24] Government regulations are no more effective than Congress. Federal regulatory agencies have limited statutory power over the GSEs and often find themselves politically unable to exercise the few powers they possess.[25]

Limited public accountability means that Congress and the president have scarcely any leverage to induce GSEs to carry out missions inconsistent with their central goal of financial profitability. For example, despite congressional legislation and pressure from the Department of Housing and Urban Development (HUD), both Fannie Mae and Freddie Mac have been slow to amend their lending standards in ways that might increase the availability of conventional mortgages to minority and working-class borrowers.[26] Instead, according to critics, both GSEs have sought to push such borrowers into the so-called subprime market, where they are charged substantially higher mortgage rates. Since Fannie and Freddie lend money to subprime lenders, both agencies may actually profit from the discrimination against subprime borrowers. In addition, despite recurrent criticism from Congress, federal regulatory agencies and consumer advocates, the GSEs have refused to pass along to consumers the borrowing, tax, and regulatory advantages that go with their quasi-governmental status. According to a study by the Congressional Budget Office, Fannie Mae and Freddie Mac retain for their shareholders approximately one-third of the subsidy they receive from the federal government. Sallie Mae, according to analysts, retains its entire subsidy as profit.[27]

The absence of accountability has also allowed the GSEs to shift their operations from less profitable markets to more profitable ones, notwithstanding their public missions. Critics call this "mission creep."[28] All the GSEs have interpreted their charters expansively, arguing that the charters contain "implied powers" allowing them to tailor their activities to changing economic conditions and to respond to circumstances that may not have been anticipated when they were chartered.[29] On these grounds, Fannie Mae and Freddie Mac have recently diverted funds from the mortgage market to potentially more profitable investment activities including financial arbitrage; home equity lending; mortgage, life, and disability insurance; and the sale of repossessed property.[30] Fannie and Freddie, chartered to operate in the secondary market, have gradually been invading primary loan markets as well. The Federal Home Loan Banks (FHLBs) offer an even more telling example of mission creep. Many

of the savings and loan associations that were to have been their principal clients were forced into bankruptcy during the 1980s. Though their
original, public purpose has evaporated, the FHLBs borrow more than a
trillion dollars each year at the discounted rate their quasi-governmental
status makes possible. They use the money to engage in complex financial arbitrage activities designed to produce a handsome—and taxpayer-
subsidized—profit.[31]

Sallie Mae has virtually completed the vertical integration and
monopolization of the student loan business. In 1997, Sallie Mae shareholders ousted the company's management and replaced it with an executive team that pledged to maximize profits. The shareholders used the
GSE's taxpayer-subsidized profits to buy out the competition. In 1999,
Sallie acquired the assets of two regional rivals for $440 million and, in
2000, purchased its largest competitor, the USA Group, for $770 million;
these purchases gave Sallie a commanding market position. Ironically,
Sallie's only serious competitor is the U.S. government's direct student
loan program. Sally, in other words, receives a federal subsidy to compete
against the federal government.

When the GSEs are criticized for losing sight of their public mission,
they typically respond with furious lobbying and public relations campaigns. Since they are private corporations, GSEs are permitted to lobby,
make political contributions, and engage in other political and public
relations activities that are forbidden to government agencies.[32] While
the GSEs claim to be public entities when it comes to borrowing money,
they are decidedly private when it comes to using the political process to
protect their privileges. All the GSEs, Fannie Mae in particular, spend
enormous amounts of money on lobbying, public relations, and political
campaigns, donating hundreds of thousands of dollars each year to political candidates.[33] In 1998, moreover, Fannie Mae and Freddie Mac
together spent nearly $8 million on Capitol Hill lobbying efforts and in
1999 increased their combined spending to $11 million. In 2000, Fannie
Mae spent more than $8 million on one advertising campaign alone.[34]

Through vigorous lobbying, Fannie and Freddie were able to resist
HUD efforts to force them to change their lending standards to the
advantage of minority borrowers and were able to defeat the Clinton
administration's recent efforts to force them to pay the customary Securities and Exchange Commission registration fees on the securities they
issue. Fannie and Freddie save tens of millions of dollars each year by
claiming exemption from these fees. Fannie and Freddie have recently
stepped up their lobbying efforts to block congressional threats to consolidate regulatory oversight of the GSEs and to strip them of their line of

credit from the U.S. Treasury—a move that might weaken Wall Street's confidence that GSE securities are backed by the government. Sallie Mae is also lobbying heavily to improve its competitive position with respect to the government's direct student-lending efforts.[35]

Fannie Mae and Freddie Mac employ advertising agencies to burnish their corporate images and counter any charges made against them. In the summer of 2000, Fannie and Freddie launched an $8 million campaign designed to influence "opinion leaders." In a series of ads in publications like the *Washington Post, Wall Street Journal,* and *New York Times,* the two corporations portrayed their critics as a "Coalition for Higher Mortgage Costs"—a cabal of anonymous bankers and bureaucrats furtively plotting to drive up interest rates for homeowners.[36]

In addition to conventional corporate advertising and public relations efforts, Fannie Mae has sought to use financial assistance to co-opt potential opponents. In 1996, Fannie created the FNMA Foundation, beginning with a gift of $350 million in stock. The foundation has awarded grants totaling $50 million to $70 million a year, usually to community organizations active in the cause of affordable housing. Critics point out that a substantial percentage of the grants seem to be awarded to groups based in districts or states represented by members of Congress who happen to serve on committees of particular importance to Fannie, such as the Senate and House Banking Committees. Still other grants have gone to groups willing to publicly endorse Fannie's lending practices.[37] In 1996, Fannie donated a total of $1.3 million to forty-one organizations in its home base, the District of Columbia. Fannie worked closely with city schools and was the leading supporter of housing and community development projects in the city. This largesse may have helped local political activists forget that Fannie's tax-exempt status cost Washington, D.C., as much as $300 million in annual tax revenues.[38] Fannie Mae representatives denied that the foundation's efforts were motivated by political concerns. One referred to the organization's critics as "paranoid."[39] Paranoid or sane, they are frustrated in their attempts to mobilize the public against Fannie Mae because Fannie's philanthropy is designed to keep the most likely activists sitting on their hands.

Though created by government to serve public purposes, the GSEs' main goal is profitability. Though their profits depend on substantial public subsidies and government-bestowed privileges, they face scarcely any public accountability. Groups and public officials who threaten to change these generous ground rules are quietly bought off. The GSEs need not appeal for public support themselves because they can finance their survival with private revenues—generated by secure public privileges.

Privatizing the Public

In the United States, privatization usually means that the government contracts with private firms to provide services formerly delivered by public agencies.[40] Private firms share the GSEs' focus on profit and lack even the nominal public purposes that are written into GSE charters. When profit and public interest pull in opposite directions, the private contractors predictably choose profit, as became apparent after September 11, 2001, in the case of the security companies responsible for airline baggage inspection at U.S. airports.

Proponents of privatization-by-contract argue that the preoccupation with profit is precisely what makes private firms more efficient in the delivery of public services than public agencies themselves, which may be so, though evidence of cost savings is hardly conclusive.[41] But some hidden costs of contracting-out are seldom taken into account. First, the government's private contractors are generally not bound by the constitutional and legal constraints under which national and state agencies operate. Basic constitutional protections like the Bill of Rights and the Fourteenth Amendment limit the actions of the federal government and the states, but not those of private firms. Second, citizen rights of more recent vintage, like those established by the Freedom of Information Act, have been held by the courts not to apply to private firms operating under government contracts.[42]

Concerns about human rights are especially acute where prisoners are concerned, and incarceration is one of the growth industries created by privatization. Tens of thousands of inmates are housed in private prisons operated by corporations, such as the Corrections Corporation of America (CCA) and Wackenhut, which are under contract with state and municipal governments and, increasingly, with the Federal Bureau of Prisons.[43]

Prisons have traditionally been public institutions, not just because they house people who have broken the laws promulgated by the state, or because they are supposed to be institutions that impose public justice, but because the prison was the visible symbol of the public's solidarity in its intolerance of crime.

The public penitentiary is by no means a perfect institution. But when the penitentiary is private, the public purposes of incarceration often disappear behind the prison walls. Rehabilitation and other services are usually the first to go. Unlike inmates in public prisons, inmates in private prisons do not have the right to bring suit in federal court if they are mistreated. Recreational activities, counseling services, and vocational training all reduce profits and are cut to the bone. Profits can also be protected by hiring fewer correctional officers than in public prisons, but this means that private institutions can operate safely only if they confine prisoners to their cells virtually all the time.[44]

For similar reasons, the conditions of incarceration and punishment tend to be harsh in private prisons. The scarcity of personnel leads guards to resort quickly to manacles and isolation for even minor infractions of prison rules. Health care is strictly rationed because medical services threaten profit margins. Low levels of staffing lead to high levels of inmate violence.[45] Prisoners in private institutions also tend to serve longer terms than prisoners in public institutions for reasons having nothing to do with the severity of their crimes. A study by one state's corrections department showed that prisoners in private facilities lost "good time," that is, credit toward an earlier release, at a rate eight times as high as the rate for inmates of public institutions.[46] The explanation was simple. The earlier the release, the less the revenue produced by the inmate for the corporate jailer.

Though private prisons have numerous critics, the correctional corporations, like GSEs, are able to keep their foes at bay and expand their domains through vigorous lobbying and public relations efforts, and they can afford to do so. Private prisons make money. Revenues were more than $1 billion in 1997 and continue to climb. The largest prison firm, CCA, showed a tenfold share price increase between 1994 and 1998.[47] The flow of cash has provided private prison firms with the means and motive to promote their interests in politics. Often they purchase services and supplies from companies owned by local and state officials. They make substantial contributions to political campaigns and use expensive lobbyists to sway state officials.[48] Like the GSEs, private prison firms also co-opt potential critics with grants. In one notable case, a well-known criminologist who published research favorable to private incarceration in general and to the CCA in particular and who often defended the corporation's treatment of inmates in media and academic commentary, turned out to have been the recipient of substantial research funding from both CCA and Wackenhut—a conflict of interest he failed to disclose.[49] Private prison firms have also lobbied the states for increased prison terms for a variety of offenders, a strategy designed to fill prison beds and corporate coffers.[50]

Many of the problems associated with private prisons can also be found where other types of private firms have taken over the duties of public agencies. Under Medicaid contracts, for example, profit-seeking chains of residential facilities have become major operators in the provision of care for the physically and mentally disabled. Like private prison firms, these corporations have an incentive to increase their profitability by skimping on service. The result, according to critics, has been a nationwide pattern of patient neglect.[51]

In many respects, however, privatization of prisons raises issues that are more serious than those raised by privatization elsewhere. Law enforcement and the punishment of offenders are defining attributes of both sovereignty and community. By imprisoning criminals, the state protects its citizens, asserts its power, and discourages people from taking the law into their own hands so as to create a condition of anarchy in which no one is safe. The public punishment of criminals also defines the boundaries of citizenship and reinforces the coherence of the political community by identifying the conduct that stands beyond the pale.[52] The privatization of punishment threatens to transform the law, justice, and punishment into mere commodities, and the private prison is an institutional declaration that we have ceased to be a public.

Vouchers

The use of vouchers may be an excellent way to achieve privatization. Contracting-out privatizes the supply of public services, but vouchers privatize their consumption as well. The citizens who receive vouchers from the government make their own private decisions about where to spend them. In the process, they create competitive markets for public services, markets in which demand is subsidized by government. These markets are supposed to generate higher-quality public services than government bureaucracies can produce, and with greater cost efficiency. In theory, the discipline of market competition will force private firms in the public service business to manufacture their products at the lowest possible cost so as to keep their prices competitive or to maximize profits and attract investment capital. But if the services that they sell are unsatisfactory to consumers, the customers will take their vouchers to competing firms that give them the kinds of services they want. The outcome—again, in theory—is that efficient producers of high-quality services will prosper while the inefficient and incompetent will founder, and the public in general will be better off than they would be if monopolistic government bureaucracies were the only suppliers of public services.

The theoretical argument apparently makes practical sense to many policymakers. States and localities have made extensive use of vouchers, and the federal government now employs them in its Food Stamp Program, in its Women, Infants, and Children nutrition program, and as one mechanism to provide low-income households with affordable housing. In addition, vouchers have been put to work in subsidizing child care, transportation, job training, prescription drugs for children, the neutering of pets, low-volume flush toilets, and the purchase of electric rather than gasoline-powered lawnmowers. Some states have converted cash welfare benefits into vouchers as a way of preventing noncompliant recipients from making non-essential or improper purchases,[53] and the practice may spread as welfare reform cuts off cash benefits to recipients who have reached the maximum permissible time on public assistance. Vouchers could be issued to proscribed welfare mothers to make sure that their children do not go unfed, unsheltered, or undiapered.

In theory, Americans at large could purchase a wide variety of public services through the use of vouchers. But in practice, reliance on vouchers seems most extensive in policies and policy proposals aimed at Americans whose circumstances are modest at best. Voucher programs in housing, nutrition, job training, and child care are all intended for citizens of low to moderate incomes. On the one hand targeting the poor is perfectly understandable. Vouchers represent public subsidies, and subsidies tend to be redistributive. On the other hand, many nonpoor Americans receive government subsidies in the form of contracts, grants, tax credits and deductions, or direct cash payments. Vouchers are rarely for the rich.

Though portrayed as passports to consumer sovereignty and instruments of choice, vouchers are actually mechanisms of control. In the first place, they restrict the consumption decisions of their recipients. Housing vouchers are to be used only for housing. In fact, the sale of vouchers for cash, as sometimes occurs in the case of food stamps, is a federal crime. Vouchers are not fungible.

In the second place, vouchers influence their recipients' political conduct as well as their consumer behavior. No other mechanism of privatization so clearly converts citizens into customers, and as customers they have little occasion to mobilize for collective action. Dissatisfied customers rarely organize in protest. They simply take their business elsewhere. Vouchers, in other words, tend to melt collective identities down into private interests and dissolve collective behavior into private consumer decisions. The substitution of housing vouchers for public housing projects eliminates the occasion for tenants' councils to make collective demands of public housing authorities. Instead, communal demands directed at public institutions are disaggregated into the private complaints that individual tenants address to private landlords. This does not mean that housing vouchers constitute bad policy or that public housing projects are good for poor people. It means that voucher programs can have profound consequences for our conceptions of citizenship and our political experience. The massive protests and school boycotts that finally drove New York City to decentralize its public school system in 1968 might never have occurred in a world of vouchers. Parents who disapproved of the schools to which their children had been assigned could have taken their children and their vouchers elsewhere.

Public education, in fact, has been the focal point for political contention about vouchers, and the targeting of poor people has become more pronounced as the controversy over school vouchers has unfolded. School vouchers were originally intended for democratic citizens in general. Universality was central to Thomas Paine's vision of government support for citizen education in *The Rights of Man.*[54] Milton Friedman had similar expectations when he offered the first explicit proposal for a system of school vouchers in 1955. It was to be a replacement for public education in general. But once launched on their long and troubled journey in American politics, school vouchers evolved into an educational policy option designed almost exclusively for low-income urban families. Experimental voucher programs in Cleveland and Milwaukee, and one approved by Congress for the District of Columbia, have all targeted children from poor families. A Florida voucher program designed to provide educational alternatives to children at academically nonperforming schools is effectively aimed at poor children. Privately financed voucher initiatives have focused on the same clientele. Recent school voucher proposals advanced by political conservatives for the nation as a whole also envision a clientele composed of the poor, and in the tradition of unlikely bedfellows, these proposals have attracted considerable support among African American parents who seek alternatives to the inner city public schools that they, along with many others, regard as academically inferior.[55]

But the new conservative case for school vouchers is not just a device to separate black voters from their traditional allies in the Democratic party. It also tends to neutralize liberal critics of educational vouchers. Middle-class white parents, the argument goes, can escape bad schools by buying a house in a better school district, but poor residents of the inner city, trapped in ghetto neighborhoods, have no options for their children except the ineffective neighborhood schools. Those schools are likely to perpetuate the educational disadvantages that have prevented the parents from escaping urban ghettoes, and may condemn many of their children to serve life sentences in the same places.

The egalitarian case for school vouchers has found favor with some Americans who are not free market enthusiasts. But the political momentum of the idea has been diminished by voter rejection of voucher referenda in California and Michigan and by an unfavorable federal court decision on Cleveland's voucher experiment. The elder President Bush proposed federal support for school vouchers and his son supported them as governor of Texas. But once exposed to the political currents in Washington, the younger Bush quietly dropped the controversial idea overboard in order to ensure a smooth passage for his education program—one that emphasized national standards, nationwide testing, and the use of federal aid to enforce school accountability. Vouchers have sunk with scarcely a trace, at least for the moment.[56]

The use of vouchers in the Food Stamp Program and the federal housing program has provoked disputes, but nothing like the seismic upheavals occasioned by proposals for educational vouchers. Food and shelter are private commodities obtained through private purchase, with few consequences for parties other than the buyers and sellers. Education has a more complex and ambiguous status. As education scholar Henry Levin points out, schooling "addresses public interests by preparing the young to assume adult roles in which they can undertake civic responsibilities; embrace a common set of values; participate in a democratic polity with a given set of rules; and embrace economic, political, and social life that constitute the foundation for the nation."[57] Simply stated, public schools are supposed to transmit public morality from one generation to the next. And they are not very good at it.

Political scientists John Chubb and Terry Moe explain why. The goals of public education cannot be defined with any precision because they must accommodate the diverse moral and cultural inclinations of a heterogeneous society. The problem is a common one in urban bureaucracies charged with upholding public morality. Almost everyone claims to know what public morality is, but there is hardly any agreement about its substance. That, according to Chubb and Moe, is precisely the problem that leaves the public schools adrift in "weak and watered down" mediocrity.[58] Instead of trying to meet the needs and wants of the children and parents whom they most immediately know and serve, the schools are forced, democratically, to answer to everyone in general. Vouchers would help to narrow each school's clientele and clarify its mission. Instead of trying to please the public at large, each school would take its cues from its own students and their parents. It could become a little community of the like-minded, as parents with similar cultural and academic values were drawn toward the schools that most nearly matched their preferences.

Substituting market control for democratic control over education means that citizens with no children in the schools would have no voice in school policy. Yet they would presumably continue to be taxed to pay for education. Taxation without representation is sometimes tolerated in the United States, old slogans notwithstanding, but such departures from principle require justification, especially when the unrepresented tax-payers constitute the public at large. The implicit rationale is that voucher schools can achieve educational excellence beyond the reach of democratically controlled public schools. The resulting increase in the competence of the voucher-school alumni as workers, citizens, and parents should make the political autonomy of the voucher schools acceptable to a majority of the people who have to live with their graduates.

But the educational effectiveness of voucher schools has been the subject of a sometimes rancorous debate. One especially intense dispute has revolved around the analysis of data from the experimental voucher programs in Milwaukee and Cleveland. The methodological sniping among social scientists—bewildering and tedious to most of the civilian bystanders—seems finally to have arrived if not at a conclusion, then at least an emergent consensus: Vouchers may conceivably have a positive effect on the academic performance of children, but not a large one. In one of the most rigorously designed analyses of data from the Milwaukee voucher experiment, Cecilia Rouse concludes that children in the program outdid a control group of children in the public schools by about 1.5 to 2.0 percentile points on math achievement scores but did no better in reading. Classroom reforms introduced within the existing framework of public education could easily produce improvements of the same or greater magnitude.[59]

The findings are inconclusive, not just because the estimated effects of vouchers seem slight but because the Milwaukee and Cleveland experiments from which the data were drawn were not full-scale school voucher systems, enrolling the poor children of an entire city. Increases in scale are likely to create a need or a demand for more administrative direction. Milton Friedman's 1955 proposal for educational vouchers envisioned little more oversight of voucher schools than the health department exercises over restaurants. But the authors of more recent variants on Friedman's plan usually call for more public regulation of private schools receiving vouchers. Racial discrimination in admission and employment practices would be prohibited by most voucher proposals currently in circulation. Even Friedman would presumably have allowed for health and safety inspections of school buildings, and he conceded the need for some curriculum controls as well. Other possible subjects for public regulation are teacher qualifications, whether and under what conditions voucher schools should be able to reject or expel students whom they do not want, what kind of information schools should be required to provide to parents, whether the schools must meet truth-in-advertising tests, and what kind of information they must supply to public authorities.[60]

Since public funds are supposed to support vouchers, it is reasonable to expect some public regulation. And if vouchers follow the usual course of politics, the body of regulation can be expected to grow. The same circumstances that make voucher proposals so controversial today would generate pressures for regulation in any future system of market-driven school choice. In time, policymakers might be pressured to augment the value of vouchers for schools that emphasize the acquisition of certain vital skills or use favored teaching techniques like phonics. They could be moved to restrict the use of vouchers in schools that practice bilingual education, supply students with condoms, or refuse to hire gay and lesbian teachers. In short, the effort to liberate education from the supposedly stifling central control of bureaucracy may succeed only in replacing a school bureaucracy with a voucher bureaucracy. If so, however, that bureaucracy will be a fortunate one whose clients are disinclined to mobilize in protest against incompetence or nonperformance. They will simply move their children from schools that they dislike to others that they dislike less. As customers in a personal democracy, these clients will have settled for less collective access to public or systemic decisions in return for the private right to make certain personal decisions themselves.

But there is likely to be one powerful control over the bureaucratic regulation of voucher schools. The business firms that run the schools can be expected to have an intense interest in the conditions imposed upon them by public authorities—and in the value of the vouchers. Unless prevented by public regulation, more profitable voucher schools may find it advantageous to buy out their less successful competitors and achieve economies of scale in everything from cafeteria food to textbook purchases. Or perhaps existing educational firms, like the Edison Company or the Sylvan Learning Corporation, will operate chains of voucher schools, doing for education what McDonald's has done for food.

This is not necessarily a bad thing. The educational franchisers who win the battle of the marketplace will presumably do so on the strength of educational performance, and just as the public schools offer different educational options for different students, corporate educators could advertise different packages of schooling for different tastes and financial resources. But as a means of escape from bureaucracy, vouchers will have failed. The scheme that was supposed to generate more choice among educational alternatives seems just as likely to give us schooling under the auspices of a voucher bureaucracy or corporate educational bureaucracies or both.

For some voucher advocates, this outcome would represent a serious disappointment. John Chubb and Terry Moe have argued that some of the most serious academic deficiencies in public school systems are the products of their organization under centralized democratic control.[61] Voucher schools are not immune to central bureaucratic controls, but they need not be conventionally democratic. Having converted citizens into customers, the privatized school system would have eliminated one of the most obvious conditions for collective mobilization—the inclination to exercise "voice" because "exit" is not an option. In a voucher system, of course, schools might be sensitive to parents' voiced complaints precisely because exit and the transfer of vouchers to another school are relatively easy if complaints go unheeded. But this means that schools will operate according to personal, not popular, democracy. Schools will be responsive to individual parents who complain. Those who do not complain will have no one to represent them, and any attempt by parents to mount a collective campaign for school improvement will be handicapped by their easy access to the exit option. The same dissatisfactions that provoke collective action will also cause potential dissidents to desert their fellow protesters for other schools.

Some research, however, seems to point in a different direction. Although claims for the academic impact of vouchers are controversial, there is general agreement that parents who select their children's schools under a voucher plan or other system of school choice tend to be more satisfied with those schools than comparable public school parents and more trustful of their children's teachers. Parents who select schools are also more likely to participate in the education of their children. Parents of children in the Milwaukee voucher experiment, for example, were more likely than nonparticipants to help their children with reading and math assignments and somewhat more likely to attend parent-teacher conferences.[62]

According to one account, "market-like reforms" promise to make parents more than mere customers, because "by expanding the options that people have over public services, citizen/consumers can also become better *citizens,* and by so doing, increase the nation's stock of social capital."[63] But this type of citizenship has a distinctive emphasis. The participatory parents of voucher schools are activists in the education of their children. Like the community service volunteers who produce public goods instead of demanding them, participatory parents are engaged primarily in supply-side citizenship, and their participation is more personal than collective. But participation is hardly evil or hurtful. On the contrary, parental involvement contributes powerfully to the effectiveness of education. In the context of school choice, parents' selection of schools that reflect their own cultural, moral, and pedagogical preferences would no doubt contribute to the effective socialization of children. Distinct interpretations of public morality, not "weak and watered down" versions, could be embodied in voucher schools espousing coherent educational philosophies reinforced by parents whose values echoed those of the schools. Their children's ethical and cultural sensibilities would reflect the enhanced energy and clarity with which the voucher school and its subcommunity had transmitted their shared moral values. But where would those values be debated?

The Nonprofit Sector: Customers and Volunteers

Voucher programs belong to a family of public policies that attempt to mobilize private interests to advance the public interest. These policies represent an alternative to so-called command-and-control policies, in which government agencies identify a public objective and then map out a trail of regulations designed to enforce the behavior that leads to the goal. One problem with the command-and-control model, however, is that it frequently operates in the dark concerning the most efficient means for reaching its ends. Its methods are never tested by market competition, and administrators may be oblivious to the unintended costs imposed on the economy by their bureaucratic pursuit of the public interest. Regulations can distort resource allocations, raise prices, and destroy jobs.

The remedy is to leave the means up to the market. That was the approach urged in Harvard's 1976 Godkin Lectures by Charles L. Schultze, soon to be President Carter's chairman of the Council of Economic Advisers. Instead of trying to specify methods of pollution control, he argued, the Environmental Protection Agency should levy effluent charges on polluting industries and then rely on the profit-maximizing imperatives of the marketplace to energize the search for the most cost-effective methods of reaching acceptable pollution levels.[64]

While command-and-control policies frequently operate in the dark where means are concerned, market-based policies that activate private interests sometimes fly blind with respect to ends. An educational voucher system, for example, need never specify what constitutes a good education. Such specificity, in fact, would violate the system's market-based rationale, which is to allow consumers the freedom to choose the kinds of education that they want. The ends of "choice" policies may never be publicly articulated, much less debated.

But there is a crucial difference between the ignorance of bureaucratic command and the blindness in policies of choice. As Schultze persuasively argues, a government that operates through bureaucratic regulations frequently does not know what it is doing. But in market-based programs, it is the people who may not know what the government is doing. If no public authorities define the kind of education that they are trying to achieve, how can anyone be held responsible for the education that results? Policies of private choice promote responsiveness, but not responsibility. The primary responsibility lies with the customers, who are expected to make intelligent choices consistent with their preferences. If they make mistakes, of course, they can often change their choices. However, the damage done by a bad choice may not be so easily reversed as the choice itself, and the collective results of good, self-interested choices may prove distasteful to the public at large. Perhaps this is what H. L. Mencken had in mind when he noted that democracy gives the people what they want—good and hard.

Implementing public policies through nonprofit organizations is one postwar innovation that stands midway between policies of command and policies of choice. Nonprofits embody a self-conscious awareness of ends along with a flexible experimentalism in the choice of means—more accountability than the market, more responsiveness than public bureaucracy. Nonprofits are private groups dedicated to public interests. Born in altruism, their ability to attract financial support depends upon their explicit espousal of worthy objectives, but they combine this commitment to their missions with "an organizational vitality free from the coercion of government laws."[65]

Nonprofit organizations, at first associated with religious denominations, have worked in cooperation with government since the first half of the nineteenth century, notwithstanding recent debates about the novelty of "faith-based" social policy. But until 1960, relationships between nonprofits and the state were limited and relatively distant. Reliance on nonprofits increased sharply, however, during and after the Great Society years of the Johnson administration. Like the New Deal, this era marked a growth spurt in the welfare state; but unlike the expansion of the 1930s, this one was accomplished largely outside the formal boundaries of the federal government, and nonprofits were among its principal vehicles. The local implementation of the Johnson administration's antipoverty program, for example, was carried out by a thousand community action agencies. Approximately 90 percent of them were nonprofit corporations rather than government agencies.

The growth in government reliance on nonprofits has been concentrated among providers of social services such as mental health treatment, family planning, legal services, treatment for alcoholism and drug abuse, health care, child protective services, job training, and shelters for battered women. Congress contributed significantly to this trend in 1967, when it approved amendments to the Social Security Act designed to provide funds to the states for social services. Aside from explicitly encouraging the states to purchase services from private, nonprofit agencies, Congress devised a matching formula that made such purchases irresistibly attractive. It said that the federal government would match private as well as state social service expenditures at a three-to-one ratio. States could help themselves to federal dollars, not just by spending their own money on social services but by going into partnership with private nonprofit agencies whose expenditures could also be counted toward the federal match. By 1971, one-fourth of all state funds for social services were being used to purchase services from nonprofits. By 1972, Congress took notice of the bonanza that it was financing and capped federal social service grants at $2.5 billion a year. But the states' contracts with private agencies continued to grow.[66]

Reagan administration cuts in grants to states and localities represented a serious setback for nonprofit service providers. By 1997 the federal government's social service funding for nonprofits was 21 percent higher than in 1980, but during the dry years that intervened, the private organizations had suffered a cumulative loss of more than $35 billion in federal support.[67]

The welfare reform legislation of 1996, however, may prove as big a boon to nonprofit social service agencies as the Social Security Amendments of 1967, but the legislation brings new pressures as well. In effect, the new regime in welfare substitutes social services for cash benefits. Its supreme objective is to move welfare recipients into the workforce. But their transformation into wage earners cannot be accomplished without remedial education, job training and job placement, transportation, and day care for their children. Many of these services are provided by nonprofits; but not all social service agencies will flourish equally as a result of welfare reform, and they will often find themselves in competition with profit-seeking firms that have recently moved into the mushrooming social service business. A preliminary study of the legislation's impact in the Cleveland area suggests that small, community- or faith-based organizations, like neighborhood centers and settlement houses, may not be prepared to respond to government and private-sector funders' demands that they become more businesslike and that they demonstrate through outcome measures that they can produce the results for which they are being paid.[68]

Government's insistence on accountability is legitimate and understandable. When public agencies contract with any service provider, they surrender direct control over public services, and monitoring the activities of their contractors is often difficult.[69] One problem is what economists call "information asymmetry." Contractors have far more information than the government about what they are doing and can often camouflage practices that government bureaucrats might question. The bureaucrats, for their part, sometimes complain that in their zeal to privatize, Congress and the state legislatures often fail to appropriate the funds necessary to hire government workers to monitor the contractors. After all, legislators see the purpose of privatization as reducing, not increasing, the size of government bureaucracies.[70]

Nonprofits present special problems of accountability. They often enjoy greater legitimacy with the public than either government authorities or profit-making businesses. Often too, their boards of directors include prominent people who will come to an organization's defense if it is subjected to criticism. Government monitoring of nonprofits is also complicated by the fact that many have a variety of funding sources including government grants, private donations, and for-profit subsidiaries. This variety allows them resist pressure from any single funding agency, though as political scientists Steven Smith and Michael Lipsky point out, the "blockiness" of government contracts means that their loss can leave a more hurtful gap in the resources of a nonprofit than a 10 percent drop in donations or a shortage of volunteers.[71]

Government oversight must also contend with fundamental changes in the behavior of nonprofits, changes that began during the lean years of the Reagan administration and may be reinforced by the very insistence on accountability and oversight now emphasized in bureaucratic monitoring of nonprofit contractors. Nonprofits have "commercialized" in order to develop streams of income independent of government contracts, foundation grants, or donor contributions. Organizations as diverse as the Girl Scouts, the Jewish Community Centers Association, and the American Cancer Society now charge fees for some of their services or make "cause-related marketing arrangements with business corporations." Nonprofit social service organizations "trade on their reputational and membership assets to expand sales of products and services that become identified with their names." Since they now recognize their reputations as marketable assets, they must also take care not to engage in business ventures that would reduce the sales value of their names or undermine the credibility of their commitments to their primary missions. But care has not saved them from criticism. AARP ran into trouble, for example, when it decided to license managed care providers. Licensing was a service of potential interest to AARP members but one that allied the organization with firms that rationed medical care as well as dispensing it.[72]

The exploitation of multiple revenue sources by nonprofits reduces the government's leverage with the organizations and threatens to weaken its policing of social service contractors. There is ample reason for oversight. The corruption of a national United Way executive called attention to the presence of venality in nonprofit agencies, and a large number of other cases suggest that corruption is not rare. Occasionally it consists simply of high salaries and bonuses for nonprofit executives; in other cases, outright fraud, usually at the expense of programs and clients.[73]

If the government's use of nonprofit agencies creates problems for public administration, however, it generates far more serious dilemmas for the nonprofits themselves. A number of studies have suggested that government funding of social service agencies can "crowd out" private contributors, frustrating the organizations' efforts to avoid heavy dependence on government contracts,[74] and possibly explaining organizations' recent adventures in capitalist commercialism. Government demands for more businesslike management and accountability in nonprofit agencies mean that "more and more organizational resources [are] being directed to administration and management and less to service delivery."[75] But the most politically significant consequence of the new contractual relationship between government and nonprofits is the redirection of organizational energy from the mobilization of public constituencies to the "treatment" of clients one by one. In the process, attention shifts to personal rather than political problems.[76]

The tendency for redirection became evident early in the era of nonprofit social services financed by government. In a national study of community action agencies receiving grants from the Johnson administration's Office of Economic Opportunity, James Vanecko found that the local organizations seemed to follow one of two paths. One group of community action agencies was devoted to the goal of "organizing the poor to increase their political power." The other concentrated on delivering social services to the poor so that they might overcome their poverty through individual rather than collective action. The difference in goal orientation proved to be associated with a difference in impact. The commitment to political mobilization was accompanied by an extensive array of changes in local institutions that served the poor—from public schools to social service agencies. They were, for example, more likely to hire minority personnel, more likely to offer services beneficial to poor people. But Vanecko found almost no evidence of institutional change in towns where the Poverty Program's community action agencies saw their role as that of service-provider.[77] When the local organizations emphasized service-delivery, they evidently soaked up the demand for social services and absorbed the pressure for change that the turbulence of the 1960s had stirred up among low-income city residents, many of whom belonged to minority groups.

A study of local Poverty Program and Model Cities agencies in Baltimore showed why the organizations sponsored by government might have difficulty in maintaining citizen involvement. The government-sponsored citizen groups were compared with neighborhood-based groups that had been formed independently by local residents, many of them in the same neighborhoods where the Model Cities and Community Action programs operated. The sharpest difference between members of the government-sponsored groups and independent community groups occurred in their responses to the question whether they and their fellow participants had problems "figuring out what the organization was supposed to be doing."[78]

Members of the government-sponsored groups were far more likely to acknowledge this problem than people belonging to the independent groups, and difficulty in defining group objectives was associated with perceptions of serious internal conflict, mutual suspicion among members, and a lack of confidence in the efficacy of the organization itself.[79]

The paradox of "maximum feasible participation" is that citizens presumably participate because they have something to say about the objectives and design of public programs. On the one hand, fully developed and clearly defined programs leave little to be shaped by the interests, imaginations, or convictions of the citizens. On the other hand, leaving significant decisions up to citizens means fielding programs with diffuse objectives and undefined strategies that may leave citizens uncertain about the purposes of their government-sponsored community organizations, and cause them to become disaffected.

Independently initiated citizen groups presumably avoid this problem because they form not because of some general legislative mandate but because their members have identified some immediate need or problem that requires their attention. There is seldom any question why the organization exists or what its objectives are. But even independent, nonprofit organizations undergo substantial changes when they provide social services under government contracts. Service delivery tends to displace collective mobilization.

The political activities of nonprofit organizations are restricted even before they become government contractors. In order to qualify as a tax-exempt group under section 501(c)(3) of the Internal Revenue Code, organizations may not engage in partisan politics, and may not spend more than one-quarter of their privately raised funds on political activity of any kind. Some groups maintain both their nonprofit status and their political freedom by establishing subsidiaries to carry out their political missions.[80] But even within the limitations of the Code's 501(c)(3) provisions governing nonprofit status, there remains room for political maneuver. Nonprofits have legally "provided the institutional base where citizens could come together and discuss their problems, thereby engaging in an active form of citizenship. Nonprofits have advocated for their client communities, giving voice to their needs in policy dialogues." But even these limited forms of grassroots mobilization may disappear once a group becomes a service-provider under government contract. Contracting contributes to the "depoliticization of nonprofits" as they are pushed "to adopt more market-oriented practices, and to meet individual client demand rather than community need."[81]

Social service nonprofits dependent on government contracts must become more circumspect about mobilizing their constituencies for political action than they would be without contracts. "If they engage in advocacy," as Smith and Lipsky observe, "they do so with the knowledge that their fate as organizations, not just clients' interests, will be affected by such initiatives." The nature of their political activism is likely to change as well. "The material interests of nonprofits under contracting tend to reduce the ideological character of political advocacy and shift it to technical issues relating to rates, funding levels, and regulations."[82]

It is not only the dependence on government that narrows the political world of social service contractors. Service delivery itself often limits the political consciousness of clients and providers alike. Social services tend to individualize social problems by treating their victims one at a time. The social services function, according to social critic Jeffrey Galper, draws the participants' attentions "away from the nature of the society at large or from necessary changes in the client's environment that go beyond what any one person can provide for another."[83] Contracting with nonprofits for social services is a device that not only expands the welfare state without expanding the state itself but also contributes to the demobilization of political activists.[84]

The rise of the new contractual welfare state has changed our understanding of activism itself. It has reshaped citizenship to fit the emerging regime of personal democracy. Social scientist David Wagner pinpoints the paradoxical connection between the political demobilization of our era and the simultaneous mobilization of community service volunteers:

Today's younger generation of activists, human service workers, and volunteers has seen no major radical movements in two decades and consequently has come to mistake the missionary zeal of service work with politics. For neophytes, the constant assertion that nonprofit social service agencies are somehow "political" reinforces the mistaking of bureaucratic organizations for social movements. The new generations do yearn for some meaningful activity. But the absence of large-scale social and political movement as well as the influence of elder siblings and the media has made the idea of volunteering with the homeless, with Habitat for Humanity, with people who have AIDS, or with battered women about the most 'radical' thing a person can do.[85]

The nonprofit social service contractors supply one of the links between the new, individualized "service" citizenship of personal democracy and its demobilization of collective movements in American politics. By expanding the scope of government into the so-called independent sector, the state has absorbed or neutralized its potential challengers. The service contract, says Stanley Aronowitz, is one of "the key mechanisms for transforming social movements from independent adversaries of the state to collaborators."[86] In the process, citizens are transformed into volunteers or customers.

Devolution

Instead of colonizing the independent sector that stands between the public and the private, perhaps government should leave the nonprofits to their independence and concentrate instead on making itself more accessible, and more responsive, to the public that it serves. In theory, at least, that has been one of the explicit justifications for a longstanding campaign to shift the business of government downward in the federal system—out of Washington and into the states and localities that are supposed to stand "closer to the people" than the insular empire on the Potomac.

Some of the most fervent exponents of federalism and decentralization, however, have preached the cause in Washington itself. In 1957, President Eisenhower, addressing the annual meeting of the National Governors Association, proposed a federal-state inquiry to identify the programs and revenues that the federal government could transfer to the states. The Joint Federal-State Action Committee, created to carry out this study, submitted its report in 1960, but it produced no reversal of the centralizing tendencies that had been building the concentration of authority in Washington through the New Deal and World War II.

The concentration, however, was not all that it seemed. To be sure, the national government was growing. The number of civilian employees of the federal government increased by approximately 400,000 during the 1960s. But state and local governments added ten times that number during the same decade, increasing their personnel by about 40 percent—hardly a sign of power concentration on the Potomac. But there was a further complexity in the era's federalism. Much of the growth in state and local governments was being financed and directed through federal programs of grants-in-aid, and while they added to the public workforce outside of Washington, they also added to the mass of regulations, deadlines, and reporting requirements that states and localities had to observe in order to sustain the flow of federal dollars.

Under the regime of "creative federalism" proclaimed by the Johnson administration, the federal government did not turn power back to the states. It "shared" power with them, and with a host of nonprofit organizations that were also parties to the proliferating programs of the Great Society. By 1969, when the Nixon administration won custody of the sprawling system of intergovernmental relations, it was a crazy quilt of more than five hundred programs, some of them operating at cross purposes, all of them carrying a heavy cargo of regulations and guidelines along with the money that they shipped from Washington to states and localities.

The explicit objective of the Nixon administration was not to abolish but to rationalize, streamline, and tame the intergovernmental behemoth. Block grants and revenue sharing were to be the principal vehicles for management reform in intergovernmental policy. Block grants, or "special revenue sharing," would have consolidated a number of federal grant programs serving the same general purpose—education, job training, or rural development, for example—and allowed the states much greater discretion in spending these funds than they had enjoyed under the existing "categorical" grants, which were tied to particular programs and bound up with regulations and reporting requirements.

General revenue sharing represented an even more drastic simplification in the system of intergovernmental aid. It sent quarterly checks to every single one of the thirty-nine thousand or so state, local, and Indian tribal governments in the country. The amount of the check was determined by a formula that accounted for population, poverty, and local tax effort; and the recipient governments could use the money for virtually any purpose they liked. General revenue sharing was conceived not only as a way to minimize federal regulation of states and localities but also as a remedy for disparities between national and subnational revenue-raising capacities. States and localities depended heavily on property taxes and sales taxes. But property taxes did not respond readily to inflation or economic growth, and the sales tax was regressive. The federal income tax, in contrast, because of its progressivity, captured a growing percentage of Americans' incomes during periods of inflation or economic expansion.

Simplification, deregulation, and revenue equalization were not the only purposes served by the Nixon "New Federalism" initiative. As political scientist Richard Nathan has pointed out, when the federal government exported its money and authority to the hinterland, it also undercut the influence of Washington-based interest groups and bureaucrats, many of whom were hostile to Nixon's agenda. By decentralizing authority over public policy, Nixon circumvented the most stubborn obstacles that he faced in Washington, and enhanced the authority of the White House in relation to the iron triangles that made public policy the captive of bureaucratic agencies, congressional subcommittees, and organized interests. In fact, the Congress initially rejected Nixon's New Federalism proposals precisely because its members feared that the new arrangements would displace the categorical grant programs that they favored and controlled.

Perhaps the political plot behind the New Federalism was too complex to succeed, but it did not fail entirely. In the end, Congress rejected most, but not all, of the President's block grant proposals and approved general revenue sharing. Though carefully plotted as a political maneuver, the most striking feature of the New Federalism as public policy was the extent to which it was plotless, and the Johnson administration's Creative Federalism pointed in the same, uncertain direction. The distribution of national political authority to states, localities, and nonprofit agencies reduced the federal government's responsibility to determine where it was headed. In the case of general revenue sharing, this sense of direction disappeared almost entirely. The legislation "lacked even the perfunctory statement of purpose that customarily served as a preamble for almost all bills introduced in Congress."[87] Policy evaluators were subsequently frustrated in their attempts to assess the success or failure of the program because they could not figure out what purposes revenue sharing was supposed to serve in the first place.[88]

Like vouchers and "maximum feasible participation," revenue sharing and block grants left the ends of national policy largely undefined. Washington decision-makers could easily agree about these policies, precisely because their purposes were so diffuse. But mobilizing a popular constituency around a political vacuum is difficult, and although ambiguity about ends might ease the approval of a program, the same lack of definition meant that rallying defenders would be difficult when the policy was under attack. The flagships of Nixon's New Federalism were susceptible to several threats. Their supposed virtue was flexibility, but flexibility meant ambiguity, and ambiguity invited efforts at clarification. States litigated in order to define their authority and responsibilities. Federal policymakers responded to the same ambiguity, and "pressures re-emerge[d] for recentralization, recategorization, and retrenchment.[89]

Revenue sharing would be one of the first triumphs of Nixon's New Federalism to suffer the consequences of its political vacuity. When the program came up for renewal in 1977, it lost one-third of its appropriation. The $2 billion in revenue-sharing funds earmarked for the states were eliminated. The surviving remnant of the program went down during the Reagan administration, along with an armada of other intergovernmental assistance programs. Many shared the same kind of vulnerability. Since they articulated no clear national purposes, they were difficult to justify and lacked strongly motivated defenders. It was no coincidence that the deepest budget cuts of the Reagan administration fell upon federal grant programs for states and localities.[90]

Reagan's New Federalism used one of the mechanisms of Nixon's New Federalism to achieve its more conservative ends. Nine new block grant programs were created in 1981 to consolidate seventy-seven categorical grant programs and reduce their funding by approximately 25 percent. Reagan's objective, as political scientist Timothy Conlan shows, was not to enhance the resources of subnational governments at the expense of Washington but to shrink the stature of government at all levels. Nixon's purpose had been to break the connection between federal grant programs and their organized constituencies. To the degree that he succeeded, he left the programs without friends in the presence of their enemies. Reagan's budget cuts demonstrated their vulnerability, and through his own block grant proposals, he created new candidates for programmatic oblivion. But he was unable to extend his New Federalism initiative beyond his first year in office, perhaps because the advocates of federal grant programs had sensed his larger strategy. As one witness testified before a congressional committee in 1981, "the problem with block grants . . . is that by removing the targeting [to specific clienteles], you remove the constituency for funding. Pretty soon you can pretend there was no need for funding at all."[91]

From the 1960s through the 1980s, the Creative and New Federalisms eroded the purposes of national policy. Decentralization made no sense, after all, unless state and local authorities could exercise their discretion to modify federal policy or design their own local versions of national programs. Allowing for this discretion, however, required that national policymakers suspend the definition of means and ends and permit both to be tailored to fit local preferences and conditions in state capitals, cities, towns, and counties. Programs that lacked clear definition, however, were difficult to defend in national politics, where they had to compete for money and attention with clear and pressing priorities like national defense and economic growth. In a sense, these up-in-the-air programs were instruments of political demobilization. They detached national policy from any particular objective or any particular constituency. The resulting political void helped to open the way for privatization, vouchers, and policies of "choice." Where public purposes evaporated, private interests were the only ones that counted.

Private interests seemed to matter more than ever after the congressional elections of 1994, which won recognition as a watershed in public policy because they shifted control of Congress to a new Republican majority whose champion, Newt Gingrich, came to Washington with an explicitly conservative legislative program that challenged the leadership of the White House. The Republican Contract with America was an alternative State of the Union message that charted a path independent of the one outlined by President Clinton. But its scheme for "devolution" simply continued the decentralizing tendencies begun in the era of Creative Federalism. Though Gingrich excoriated the supposed liberal excesses of the Great Society, he was in fact living on their legacy.

Great Society government often operated outside the bureaucratic agencies that had been the workhorses of the New Deal policy. Long before Gingrich raged against the "Great Society structure of bureaucracy," the heralds of the Great Society itself expressed a Kennedyesque disdain for the stolid routines and stunted imaginations of Washington bureaucrats. The War on Poverty was initially waged by bureaucratic guerilla fighters whose aim was to prevent their program from falling into the hands of mere civil servants. By design, most of the action took place far from the capital, in cities and towns where local people, not national administrators, were supposed to figure out how to fight poverty and what "maximum feasible participation" had to do with the fight. With the possible exception of Medicare, the same decentralization of effort characterized the Great Society in general. The Great Society was not a creature of Washington, and its policies frequently abandoned the direct approach of bureaucratic command and control. The evident purpose was to create a Great Society without a big government.[92]

The Great Society's visionaries were no doubt aware that their policies would have to pass muster with people who shared Gingrich's animus toward national government. They were also aware that they were dealing with one of the most explosive issues in American politics—race. It was the unspoken theme of the War on Poverty. Instead of launching a general ground offensive against poverty, it concentrated its resources where African Americans were concentrated. The localization of the antipoverty initiative may have helped to keep racial confrontation at a distance from Washington, but it could hardly banish the race issue from national politics; and critics would subsequently argue that localities were not the arenas in which to fight poverty in any case.

The devolutionary provisions of the 1994 Contract with America would meet a similar objection. The central contention of the critics of the contract was that programs benefiting the poor at the expense of the nonpoor could not succeed or survive if entrusted to states or localities. States had to compete with one another for taxpayers and investment capital. From the perspective of these revenue producers, antipoverty programs represented costs without any corresponding benefits. States therefore had an incentive to reduce their "redistributive" expenditures so as to make themselves more attractive to the people who paid taxes and to the capitalists who created jobs. Antipoverty programs run by the states were doomed losers in a "race to the bottom"—a race in which competing governments sought to outdo one another in cutting their social welfare expenditures.[93]

In the 1990s, however, programs for the poor became prime candidates for devolution to the states. An attempt to convert Medicaid into a block grant failed,[94] but in 1996 the Aid for Families with Dependent Children Program fell to devolution. Renamed Temporary Assistance for Needy Families, it lost its status as an entitlement program, and the states gained broad authority to divert the funds from cash benefits for poor people to a variety of other uses.

In this case, however, devolution did not set off the predicted race for the bottom, perhaps because it occurred at a time of national economic prosperity, when grants to the states were based on the large welfare expenditures of less prosperous years preceding the boom. The states had welfare money to spare. The welfare reform legislation also contained a maintenance-of-effort provision that prohibited the states from reducing their welfare expenditures below 80 percent of their pre-reform spending levels.

But devolution made a difference. In a study comparing welfare policymaking at the national level with welfare policymaking in the states, Pamela Winston found that a narrower range of groups mobilized when authority over welfare moved to the states.[95] The political pattern of state policymaking matched the one outlined by political scientist Grant McConnell, who argued that the likelihood of elite control increased along with the decentralization of political authority. Being "closer to the people" did not necessarily mean more fully democratic participation. Margaret Brassil encountered a similar result in a study of the de facto devolution of affordable housing policy under the Reagan administration, when federal funds for the construction of low-income housing were drastically cut. The states did not abandon the poor to the housing market. Instead of racing for the bottom, they began their own programs for the construction of affordable housing. But they did not do so in response to political mobilization among the poor or their advocates. Federal housing programs had encouraged the establishment of state housing bureaucracies. They survived the Reagan housing cuts and provided a political base for the continuation of affordable housing policies after direct federal funding dried up. Additional support for the construction of low-income housing came from business groups. Low-income housing was promoted as an economic development measure rather than a redistributive policy—a means to accommodate the low-wage workers employed in local business firms.[96]

Like other efforts to make national policy more flexible and responsive, devolution also contributes to public demobilization. It does so in two ways. First, along with the New Federalism initiatives of Nixon and Reagan, devolution tends to dissolve the national purposes of national policies. In order to leave discretion to the states or localities, block grants and other devices of devolution must refrain from fully specifying a policy's means or ends. The result is a diffuse policy with a diffuse and probably passive or inactive constituency. Second, by decentralizing decision-making authority from the national government to smaller units, devolution tends to reduce political participation in those decisions. Some portion of this reduction may simply be a failure to achieve critical mass. In the nation as a whole, for example, piano tuners may be numerous enough to form a national association with an interest in arts policy or small business loans. But in Idaho or Oklahoma, piano tuners may be too scarce to field a softball team, much less play politics. In addition, Madisonian logic suggests that small constituencies are more likely than large ones to fall under the domination of a single interest. Its hegemony may discourage opposing interests from mobilizing, or it may use its political privilege to structure local institutions so that other interests find it difficult to organize. Organization, as E. E. Schattschneider observed, is the mobilization of bias; some interests can be organized into politics while others are organized out.[97]

There is a common denominator that links devolution with privatization, vouchers, and policies of "choice." They are all instruments for circumventing the federal bureaucracy and its hierarchical mechanisms of policy implementation. The difference among them is that devolution is frequently an intermediate stage on the way to a more thoroughgoing disaggregation of public purposes and public constituencies. Devolution tends to divorce public policies from the organized groups that support them and leaves policies vulnerable to elimination, downsizing, "outsourcing," and privatization. Devolution and block grants are stepping stones on the path from citizenship to customerhood and clienthood. Devolution leads not to a new public philosophy but to the absence of such a policy.

Chapter 10

Does Anyone Need Citizens?

AMERICANS ARE entering a political world in which citizens have ceased to compose a public. Americans continue to participate in politics (at reduced levels and with diminished influence), but they do so increasingly on their own. America is becoming a nation of emphatically *private* citizens—customers and clients who find it difficult to express coherent, common interests through collective political action. In fact, Americans have sacrificed something of citizenship itself. Proper citizens have a collective identity. That is precisely what has been lost in the era of personal democracy.

So far, citizens have done little to reassert their collective status, though the profound alienation from politics that surfaces in public opinion polls and political commentary suggests that they are hardly satisfied with their current standing. Unless apathy and withdrawal are regarded as forms of political participation, however, citizens have made no concerted effort to change their standing. Personal democracy creates a Catch-22 for the collective mobilization of citizens. If citizens are to be roused from apathy to action, someone in a position to arouse them must have an interest in doing so, but one of the essential features of today's personal democracy is that hardly anyone in power fits that description.

Historians can point to some instances of spontaneous popular mobilization—urban mobs or peasant uprisings—that erupted without elite sponsorship.[1] The protests of ordinary people, often driven by deprivation and injustice, have overthrown dynasties.[2] Ordinary people swept away the old order in eighteenth-century France and prepared the way for the collapse of the Romanovs and the rise of Bolshevism in Russia.[3] More recently, they assembled for nightly vigils in the city squares of East Germany until the rulers lost confidence in their own capacity to govern.

But spontaneous popular action, though sometimes decisive, is usually ephemeral. It takes place in what political scientist Aristide Zolberg calls a "moment of madness," a short burst of intense, sometimes violent political agitation that soon subsides.[4] Ordinary citizens, after all, have to reconcile their political roles with their responsibilities as parents and breadwinners. If they are to play a continuing role in collective politics, their participation must be structured or subsidized by others who can reduce the costs of political activism or intensify the motives that stimulate it. Students and practitioners of mass politics have long recognized that spontaneous citizen movements seldom amount to much and last only briefly. Lenin, for example, argued that the working class on its own was capable of only very fitful and limited forms of political action. They needed a vanguard drawn from the bourgeois intelligentsia to develop their political consciousness and revolutionary ardor.[5] Like proletarians, organized interest groups also require elite stimulation. The origins of modern interest groups have been traced to the activities of "organizational entrepreneurs" who had resources to invest in gathering together a membership.[6]

Historically, the "assistance" needed to sustain popular political involvement has come from two sources. First, there was government, which sought to promote the political engagement of citizens in order to solidify the state. During the eighteenth and nineteenth centuries, Western governments learned that popular participation helped give the state access to a stabilizing base of taxpayers, soldiers, and citizen administrators. The expansion of suffrage, political representation, and civil rights from the time of the American Revolution to the early decades of the twentieth century signified that popular support was the principal source of political power and state legitimacy.[7]

Competition for that citizen-based power produced the second stimulus to grassroots political participation. Political elites tried to mobilize popular support for their struggles against their political antagonists. When Western democracies expanded the electorate, they created a new realm of political possibilities in which the active support of ordinary citizens could be put to political use by leaders competing for power or struggling to achieve their policy objectives. In the United States, from the time of the Jeffersonians and Federalists, competing elites appealed for popular support through political party organizations and their programs. Parties won control of government offices by bringing voters to the polls. Control of government gave the parties access to the patronage that brought activists into party organizations and enhanced the capacity to mobilize the electorate, which in turn enabled the party to win more offices. As long as elites needed the support of common citizens, they encouraged collective activism and fashioned their policies to attract wide support.

But the old patterns of leadership competition and state building have faded, and the elite encouragement of mass participation has weakened along with those patterns. To begin with, governments are no longer so dependent as they once were upon mobilized citizens. State construction eventually gives way to state conservation. Public administration, revenue collection, and the waging of war do not rely so heavily as they once did on popular activism and enthusiasm. Government today cultivates satisfied customers rather than mobilized citizens. This change is reflected in new forms of civic education that stress individual participation in noncontroversial public service activities rather than public demands, debate, and collective engagement. In government bureaucracies, public service has been transformed into customer relations. The military today recruits volunteers by promising to make each soldier an "army of one." Instead of national health insurance, Congress produces a "patient's bill of rights." In one public setting after another, government disaggregates the public into a mass of individual clients, consumers, and contributors.

Not only has government found new and nonparticipatory ways of doing business, but the competing political elites that once activated and organized popular constituencies to influence or run the government have found other ways to achieve their ends. They rely on litigation, privileged access to bureaucratic regulatory processes, official recognition as "stakeholders," access to "insider" interest-group politics, and membership in the "political-donor class." Contemporary elites have found that they need not engage in the arduous task of building popular constituencies. Public interest groups and environmental groups have large mailing lists but few active members; civil rights groups field more attorneys than protestors; and national political parties activate a familiar few rather than risk mobilizing anonymous millions.

Political Currents in Personal Democracy

The new politics of partial and selective mobilization has imposed limits not just on political participation but also on the substance of politics itself. The Democratic party, historically the party of blacks and blue-collar workers, has reinvented itself as the champion of suburban "soccer moms." President Clinton's tactic of "triangulation," or capturing the middle, indicated that the Democratic party had turned its face from economically vulnerable factory workers and the poor and uneducated. Over the protests of organized labor, the Clinton administration promoted trade deregulation that threatened the jobs of American workers. The administration embraced a welfare reform proposal that succeeded in moving thousands of poor Americans off the public assistance rolls, but not out of poverty.

The latest thing in mainstream American liberalism is "postmaterialism," the civilian counterpart of the powerful public ideas that guide government policymakers. Postmaterialism levitates above the sordid scuffle of the special interests and sets its sights on enhancing the quality of life, often without regard to economic considerations. Postmodernism is for saving the whales and the wilderness, preserving a woman's right to choose, building self-esteem, conserving energy, and reforming campaign finance. It is against AIDS, fundamentalist intolerance, offshore drilling, gay bashing, and the gun lobby. And its adherents have discovered a different color loop of ribbon for every noble cause. The causes, by and large, *are* noble. But they are the causes of the comfortable.

Postmaterialism is the faith of citizens who have escaped want. They are not oblivious to the needs of the needy—they probably account for a disproportionate part of the army of individual volunteers who deliver soup and services to the poor and homeless—but the political mobilization of the unfortunate is not on their agenda. When the left-of-center loses interest in the tangible goods of public policy, it distances itself from the silent ranks of citizens who live in straitened circumstances—not just the poor but also working-class families trying to stay afloat in an economy in which manufacturing has ebbed and a high school diploma no longer assures economic self-sufficiency. These are citizens whose material needs are too compelling, too substantial, too urgent to ignore. They are the Americans who cannot afford postmaterialism, and their political voicelessness contributes not only to their own deprivation but also to the impoverishment of the political system as a whole.

The rightward drift of American politics since the 1970s is, at least in part, a by-product of leftward demobilization. Today's progressives, unlike their Jeffersonian forebears, seldom seek to advance the interests of the disfavored by enlisting them in grassroots political movements. Today's conservatives, therefore, unlike their Federalist predecessors, are not so driven to compete for popular support as a means of political self-preservation. Though they sometimes strike a populist and patriotic stance on morally symbolic issues, there is little to deter them from public advocacy of tax and economic policies sharply slanted toward the royalists of wealth. It would be difficult for conservatives to mobilize broad popular support for a repeal of inheritance taxes, a reduction of capital gains levies, or a repeal of the alternative minimum tax for business corporations. Conservatives are spared the inconvenience, in part, because postmaterial progressives abstain from popular mobilization themselves.

Crusaders for a variety of progressive causes have looked to the civil rights movement as a model of mass mobilization. None can emulate it, and as we have seen, the embers of the civil rights movement itself gradually lose their fire amid the legal and bureaucratic particularities of affirmative action and minority contracting. These remedies for racial inequality have their value, but they are the concerns of W.E.B. DuBois's "talented tenth." The disadvantaged majority of the nation's minority groups are not the beneficiaries of these remedies. But they are not entirely ignored.

The latest form of justice urged on behalf of these groups is reparations. Whatever the rights and wrongs of the proposal itself, it promises material benefits for a sizeable constituency consisting disproportionately of the poor and economically marginal. The demand for reparations is tailored to the mass mobilization of political outsiders, but it is being advanced through litigation, not mobilization. Reparations advocates have filed suit against several corporations alleged to have profited from slavery. The case is likely to focus narrowly on the actions of the companies, not the institution of slavery. "If a lawsuit does not lead to a general discussion in society about slavery," argues political theorist Elazar Barkan, "then the lawsuits are not very helpful."[8]

Like many other manifestations of personal democracy, reparations would function as a mechanism for political demobilization. They would disaggregate a morally coherent demand into 20 million private claims, as though the historical crimes of a nation against a race could be redeemed by cash indemnities, a sorry stand-in for political justice—and, one might argue, a sorry kind of citizenship, energized by private gain rather than a commitment to public service. It may be a measure of how far we have fallen from the patriotic state of grace in which Tom Brokaw's "greatest generation" soldiered through a depression and suffered through a war to give us the American century. We seem to have frittered that grace away in private self-indulgence.

No wonder public schools have made community service a graduation requirement. Academic lamentations about the loss of "civic community" and "social capital" strike a responsive chord among journalists and opinion leaders who trace the unraveling of citizenship to a decline of neighborliness or to the passing of a world in which families sat down together for dinner without a place at the table for television.

Yet there are unmistakable signs that citizens stand ready to respond to the call of justice alone—without reparations or reward. As this book reaches its close, salvage workers are sifting the cinders of what was the World Trade Center, and we learn that the U.S. mails carry contagion. Americans are frightened, but they are also ready and even eager to be of use to their nation and their fellow citizens. Contributions have poured into relief funds; volunteers stand ready to demonstrate generosity of a more personal kind; blood donors have waited patiently in long lines to give something of themselves to fellow citizens; flags are everywhere. But there is hardly anything for citizens to do.

In an appearance before a joint session of Congress, President Bush declared war on terrorism. In another time, he might have called young men to the recruiting stations and women to the defense plants, and he might have prepared the nation at large for sacrifice. Instead the only demand he made of Americans was "to live their lives and hug their children"—in other words, to go on as though nothing had happened. We are exhorted to have the courage to consume, to patronize the travel and hospitality industries, to do our business, lest a reduction of household expenditures undermine the economy needed to produce smart bombs and cruise missiles. The president's annual State of the Union message calls on the nation to ready itself for a prolonged war but asks no one to pay for it, and even recommends a reduction in taxes. He is the first wartime president to do so. No indictment of ours could demonstrate so decisively the extent to which our government is able to dispense with active citizen support, or the degree to which it has lost its regard for its own citizens.

Solutions Are the Problem

How can we make rulers take us seriously as citizens? The question itself assumes that the remedy lies with the citizens themselves. It suggests that we have not taken citizenship seriously enough—because we spend too much time watching television instead of attending to public affairs, because we have allowed the country's vital civic institutions to deteriorate, because we are insufficiently attentive to understand complex policy issues. In fact, the role of citizens has contracted not so much because citizens themselves have neglected their responsibilities but because the country's leaders have less use for citizens than they once did. If the ties that bind citizens to one another have weakened, one reason may be that today's political elites create few occasions to bring Americans together through the collective mobilization of grassroots support.

Any measures designed to encourage the vigorous exercise of American citizenship must be aimed at least as much at political leaders as at the citizens themselves. But because the target is so diffuse, the aim cannot be precise. Personal democracy is a political culture that reflects systemic changes in American politics. It will not give way to institutional tinkering alone. Our fondness for institutional remedies, in fact, may actually contribute to citizen disengagement. It draws us toward mechanical solutions, like term limits, that promise to provide for the general welfare without the intervention of public-spirited citizens. In fabricating their government, Americans aspired to create a "machine that would run of itself"—a government of laws resistant to human failings. It was designed to get by with leaders who were less than Washingtonian. It could hardly demand much of its citizens. This convenient fiction concealed the essential character of citizenship. It is hard work.

Americans have willingly undertaken the unglamorous work of citizenship in response to the incentives or inspiration offered by their political leaders. For a small minority, the work is its own reward. But for most, political activism is a chore undertaken only when vital interests are threatened and their leaders summon them compellingly to serve. Today the leaders seldom call, and they ask little when they do. Citizenship has withered as a result.

Leaders can motivate citizens, but they are unlikely to do so when they have few political incentives to mobilize popular constituencies. Too often, they find that they can achieve their aims more easily through lawsuits than by appeals to the public. Reducing leaders' opportunities to make public policy by litigation could reenergize citizens by encouraging leaders to address the public rather than the judiciary. Campaign finance reform could also help—but not the kind recently enacted by Congress. Reforms adopted in 2002 seek to restrict the soft money contributed to the national parties. These reforms will probably hasten the final stages of organizational decomposition that have made political parties incoherent congregations whose members adhere to no faith in particular.

Rather than destroy parties, America should adopt reforms that would make the parties the principal institutions for campaign finance. Such reforms might bolster the possibilities for collective political action and refill the nation's empty voting booths. But would the parties risk mobilizing voters whose political inclinations may not be fully known and tested? Perhaps the parties could be induced to take the risk by electoral regulations that invalidated the results of any contest in which a majority of the eligible public did not participate.

These remedies hardly add up to a comprehensive program of reform. They are simply examples of the kinds of measures that might help to reconstitute American citizens as an American public. What is at stake in this effort is not merely the distribution of the nation's power and wealth but also its identity. Imagine a society whose members no longer look for connections between their own interests and those of their neighbors, or become insensitive to the resonance between their own aspirations and those of their fellow citizens. Imagine a country whose inhabitants see no reason to explain their hopes to one another, or to justify their anxieties. That country may not remain imaginary much longer. Under the regime of personal democracy, citizens have scarcely any reason to explain themselves to one another or to justify their wants. The experience of collective mobilization encourages citizens to form their own interests within a framework of common goods. Without collective mobilization we become a nation of occupants. We will no doubt remain on speaking terms, and we may even argue with one another less frequently, but there will be fewer reasons for us to be interested in one another or to engage one another politically.

End of an Era

We are approaching the end of a political epoch, one in which citizens jointly inhabited a public sphere. They were gathered there because they mattered. Because the people were essential to the development and functioning of the state, elites could not govern without them. In the era of popular democracy, the support of this public was also essential to political leaders who wanted to win control of the state. Today the competition for power and the operation of government no longer depend so vitally upon the mass public.

Both the public and the citizens who make it up have become obsolete. They could hardly have been expected to go on forever. The public sphere was an artifact of modernity. It provided a place in which mere political subjects evolved into political actors and full citizens. The public sphere enabled them to become a public.[9] Since these developments had a starting point in history, it is only reasonable to suppose that they may also come to an end. That end is now in sight. What will come after it is not yet visible, but we can imagine two futures for democracy—one dark and one somewhat brighter.

What lies ahead, perhaps, is a dissonant echo of the past. For the better part of its first two centuries, the American Republic experienced cycles of mobilization as competing elites vied with one another to expand their popular support. But the nation's new elites have discovered a succession of arrangements to achieve their aims without popular support. That process of discovery may not yet be over. The progressive demobilization of the public may continue as leaders find new ways to insulate themselves from the uncertainties of popular participation or to reduce the resources that must be devoted to popular mobilization. In other words, recurrent cycles of demobilization may go on unraveling popular democracy—a replay in reverse of the processes that once knit together the American public and integrated it into American politics.

The new terms of political combat may accelerate this downward spiral of demobilization. Political candidates already wage campaigns of attack designed not so much to mobilize supporters as to keep their opponents' partisans away from the polls. Another battle tactic in national politics is to disable the institutional support base of one's antagonists. Parties and politicians sustain themselves by colonizing institutions in and around government. They live off the "new patronage"—the grants, contracts, tax benefits, and programs that employ or finance their allies—and they seek victory by paralyzing or dismantling the institutional infrastructure that sustains their opponents. Budget cuts, devolution, privatization, and the launching of independent prosecutors on open-ended investigations are all employed to disable opponents. Among the institutions disabled may be some that still function to rouse citizens to action. Wrecking them will further reduce the scope of the politically active public.

The members of that public may not go quietly into political retirement. Inducing them to accept their new status depends on their ability to get what they want from government without resorting to collective mobilization. Personal democracy "empowers" citizens to get what they want on their own. It disaggregates the public into a collection of private customers, clients, cases, or consumers whose personal interests seldom grow into collective demands because government provides channels for satisfying those interests through market mechanisms, litigation, or administrative adjudication.

This does not mean that political elites are engaged in a conscious conspiracy to atomize the public. Some of the measures that moved us in this direction promised increases in institutional effectiveness or responsiveness. Others were popular. The government's support of home mortgages, highway construction, and low gasoline taxes combined to create a nation of suburbanites who pursued happiness and the good life not by pressing demands on local governments but by moving from one political jurisdiction to another. Instead of joining with their neighbors to voice demands for better public services or amenities, they exercise the quiet, private "exit" option.

There is nothing new about private solutions for public problems. The open frontier of the nineteenth century is sometimes invoked to explain why working-class insurgency played such a small role in American political history. Malcontents, the argument goes, moved west. Suburban commuters, however, have much less distance to travel, and private solutions in general have become more plentiful and easily accessible than they were in the past. The technology of governing now includes many mechanisms for translating public policy into private choices. In fact, the public use of private interest is consciously promoted as a technique of effective governance. It is a convenience not just for government but for citizens too. Collective action is complicated and time consuming. But convenience, as we have seen, comes at a cost.

Pluralists as long ago as Arthur Bentley have argued that the public was an empty abstraction; the public interest, non-existent. But the terms "public" and "public interest" continued to carry weight in political debate, and they have proven solid enough to curb some of the excesses of special interest and political self-dealing. Special prosecutors still depend upon some conception of a public interest. The public, however, is eroding. In time, it may become just as insubstantial as Bentley imagined it.

Politics without a public could be an Orwellian nightmare, but with multiple Big Brothers locked in political conflict high above the people that they presumably represent. Elites would not be completely free of democratic constraint. Government would still have to assure that its "customers" remained satisfied. If it failed to do so, the processes of demobilization outlined here could be interrupted as a result. Political leaders, after all, are not politically infallible. Because they are leaders, their mistakes often originate in hubris. Sometimes entire institutions are infected by it. In this case, hubris might lead them to believe that they could dispense with citizens or institutions still indispensable—and capable of retaliation. Even more likely is the possibility that combat among political elites may so damage public institutions that they are no longer able to deliver services that citizens regard as essential. Popular backlash might then halt the drift toward personal democracy, especially if popular leaders stood ready to take advantage of the backlash by mobilizing a popular constituency of angry citizens.

Personal democracy may therefore suffer from an internal contradiction that makes it inherently unstable. The institutional casualties of elite combat could impair the programs and organizations necessary for maintaining popular quiescence. Public reaction to the 1995 shutdown of the federal government may be an early sign of future possibilities. The Republican-controlled 104th Congress refused to grant funds for continuing government operations while it worked out a budget compromise with President Clinton. The maneuver backfired. Instead of demonstrating that the country could do without its government, Congress lost public support for paralyzing public authority in the cause of ideological correctness.

Finding hope for a reanimation of the public in government gridlock is not a happy prospect, but a functioning government with a disabled public is unlikely to serve the public good. Today, however, the vitality of the public as a force in American politics is crumbling, and the time may soon arrive when the most pressing and yet disturbing question in American politics is "Who cares?"

Notes

Chapter 1: From Popular to Personal Democracy

1. William N. Chambers and Philip C. Davis, "Party Competition and Mass Participation, 1824–1852," in *The History of American Electoral Behavior*, ed. Joel Silbey, Allan Gogue, and William Flanigan (Princeton, N.J.: Princeton University Press, 1978), 180–185; Paul Kleppner, *Who Voted? The Dynamics of Electoral Turnout, 1870–1980* (New York: Praeger, 1982), 18–19.
2. Michael McGerr, *The Decline of Popular Politics: The American North, 1865–1928* (New York: Oxford University Press, 1986).
3. Sidney Verba, Kay Schlozman, and Henry Brady, *Voice and Equality: Civic Voluntarism in American Politics* (Cambridge, Mass.: Harvard University Press, 1995), 72–73, 531; Steven J. Rosenstone and John Mark Hansen, *Mobilization, Participation, and Democracy in America* (New York: Macmillan, 1993), 61.
4. William Glaberson, "Juries, Their Powers under Siege, Find Their Role Is Being Eroded," *New York Times*, March 2, 2001, 1.
5. R. W. Apple, "So Far, Bush Has Asked Not What You Can Do," *New York Times*, October 15, 2001, B1.
6. Michael Schudson, *The Good Citizen: A History of American Civic Life* (New York: Free Press, 1998), 299.
7. Norman Nie, Jane Junn, and Kenneth Stehlik-Berry, *Education and Democratic Citizenship in American Politics* (Chicago: University of Chicago Press, 1996), 131: Verba, Schlozman, and Brady, *Voice and Equality*, 530.

8. Jeffrey M. Berry, *The Interest Group Society,* 2d ed. (Glenview, Ill.: Scott, Foresman, 1989), chap. 4 (for the phrase "advocacy explosion," see p. 16); Frank Baumgartner and Jeffrey Talbert, "Interest Groups and Political Change," in *The New American Politics,* ed. Bryan Jones (Boulder, Colo: Westview Press, 1995), 87–104; Verba, Schlozman, and Brady, *Voice and Equality,* 72–73; Rosenstone and Hansen, *Mobilization, Participation, and Democracy in America,* 61.

9. Sidney Milkis has offered one persuasive account of the origins of the public's detachment from conflict; see *The President and the Parties: The Transformation of the American Party System* (New York: Oxford University Press, 1993), 16–17.

10. V. O. Key, *Politics, Parties, and Pressure Groups,* 4th ed. (New York: Crowell, 1958), 221–223.

11. Benjamin Ginsberg, Walter Mebane, and Martin Shefter, "The Changing Relationship between Conflict and Mobilization in American Politics" (paper presented to the 1993 annual meeting of the Social Science History Association, Baltimore, Md., November 1993).

12. Wilson is quoted in Max Farrand, ed., *The Records of the Federal Convention of 1787* (New Haven, Conn.: Yale University Press, 1966), 1:49.

13. See Michale X. Delli Carpini and Scott Keeter, *What Americans Know about Politics and Why It Matters* (New Haven, Conn.: Yale University Press, 1996); and Michael J. Avey, *The Demobilization of American Voters: A Comprehensive Theory of Voter Turnout* (New York: Westport Press, 1989), 27–28.

14. See E. Pendleton Herring, *Group Representation before Congress* (Baltimore: Johns Hopkins Press, 1929).

15. See Brooks Jackson, *Honest Graft: Big Money and the American Political Process* (New York: Alfred A. Knopf, 1988).

16. Charles Merriam, *The Making of Citizens* (Chicago: University of Chicago Press, 1931).

17. Guidelines provided to teachers by the New York State Education Department reflect the lessons in electoral politics designed for very young children:

> To illustrate the voting process provide an illustration such as: Chuck and John would both like to be the captain of the kickball team. How will we decide which boy will be the captain? Help the children to understand that the fairest way to choose a captain is by voting.
>
> Write both candidates' names on the chalk board. Pass out slips of paper. Explain to the children that they are to write the name of the boy they would like to have as their captain. Collect and tabulate the results on the chalk board.
>
> Parallel this election to that of the election for the Presidency.

The New York State Education Department, Bureau of Elementary Curriculum Development, *Social Studies-Grade 1, A Teaching System* (Albany,
N.Y.: The University of the State of New York, 1971), 32.

18. Karlene Hanko, "College, University Presidents Pledge to Encourage Participation in Politics," *Daily Pennsylvanian,* July 13, 1999, 1.

19. Dale Blyth, Rebecca Saito, and Tom Berkas, "A Quantitative Study of the
Impact of Service Learning Programs," in *Service Learning: Applications from
the Research,* ed. Alan Waterman (Mahwah, N.J.: Lawrence Erlbaum, 1997),
42–43; Jianjung Wang, Betty Greathouse, and Veronica Falcinella, "An
Empirical Assessment of Self-Esteem Enhancement in a High School Challenge Service-Learning Program," *Education* 99 (Fall 1998): 99–105. Only 19
percent of service-learning students interviewed indicated that their activities were "political"—for example, making an effort to change laws or collecting signatures on petitions.

20. Elizabeth Crowley, "More Young People Turn Away from Politics and Concentrate Instead on Community Service," *Wall Street Journal,* June 16, 1999,
A28.

21. Nina Eliasoph, *Avoiding Politics: How Americans Produce Apathy in Everyday
Life* (New York: Cambridge University Press, 1998), 61.

22. Dana Milbank, "Bush Makes a Pitch for Teaching Patriotism," *Washington
Post,* November 2, 2001, A2.

23. U.S. Commission on Reorganization of the Executive Branch of the Gov-
ernment, *General Management of the Executive Branch* (Washington, D.C.:
Government Printing Office, 1949), 1; James Q. Wilson, "Reinventing
Public Administration," *PS* 27 (December 1994): 668; Al Gore, *From Red
Tape to Results: Creating a Government That Works Better and Costs Less,*
Report of the National Performance Review (Government Printing Office,
1993), 43.

24. Fritz Morstein Marx, *The Administrative State* (Chicago: University of
Chicago Press, 1957), 44.

25. Steven Cohen and William Eimicke, *The New Effective Public Manager* (San
Francisco: Josey-Bass, 1995), chap. 10.

26. Will Kymlicka and Wayne Norman, "The Return of the Citizen: A Survey of
Recent Work on Citizenship Theory," *Ethics* 104 (January 1994): 352.

27. Tom Brokaw, *The Greatest Generation* (New York: Random House, 1998).

28. For influential explanations along these lines, see Robert D. Putnam, "The
Strange Disappearance of Civic America," *The American Prospect,* no. 24
(winter 1996): 34–48; Robert N. Bellah, Richard Madsen, William M. Sulli-
van, Ann Swidler, and Steven M. Tipton, *Habits of the Heart: Individualism
and Commitment in American Life* (Berkeley: University of California Press,
1985); and Lawrence Mead, *Beyond Entitlement: The Social Obligations of Citizenship* (New York: Free Press, 1986).

29. Putnam, "The Strange Disappearance of Civic America," 34–48; Putnam, "Bowling Alone: America's Declining Social Capital," *Journal of Democracy* 6, no. 1 (January 1995): 65–78.
30. Robert D. Putnam, *Bowling Alone: The Collapse and Revival of American Community* (New York: Simon & Schuster, 2000), 128–131.
31. Ibid., 223, 231.
32. C. Everett Ladd, "Bowling with Tocqueville: Civic Engagement and Social Capital" (Bradley Lecture, American Enterprise Institute for Public Policy Research, Washington, D.C., September 15, 1998), 8.
33. Theda Skocpol, "Unraveling from Above," *The American Prospect*, no. 25 (March–April 1996): 24.
34. Theda Skocpol, "Advocates without Members: The Recent Transformation of American Civic Life," in *Civic Engagement in American Democracy*, ed. Theda Skocpol and Morris P. Fiorina (Washington, D.C.: Brookings Institution Press; New York: Russell Sage Foundation, 1999), 491.
35. Sidney Tarrow, "Making Social Science Work across Space and Time: A Critical Reflection on Robert Putnam's 'Making Democracy Work,'" *American Political Science Review* 90 (June 1996): 389–397.
36. Peter Riesenberg, *Citizenship in the Western Tradition: Plato to Rousseau* (Chapel Hill: University of North Carolina Press, 1992), xvii.
37. Thucydides, *The History of the Peloponnesian War*, trans. Sir Richard Livingstone (New York: Oxford University Press, 1960), 117.
38. Otto Hintze, "Military Organization and State Organization," in *The Historical Essays of Otto Hintze*, ed. Felix Gilbert (New York: Oxford University Press, 1975), 196, 211. See also Edward W. Fox, *The Emergence of the Modern European World: From the Seventeenth to the Twentieth Century* (Cambridge, Mass.: Blackwell, 1993), 189.
39. Derek Sayer, "A Notable Administration: English State Formation and the Rise of Capitalism," *American Journal of Sociology* 97 (March 1992): 1382–1415; David H. Sacks, "The Paradox of Taxation: Fiscal Crises, Parliament, and the Liberty of England," in *Fiscal Crises, Liberty, and Representative Government, 1450–1789*, ed. Philip T. Hoffman and Kathryn Norberg (Stanford, Calif.: Stanford University Press, 1994), 7–66.
40. Charles Tilly, *Coercion, Capital, and European States, a.d. 990–1990* (Cambridge, Mass.: Blackwell, 1992), 74–75; Kathryn Norberg, "The French Fiscal Crisis of 1788," in *Fiscal Crises, Liberty, and Representative Government, 1450–1789*, ed. Philip T. Hoffman and Kathryn Norberg (Stanford, Calif.: Stanford University Press, 1994), 253–298.
41. Rogers Brubaker, *Citizenship and Nationhood in France and Germany* (Cambridge, Mass.: Harvard University Press, 1992), 41; Sayer, "A Notable Administration," 1398–1399.

42. Martin Shefter, *Political Parties and the State: The American Historical Experience* (Princeton, N.J.: Princeton University Press, 1994), 75–81.

43. Ruth O'Brien, "Taking the Conservative State Seriously: Statebuilding and Restrictive Labor Practices in Postwar America," *Journal of Labor Studies* 21 (Winter 1997): 33–63; Ronald A. Cass, "Models of Administrative Action," *Virginia Law Review* 72 (1986): 377.

44. O'Brien, "Taking the Conservative State Seriously," 50.

45. Ibid., 61; Susan Sterett, "Legality in Administration in Britain and the United States: Toward an Institutional Explanation," *Comparative Political Studies* 25 (July 1992): 210–211.

46. R. Shep Melnick, *Regulation and the Courts: The Case of the Clean Air Act* (Washington, D.C.: Brookings Institution, 1983).

47. Jeffrey M. Berry, "Citizen Groups and the Changing Nature of Interest Group Politics in America," *The Annals of the American Academy of Political and Social Science* 528 (July 1983): 31–32. On government and foundation funding of interest groups, see Michael S. Greve, "Why 'Defunding the Left' Failed," *The Public Interest*, no. 89 (Fall 1987): 93–99; Theda Skocpol, "Associations without Members," *The American Prospect* 10, no. 45 (July–August 1999): 66–73.

48. Mary Ann Glendon, *Rights Talk: The Impoverishment of Political Discourse* (New York: Free Press, 1991), 171.

49. Andrew Koshner, *Solving the Puzzle of Interest Group Litigation* (Westport, Conn.: Greenwood Press, 1998).

50. Steven E. Schier, *By Invitation Only: The Rise of Exclusive Politics in the United States* (Pittsburgh, Penn.: University of Pittsburgh Press, 2000).

51. Skocpol, "Associations without Members," 68.

52. Matthew A. Crenson and Francis E. Rourke, "American Bureaucracy since World War II," in *The New American State: Bureaucracies and Policies since World War II*, ed. Louis Galambos (Baltimore: Johns Hopkins University Press, 1987).

53. Richard A. Cloward and Frances Fox Piven, *Regulating the Poor: The Functions of Public Welfare* (New York: Pantheon, 1971), 275–276; Robert Kerstein and Dennis R. Judd, "Achieving Less Influence with More Democracy: The Permanent Influence of the War on Poverty," *Social Science Quarterly* 61 (September 1980): 208–220; Matthew A. Crenson, "Organizational Factors in Citizen Participation," *Journal of Politics* 36 (May 1974): 356–378.

54. Theodore J. Lowi, *The End of Liberalism* (New York: W. W. Norton, 1969), 234–235.

55. Timothy Conlan, *From New Federalism to Devolution: Twenty-Five Years of Governmental Reform* (Washington, D.C.: Brookings Institution, 1998) chap. 8.

Chapter 2: The Rise and Fall of the Citizen

1. E. E. Schattschneider, *The Semisovereign People: A Realist's View of Democracy in America* (New York: Holt, Rinehart, and Winston, 1960).
2. Hans J. Morgenthau, *The Purpose of American Politics* (New York: Vintage Books, 1964), 11.
3. Stewart Mitchell, ed., *Winthrop Papers* (Boston: Massachusetts Historical Society, 1931), 2:292, 295.
4. Seymour Martin Lipset, *American Exceptionalism: A Double-Edged Sword* (New York: W. W. Norton, 1996), 19, 31; G. K. Chesterton, *Collected Works* (San Francisco: Ignatius Press, 1990), 21:45; Samuel Huntington, *American Politics: The Promise of Disharmony* (Cambridge, Mass.: Harvard University Press, 1981); Louis Hartz, *The Liberal Tradition in America* (New York: Harcourt, Brace, 1955).
5. D. W. Meinig, *The Shaping of America: A Geographic Perspective on 500 Years of History,* vol. 2, *Continental America, 1800–1867* (New Haven, Conn.: Yale University Press, 1993), 12–17.
6. Alexis de Tocqueville, *Democracy in America,* trans. Henry Reeve (New York: Vintage Books, 1961) 1:72–73.
7. John A. Crow, *Spain: The Root and the Flower,* 3d ed. (Berkeley: University of California Press, 1985). Also see Henry Kammen, *Inquisition and Society in Spain in the Sixteenth and Seventeenth Centuries* (Bloomington: Indiana University Press, 1985).
8. John Brewer, *Sinews of Power: War, Money, and the English State, 1688–1783* (New York: Alfred A. Knopf, 1989), 75. See also Vernon Dibble, "The Organization of Traditional Authority in English Country Government, 1558–1640," in *The Handbook of Organization,* ed. James G. March (Chicago: Rand McNally, 1965), 884–885.
9. Martin Shefter, *Political Parties and the State: The American Historical Experience* (Princeton, N.J.: Princeton University Press, 1994), 21–60.
10. Ibid., chap. 3.
11. James D. Richardson, comp., *Messages and Papers of the Presidents* (Washington, D.C.: Government Printing Office, 1896–1899), 2:448.
12. Matthew A. Crenson, *The Federal Machine: Beginnings of Bureaucracy in Jacksonian America* (Baltimore: Johns Hopkins University Press, 1975), 175.
13. Harold Gosnell, *Machine Politics: Chicago Model,* rev. ed. (Chicago: University of Chicago Press, 1968).
14. Robert K. Merton, *Social Theory and Social Structure,* rev. ed. (Glencoe, Ill.: Free Press, 1968), 74.
15. Richard Jensen, *The Winning of the Midwest* (Chicago: University of Chicago Press, 1971).

16. See Robert H. Wiebe, *The Search for Order, 1877–1920* (New York: Hill and Wang, 1967).
17. Samuel Haber, *Efficiency and Uplift: Scientific Management in the Progressive Era, 1890–1920* (Chicago: University of Chicago Press, 1964).
18. Shefter, *Political Parties and the State*, 78–79.
19. Paul Van Riper, *History of the United States Civil Service* (Evanston, Ill.: Row, Peterson, 1958).
20. Ibid., 219.
21. Harold Seidman, *Politics, Position, and Power: The Dynamics of Federal Organization*, 5th ed. (New York: Oxford University Press, 1998).
22. Rudolf Braun, "Taxation, Socio-Political Structure, and State-Building: Great Britain and Brandenburg-Prussia," in *The Formation of National States in Western Europe*, ed. Charles Tilly (Princeton, N.J.: Princeton University Press, 1975), 243–327.
23. Margaret G. Myers, *A Financial History of the United States* (New York: Columbia University Press, 1970), 15.
24. Ibid., 6.
25. Ibid., 12.
26. Richard Franklin Bensel, *Yankee Leviathan: The Origins of Central State Authority in America, 1859–1877* (New York: Cambridge University Press, 1990), 248.
27. John F. Witte, *The Politics and Development of the Federal Income Tax* (Madison: University of Wisconsin Press, 1985), chap. 4.
28. Ellis Paxson Oberholtzer, *Jay Cooke: Financier of the Civil War* (Philadelphia: Jacobs, 1907).
29. Eric L. McKitrick, "Party Politics and the Union and Confederate War Efforts," in *The American Party Systems: Stages of Political Development*, ed. William Nisbet Chambers and Walter Dean Burnham, 2d ed. (New York: Oxford University Press, 1975), 147.
30. Irwin Unger, *The Greenback Era: A Social and Political History of American Finance, 1865–1879* (Princeton, N.J.: Princeton University Press, 1964). Also see Robert Sharkey, *Money, Class, and Party: An Economic History of Civil War and Reconstruction* (Baltimore: Johns Hopkins University Press, 1959).
31. Sidney Ratner, *American Taxation: Its History as a Social Force in Democracy* (New York: W. W. Norton, 1942), 178.
32. Ray Stannard Baker and William Edward Dodd, eds., *Public Papers of Woodrow Wilson* (New York: Harper and Brothers, 1925–1927), 3:421.
33. Myers, *Financial History of the United States*, 270.
34. Donald R. Stabile and Jeffrey A. Cantor, *The Public Debt of the United States: An Historical Perspective, 1775–1990* (New York: Praeger, 1990), 79.
35. David C. Elliott, "The Federal Reserve System, 1914–29," in *The Federal Reserve System*, ed. Herbert Prochnow (New York: Harper & Brothers, 1960), 295–316.
36. Myers, *Financial History of the United States*, chap. 15.

37. Stabile and Cantor, *Public Debt of the United States,* chap. 6.
38. Ratner, *American Taxation,* 72.
39. See Benjamin Ginsberg and Martin Shefter, *Politics by Other Means,* 2d rev. ed. (New York: W. W. Norton, 1999), chap. 4 .
40. Michael J. Graetz, *The Decline and Fall of the Income Tax* (New York: W. W. Norton, 1997), 93.
41. Dan Morgan, "House Authorizes War Bonds," *Washington Post,* October 24, 2001, A23.
42. Samuel E. Finer, "State and Nation-Building in Europe: The Role of the Military," in *The Formation of National States in Western Europe,* ed. Charles Tilly (Princeton, N.J.: Princeton University Press, 1975), 84–163.
43. Goran Therborn, "The Rule of Capitalism and the Rise of Democracy," *New Left Review,* no. 103 (May 1977): 3–41.
44. Catherine Lyle Cleverdon, *The Woman Suffrage Movement in Canada* (Toronto: University of Toronto Press, 1950).
45. John K. Mahon, *History of the Militia and the National Guard* (New York: Macmillan, 1983), chap. 3.
46. D. Christopher Leins, "The American Experience with an Organized Militia" (unpublished seminar paper, Johns Hopkins University, 1999).
47. Mahon, *History of the Militia and the National Guard,* 84.
48. Otis A. Singletary, *Negro Militias and Reconstruction* (Austin: University of Texas Press, 1957).
49. Allen W. Trelease, *White Terror: The Ku Klux Klan Conspiracy and Southern Reconstruction* (New York: Harper, 1971).
50. Mahon, *History of the Militia and the National Guard,* 161.
51. Allan Millett and Peter Maslowski, *For the Common Defense: A Military History of the United States of America* (New York: Free Press, 1994), 350.
52. Martin Binkin and William F. Kaufman, *U.S. Army Guard and Reserve: Rhetoric, Realities, Risk* (Washington, D.C.: Brookings Institution, 1989), 49.
53. See Robert Leonhard, *The Principles of War for the Information Age* (San Francisco: Presidio Press, 1998); Bill Owen and Ed Offley, *Lifting the Fog of War* (New York: Farrar, Straus and Giroux, 1999); Andrew Krepinevich, "Two Cheers for Air Power," *Wall Street Journal,* June 11, 1999, A18; and Michael Ignatieff, "The New American Way of War," *New York Review of Books,* July 20, 2000, 42–46.
54. Theda Skocpol, *Protecting Soldiers and Mothers: The Political Origins of Social Policy in the United States* (Cambridge, Mass.: Belknap Press of Harvard University Press, 1992).
55. Michael D. Pearlman, *Warmaking and American Democracy* (Lawrence: University Press of Kansas, 1999), 57.
56. Chilton Williamson, *American Suffrage from Property to Democracy, 1760–1860*

(Princeton, N.J.: Princeton University Press, 1960), chap. 6 (quotation on p. 188).

57. Benjamin Ginsberg, *The Consequences of Consent* (New York: Random House, 1982), chap. 1.

58. Emory Upton, *The Military Policy of the United States* (Washington, D.C.: Government Printing Office, 1917).

Chapter 3: Elections without Voters

1. See Steven J. Rosenstone and John Mark Hansen, *Mobilization, Participation, and Democracy in America* (New York: Macmillan, 1993), 231–232.

2. Richard Jensen, *The Winning of the Midwest* (Chicago: University of Chicago Press, 1971), chap. 6.

3. See Mark Wahlgren Summers, *The Press Gang: Newspapers and Politics, 1863–1878* (Chapel Hill, N.C.: University of North Carolina Press, 1994).

4. The classical description of nineteenth-century American political parties in action is Moisei Ostrogorski's *Democracy and the Organization of Political Parties* (New York: Macmillan, 1902).

5. See Philip E. Converse, "Change in the American Electorate," in *The Human Meaning of Social Change,* ed. Angus Campbell and Philip E. Converse (New York: Russell Sage Foundation, 1972), 263–337.

6. J. Morgan Kousser, *The Shaping of Southern Politics: Suffrage Restriction and the Establishment of the One-Party South, 1890–1910* (New Haven, Conn.: Yale University Press, 1974).

7. U.S. Bureau of the Census, *Statistical Abstract of the United States* (Washington, D.C., 2000).

8. Melissa Feld, "Campaign Spending in the United States" (master's thesis, Johns Hopkins University, 1999), 76.

9. Steven E. Schier, *By Invitation Only: The Rise of Exclusive Politics in the United States* (Pittsburgh, Penn.: University of Pittsburgh Press, 2000).

10. Dana Milbank, "Virtual Politics: Candidates' Consultants Create the Customized Campaign," *The New Republic,* July 5, 1999, 22–27.

11. See Robert Shogan, "Politicians Embrace Status Quo as Nonvoter Numbers Grow," *Los Angeles Times,* May 4, 1998, A5; and Lars-Erik Nelson, "Undemocratic Vistas," *The New York Review of Books,* August 12, 1999, 9–12.

12. Stephen Ansolabehere and Shanto Iyengar, *Going Negative: How Political Advertisements Shrink and Polarize the Electorate* (New York: Free Press, 1995).

13. Elizabeth Drew, *The Corruption of American Politics: What Went Wrong and Why* (New York: Birch Lane, 1999); E. J. Dionne Jr., *Why Americans Hate Politics* (New York: Simon and Schuster, 1991); Joseph S. Nye, Philip D. Zelikow, and David C. King, eds., *Why People Don't Trust Government* (Cambridge, Mass.: Harvard University Press, 1997).

14. See David Canon, "A Pox on Both Your Parties," in *The Enduring Debate,* ed. David Canon, Anne Khademian, and Kenneth R. Mayer (New York: W. W. Norton, 2000), 3.
15. E. E. Schattschneider, *The Semisovereign People: A Realist's View of Democracy in America* (New York: Holt, Rinehart, and Winston, 1960), chap. 4.
16. Maurice Duverger, *Political Parties* (New York: Wiley, 1963), 426.
17. Shogan, "Politicians Embrace Status Quo," A5.
18. Ibid.
19. Joan Didion, "Uncovered Washington," *The New York Review of Books,* June 24, 1999, 72–80.
20. See Ruy Teixeira and Joel Rogers, *America's Forgotten Majority: Why the White Working Class Still Matters* (New York: Basic Books, 2000). Also see Milton J. Esman, *Government Works: Why Americans Need the Feds* (Ithaca, N.Y.: Cornell University Press, 2000).
21. Christopher Lasch, *The Revolt of the Elites: And the Betrayal of Democracy,* 1st ed. (New York: W. W. Norton, 1995).
22. Helen Dewar, "Motor Voter Agreement Is Reached," *Washington Post,* April 28, 1993, A6.
23. Peter Baker, "Motor Voter Apparently Didn't Drive Up Turnout," *Washington Post,* November 6, 1996, B7.
24. Chilton Williamson, *American Suffrage from Property to Democracy, 1760–1860* (Princeton, N.J.: Princeton University Press, 1960), 25–28. Also see Robert E. Brown, *Middle-Class Democracy and the Revolution in Massachusetts* (Ithaca, N.Y.: Cornell University Press, 1955).
25. Max Farrand, ed., *The Records of the Federal Convention of 1787* (New Haven, Conn.: Yale University Press, 1966), 1:132.
26. Williamson, *American Suffrage,* chap. 5.
27. *The Hornet,* vol. 1, no. 6, 1802.
28. *Continental Journal,* January 9, 1777.
29. Williamson, *American Suffrage,* 133.
30. Ibid.
31. Kirk H. Porter, *A History of the Suffrage in the United States* (Chicago: University of Chicago Press, 1918). Also see Jacob Frieze, *A Concise History of Efforts to Obtain an Extension of the Suffrage in Rhode Island* (Providence, R.I.: Thomas S. Hammond, 1842).
32. John Hope Franklin, *The Militant South, 1800–1861* (Cambridge, Mass.: Belknap Press of Harvard University Press, 1956).
33. See Eric Foner, *Reconstruction: America's Unfinished Revolution, 1863–1877* (New York: Harper & Row, 1988).
34. Kousser, *Shaping of Southern Politics.*
35. Harold Gosnell, *Democracy, the Threshold of Freedom* (New York: Ronald Press, 1948).

36. Walter Dean Burnham, "Change in the American Electorate," in *The Human Meaning of Social Change,* ed. Angus Campbell and Philip E. Converse (New York: Russell Sage Foundation, 1972).

37. Joseph P. Harris, *Registration of Voters in the United States* (Washington, D.C.: Brookings Institution, 1929).

38. Minnesota is the only state that currently permits day-of-the-election registration. Interestingly, approximately 10 percent of those voting in the 1998 statewide contest that elected colorful former wrestler Jesse Ventura as Minnesota's governor were first-time voters who registered on election day.

39. See Robert H. Wiebe, *The Search for Order, 1877–1920* (New York: Hill and Wang, 1967).

40. Samuel Haber, *Efficiency and Uplift: Scientific Management in the Progressive Era, 1890–1920* (Chicago: University of Chicago Press, 1964).

41. Martin Shefter, *Political Parties and the State: The American Historical Experience* (Princeton, N.J.: Princeton University Press, 1994), 78–79.

42. Paul Van Riper, *History of the United States Civil Service* (Evanston, Ill.: Row, Peterson, 1958).

43. Ibid., 219.

44. See Grant McConnell, *Private Power and American Democracy* (New York: Alfred A. Knopf, 1966). Also see Shefter, *Political Parties and the State,* chap. 3.

45. The public relations effort is described in George Creel, *How We Advertised America* (New York: Harper, 1920).

46. McConnell, *Private Power and American Democracy.*

47. Kristi Andersen, *The Creation of a Democratic Majority, 1928–1936* (Chicago: University of Chicago Press, 1982).

48. James Sundquist, *Dynamics of the Party System* (Washington, D.C.: Brookings Institution, 1975).

49. Shefter, *Political Parties and the State,* chap. 3.

50. J. David Greenstone, *Labor in American Politics,* 2d ed. (Chicago: University of Chicago Press, 1977).

51. Shefter, *Political Parties and the State,* chap. 3.

52. M. Elizabeth Sanders and Richard Bensel, "The Impact of the Voting Rights Act on Southern Welfare Systems," in *Do Elections Matter?* ed. Benjamin Ginsberg and Alan Stone, 2d ed. (Armonk, N.Y.: M. E. Sharpe, 1991).

53. Michael Goldfield, *The Decline of Organized Labor in the United States* (Chicago: University of Chicago Press, 1987).

54. Richard Keller, "Pennsylvania's 'Little New Deal,'" in *The New Deal,* ed. John Braeman, Robert H. Bremner, and David Brody, vol. 2, *State and Local Levels* (Columbus: Ohio State University Press, 1975).

55. See Mike Davis, *Prisoners of the American Dream* (London: Verso, 1986).

56. Benjamin Ginsberg, "Money and Power: The New Political Economy of

American Elections," in *The Political Economy: Readings in the Politics and Economics of American Public Policy,* ed. Thomas Ferguson and Joel Rogers (New York: M. E. Sharpe, 1984).

57. See Wilfred Binkley, *President and Congress* (New York: Vintage Books, 1962), chap. 15.

58. Frances Fox Piven and Richard A. Cloward, *Why Americans Don't Vote* (New York: Pantheon, 1988), chap. 5.

59. Hugh Davis Graham, *The Civil Rights Era: Origins and Development of National Policy, 1960–1972* (New York: Oxford University Press, 1990), pt. 1.

60. Arthur Schlesinger Jr., *A Thousand Days* (Boston: Houghton-Mifflin, 1965).

61. Frances Fox Piven and Richard A. Cloward, *Poor People's Movements: Why They Succeed, How They Fail* (New York: Vintage Books, 1979).

62. August Meier and Elliott Rudwick, *CORE: A Study in the Civil Rights Movement, 1942–1968* (Urbana: University of Illinois Press, 1975).

63. Theodore Sorenson, *Kennedy* (New York: Harper, 1965).

64. Howard Zinn, *SNCC: The New Abolitionists* (Boston: Beacon Press, 1964).

65. For New Deal and postwar liberal views of the presidency, see Grant McConnell, *The Modern Presidency* (New York: St. Martin's, 1967). Also see James MacGregor Burns, *Presidential Government: The Crucible of Leadership* (Boston: Houghton-Mifflin, 1965).

66. See Walter Goodman, *The Committee: The Extraordinary Career of the House Committee on Un-American Activities* (New York: Farrar, Straus and Giroux, 1968). Also see Allen Weinstein, *Perjury: The Hiss-Chambers Case,* updated ed. (New York: Random House, 1997).

67. Benjamin Ginsberg, *The Fatal Embrace: Jews and the State* (Chicago: University of Chicago Press, 1993), 118–119.

68. Frances Fox Piven and Richard A. Cloward, *Regulating the Poor: The Functions of Public Welfare* (New York: Pantheon, 1971), 227–239.

69. Thomas Ferguson and Joel Rogers, *Right Turn: The Decline of the Democrats and the Future of American Politics* (New York: Hill and Wang, 1986), 54–55.

70. Network correspondent Robert Schakne is discussed in Edward Bliss Jr., *Now the News* (New York: Columbia University Press, 1991).

71. See David Garrow, *Bearing the Cross: Martin Luther King, Jr., and the Southern Christian Leadership Conference* (New York: Random House, 1986).

72. See Doug McAdam, *Freedom Summer* (New York: Oxford University Press, 1988).

73. Graham, *Civil Rights Era,* 165.

74. David Garrow, *Protest at Selma: Martin Luther King and the Voting Rights Act of 1965* (New Haven, Conn.: Yale University Press, 1978).

75. Stephen Lawson, *Black Ballots: Voting Rights in the South, 1944–1969* (New York: Columbia University Press, 1976).

76. Howell Raines, *My Heart Is Rested* (New York: Putnam's, 1977).

77. Taylor Branch, *Pillar of Fire: America in the King Years, 1963–1965* (New York: Simon and Schuster, 1998).
78. See Alexander P. Lamis, ed., *Southern Politics in the 1990s* (Baton Rouge: Louisiana State University Press, 1999).
79. J. David Greenstone and Paul Peterson, in *A Decade of Antipoverty Policies,* ed. Robert Haveman (New York: Academic Press, 1977); Nicholas Lemann, *The Promised Land: The Great Black Migration and How It Changed America* (New York: Alfred A. Knopf, 1991).
80. See Michael Lipsky, "Toward a Theory of Street-Level Bureaucracy," in *Theoretical Perspectives on Urban Politics,* ed. Willis Hawley (Englewood Cliffs, N.J.: Prentice Hall, 1976), 199, 203–204.
81. See Robert Salisbury, "Urban Politics: The New Convergence of Power," *Journal of Politics* 26 (November 1964): 775–797.
82. See Walter Dean Burnham, "Party Systems and the Political Process," in *The American Party Systems: Stages of Political Development,* ed. William Nisbet Chambers and Walter Dean Burnham, 2d ed. (New York: Oxford University Press, 1975).
83. Joseph A. Califano Jr., *The Triumph and Tragedy of Lyndon Johnson: The White House Years* (New York: Simon and Schuster, 1991).
84. Doris Kearns Goodwin, *Lyndon Johnson and the American Dream* (New York: Harper and Row, 1976), chap. 11.
85. See Ronald Radosh, *Divided They Fell: The Demise of the Democratic Party, 1964–1996* (New York: Free Press, 1996), chap. 3.
86. Christopher Lasch, *Revolt of the Elites.*
87. Walter Sheridan, *The Rise and Fall of Jimmy Hoffa* (New York: Saturday Review Press, 1972).
88. Robert O'Reilly, *Racial Matters: The FBI's Secret File on Black America, 1960–1972* (New York: Free Press, 1989). Also see Gerald D. McKnight, *The Last Crusade: Martin Luther King, Jr., the FBI, and the Poor People's Campaign* (Boulder, Colo.: Westview Press, 1998).
89. Arthur Schlesinger Jr., *Robert Kennedy and His Times* (New York: Ballantine, 1978), 675.
90. Jean Stein and George Plimpton, *American Journey: The Times of Robert Kennedy* (New York: Signet, 1969).
91. Ibid., 221.
92. Brian Dooley, *Robert Kennedy: The Final Years* (New York: St. Martin's, 1996), 126.
93. Ibid., 60.
94. Abbie Hoffman, *Revolution for the Hell of It* (New York: Dial, 1968), 240.
95. Dooley, *Robert Kennedy,* chap. 5.
96. Paul Cowan, "Wallace in Yankeeland," *Village Voice,* July 18, 1968; Robert Coles, "Ordinary Hopes, Ordinary Fears," in *Conspiracy: The Implications of*

the Harrisburg Trial for the Democratic Tradition, ed. J. C. Raines (New York: Harper and Row, 1974), 99.

97. Dooley, *Robert Kennedy,* chap. 4, 126, 108.

98. Nelson Polsby, *Consequences of Party Reform* (New York: Oxford University Press, 1983), chap. 2.

99. David Vogel, *Fluctuating Fortunes: The Political Power of Business in America* (New York: Basic Books, 1989), chap. 5.

100. Jeffrey M. Berry, *The New Liberalism: The Rising Power of Citizen Groups* (Washington, D.C.: Brookings Institution, 1999).

101. See Harold Seidman, *Politics, Position, and Power: The Dynamics of Federal Organization,* 5th ed. (New York: Oxford University Press, 1998); and Ginsberg and Shefter, *Politics by Other Means,* 2d rev. ed. (New York: W. W. Norton, 1999), chap. 3.

102. Ibid., chap. 1.

103. See Theodore J. Lowi, *The End of Liberalism* (New York: W. W. Norton, 1969). Also see William Niskanan, *Bureaucracy and Representative Government* (Chicago: Aldine, 1971); and Richard A. Harris and Sidney M. Milkis, *The Politics of Regulatory Change* (New York: Oxford University Press, 1995).

104. On the expanded role of the courts, see Gerald N. Rosenberg, *The Hollow Hope: Can Courts Bring About Social Change?* (Chicago: University of Chicago Press, 1991).

105. See, for example, John Rawls, *A Theory of Justice* (Cambridge, Mass.: Harvard University Press, 1971); and Ronald Dworkin, *Taking Rights Seriously* (Cambridge, Mass.: Harvard University Press, 1977). A more explicit statement of the same theme is presented by Herbert Gans in "We Won't End the Urban Crisis until We End Majority Rule," *New York Times Magazine,* August 3, 1969.

106. Conservative strategist Paul Weyrich declares, "I don't want everyone to vote. Our leverage in the electorate goes up . . . as the voting populace goes down" (Thomas Ferguson and Joel Rogers, eds., *The Hidden Election: Politics and Economics in the 1980 Presidential Campaign* [New York: Pantheon, 1981], 4).

107. Ginsberg and Shefter, *Politics by Other Means,* chap. 4.

108. Sidney Verba, Kay Schlozman, and Henry Brady, *Voice and Equality: Civic Voluntarism in American Politics* (Cambridge, Mass.: Harvard University Press, 1995), chap. 16.

Chapter 4: The Old Patronage and the New

1. Anthony Downs, *An Economic Theory of Democracy* (New York: Harper & Row, 1957).

2. On Progressivism, see George Mowry, *The California Progressives* (Berkeley: University of California Press, 1951); and Samuel Haber, *Efficiency and*

Uplift: Scientific Management in the Progressive Era, 1890–1920 (Chicago: University of Chicago Press, 1964). On the role of business elites, see Robert H. Wiebe, *Businessmen and Reform* (Chicago: Quadrangle Books, 1962).

3. See Benjamin Ginsberg and Martin Shefter, *Politics by Other Means*, 2d rev. ed. (New York: W. W. Norton, 1999).

4. Jill Quadagno, *The Color of Welfare: How Racism Undermined the War on Poverty* (New York: Oxford University Press, 1994), 20–24; Robert C. Lieberman, *Shifting the Color Line: Race and the American Welfare State* (Cambridge, Mass.: Harvard University Press, 1998), 6–9.

5. Martin Shefter, *Political Parties and the State: The American Historical Experience* (Princeton, N.J.: Princeton University Press, 1994), chap. 3.

6. William Schneider, quoted in Frances Fox Piven and Richard A. Cloward, *Why Americans Still Don't Vote: And Why Politicians Want It That Way* (Boston: Beacon Press, 2000), 118.

7. See, for example, Walter Dean Burnham, *Critical Elections and the Mainsprings of American Electoral Politics* (New York: W. W. Norton, 1970); Martin Wattenberg, *The Decline of American Political Parties* (Cambridge, Mass.: Harvard University Press, 1990); and David Broder, *The Party's Over: The Failure of Politics in America* (New York: Harper & Row, 1972).

8. See John Bibby, "Party Networks: National-State Integration, Allied Groups, and Issue Activists," in *The State of the Parties: The Changing Role of Contemporary Parties*, ed. John Green and Daniel Shea, 3d ed. (New York: Rowman & Littlefield, 1999), 69–85; and Paul S. Herrnson, "National Party Organizations at the Century's End," in *The Parties Respond: Changes in American Parties and Campaigns*, ed. L. Sandy Maisel, 3d ed. (Boulder, Colo.: Westview Press, 1998), 50–82.

9. Ginsberg and Shefter, *Politics by Other Means*.

10. Steven E. Schier, *By Invitation Only: The Rise of Exclusive Politics in the United States* (Pittsburgh, Penn.: University of Pittsburgh Press, 2000).

11. Matthew A. Crenson and Francis E. Rourke, "The Federal Bureaucracy since World War II," *The New American State: Bureaucracies and Policies since World War II*, ed. Louis Galambos (Baltimore: Johns Hopkins University Press, 1987).

12. See Roger Kimball, *Tenured Radicals: How Politics Has Corrupted Our Higher Education* (New York: Harper & Row, 1990).

13. Joel Aberbach and Bert Rockman, "Clashing Beliefs within the Executive Branch," *American Political Science Review* 70 (June 1976): 456–468.

14. Ginsberg and Shefter, *Politics by Other Means*, 123–124.

15. Michael S. Greve, "Why 'Defunding the Left' Failed," *The Public Interest*, no. 89 (Fall 1987): 91–106.

16. Timothy Conlan, *From New Federalism to Devolution: Twenty-Five Years of Intergovernmental Reform* (Washington, D.C.: Brookings Institution Press,

1998); Richard Nathan, *The Plot That Failed: Nixon and the Administrative Presidency* (New York: Wiley, 1975).

17. Pamela Winston, "The Devil in Devolution: Welfare, the Nation, and the States" (Ph.D. diss., Johns Hopkins University, 1999).

18. *Atlanta Constitution,* April 3, 1993, A8.

19. Robert Garrett, "Twenty Four Years of House Work," *Louisville Courier-Journal,* January 3, 1999, 5.

20. Dana Priest, "Risk and Restraint: Why the Apaches Never Flew in Kosovo," *Washington Post,* December 29, 1999, 1.

21. Helen Dewar, "Embattled Court Nominees Are Confirmed: Senate Conservatives Opposed Two for Ninth Circuit; Paez's Four-Year Wait Ends," *Washington Post,* March 10, 2000, A10.

22. Ginsberg and Shefter, *Politics by Other Means,* chap. 1.

23. Peter Baker and Susan Schmidt, "Starr Searches for Sources of Staff Criticism: Private Investigator Says Clinton Team Hired Him," *Washington Post,* February 24, 1998, 1.

24. John F. Harris, "Office of Damage Control," *Washington Post,* January 31, 1998, 1.

25. "In the Courts," *San Diego Union-Tribune,* December 7, 2000, A14.

26. Kerry Lauerman, "Block the Vote," *New York Times Magazine,* January 23, 2001, 16.

27. Al Gore, quoted in "Today's News: Gore Pushes On," *Washington Post,* November 29, 2000, C15.

28. Schier, *By Invitation Only,* chap. 4.

29. George Gallup and Saul Rae, *The Pulse of Democracy: The Public Opinion Poll and How It Works* (New York: Simon and Schuster, 1940), 14. See also Charles W. Roll Jr. and Albert H. Cantril, *Polls: Their Use and Misuse in Politics* (Cabin John, Md.: Seven Locks Press, 1972).

30. See Benjamin Ginsberg, *The Captive Public: How Mass Opinion Promotes State Power* (New York: Basic Books, 1986); Susan Herbst, *Numbered Voices: How Opinion Polling Has Shaped American Politics* (Chicago: University of Chicago Press, 1993); and J. D. Peters, "Historical Tensions in the Concept of Public Opinion," in *Public Opinion and the Communication of Consent,* ed. T. L. Glasser and C. T. Salmon (New York: Guilford Press, 1995), 3–32.

31. Chester F. Barnard, *Public Opinion in a Democracy,* pamphlet (Princeton, N.J.: Herbert Baker Foundation, Princeton University, 1939), 13.

32. Of course, not all polls claim scientific objectivity. The nonbinding Iowa Republican presidential straw poll, for example, does not make use of a random sample of Iowans. This poll counts only the votes of those Iowa Republicans who make the effort to travel to Iowa State University in Ames to indicate which aspirants for the Republican presidential nomination they prefer. Political professionals and the media see the Iowa straw poll as

an early indication of each candidate's strength. However, in its twenty-year history, the straw poll has never predicted the eventual presidential winner (Richard L. Berke, "Iowa Straw Poll Proving a Little Can Mean a Lot," *New York Times,* August 13, 1999, 1).

33. See Eugene Webb et al., *Unobtrusive Measures: Nonreactive Research in the Social Sciences* (Chicago: Rand McNally, 1966).

34. This discussion is based upon Ginsberg, *The Captive Public.* For a critique of this argument see Philip E. Converse, "The Advent of Polling and Political Research," *PS* 29 (December 1996): 653–654.

35. For an excellent review of the actual process of opinion polling, see Michael Traugott and Paul Lavrakas, *The Voter's Guide to Election Polls* (Chatham, N.J.: Chatham House, 1996).

36. Hadley Cantril, "The Intensity of an Attitude," *Journal of Abnormal and Social Psychology* 41 (1946): 129–135.

37. Aage R. Clausen, Philip Converse, and Warren Miller, "Electoral Myth and Reality: The 1964 Election," *The American Political Science Review* 59 (June 1965): 321–332.

38. Converse, "The Advent of Polling."

39. Dan Balz, "Rallying the Faithful for Gore: As Candidate Takes the Reins, Speakers Aim at Core Voters," *Washington Post,* August 16, 2000, 1.

40. Roll and Cantril, *Polls,* 153.

41. See Richard Jensen, "American Election Analysis," in *Politics and the Social Sciences,* ed. Seymour Martin Lipset (New York: Oxford University Press, 1969), 229.

42. Rich Morin, "Telling Polls Apart," *Washington Post,* August 16, 2000, A35.

Chapter 5: Disunited We Stand

1. For a classic statement of this position, see David B. Truman, *The Governmental Process: Political Interests and Public Opinion* (New York: Alfred A. Knopf, 1951).

2. Elisabeth S. Clemens, *The People's Lobby: Organizational Innovation and the Rise of Interest Group Politics in the United States, 1890–1925* (Chicago: University of Chicago Press, 1997), 85.

3. Ibid., 73.

4. E. Pendleton Herring, *Group Representation before Congress* (Baltimore: Johns Hopkins Press, 1929), 41.

5. Ibid., 46–50. See also Clemens, *The People's Lobby,* 73.

6. Charles Nagel, quoted in Grant McConnell, *Private Power and American Democracy* (New York: Alfred A. Knopf, 1966), 59–60.

7. Grant McConnell, *The Decline of Agrarian Democracy* (Berkeley: University of California Press, 1953), 30–32, 49; Herring, *Group Representation,* 117–118.

8. Theodore Lowi, *The Politics of Disorder* (New York: W. W. Norton, 1971), 5, 12.

9. Frances Fox Piven and Richard A. Cloward, *Poor People's Movements: Why They Succeed, How They Fail* (New York: Vintage Books, 1979), xxii.

10. Clemens, *The People's Lobby*, 211. See also Christopher Howard, "Sowing the Seeds of 'Welfare': The Transformation of Mothers' Pensions, 1900–1940," *Journal of Policy History* 4 (1992): 207; Molly Ladd-Taylor, *Mother Work: Women, Welfare, Child Welfare, and the State, 1890–1930* (Urbana: University of Illinois Press, 1994), 64–65; Robyn Muncy, *Creating a Female Dominion in American Reform, 1890–1935* (New York: Oxford University Press, 1991), 121; Matthew A. Crenson, *Building the Invisible Orphanage: A Prehistory of the American Welfare System* (Cambridge, Mass.: Harvard University Press, 1998), 281. Theories of interest group decadence and oligarchy find their locus classicus in Robert Michels, *Political Parties: A Sociological Study of the Oligarchical Tendencies of Modern Democracy* (1915; New York: Dover Publications, 1959).

11. On the Progressive affinity for independent regulatory commissions, see Marver Bernstein, *Regulating Business by Independent Commission* (Princeton, N.J.: Princeton University Press, 1955), 36–37.

12. Murray Edelman, *The Symbolic Uses of Politics* (Urbana: University of Illinois Press, 1967), 23–25, 57.

13. See, for example, Morton Keller, *Regulating a New Economy: Public Policy and Economic Change in America, 1900–1930* (Cambridge, Mass.: Harvard University Press, 1990).

14. Gabriel Kolko, *Railroads and Regulation, 1877–1917* (Princeton, N.J.: Princeton University Press, 1965); George J. Stigler, "The Theory of Economic Regulation," *Bell Journal of Economics and Management Science* 2 (Spring 1971): 3–21. For an up-do-date and concise survey of academic views concerning the origins of the Interstate Commerce Commission, see Elizabeth Sanders, *Roots of Reform: Farmers, Workers, and the American State, 1877–1917* (Chicago: University of Chicago Press, 1999) 179–181.

15. William Hepburn and Robert LaFollette are quoted in Robert E. Cushman, *The Independent Regulatory Commissions* (New York: Oxford University Press, 1941), 48.

16. George Miller, *Railroads and the Granger Laws* (Madison: University of Wisconsin Press, 1971), 94–96; Stephen Skowronek, *Building a New American State: The Expansion of National Administrative Capacities, 1877–1920* (New York: Cambridge University Press, 1982), 126–127.

17. Skowronek, *Building a New American State*, 131.

18. Ibid., chap. 2. For a theory of regulation based on the intensity and strength of the affected interests, see James Q. Wilson, "The Politics of Regulation," in *The Politics of Regulation*, ed. James Q. Wilson (New York: Basic Books, 1980), 357–394.

19. Ari Hoogenboom and Olive Hoogenboom, *A History of the ICC: From*

Panacea to Palliative (New York: W. W. Norton, 1976), 52–53; Cushman, *Independent Regulatory Commissions,* 70; Sanders, *Roots of Reform,* 199–201.

20. On support for more potent regulation, see Richard H. K. Vietor, "Businessmen and the Political Economy: The Railroad Rate Controversy of 1905," *Journal of American History* 64, no. 1 (June 1997): 47–66. On the number of complaints, see Sanders, *Roots of Reform,* 201.

21. Keller, *Regulating a New Economy,* 47.

22. Alan Stone, *Economic Regulation and the Public Interest: The Federal Trade Commission in Theory and Practice* (Ithaca, N.Y.: Cornell University Press, 1977), 22; Cushman, *Independent Regulatory Commissions,* 179–180, 187.

23. Gretchen Ritter, *Goldbugs and Greenbacks: The Antimonopoly Tradition and the Politics of Finance in America* (New York: Cambridge University Press, 1997).

24. Keller, *Regulating a New Economy,* 203.

25. E. Pendleton Herring, "Special Interests and the Interstate Commerce Commission. I. Cooperation in Regulation," *American Political Science Review* 27, no. 2 (April 1933): 746–748, 750.

26. Ibid., 743.

27. Ibid., 743–744.

28. Ibid., 912–913.

29. Charles E. Cotterill, Address to Traffic Clubs, *Railway Age,* May 3, 1930, 1070.

30. Lawrence S. Rothenberg, *Regulation, Organization, and Politics: Motor Freight Policy at the Interstate Commerce Commission* (Ann Arbor: University of Michigan Press, 1994), 42–47; Hoogenboom and Hoogenboom, *History of the ICC,* 130.

31. Theodore J. Lowi, *The End of Liberalism* (New York: W. W. Norton, 1969), 75.

32. E. Pendleton Herring, *Public Administration and the Public Interest* (New York: McGraw-Hill, 1936), 28–29, 350, 394.

33. For classic statements of this argument, see McConnell, *Private Power and American Democracy,* and Lowi, *End of Liberalism.*

34. McConnell, *Private Power and American Democracy,* chap. 5.

Chapter 6: From Masses to Mailing Lists

1. Theodore Lowi, *The Politics of Disorder* (New York: W. W. Norton, 1971), 75.

2. Robert F. Himmelberg, *The Origins of the National Recovery Administration: Business, Government, and the Trade Association Issue, 1921–1933* (New York: Fordham University Press, 1976); Ellis W. Hawley, *The New Deal and the Problem of Monopoly: A Study in Economic Ambivalence* (Princeton, N.J.: Princeton University Press, 1966).

3. Leverett S. Lyon, Paul T. Homan, Lewis L. Lorwin, George Terborgh, Charles L. Dearing, Leon C. Marshall, *The National Recovery Administration: An Analysis and Appraisal* (Washington, D.C.: Brookings Institution, 1935),

25–26, 871; J. Joseph Huthmacher, *Senator Robert F. Wagner and the Rise of Urban Liberalism* (New York: Atheneum, 1968), 149–150; Michael M. Weinstein, *Recovery and Redistribution under the NIRA* (New York: North-Holland, 1980), 2–4.

4. Hawley, *New Deal and the Problem of Monopoly*, 20–21; Lyon et al., *National Recovery Administration*, 25.

5. Mancur Olson, *The Logic of Collective Action: Public Goods and the Theory of Groups* (Cambridge, Mass.: Harvard University Press, 1971), 9–11.

6. The NRA lacked the enforcement authority to support collective action among competing business firms by legal coercion. The National Labor Board, for example, which was responsible for monitoring employer compliance with Section 7(a) discovered that the law had armed it with few sanctions. It could report violations to the NRA Compliance Division, whose ultimate weapon was the removal of a company's Blue Eagle emblem. Harry A. Millis and Emily Clark Brown, *From the Wagner Act to Taft-Hartley: A Study of National Labor Policy and Labor Relations* (Chicago: University of Chicago Press, 1950), 423–425.

7. Bernard Bellush, *The Failure of the NRA* (New York: W. W. Norton, 1975), 50–51.

8. Martin Shefter, *Political Parties and the State: The American Historical Experience* (Princeton, N.J.: Princeton University Press, 1994), 153–154; Theda Skocpol, *Protecting Soldiers and Mothers: The Political Origins of Social Policy in the United States* (Cambridge, Mass.: Belknap Press of Harvard University Press, 1992), 226–229.

9. David Plotke, "The Wagner Act, Again: Politics and Labor, 1935–37," *Studies in American Political Development* 3 (1989): 115, 140; Mark Barenberg, "The Political Economy of the Wagner Act: Power, Symbol, and Workplace Cooperation," *Harvard Law Review* 106 (May 1993): 1393–1394; Stanley Vittoz, *New Deal Labor Policy and the American Industrial Economy* (Chapel Hill: University of North Carolina Press, 1987), 79.

10. Lawrence G. Flood, ed., *Unions and Public Policy: The New Economy, Law, and Democratic Politics* (Westport, Conn.: Greenwood Press, 1995), 9.

11. Ken Kolman, *Outside Lobbying: Public Opinion and Interest Group Strategies* (Princeton, N.J.: Princeton University Press, 1998), 18–19. See also Jack L. Walker Jr., *Mobilizing Interest Groups in America: Patrons, Professions, and Social Movements* (Ann Arbor: University of Michigan Press, 1991), 11.

12. Lyon et al., *National Recovery Administration*, 417.

13. Millis and Brown, *From the Wagner Act to Taft-Hartley*, 20–21; Huthmacher, *Senator Robert F. Wagner*, 66. Tactical considerations may also have played a part in support for Section 7(a). President Roosevelt used the section as a replacement for other legislation to which he and many business groups objected. The most popular of these was the Thirty Hours Bill sponsored by

Senator Hugo Black. It would have prohibited shipment in interstate commerce of goods produced by workers who were employed for more than six hours a day and five days a week. The measure, which was designed to spread work and reduce unemployment, enjoyed strong support from organized labor; but Roosevelt regarded it as inflexible and infeasible. Though lukewarm about Section 7(a), he found it less objectionable than Black's bill, and he offered the section as a substitute that was acceptable to the White House. Kenneth Finegold and Theda Skocpol, *State and Party in America's New Deal* (Madison: University of Wisconsin Press, 1995), 70–71; Vittoz, *New Deal Labor Policy*, 83–85.

14. Donald R. Brand, *Corporatism and the Rule of Law: A Study of the National Recovery Administration* (Ithaca, N.Y.: Cornell University Press, 1988), 312. David Plotke also assigns a central role to political ideas in the passage of the Wagner Act, but he emphasizes the importance of labor disruptions in 1934–1935 ("Wagner Act, Again," 118). A recent revisionist account of New Deal labor legislation credits liberal political ideas, shared by Democrats and Republicans alike, with a formative influence on the government's policies toward unions (Ruth O'Brien, *Workers' Paradox: The Republican Origins of New Deal Labor Policy, 1886–1935* [Chapel Hill: University of North Carolina Press, 1998]).
15. Huthmacher, *Senator Robert F. Wagner*, 49, 66, 146–147 (quotation on p. 66). On the Wagner Act's "collaborationist" intentions, see Barenberg, "Political Economy of the Wagner Act," 1381–1496.
16. Michael Goldfield, "Worker Insurgency, Radical Organization, and New Deal Labor Legislation," *American Political Science Review* 83 (December 1989): 1257–1282; Plotke, "Wagner Act, Again," 112. See also Plotke, *Building a Democratic Political Order: Reshaping American Liberalism in the 1930s and 1940s* (Cambridge: Cambridge University Press, 1996), 117–120.
17. Frances Fox Piven and Richard A. Cloward, *Poor People's Movements: Why They Succeed, How They Fail* (New York: Vintage Books, 1979).
18. Kenneth Casebeer, "Drafting Wagner's Act: Leon Keyserling and the Precommittee Drafts of the Labor Disputes Act and the National Labor Relations Act," *Industrial Relations Law Journal* 11 (1989), 73–141.
19. Finegold and Skocpol, *State and Party in America's New Deal*. See also Theda Skocpol, Kenneth Finegold, and Michael Goldfield, "Explaining New Deal Labor Policy," *American Political Science Review* 84 (December 1990): 1297–1316.
20. Kenneth Finegold and Theda Skocpol, "State, Party, and Industry: From Business Recovery to the Wagner Act in America's New Deal," in *Statemaking and Social Movements: Essays in History and Theory*, ed. Charles Bright and Susan Harding (Ann Arbor: University of Michigan Press, 1984), 165, 175.
21. Terry M. Moe, "Interests, Institutions, and Positive Theory: The Politics of

the NLRB," *Studies in American Political Development: An Annual* 2 (1987): 239.

22. Millis and Brown, *From the Wagner Act to Taft-Hartley*, 49

23. Moe, "Interests, Institutions, and Positive Theory," 244–245.

24. Taylor Dark, *The Unions and the Democrats: An Enduring Alliance* (Ithaca, N.Y.: Cornell University Press, 1999), 78–79.

25. Ibid., 38, 53.

26. Marick Masters and John Thomas Delaney, "Union Political Activities: A Review of the Empirical Literature," *Industrial and Labor Relations Review* 40 (April 1987): 338.

27. Michael Burawoy, *Manufacturing Consent: Changes in the Labor Process under Monopoly Capitalism* (Chicago: University of Chicago Press, 1979), 114–115 (emphasis in original).

28. Daniel Bell, *The End of Ideology: On the Exhaustion of Political Ideas in the Fifties*, new rev. ed. (New York: Collier Books, 1962), 214–215.

29. Moe, "Interests, Institutions, and Positive Theory," 245; Clinton S. Golden and Virginia D. Parker, eds., *Causes of Industrial Peace under Collective Bargaining* (New York: Harper Brothers, 1955), 25–26, 30–31.

30. Katherine V. W. Stone, "The Post-War Paradigm in American Labor Law," *The Yale Law Journal* 90 (June 1981): 1523, 1525–1529, 1533; Christopher L. Tomlins, *The State and the Unions: Labor Relations, Law, and the Organized Labor Movement in America, 1880–1960* (Cambridge: Cambridge University Press, 1985), 320–322.

31. Judith Stepan-Norris and Maurice Zeitlin, "'Red' Unions and 'Bourgeois' Contracts?" *American Journal of Sociology* 96 (March 1991): 1151–1200.

32. James A. Gross, *Broken Promise: The Subversion of U.S. Labor Relations Policy, 1947–1994* (Philadelphia: Temple University Press, 1995), 27–30; Tomlins, *State and the Unions*, 323–324.

33. J. David Greenstone, *Labor in American Politics*, 2d ed. (Chicago: University of Chicago Press, 1977), xiii.

34. Dark, *Unions and the Democrats*, 84–87; Tracy Roof, "The AFL-CIO's Electoral Activities from the 1960's to the Present" (paper presented at the annual meeting of the Northeastern Political Science Association, Philadelphia, 1999), 6.

35. Dark, *Unions and the Democrats*, 108–111; Gross, *Broken Promise*, 237–238; Moe, "Interests, Institutions, and Positive Theory," 263.

36. James T. Bennett, "Private Sector Unions: The Myth of Decline," *Journal of Labor Research* 12 (winter 1991): 1–28.

37. John Thomas Delaney, Jack Fiorito, and Marick F. Masters, "The Effects of Union Organizational and Environmental Characteristics on Union Political Action," *American Journal of Political Science* 32 (August 1988): 632. The notion that there is a negative relationship between union

organizing and union political activity is confirmed by Bennett ("Private Sector Unions," 8).

38. Quoted in Moe, "Interests, Institutions, and Positive Theory, 263–264; Gross, *Broken Promise,* 256, 270.

39. Roof, "AFL-CIO's Electoral Activities," 7.

40. Dark, *Unions and the Democrats,* 130.

41. Ibid., 132.

42. Michael Goldfield, *The Decline of Organized Labor in the United States* (Chicago: University of Chicago Press, 1987), 182–217; Kim Moody, *An Injury to All: The Decline of American Unionism* (London: Verso, 1988).

43. Dark, *Unions and the Democrats,* 152.

44. Ibid., 172, 175–176.

45. Tracy Roof, "Down to the Grassroots: The Causes and Consequences of the AFL-CIO's Changing Legislative Strategies" (paper presented at the annual meeting of the American Political Science Association, Atlanta, 1999), 18. See also Dark, *Unions and the Democrats,* 168–169.

46. Roof, "AFL-CIO's Electoral Activities," 9.

47. Gary Jacobson, "The Effect of the AFL-CIO's Voter Education Campaigns," *The Journal of Politics* 61 (February 1999): 187.

48. Roof, "AFL-CIO's Electoral Activities," 11; Thomas B. Edsall, "Unions Mobilize to Beat Bush, Regain House," *Washington Post,* March 27, 2000, 10.

49. John M. Broder and Richard A. Oppel Jr., "Companies Join Big-Donor List for Democrats," *New York Times,* August 13, 2000.

50. Dark, *Unions and the Democrats,* 130–131, 140. See also Edsall, "Unions Mobilize to Beat Bush."

51. Roof, "Down to the Grassroots," 18.

52. Michael Eisenscher, "Labor: Turning the Corner Will Take More Than Mobilization," in *The Transformation of U.S. Unions: Voices, Visions, and Strategies from the Grassroots,* ed. Ray M. Tillman and Michael S. Cummings (Boulder, Colo.: Lynne Rienner, 1999), 74–75.

53. On the racial dimension of the Community Action Program, see J. David Greenstone and Paul Peterson, *Race and Authority in Urban Politics: Community Participation and the War on Poverty* (New York: Russell Sage Foundation, 1973). On race in the Model Cities Program, see Nicholas Lemann, *The Promised Land: The Great Black Migration and How It Changed America* (New York: Alfred A. Knopf, 1991), 197–198.

54. Daniel Patrick Moynihan, *Maximum Feasible Misunderstanding* (New York: Free Press, 1969) 142–143.

55. Sanford D. Horwitt, *Let Them Call Me Rebel: Saul Alinsky—His Life and Legacy* (New York: Alfred A. Knopf, 1989) 472; Howard Hallman, "The Community Action Program: An Interpretive Analysis," in *Power, Poverty, and Urban Policy,* ed. Warner Bloomberg Jr. and Henry J. Schmandt, Urban Affairs Annual

Review (Beverly Hills, Calif., Sage Publications, 1968), 2:289; Matthew A. Crenson, "Organizational Factors in Citizen Participation," *Journal of Politics* 36 (May 1974): 375–376.

56. Greenstone and Peterson, *Race and Authority in Urban Politics,* 179–199; Crenson, "Organizational Factors in Citizen Participation," 356–378.

57. Gary Bryner, "Congress, Courts, and Agencies: Equal Employment and the Limits of Policy Implementation," *Political Science Quarterly* 96 (fall 1981): 418.

58. Maurice E. R. Munroe, "The EEOC: Pattern and Practice Imperfect," *Yale Law and Policy Review* 13 (1995): 220, 254, 260–261.

59. Ibid., 261–263; Hanes Walton Jr., *When the Marching Stopped: The Politics of Civil Rights Regulatory Agencies* (Albany: State University of New York Press, 1988), 148; Hugh Davis Graham, "The Civil Rights Act and the American Regulatory State," in *Legacies of the 1964 Civil Rights Act,* ed. Bernard Grofman (Charlottesville: University Press of Virginia, 2000), 53; Harrell R. Rodgers Jr., "Fair Employment Laws for Minorities: An Evaluation of Federal Implementation," in *Implementation of Civil Rights Policy,* ed. Charles S. Bullock III and Charles M. Lamb (Monterey, Calif.: Brooks/Cole, 1984), 97–98.

60. Gary Orfield, *The Reconstruction of Southern Education* (New York: Wiley-Interscience, 1969).

61. Stephen C. Halpern, *On the Limits of the Law: The Ironic Legacy of Title VI of the 1964 Civil Rights Act* (Baltimore: Johns Hopkins University Press, 1995), 67–68.

62. Jeffrey S. Brand, "The Second Front in the Fight for Civil Rights: The Supreme Court, Congress, and Statutory Fees," *Texas Law Review* 69 (December 1990): 306, 310–311.

63. Graham, "Civil Rights Act," 51.

64. Hugh Heclo, *A Government of Strangers: Executive Politics in Washington* (Washington, D.C.: Brookings Institution, 1977), 111.

65. Walker, *Mobilizing Interest Groups,* 62–64; Richard A. Harris, "Politicized Management: The Changing Face of Business in American Politics," in *Remaking American Politics,* ed. Richard A. Harris and Sidney M. Milkis (Boulder, Colo.: Westview Press, 1989), 261–263; Jeffrey M. Berry, *The Interest Group Society,* 2d ed. (Glenview, Ill.: Scott Foresman/Little, Brown, 1989), chap. 2; Berry, *The New Liberalism: The Rising Power of Citizen Groups* (Washington, D.C.: Brookings Institution, 1999), 35–36.

66. Hugh Davis Graham makes a similar point about the regulatory agencies created during the 1960s and 1970s ("Civil Rights Act," 45).

67. Harris, "Politicized Management," 264–265.

68. Ibid., 265; Michael W. McCann, *Taking Reform Seriously: Perspectives on Public Interest Liberalism* (Ithaca, N.Y.: Cornell University Press, 1986), 112–113.

69. Jeffrey M. Berry, *Lobbying for the People: The Political Behavior of Public Interest Groups* (Princeton, N.J.: Princeton University Press, 1977), 186–188.
70. McCann, *Taking Reform Seriously,* 176; Theda Skocpol, "Advocates without Members: The Recent Transformation of American Civic Life," in *Civic Engagement in American Democracy,* ed. Theda Skocpol and Morris P. Fiorina (Washington, D.C.: Brookings Institution Press; New York: Russell Sage Foundation, 1999), 478.
71. Michael T. Hayes, "The New Group Universe," in *Interest Group Politics,* ed. Allen J. Cigler and Burdett A. Loomis, 2d ed. (Washington, D.C.: CQ Press, 1986), 142–143; Theda Skocpol, "Advocates without Members," 462, 480.
72. Berry, *New Liberalism,* 26.
73. Carl Tobias, "Essay: Participant Compensation in the Clinton Administration," *Connecticut Law Review* 27 (winter 1995): 563–568.
74. Allen J. Cigler and Anthony J. Nownes, "Public Interest Entrepreneurs and Group Patrons," in *Interest Group Politics,* ed. Allen J. Cigler and Burdett A. Loomis, 4th ed. (Washington, D.C.: CQ Press, 1995), 82–84.
75. Michael S. Greve, "Why 'Defunding the Left' Failed," *The Public Interest,* no. 89 (fall 1987): 91–106; Jeff Shear, "The Ax Files," *National Journal* 27 (April 15, 1995): 924–927.
76. Shear, "Ax Files," 925.
77. Martin Shapiro, "Of Interests and Values: The New Politics and the New Political Science," in *The New Politics of Public Policy,* ed. Marc K. Landy and Martin A. Levin (Baltimore: Johns Hopkins University Press, 1995), 7.
78. Berry, *Interest Group Society,* chap. 7; Skocpol, "Advocates without Members," 489.
79. Steven P. Croley and William F. Funk, "The Federal Advisory Committee Act and Good Government," *Yale Journal on Regulation* 14 (spring 1997): 462.
80. Ibid., 451–557 (quotations on p. 499).
81. Steven E. Schier, *By Invitation Only: The Rise of Exclusive Politics in the United States* (Pittsburgh, Penn.: University of Pittsburgh Press, 2000), 14, 31, 36 (quotations on p. 31).
82. Ibid., 175, 179–184.
83. Kenneth M. Goldman, *Interest Groups, Lobbying, and Participation in America* (Cambridge: Cambridge University Press, 1999), 125; Ken Kolman, *Outside Lobbying* (Princeton, N.J.: Princeton University Press, c1998), 63–64, 162.

Chapter 7: The Jurisprudence of Personal Democracy

1. David Adamany, "The Supreme Court," in *The American Courts,* ed. John B. Gates and Charles A. Johnson (Washington, D.C.: CQ Press, 1991), 5–34.
2. Andrew Jay Koshner, *Solving the Puzzle of Interest Group Litigation* (Westport, Conn.: Greenwood Press, 1998).
3. Martin Shapiro, "The Supreme Court: From Warren to Burger," in *The New*

American Political System, ed. Anthony King (Washington, D.C.: American Enterprise Institute, 1978), 179–212. Also see Martin Shapiro, "Fathers and Sons: The Court, the Commentators, and the Search for Values," in *The Burger Court: The Counter-Revolution That Wasn't,* ed. Vincent Blasi (New Haven, Conn.: Yale University Press, 1983), 218–238.

4. Koshner, *Solving the Puzzle,* 13.
5. Lee Epstein, *Conservatives in Court* (Knoxville: University of Tennessee Press, 1985).
6. Susan Olson, "The Political Evolution of Interest Group Litigation," in *Governing through the Courts,* ed. Richard Gambitta, Marlynn May, and James Foster (Beverly Hills, Calif.: Sage Publications, 1981), 225–258. Also see Karen Orren, "Standing to Sue: Interest Group Conflict in the Federal Courts," *American Political Science Review* 70 (1976): 723–741.
7. Stephen C. Yeazell, *From Medieval Group Litigation to the Modern Class Action* (New Haven, Conn.: Yale University Press, 1987). Also see Jack B. Weinstein, *Individual Justice in Mass Tort Litigation: The Effects of Class Actions, Consolidations, and Other Multiparty Devices* (Evanston, Ill.: Northwestern University Press, 1995).
8. Samuel Issacharoff, "Governance and Legitimacy in the Law of Class Actions," *Supreme Court Review* 1999 (1999): 337.
9. Jeremy Rabkin, *Judicial Compulsions* (New York: Basic Books, 1989).
10. *Newman v. Piggie Park Enterprises, Inc.,* 390 U.S. 400 (1968). In the May 2001 case of *Buckhannon Board and Care Home v. West Virginia Department of Health and Human Resources* (no. 99–1848), the U.S. Supreme Court placed limits on fee shifting by ruling that a plaintiff could not be awarded fees if a suit achieved its aim by producing "a voluntary change" in a defendant's conduct. Some public interest lawyers asserted that this decision would undermine public interest litigation by discouraging plaintiffs from incurring costs for which they might ultimately not be reimbursed even if they prevailed. Other experts, however, said there were a number of tactics that public interest litigators could use to circumvent the *Buckhannon* ruling. For a discussion, see Marcia Coyle, "Fee Change Is a Sea Change," *The National Law Journal,* June 11, 2001, A1.
11. Michael Greve, "The Private Enforcement of Environmental Law," *Tulane Law Review* 65 (1990): 339.
12. Robert Percival and Geoffrey Miller, "The Role of Attorney Fee Shifting in Public Interest Litigation," *Law and Contemporary Problems* 47 (1984): 233.
13. Natalie Bussan, "All Bark and No Bite: Citizen Suits after Steel Company v. CBE," *Wisconsin Environmental Law Journal* 6 (1999): 195. Important cases include *Lujan v. Defenders of Wildlife,* 504 U.S. 555 (1992); and *Chicago Steel and Pickling Company v. Citizens for a Better Environment,* 118 Sup. Ct. 1003 (1998).

14. See Jeremy Rabkin, "Government Lawyering: The Secret Life of the Private Attorney General," *Law and Contemporary Problems* 61 (winter 1998): 179. See also Karen O'Conner and Lee Epstein, *Public Interest Law Groups* (Westport, Conn.: Greenwood Press, 1989).

15. Joseph Ward, "Corporate Goliaths in the Costume of David: The Question of Association Aggregation under the Equal Access to Justice Act—Should the Whole Be Greater Than Its Parts," *Florida State University Law Review* 26 (1998): 151.

16. *Buckhannon Board and Care Home v. West Virginia Department of Health and Human Resources,* 532 U.S. 598 (2001).

17. Coyle, "Fee Change Is a Sea Change," A1.

18. See Richard Neely, *How Courts Govern America* (New Haven, Conn.: Yale University Press, 1981). Also see Michael McCann, "How the Supreme Court Matters in American Politics," in *The Supreme Court in American Politics,* ed. Howard Gillman and Cornell Clayton (Lawrence: University Press of Kansas, 1999).

19. Lee Epstein and Thomas Walker, "The Role of the Supreme Court in American Society," in *Contemplating Courts,* ed. Lee Epstein (Washington, D.C.: CQ Press, 1995), 315–346.

20. For example, for nearly two decades economic interests affected by government actions under the Endangered Species Act were generally denied standing in federal court to pursue their claims. See William Z. Buzbee, "Expanding the Zone, Tilting the Field," *Administrative Law Review* 49 (1997): 763.

21. Randall Ripley and Grace A. Franklin, *Bureaucracy and Policy Implementation* (Homewood, Ill.: Dorsey Press, 1982).

22. For a detailed history of tobacco litigation, see Tucker S. Player, "After the Fall: The Cigarette Papers, the Global Settlement, and the Future of Tobacco Litigation," *South Carolina Law Review* 49 (1998): 311.

23. Ibid., 318.

24. See Stanton Glantz and Edith Balbach, *Tobacco War: Inside the California Battles* (Berkeley: University of California Press, 2000).

25. Milo Geyelin, "Philip Morris Hit with Record Damages," *Wall Street Journal,* March 31, 1999, A3.

26. See Junda Woo, "Mississippi Wants Tobacco Firms to Pay Its Cost of Treating Welfare Recipients," *Wall Street Journal,* May 24, 1994, A2.

27. Hanach Dagan and James White, "Governments, Citizens, and Injurious Industries," *New York University Law Review* 75 (2000): 354.

28. Ibid., 360.

29. See Maria Bianchini, "The Tobacco Agreement That Went up in Smoke," *California Law Review* 87 (1999): 703.

30. Myron Levin, "Unwittingly Allied Forces Laid Tobacco Bill to Rest," *Los Angeles Times,* June 23, 1998, A1.

31. Ann Davis, "Antitobacco Lawyers in Massachusetts Suit Awarded $775 Million," *Wall Street Journal,* July 30, 1999, A3.
32. Stuart Taylor, "How a Few Rich Lawyers Tax the Rest of Us," *National Journal* 31 (June 26, 1999): 1866.
33. Dagan and White, "Governments, Citizens, and Injurious Industries," 378.
34. Ibid., 381.
35. See Eric Pianin, "House Votes to Curb Tobacco Suit Funding," *Washington Post,* June 20, 2000, 1.
36. Barry Meier, "Industry Crosses Troubling Line: But Challenging Award May Be Easy for Tobacco Companies," *New York Times,* July 11, 2000, A10.
37. Dagan and White, "Governments, Citizens, and Injurious Industries," 381.
38. Gordon Fairclough, "Tobacco Deal Has Unintended Effect: New Discount Smokes; Rise of Small Manufacturers Means Big Companies Pay Less to the States," *Wall Street Journal,* May 1, 2001, 1.
39. "Saved By Smokers: States Are Frittering Away the Money They Extorted from Tobacco Firms," *The Economist,* November 24, 2001, 33.
40. See Michael Barone, "Trying the Lawyers," *U.S. News and World Report,* June 28, 1999, 34.
41. Thomas W. Merrill, "Capture Theory and the Courts, *Chicago-Kent Law Review* 72 (1997): 1039.
42. The classical discussion of the phenomenon is Philip Selznick, *T.V.A. and the Grass Roots* (Berkeley: University of California Press, 1949). On the courts' search for a constituency, see Orren, "Standing to Sue."
43. Deanne M. Barney, "The Supreme Court Gives an Endangered Act New Life," *North Carolina Law Review* 73 (1998): 1889.
44. Ibid. See also the Ninth Circuit's decisions in *Nevada Land Association v. U.S. Forrest Service,* 8 F. 3d 713 (1993); and *Dan Caputo v. Russian River County Sanitation District,* 749 F. 2d 571 (1984).
45. *TVA v. Hill,* 437 U.S. 153 (1978).
46. *Association of Data Processing Service Organizations v. Camp,* 397 U.S. 150 (1970).
47. Kathleen Becker, "Bennett v. Plenart: Environmental Citizen Suits and the Zone of Interest Test," *Environmental Law* 26 (1996): 107.
48. *Babbitt v. Sweet Home Chapter of Communities for a Greater Oregon,* 516 U.S. 687 (1995).
49. Fiona M. Powell, "Defining Harm under the Endangered Species Act: Implications of Babbitt v. Sweet Home," *American Business Law Journal* 33 (1995): 131.
50. Daniel R. Dinger, "Throwing *Canis Lupus* to the Wolves: *United States v. McKittrick* and the Existence of the Yellowstone and Central Idaho Experimental Wolf Populations under a Flawed Provision of the Endangered Species Act," *Brigham Young University Law Review* 2000 (2000): 377.

51. *Sickman v. United States,* 184 F. 2d 616 (7th Cir. 1950).
52. *United States v. McKittrick,* 142 F. 3d 1170 (9th Cir. 1998).
53. Oliver Houck, "The Endangered Species Act and Its Implementation by the U.S. Departments of Interior and Commerce," *University of Colorado Law Review* 64 (1993): 277.
54. Stuart Hardy, "The Endangered Species Act: On a Collision Course with Human Needs," *Public Land Law Review* 13 (1992): 87. Also see Craig Baldauf, "Courts, Congress, and Common Killers Conspire to Drive Endangered Species into Extinction," *Wake Forest Law Review* 30 (1995): 113.
55. Andrew Revkin, "Rules Shielding the Gray Wolf May Soon Ease," *New York Times,* July 3, 2000, 1.
56. Anita Huslin, "Grizzly Proposition Aims to Return Bears to Idaho," *Washington Post,* July 3, 2000, A3.
57. *Bennett v. Spear,* 117 S. Ct. 1154 (1997).
58. Barney, "Supreme Court."
59. The dismemberment of AT&T is discussed in Alan Stone, *Wrong Number: The Breakup of AT&T* (New York: Basic Books, 1989).
60. Steve Lohr, "U.S. Pursuit of Microsoft: Rare Synergy with Company's Rivals," *New York Times,* June 12, 2000, C1.
61. Ibid., C12.
62. Ted Bridis, "Microsoft-Tied Groups Report Weird Incidents," *Wall Street Journal,* June 19, 2000, A48.
63. Ibid.
64. Ted Bridis, Glenn R. Simpson, and Mylene Mangalindan, "How Piles of Trash Became Latest Focus in Bitter Software Feud," *Wall Street Journal,* June 29, 2000, 1. Also see Glenn R. Simpson, "Investigative Firm Played a Role in Microsoft Case," *Wall Street Journal,* June 19, 2000, A48.
65. For additional examples of the ways in which competing interests endeavor to use the courts against one another, see Michael Catanzaro, "The Antitrust Club," *National Review,* September 25, 2000, 27–31.
66. Yeazell, *From Medieval Group Litigation,* 248.
67. Gerald N. Rosenberg, *The Hollow Hope: Can Courts Bring About Social Change?* (Chicago: University of Chicago Press, 1991). For an alternative view, see Michael McCann and Helena Silverstein, "Rethinking Law's Allurements," in *Cause Lawyering,* ed. Austin Sarat and Stuart Scheingold (New York: Oxford University Press, 1998), 261–292. Also see Ann Southworth, "Lawyers and the 'Myth of Rights' in Civil Rights and Poverty Practice," *Boston University Public Interest Law Journal* 8 (1999): 469.
68. See George Stigler, "The Theory of Economic Regulation," *Bell Journal of Economics and Management Science* 2 (1971): 3–21.
69. See Seymour Martin Lipset, Martin Trow, and James Coleman, *Union Democracy* (Glencoe, Ill.: Free Press, 1956).

70. William Simon, "Visions of Practice in Legal Thought," *Stanford Law Review* 36 (1984): 469.

71. John Judis, "The Contract with K Street," *The New Republic*, December 4, 1995, 18–25.

72. Mancur Olson, *The Logic of Collective Action: Public Goods and the Theory of Groups* (Cambridge, Mass.: Harvard University Press, 1971).

73. Donald Wittman, "Parties as Utility Maximizers," *American Political Science Review* 67 (June 1973): 490–498.

74. See John Coffee, "Understanding the Plaintiff's Attorney: The Implication of Economic Theory for Private Enforcement of Law through Class and Derivative Actions," *Columbia Law Review* 86 (1986): 669. Also see Abraham Cheyes, "The Role of the Judge in Public Law Litigation," *Harvard Law Review* 89 (1976): 1281.

75. Samuel Issacharoff, "Class Action Conflicts," *University of California Davis Law Review* 30 (1997): 805.

76. Jonathan Macey and Geoffrey Miller, "The Plaintiff's Attorney's Role in Class Action and Derivative Litigation," *University of Chicago Law Review* 58 (1991): 1.

77. Derrick Bell, "Serving Two Masters: Integration Ideals and Client Interests in School Desegregation Decisions," *Yale Law Journal* 85 (1976): 505.

78. See Bryant Garth, Ilene Nagel, and Jay Plager, "The Institution of the Private Attorney General: Perspectives from an Empirical Study of Class Action Litigation," *University of Southern California Law Review* 61 (1988): 353.

79. Weinstein, *Individual Justice in Mass Tort Litigation*, 135.

80. Issacharoff, "Governance and Legitimacy," 339. See also *Deposit Guarantee Bank v. Roper*, 445 U.S. 326 (1980).

81. See John Brewer, *The Sinews of Power: War, Money, and the English State, 1688–1783* (New York: Alfred A. Knopf, 1989).

82. Coffee, "Understanding," 681.

83. Terry Anderson, *The Movement and the Sixties* (New York: Oxford University Press, 1995).

84. John Coffee, "Class Action Accountability," *Columbia Law Review* 100 (2000): 243.

85. John Coffee, "The Regulation of Entrepreneurial Litigation: Balancing Fairness and Efficiency in the Large Class Action," *University of Chicago Law Review* 54 (1987): 886.

86. For a discussion of class certification, see Sofia Androgue, "Mass Tort Class Actions in the New Millennium," *Review of Litigation* 17 (1998): 427. Also see Androgue, "Developments in the Law—The Paths of Civil Litigation. IV. Class Action Reform: An Assessment of Recent Judicial Decisions and Legislative Initiatives," *Harvard Law Review* 113 (2000): 1806. For a discussion of a major case involving future interests, see Susan P. Koniak, "Feasting While

the Widow Weeps: Georgine v. Amchem Products, Inc.," *Cornell Law Review* 80 (1995): 1045.

87. Coffee, "Regulation," 883.
88. See "Note: In-Kind Class Action Settlements," *Harvard Law Review* 109 (1996): 810.
89. Susan Koniak and George M. Cohen, "Under Cloak of Settlement," *University of Virginia Law Review* 82 (1996): 1051.
90. Ibid.
91. Coffee, "Understanding," 691.
92. John Coffee, "Class Action Accountability," *Columbia Law Review* 100 (2000): 370.
93. Coffee, "Understanding," 691.
94. Steven Shavell, "The Social versus the Private Incentive to Bring Suit in a Costly Legal System," *Journal of Legal Studies* 11 (1982): 333.
95. See Coffee, "Understanding," 681.
96. Paula Wilson, "Attorney Investment in Class Action Litigation: The Agent Orange Example," *Case Western Reserve Law Review* 45 (1994): 291.
97. Marshall Breger, "Accountability and the Adjudication of the Public Interest," *Harvard Journal of Law and Public Policy* 8 (1985): 2. Also see Kenney Hegland, "Beyond Enthusiasm and Commitment," *Arizona Law Review* 13 (1971): 805; and Gerald P. Lopez, *Rebellious Lawyering: One Chicano's Vision of Progressive Law Practice* (Boulder, Colo.: Westview Press, 1992).
98. "Developments in the Law—The Paths of Civil Litigation. III. Problems and Proposals in Punitive Damages Reform," *Harvard Law Review* 113 (2000): 1783.
99. See Jeremy Rabkin, "Government Lawyering."
100. Ibid., 183. For Judge Frank's opinion, see 134 F. 2d 694 (2d Cir. 1943).
101. Robert Anthony, "Zone-Free Standing for Private Attorneys General," *George Mason Law Review* 7 (1999): 237. See Also see Danielle R. Axelrad, "Current Developments in the Law: Ericson v. Syracuse University," *Boston University Public Interest Law Journal* 9 (1999): 155.
102. Rabkin, "Government Lawyering," 179.
103. Stephen Yeazell, "Collective Litigation as Collective Action," *University of Illinois Law Review* 1989 (1986): 55.
104. Bell, "Serving Two Masters," 482.
105. Martha Matthews, "Ten Thousand Tiny Clients: The Ethical Duty of Representation in Children's Class-Action Cases," *Fordham Law Review* 64 (1996): 1444. Also see Deborah Rhode, "Class Conflicts in Class Actions," *Stanford Law Review* 34 (1982): 1211; and Charles K. Rowley, *The Right to Justice* (Aldershot, Hants, England: Elgar Publishing, 1992).
106. Matthews, "Ten Thousand Tiny Clients," 1444.
107. See William B. Rubenstein, "Divided We Litigate: Addressing Disputes

among Group Members and Lawyers in Civil Rights Campaigns," *Yale Law Journal* 106 (1997): 1623.

108. Duncan Black, *The Theory of Committees and Elections* (Cambridge: Cambridge University Press, 1968).

109. In a small number of cases, courts have held advocacy to be inadequate when a vote taken among class members indicated strong opposition to advocates' proposals. In other cases, the courts have ignored such evidence (Rhode, "Class Conflicts," 1232).

110. A number of examples are discussed in Rhode, "Class Conflicts."

111. Greve, "Private Enforcement," 339.

112. This particular sort of environmental litigation may have been brought to an end by the Supreme Court's decision in *Chicago Steel and Pickling Co. v. Citizens for a Better Environment* (1003), which suggested that a plaintiff lacked standing to sue when the only remedy available to the court was a fine payable to the federal treasury.

113. Stanley Holmes, "Judge to Rule Next Week in Seattle Bias Case," *Seattle Times,* September 24, 1999, C1.

114. "Once United Boeing's Black Workers Split over Discrimination Settlement," *The Associated Press State and Local Wire,* June 7, 1999.

115. Rebecca Cook, "Judge Puts Settlement on Hold While Objectors Make Their Case," *The Associated Press State and Local Wire,* May 27, 1999. For examples of similar cases, see Dinesh D'Souza, *The End of Racism* (New York: Free Press, 1995).

116. Mark Hosenball and Evan Thomas, "Jesse and Al's Food Fight," *Newsweek,* April 9, 2001, 41.

117. For a discussion and bibliography, see David O'Brien, *Storm Center: The Supreme Court in American Politics,* 5th ed. (New York: W. W. Norton, 2000).

118. Rosenberg, *Hollow Hope,* chap. 2.

Chapter 8: Movements without Members

1. For a discussion of such groups and their goals, see Jeffrey M. Berry, *The New Liberalism: The Rising Power of Citizen Groups* (Washington, D.C.: Brookings Institution, 1999), chap. 3.

2. Benjamin Ginsberg, *The Fatal Embrace: Jews and the State* (Chicago: University of Chicago Press, 1993), chap. 4.

3. Hugh Davis Graham, *The Civil Rights Era: Origins and Development of National Policy, 1960–1972* (New York: Oxford University Press, 1990), 286.

4. See Faye Crosby and Cheryl VanDeVeer, eds., *Sex, Race, and Merit: Debating Affirmative Action in Education and Employment* (Ann Arbor: University of Michigan Press, 2000). Also see Terry Eastland, *Ending Affirmative Action: The Case for Colorblind Justice* (New York: Basic Books, 1996).

5. William Raspberry, "The Incredible Shrinking Black Agenda," *Washington Post,* February 9, 2001, A29. Raspberry indicates that an end to "racial profiling" is another item on the civil rights agenda. African Americans charge that the police are more likely to stop and question blacks than whites because of a police profile equating black skin with criminality. Racial profiling by the police should be seen as another mainly middle-class issue, insofar as it is especially intolerable to black business people, professionals, and white-collar employees to be subjected to police harassment that ignores their social status. During the 2000 vice presidential debate, both candidates were asked about an alleged case of racial profiling in Silver Spring, Maryland, involving a White House staffer. To upper-middle-class African American professionals, this case indicated that their social and economic status did not protect them from the sort of treatment the police usually reserve for members of the working class or the lower class.

6. William Julius Wilson, "Race-Neutral Programs and the Democratic Coalition," in *Affirmative Action,* ed. Francis Beckwith and Todd Jones (Amherst, N.Y.: Prometheus, 1997), chap. 10.

7. Ibid., 153. Also see Thomas Sowell, "From Equal Opportunity to Affirmative Action," in *Affirmative Action,* ed. Francis Beckwith and Todd Jones (Amherst, N.Y.: Prometheus, 1997), 109–111.

8. Orlando Patterson, *The Ordeal of Integration: Progress and Resentment in America's Racial Crisis* (Washington, D.C.: Civitas/Counterpoint, 1997), 155.

9. Robert Gottlieb, *Forcing the Spring: The Transformation of the American Environmental Movement* (Washington, D.C.: Island Press, 1993), 125.

10. Mark Dowie, *Losing Ground: American Environmentalism at the Close of the Twentieth Century* (Cambridge, Mass.: MIT Press, 1995), 5.

11. Gottlieb, *Forcing the Spring,* 126.

12. Dowie, *Losing Ground,* 4.

13. Samuel P. Hayes, "From Conservation to Environment: Environmental Politics in the United States since World War II," *Environmental History Review* 6, no. 2 (fall 1982): 14–41.

14. Dowie, *Losing Ground,* 33.

15. Ibid., 32.

16. Samuel P. Hayes, *Explorations in Environmental History* (Pittsburgh, Penn.: University of Pittsburgh Press, 1998), 422–431.

17. Dowie, *Losing Ground,* 34–38.

18. Gerald N. Rosenberg, *The Hollow Hope: Can Courts Bring About Social Change?* (Chicago: University of Chicago Press, 1991), 272.

19. Gottlieb, *Forcing the Spring,* 130.

20. Dowie, *Losing Ground,* 179.

21. Ibid., chap. 7.

22. Frank Fischer, *Citizens, Experts, and the Environment* (Durham, N.C.: Duke University Press, 2000), 113.
23. David Schlosberg, *Environmental Justice and the New Pluralism* (New York: Oxford University Press, 1999), 9.
24. See Robert D. Bullard, ed., *Unequal Protection: Environmental Justice and Communities of Color* (San Francisco: Sierra Club Books, 1994).
25. Robert N. Mayer, *The Consumer Movement* (Boston: Twayne Publishers, 1989).
26. John D. McCarthy and Mayer N. Zald, *The Trend of Social Movements in America: Professionalization and Resource Mobilization* (Morristown, N.J.: General Learning Press, 1973).
27. Michael Pertschuk, *Giant Killers* (New York: W. W. Norton, 1986).
28. Mayer, *Consumer Movement*, 114.
29. Ibid., 46.

Chapter 9: Privatizing the Public

1. Robert A. Dahl and Charles E. Lindblom, *Politics, Economics, and Welfare: Planning and Politico-Economic Systems Resolved into Basic Social Processes* (New York: Harper and Row, 1953), 7, 16.
2. Daniel Bell, *The End of Ideology: On the Exhaustion of Political Ideas in the Fifties* (Cambridge, Mass.: Harvard University Press, 1988), 404–405.
3. The classic statement of this perspective on rational decision making is Herbert A. Simon's *Administrative Behavior: A Study of Decision-Making Processes in Administrative Organizations* (New York: Macmillan, 1945).
4. Dahl and Lindlom, *Politics, Economics, and Welfare*, 266–267.
5. Daniel Guttman, "Public Purpose and Private Service: The Twentieth Century Culture of Contracting Out and the Evolving Law of Diffused Sovereignty," *Administrative Law Review* 52 (summer 2000): 865–872.
6. See David Osborne and Ted Gaebler, *Reinventing Government: How the Entrepreneurial Spirit Is Transforming the Public Sector from Schoolhouse to Statehouse, City Hall to Pentagon* (Reading, Mass.: Addison-Wesley, 1992), esp. chaps. 6 and 10.
7. Ronald C. Moe, "The 'Reinventing Government' Exercise: Misinterpreting the Problem, Misjudging the Consequences," *Public Administration Review* 54 (March/April 1994): 111–123.
8. Daniel Patrick Moynihan, *The Politics of a Guaranteed Annual Income: The Nixon Administration and the Family Assistance Plan* (New York: Random House, 1973), 53.
9. The contemporary history of privatization is discussed in Guttman, "Public Purpose and Private Service." On the "shadow government," see Paul C. Light, *The True Size of Government* (Washington, D.C.: Brookings Institution, 1999).

10. Light, *True Size of Government*, 25.
11. Harold Seidman, *Politics, Position, and Power: The Dynamics of Federal Organization*, 5th ed. (New York: Oxford University Press, 1998), chap. 6.
12. Michael A. Froomkin, "Reinventing the Government Corporation," *University of Illinois Law Review*, vol. 1995, 548.
13. Lester M. Salamon, *Partners in Public Service* (Baltimore: Johns Hopkins University Press, 1995), pt. 3.
14. See, for example, Al Gore, *From Red Tape to Results: Creating a Government That Works Better and Costs Less*, Report of the National Performance Review (Government Printing Office, 1993). Also Osborne and Gaebler, *Reinventing Government*.
15. Jeffrey R. Henig, "Privatization in the United States: Theory and Practice," *Political Science Quarterly* 104 (winter 1989–1990): 656, 664.
16. David Wagner, *What's Love Got to Do with It? A Critical Look at American Charity* (New York: New Press, 2000), 148.
17. Thomas H. Stanton, *Government-Sponsored Enterprises: Mercantilist Companies in the Modern World* (Washington, D.C.: AEI Press, 2001).
18. Ibid., 16.
19. Froomkin, "Reinventing," 18.
20. Kathleen Day, "Greenspan Urges Review of Fannie, Freddie Subsidies," *Washington Post*, May 24, 2000, E3.
21. Stanton, *Government-Sponsored Enterprises*, 12
22. Ibid., 44.
23. On fiduciary responsibility, see Froomkin, "Reinventing," 34, 51. On the freezing out of public directors, see Herman Schwartz, "Governmentally Appointed Directors in a Private Corporation," *Harvard Law Review* 79 (1965): 350; and Ronald Gilson and Reinier Kraakman, ""Reinventing the Outside Director," *Stanford Law Review* 43 (1991): 863.
24. Stanton, *Government-Sponsored Enterprises*, 37.
25. Ibid., 45, 48, 61.
26. Urban Institute, "A Study of the GSEs' Single Family Underwriting Guidelines: Final Report" (prepared for the U.S. Department of Housing and Urban Development, April 1999). Also see Michele Derus, "Mortgage Finance Giants Fail Those Who Earn Less, Critics Say," *Milwaukee Journal Sentinel*, May 14, 2000, F1; and H. Jane Lehman, "Loan Goals Fall Short in Central Cities," *Washington Post*, April 23, 1994, E1.
27. Mary Kane, "Critics Say Home-Buying Push Puts Some Consumers at Risk," *Minneapolis Star Tribune*, April 15, 2000, H7; Marvin Phaup, *Assessing the Public Costs and Benefits of Fannie Mae and Freddie Mac* (Washington, D.C.: Congress of the United States, Congressional Budget Office, 1996), xii; Froomkin, "Reinventing," 63.

28. Jerry Knight, "Fannie, Freddie in the Political Spotlight," *Washington Post,* July 31, 2000, Business section, 7.

29. Stanton, *Government-Sponsored Enterprises,* 55.

30. Ibid., 17; Knight, "Fannie, Freddie in the Political Spotlight," Business section, 7.

31. David Ignatius, "A U.S. Government Hedge Fund?" *Washington Post,* May 10, 1999, A23.

32. Froomkin, "Reinventing," 60.

33. Bloomberg News, "Freddie, Fannie Increase Giving to Campaigns," *Milwaukee Journal Sentinel,* April 30, 2000, F5.

34. Patrick Barta, "Fannie Mae, Freddie Mac Counter Critics," *Wall Street Journal,* July 19, 2000, B6.

35. Stephen Burd, "Should Borrowers Fear a Student-Loan Behemoth?" *The Chronicle of Higher Education,* August 11, 2000, A24.

36. Barta, "Fannie Mae, Freddie Mac Counter Critics," B6.

37. Mary Jacoby, "Critics Question Fannie Mae's Influence," *St. Petersburg Times,* July 17, 2000, A1.

38. Albert Crenshaw, "This Foundation Director Says Charity Begins at Home," *Washington Post,* May 6, 1996, F9.

39. Jacoby, "Critics Question."

40. Donald Kettl, *Government By Proxy: (Mis)Managing Federal Programs* (Washington, D.C.: CQ Press, 1988).

41. For a review of the evidence, see Elliott D. Sclar, *You Don't Always Get What You Pay For: The Economics of Privatization* (Ithaca, N.Y.: Cornell University Press, 2000).

42. On constitutional protections, see Robert Gilmour and Laura Jensen, "Reinventing Government Accountability: Public Functions, Privatization, and the Meaning of State Action," *Public Administration Review* 58, no. 3 (May/June 1998): 247–257. On citizen rights, see Guttman, "Public Purpose and Private Service," 46.

43. Joseph T. Hallinan, "Shaky Private Prisons Find Vital Customer in Federal Government," *Wall Street Journal,* May 9, 2001, 1.

44. Eric Bates, "Private Prisons," *The Nation,* January 5, 1998, 11–18; Suzanne Smalley, "A Stir over Private Pens," *National Journal* 31 (May 1, 1999): 1168–1173.

45. The Justice Department recently filed suit against the Wackenhut Corrections Corporation, charging that conditions in one of its prisons were dangerous and life threatening and asking a federal judge to take emergency action to protect the inmates (Fox Butterfield, "Justice Department Sues to Alter Conditions at a Prison," *New York Times,* March 31, 2000, A16). See Ira P. Robbins, "Managed Health Care in Prisons as Cruel and Unusual Punish-

ment," *Journal of Criminal Law and Criminology* 90, no. 1 (fall 1999): 195–237; and Bates, "Private Prisons."

46. Bates, "Private Prisons."
47. Smalley, "A Stir."
48. Bates, "Private Prisons."
49. Gilbert Geis, Alan Mobley, and David Sichor, "Private Prisons, Criminological Research, and Conflict of Interest: A Case Study," *Crime and Delinquency* 45, no. 3 (July 1999): 372–389.
50. Bates, "Private Prisons."
51. See Eyal Press and Jennifer Washburn, "Neglect for Sale," *The American Prospect* 11, no. 12 (May 8, 2000): 22–29.
52. Kai T. Erikson, *Wayward Puritans* (New York: Wiley, 1966).
53. Paul Posner, Robert Yetvin, Mark Schneiderman, Christopher Spiro, and Andrea Barnett, "A Survey of Voucher Use: Variations and Common Elements," in *Vouchers and the Provision of Public Services,* ed. C. Eugene Steuerle, Van Doorn Ooms, George E. Peterson, and Robert D. Reischauer (Washington, D.C.: Brookings Institution Press, 2000), 504–513.
54. See Jeffrey R. Henig, *Rethinking School Choice: Limits of the Market Metaphor* (Princeton, N.J.: Princeton University Press, 1994), 67.
55. Pedro A. Noguera, "More Democracy Not Less: Confronting the Challenge of Privatization in Public Education," *Journal of Negro Education* 63 (1994): 238.
56. Richard Rothstein, "Lessons: Vouchers Dead, Alternatives Weak," *New York Times,* June 20, 2001, B8.
57. Henry M. Levin, "The Public-Private Nexus in Education," *American Behavioral Scientist* 43 (September 1999): 124.
58. John Chubb and Terry Moe, *Politics, Markets, and America's Schools* (Washington, D.C.,: Brookings Institution, 1990), 54; Matthew A. Crenson, "Urban Bureaucracy in Urban Politics: Notes toward a Developmental Theory," in *Public Values and Private Power in American Bureaucracy,* ed. J. David Greenstone (Chicago: University of Chicago Press, 1982), 231–232.
59. Cecilia Rouse, "Private School Vouchers and Student Achievement: An Evaluation of the Milwaukee Parental Choice Program," *Quarterly Journal of Economics* 113 (May 1998): 553–602.
60. Henig, *Rethinking School Choice,* 175–178,
61. Chubb and Moe, *Politics, Markets, and America's Schools,* 36–37.
62. Janet R. Beales and Maureen Wahl, "Private Vouchers in Milwaukee: The PAVE Program," in *Private Vouchers,* ed. Terry M. Moe (Stanford, Calif.: Hoover Institution Press, 1995), 57–59; Amy Stuart Wells, "African-American Students' View of School Choice," in *Who Chooses? Who Loses?: Culture, Institutions, and the Unequal Effects of School Choice,* ed. Bruce Fuller and

Richard F. Elmore (New York: Teachers College Press, 1996), 32, 35–36; R. Kenneth Godwin, Frank R. Kemerer, and Valerie J. Martinez, "Comparing Public Choice and Private Voucher Programs in San Antonio," in *Learning from School Choice,* ed. Paul E. Peterson and Bryan C. Hassel (Washington, D.C.: Brookings Institution Press, 1998), 281–282.

63. Mark Schneider, Paul Teske, Melissa Marschall, Michael Mintrom, and Christine Roch, "Institutional Arrangements and the Creation of Social Capital: The Effects of Public School Choice," *American Political Science Review* 91 (March 1997): 82 (italics in original).

64. Charles L. Schultze, *The Public Use of Private Interest* (Washington, D.C.: Brookings Institution, 1977).

65. Steven Rathgeb Smith and Michael Lipsky, *Nonprofits for Hire: The Welfare State in the Age of Contracting* (Cambridge, Mass.: Harvard University Press, 1993), 3.

66. Ibid., 55–56.

67. Alan J. Abramson, Lester M. Salamon, and C. Eugene Steuerle, "The Nonprofit Sector and the Federal Budget: Recent History and Future Directions," in *Nonprofits and Government: Collaboration and Conflict,* ed. Elizabeth T. Boris and C. Eugene Steuerle (Washington, D.C.: Urban Institute Press, 1999), 112.

68. Jennifer Alexander, Renee Nank, and Camilla Stivers, "Implications of Welfare Reform: Do Nonprofit Survival Strategies Threaten Civil Society?" in *Understanding Nonprofit Organizations: Governance, Leadership, and Management,* ed. J. Steven Ott (Boulder, Colo.: Westview Press, 2001), 277.

69. Scott Gates and Jeffrey Hill, "Democratic Accountability and Governmental Innovation in the Use of Nonprofit Organizations," *Policy Studies Review* 14 (spring/summer 1995): 137–148.

70. Jocelyn Johnston and Barbara Romzek, "Contracting and Accountability in State Medicaid Reform," *Public Administration Review* 59, no. 5 (September/October 1999): 383–399.

71. Gates and Hill, "Democratic Accountability," 1; Smith and Lipsky, *Nonprofits for Hire,* 10.

72. Dennis R. Young, "Commercialism in Nonprofit Social Service Associations: Its Character, Significance, and Rationale," in *To Profit or Not to Profit: The Commercial Transformation of the Nonprofit Sector,* ed. Burton Weisbrod (Cambridge: Cambridge University Press, 1998), 195–216 (quotation on p. 209).

73. For examples of fraud, see Alan Finder and Joe Sexton, "Reform Gone Awry: How Haste Made a Shambles of a Plan to Privatize Welfare," *New York Times,* April 8, 1996, A1; George Snell, "State Alleges Billing Abuses," *Worcester Telegram and Gazette,* February 17, 1999, A1; Martha Shirk, "State Contracts Can Be Lucrative: Fewer Services, Like Counseling, Means Fewer Expenses,"

St. Louis Post-Dispatch, May 26, 1996, B5; Debra Jasper and Elliot Jaspin, "Bottom Line, Not Kids' Welfare, Drives Foster System: Nonprofit Agencies Make Profit from Public Money," *Dayton Daily News*, September 29, 1999, 9A; and Robert Anglen and Mark Curnutte, "Housing Group Made Deals with Insiders, Relatives," *Cincinnati Inquirer*, February 11, 2000, A1.

74. Arthur C. Brooks, "Is There a Dark Side to Government Support for Non-profits?" *Public Administration Review* 60, no. 3 (May/June 2000): 211–218.

75. Alexander, Nank, and Stivers, "Implications of Welfare Reform," 278.

76. Smith and Lipsky cite the reliance on Medicaid as one factor turning non-profit mental health agencies to the treatment of personal problems instead of collective ones. Qualifying for Medicaid reimbursement meant "the 'medicalization' of social work and counseling practice. . . . Consequently, a social worker's focus may move away from the community or support network or the circumstantial source of a person's difficulty to an individual pathology" (Smith and Lipsky, *Nonprofits for Hire*, 68).

77. James Vanecko, "Community Mobilization and Institutional Change: The Influence of the Community Action Program in Large Cities," *Social Science Quarterly* 50 (December 1969): 609–630.

78. Matthew A. Crenson, "Organizational Factors in Citizen Participation," *Journal of Politics* 36 (May 1974): 370–371.

79. Ibid., 375.

80. See Jon S. Vernick, "Lobbying and Advocacy for the Public's Health: What Are the Limits for Nonprofit Organizations?" *American Journal of Public Health* 89, no. 9 (September 1999): 1425–1429. Also see Mary Deibel, "AARP Pays Back Taxes, Spins Off Unit," *Chicago Sun-Times*, July 15, 1999, 30.

81. Alexander, Nank, and Stivers, "Implications of Welfare Reform," 279,

82. Smith and Lipsky, *Nonprofits for Hire*, 186–187.

83. Jeffrey Galper, quoted in Wagner, *What's Love Got to Do with It?* 163.

84. Stanley Aronowitz, *The Death and Rebirth of American Radicalism* (New York: Routledge, 1996), 133–134.

85. Wagner, *What's Love Got to Do with It?* 168–169.

86. Aronowitz, *Death and Rebirth of American Radicalism*, 133.

87. Matthew A. Crenson and Francis E. Rourke, "The Federal Bureaucracy since World War II," in *The New American State: Bureaucracies and Policies since World War II*, ed. Louis Galambos (Baltimore: Johns Hopkins Press, 1987), 157.

88. Richard Nathan, Allen D. Manvel, and Susannah E. Calkins, *Monitoring Revenue Sharing* (Washington, D.C.: Brookings Institution, 1975), 5.

89. Paul Posner and Margaret T. Wrightson, "Block Grants: A Perennial, but Unstable, Tool of Government," *Publius* 26 (summer 1996): 93.

90. Timothy Conlan, *From New Federalism to Devolution: Twenty-Five Years of Intergovernmental Reform* (Washington, D.C.: Brookings Institution Press, 1998), 109.

91. Ibid., 109, 157, 295 (quotation on p. 157).
92. See John D. Donahue, *Disunited States* (New York: Basic Books, 1997), 27.
93. See Paul Peterson, *The Price of Federalism* (Washington, D.C.: Brookings Institution, 1995).
94. See Frank J. Thompson, "The Faces of Devolution," in *Medicaid and Devolution: The View from the States,* ed. Frank J. Thompson and John DiIulio Jr. (Washington, D.C.: Brookings Institution Press, 1998), 14–55.
95. Pamela Winston, "The Devil in Devolution: Welfare, the Nation, and the States" (Ph.D. diss., Johns Hopkins University, 1999).
96. Margaret Brassil, "De Facto Devolution: Affordable Housing in the States" (Ph.D. diss., Johns Hopkins University, 2001).
97. E. E. Schattschneider, *The Semisovereign People: A Realist's View of Democracy in America* (New York: Holt, Rinehart, and Winston, 1960), 71.

Chapter 10: Does Anyone Need Citizens?

1. See, for example, E. J. Hobsbawm, *Primitive Rebels* (New York: W. W. Norton, 1959).
2. George Rudé, *The Crowd in the French Revolution* (New York: Oxford University Press, 1959), chap. 15. See also Barrington Moore Jr., *Injustice: The Social Bases of Obedience and Revolt* (New York: M. E. Sharpe, 1978).
3. Leon Trotsky, *The Russian Revolution,* trans. Max Eastman (New York: Simon and Schuster, 1932).
4. Aristide Zolberg, "Moments of Madness," *Politics and Society* 2 (April 1972): 183.
5. V. I. Lenin, *What Is to Be Done? Burning Questions of Our Movement* (New York: International Publishers, 1929), chap. 2.
6. Robert H. Salisbury, "An Exchange Theory of Interest Groups," *Midwest Journal of Political Science* 13 (February 1969): 1–32.
7. Reinhard Bendix, *Nation-Building and Citizenship: Studies of Our Changing Social Order* (New York: Wiley, 1964), esp. pt. 1.
8. "Slavery and the Law: Time and Punishment," *The Economist,* April 13, 2002, 31.
9. Jürgen Habermas, *The Structural Transformation of the Public Sphere: An Inquiry into a Category of Bourgeois Society,* trans. Thomas Burger (Cambridge, Mass.: MIT Press, 1992).

Index

National Labor Relations Board (NLRB), 63, 125, 127–34
National Organization of Women, 143
National Performance Review, viii, 8
National Recovery Administration (NRA), 122–25, 264n6
National Rifle Association, 78, 136
National Right to Work Committee, 128
National War Labor Board, 129
National Wildlife Federation, 144, 189
Nelson, Gaylord, 190
Netscape Communications Corporation, 167–68
New Deal: Democratic Party's institutional base, 85; interest group politics, 122–27; labor unions in, 60–61, 62, 124–26, 128; legislation, 62, 265n14; mass mobilization, 59–63; turnout by voters, 61
New Federalism, 227–29, 232
New Politics, 71–79, 82
NIMBY ("not in my backyard"), 192–93
Nixon, Richard: appointment of federal judges, 90; Democrats supporting, 71; environmental movement and, 190; presidential power, 92; in public opinion polls, 98; resignation, 50; silent majority, 101; social programs, 87
Nofziger, Lynn, 93
nonprofit organizations, 219–26
Norris-LaGuardia Act (1932), 125, 126
North, Oliver, 93
North American Free Trade Agreement (NAFTA), 134
Norton, Eleanor Holmes, 140

Occupational Safety and Health Administration (OSHA), 77, 190
Office of Economic Opportunity (OEO), 84, 223–24
Office of Federal Contract Compliance Programs (OFCCP), 187
Office of Management and Budget, 92
Office of the Independent Council, 94
Olson, Mancur, 123
opinion leaders, 14, 101–2
Oracle Corporation, 168
Ousley, Clarence, 110

Paez, Richard, 91
Paine, Thomas, 214
patronage, 80–105; in Chicago, 27; in England, 24–25; political parties and, 25–27, 86–87, 104, 236; Progressive opposition to, 15, 28, 56; in public administration, 24–27; spoils system, 25; turnout of voters and, 27

Patterson, Orlando, 188
Pericles, 13
Perot, Ross, 194
Perry, William, 89
personal democracy: class bias, 104; collective identity lost, 234; compared to popular democracy, viii, 241; defined, viii; formative influences, 3; government by litigation, 152; history of, 14–19; internal contradictions, 243–44; litigation rather than mass mobilization, 181; political currents in, 236–39; in privatizer's belief system, 203; "representational distortion" in, 78–79
personnel administration, 28, 58
Pertschuk, Michael, 195
Peterson, Paul, 139
Philadelphia Committee of Privates, 44
Pinehurst State School and Hospital, 177
Piven, Frances, 110, 126
Planned Parenthood, 84
Plotke, David, 126, 265n14
policymaking: command-and-control versus market-based policies, 219–20; devolution of federal authority, 226–33; directness of bureaucratic control, 201–2; in domestic agencies, 85; entanglement of public policy and private interests in regulatory agencies, 118–19; expertise and ideas in, 147; by interest groups, 110; lack of clear objectives, 18; litigation in, 16–17, 48, 77–78, 152, 156, 162, 170–75, 181; "maximum feasible participation" in, 17–18, 138; by political parties, 108; "social techniques" in, 198–202; think tanks, 200; thwarting via institutional warfare, 93, 104
political leaders, 11, 240
political participation: Americans unfit for, 51; benefits given for, 4–5, 20–21; decline of, causes of, 151; devolution of federal authority and, 232; effect of citizen administrators on, 27; financial donations as, 2, 3, 151; government and, 53–54, 235; incentives for, 14; by interest groups in regulatory agencies, 119–20; "making a difference," 7; marginalization of, 78, 98, 258n106; opportunities for, 2–3; of poor people, 138; self-esteem and, 6–7; stagnation in, 2. *See also* demobilization of the public; mass mobilization
political parties: "activation" strategy, 83; attacks on opposing party's institutional base, 87–88, 242; campaign finance reform, 240–41; community action groups versus, 69;